The Danger of Dreams

The Danger of Dreams

German and American Imperialism in Latin America

Nancy Mitchell

The University of North Carolina Press

Chapel Hill and London

Designed by Jacquline Johnson
Set in Sabon
by Tseng Information Systems

Manufactured in the United States of America

The paper in this book meets the guidelines for permanence
and durability of the Committee on Production Guidelines
for Book Longevity of the Council on Library Resources.

Portions of this book have appeared previously in the following
articles:

Nancy Mitchell, "The Height of the German Challenge: The
Venezuela Blockade, 1902–3," *Diplomatic History* 20 (Spring 1996):
185–209. Reprinted by permission of Blackwell Publishers.

Nancy Mitchell, "Protective Imperialism versus Weltpolitik in Brazil:
Part One: Pan-German Vision and Mahanian Response," *International
History Review* 18, no. 2 (May 1996): 253–78, and "Protective
Imperialism versus Weltpolitik in Brazil: Part Two: Settlement, Trade,
and Opportunity," *International History Review* 18, no. 3 (August
1996): 546–72. Reprinted by permission of *International History
Review*.

Library of Congress Cataloging-in-Publication Data
Mitchell, Nancy, 1952–
The danger of dreams: German and American imperialism in
Latin America / Nancy Mitchell.
   p. cm.
Includes bibliographical references (p.) and index.
ISBN 0-8078-2489-5 (cloth: alk. paper). —
ISBN 0-8078-4775-5 (pbk.: alk. paper)
1. Germans—Latin America—History. 2. Germany—
Foreign relations—Latin America. 3. Latin America—
Foreign relations—Germany. 4. Americans—Latin America—
Attitudes. 5. United States—Foreign relations—1865–1921.
6. Latin America—Foreign relations. I. Title.
F1416.G3M58 1999
980'.00431—dc21   98-49537
           CIP

03 02 01 00 99   5 4 3 2 1

To my mother and friend,
Hope Mitchell

Contents

Illustrations

Maps

Acknowledgments

If I were a cat, I would be purring. It makes me happy to think about the people who have helped me write this book.

My intellectual debt to Piero Gleijeses is profound. He listens. Then he asks difficult questions, which frequently irritate me, and then, invariably, he helps me to find the answers. He is my sounding board and my good friend.

Walter LaFeber has been astounding. Quietly and steadfastly, he has nurtured me. In the face of his generosity, I, who am rarely at a loss for words, am.

Alex DeGrand has supported this project with deft and delightful grace. Lars Schoultz and Lloyd Ambrosius read the manuscript with extraordinarily gentle and rigorous care. Edward Ingram's probing editing challenged me to improve the chapter on Brazil. Michael Hogan helped me to sharpen the chapter on Venezuela. John Röhl has guided me through the intricacies of Wilhelmine Germany with generous passion. Fred Holborn offered unfailing encouragement and guidance.

I feel very lucky to work in the history department at N.C. State. I have fun at work. In part that's because of several friends who have been exceptionally supportive in their own very varied ways: Gail O'Brien, Stephanie Spencer, John David Smith, Tony LaVopa, and David Zonderman.

Meredith Lewis was my research assistant for two years. I wish she could have stayed forever. Gary Wilson and Mimi Riggs, two of the interlibrary loan specialists at N.C. State, are a cross between magicians and Santa Claus.

Lewis Bateman and Pamela Upton at the University of North Carolina Press have shepherded this manuscript with delightfully tender precision.

Bill Felice and Dale Lappe, two men of integrity and courage, know how deep my debt is to them. Much of this book was hammered out while walking and walking with Nancy Roman. When I was in London, I stayed with Úna Sheehan, which was one of the great pleasures of doing research there. And on my frequent trips to Washington, Debbie, Luin, Sarah, and Henry Fitch spoiled me rotten.

All these people, and many more, have been generous to me. I smile as I remember.

The Danger of Dreams

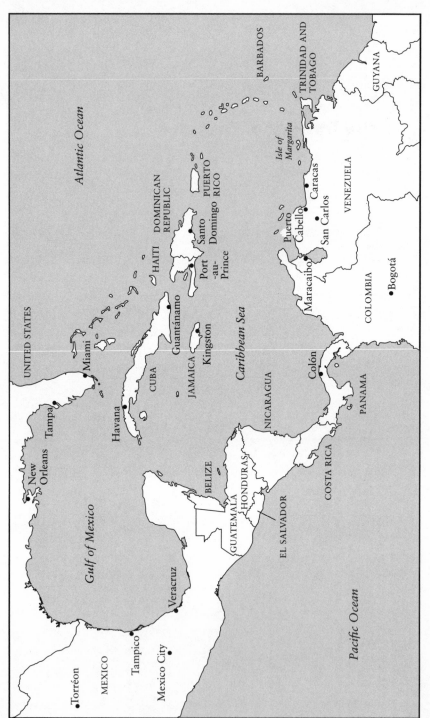

Map 1. The Caribbean Region

Introduction

In November 1914, Colonel Edward House, Woodrow Wilson's right-hand man, told the president that he "had it on fairly good authority that the Kaiser had it in mind to suggest to us that the Monroe Doctrine should extend only to the equator which would leave Germany free to exploit Brazil and other South American countries. Brazil seems to be the main object of Germany's desires." The president replied philosophically, "Perhaps the war was a godsend to us for had it not come, we might have been embroiled in war ourselves."[1] A few months later, the secretary of state, William Jennings Bryan, warned the president, "There seems to be some sympathetic cooperation between the French and German interests in Haiti." Wilson was alarmed. "This whole matter has a most sinister appearance," he responded, a bare four months before the U.S. Marines landed in Port au Prince.[2] And in 1931, Robert Lansing, Wilson's second secretary of state, wrote in the *New York Times Magazine* that in 1917 the secretary of the navy had told the president "very bluntly that there was a danger that Germany might absorb Denmark and that she might do so to obtain legal title to the Danish West Indies, which the German government coveted." It was allegedly to prevent this that the United States bought the Danish West Indies. "We would never permit the group to become German," the former secretary of state asserted.[3]

It is striking that Colonel House was worrying about Berlin's designs on Brazil in late 1914, when Germany was embroiled in the early months of World War I. It is startling to read that Wilson imagined that the French and Germans could be cooperating in Haiti in the spring of 1915, when they were slaughtering each other in Europe. It is surprising that in 1931 Lansing considered his assertion that Germany wanted to annex Denmark in order to obtain its Caribbean islands so credible that he felt no need to offer any explanation of it.

Wilson and his senior advisers had been overwhelmed by a fear that had been incubating for more than a decade: Germany would grab a chunk of Latin America if ever America's back was turned. Germany was the hungry, dissatisfied power. Germany alone chafed against President James Monroe's

"Move for move." At the turn of the century, American political cartoonists often depicted the German threat to the Monroe Doctrine. In this 1902 cartoon, the artist alludes to the U.S. Navy's well-publicized war games to show the German squadron and the North Atlantic Squadron face to face, with Uncle Sam and the Monroe Doctrine protecting the South American customhouse. In fact, both the U.S. and German navies had developed war plans against each other. (*Boston Herald*, 1902; reprinted in *American Monthly Review of Reviews* 25 [January 1902])

famous assertion that there was to be no further colonization in the Western hemisphere. The United States must be on guard.

To understand this perception of a German threat, it is necessary to claw backward through the archives to the turn of the century. It was then that the idea of a German challenge to the Monroe Doctrine became lodged in American minds. Americans had grown wary of German competition shortly after the creation of the German empire in 1871. Trade tensions between the two countries not only soured relations but also were widely presumed to be the most likely cause of war. "There is no rivalry more bitter than trade rivalry," an American admiral opined at the time. "There is no thing more dangerous to peace. There is no thing for which men will fight more savagely than for money."[4] American apprehensions hardened into distrust and fear during the Spanish-American War, when German admiral Otto von Diederichs allegedly hounded U.S. admiral George Dewey at Manila Bay. Furthermore, Darwinian assumptions had led to the widespread conviction that Germany had to expand, and many Americans believed that Latin America was the most likely place for this expansion: it had not yet been carved up by the great powers, German industrialists and bankers were already there seeking opportunities, and Germans had immigrated there in large numbers, retaining their German customs and establishing trade links with the motherland. These fears were whipped up by two mighty bellows: the growth of the German navy and the incendiary rhetoric of many German ultranationalists. In 1898, the Reich's commitment to build a world-class fleet was signaled by the First Fleet Bill; German ships increasingly prowled Latin American waters. And many prominent Germans, including the kaiser, publicly railed against the Monroe Doctrine—that "special manifestation of American arrogance," as Bismarck deemed it.[5]

While Germany was elbowing its way onto the world stage, so too was the United States. In the 1890s the Monroe Doctrine, which for seven decades had been but the chronicle of a dream, began to acquire teeth. This was in part due to the growth of the U.S. Navy, but it was also simply the serendipitous spoils of Britain's imperial overstretch. During the first Venezuela crisis of 1895-96, England had bowed to the Monroe Doctrine. Curbing further colonization of the hemisphere suited Britain, a fellow American power and sated colonizer. Over the next decade, the Royal Navy handed the baton of policing the hemisphere to the U.S. Navy, and British interest in Latin America grew more informal, focusing on the financial and service sectors. These "gentlemanly" pursuits lubricated U.S. trade with the region, rather than inhibiting it, and were not seen as a threat to the Monroe Doctrine.[6] Nor did the Spaniards pose a threat. In 1898, the United States had tossed that exhausted power from the hemisphere and assumed control of Cuba and Puerto Rico. Russia and Japan showed no interest in the region, and, by the late nineteenth century, the French, too, appeared uninterested.

At the turn of the century, however, the Monroe Doctrine's reach still exceeded its grasp. Kaiser Wilhelm II's Germany, with its policy of Weltpolitik and its rapidly growing navy, was thought to have the motivation to challenge the Monroe Doctrine and, conceivably, the means. Its navy was expanding even faster than the American, and it was, by both German and American estimates, much better trained. Given the rivalry between the two rising powers, the intemperate language of some Germans, the docility of all other European powers to America's ascent, and the vulnerability of the Monroe Doctrine, the idea of a German threat is understandable.

What is striking is not the existence of the image but its durability—that it was accepted as fact not only during the changed circumstances of World War I but also by many analysts to the present day despite the absence of extensive scholarly investigation or debate on the issue.

The analysis of Wilhelmine policy toward Latin America has been a tranquil eddy of scholarship. For historians of the United States, it has been a persistent but curiously unanalyzed refrain in the literature on the much debated topic of U.S. expansionism from the Spanish-American War to the First World War. For historians of Latin America, it has been subsumed into the story of German immigration. Historians of Germany have by and large considered it a minor blip across the crowded screen of pre–World War I diplomacy; if they have looked at Wilhelmine expansionism at all, they have preferred to focus on Germany's colonies in Africa and the Pacific.

It was not until Alfred Vagts published his brilliant *Deutschland und die Vereinigten Staaten in der Weltpolitik* that there was a serious analysis of German aims and actions in the hemisphere.[7] Vagts's work, however, appeared in the 1930s and was based on a very limited array of sources. It was untranslated and was followed, for decades, by silence.

Although the notion that U.S. expansionism was reactive and defensive predates Samuel Flagg Bemis, his *The Latin American Policy of the United States* remains the quintessential statement of the heroic explanation of American imperialism, one that stresses both the security and the humanitarian motives —the German threat to the soon-to-be-opened Panama Canal and the desire to "uplift" the benighted Latins. Bemis dubbed U.S. expansionism between the Spanish-American War and the First World War "protective imperialism." The name is telling. It separates U.S. imperialism from European imperialism. It implies that the Europeans acted aggressively for their own good, whereas the Americans reacted protectively for the good of others. It implies that Europe's imperialism was ordinary and America's exceptional. Yet Bemis did not investigate the validity of the claim that the region needed protection, despite the fact that it was central to his argument. In the absence of scholarly debate, he assumed that the aggressive rhetoric of the German ultranationalists and the widespread perception that the Germans were planning to challenge the Monroe Doctrine meant that there was in fact a German threat.[8]

William Appleman Williams, who challenged all previous explanations of U.S. imperialism with the elegant, decisive strokes of an Errol Flynn, sidestepped the idea that the region needed protection. He did not debunk it.[9] American exceptionalism survived Williams. Many of those scholars who reject the centrality of his economic motive, either for philosophical reasons or for specific ones (such as doubts that economic motivations explain the U.S.

intervention in Haiti in 1915), continue to dismiss the German threat as irrelevant, but others resurrect the security and humanitarian motives and return, implicitly or explicitly, to the basic premise of "protective imperialism." German policy—what Berlin actually did—has remained unexamined.[10]

The scholarship on Wilhelmine imperialism has tended to be the inverse of that on U.S. imperialism: in the former, operating in the shadow of Hitler, Germany's disposition to expand has been accepted as the fact that has needed explanation, while in the latter, America's expansion, despite its purported disposition against it, has usually been considered the phenomenon that needed explanation. Thus, German historiography has sought deep structural causes for Berlin's imperialism, while American historiography has more often sought particular triggers for U.S. expansion.

Until the publication of Fritz Fischer's *Griff nach der Weltmacht* in 1961, German historians after Vagts had displayed little interest in Wilhelmine expansionism. Then Fischer, like Williams in the United States, poked the hornets' nest with his apostasy of asserting that Germany's foreign policy could only be understood in the context of its particular domestic situation; that is, like Eckart Kehr, he challenged the reigning dogma in German historiography of the primacy of foreign policy. But even more radically, Fischer dared to argue that Wilhelmine Germany had been a recklessly expansionist state and that Wilhelm II—like Hitler after him—had deliberately marched to war. Thus Fischer penetrated to the bone, and the controversy surrounding his work rages to this day.[11]

Post-Fischer scholarship on German imperialism has continued to investigate the peculiarities of Wilhelmine Germany's domestic situation in order to shed light on the appeal of expansionism. Many, following Hans-Ulrich Wehler, have looked at the social structure of post-Bismarckian Germany, particularly the unusual stresses produced by rapid industrialization combined with the vagaries of the German state. These scholars, who emphasize the view "from below," see expansionism as a useful unifying tool. Others have stressed the importance of the rise of the radical right or of particular pressure groups, such as the Navy League or the pan-Germans, in fueling the drive toward expansion. If they have looked abroad at all, it has been to Germany's formal colonies. They ignore Latin America. Fischer himself barely mentioned it.[12]

Recently, however, a number of scholars have cast their gaze toward Latin America—notably Ragnhild Fiebig-von Hase, Jürgen Hell, Thomas Baecker, Gerhard Brunn, Friedrich Katz, and Holger Herwig. Without exception, they argue that Germany had designs on the region. Herwig's analysis of the German naval war plans against the United States and Katz's study of German policy toward Mexico have been widely cited to buttress the idea of a German threat.[13] On the basis of evidence from the German, American, and British archives, I challenge this interpretation.

Like the mind in a dream, historians are faced with the detritus of the day—the memo, the letter, the scribble in the margin—and must tease a story from it, and our stories vary. Given the complexity of reality, this is inevitable. Interpreters of German policy in Latin America, for example, confront the ambivalence, even the chaos, of Wilhelmine policy making. They must not only determine the purpose of Wilhelm's foreign policy, a hazardous task at best, but also weigh German capabilities against intentions, and this is always a subtle undertaking, an art. Furthermore, the thick mist of hindsight clouds the enterprise: it is tempting to assume that because the kaiser gambled for high stakes in Europe he was ready to do likewise in Latin America. And Wilhelm and the pan-Germans have left a myriad of catchy and startling comments to support the interpretation, not to mention the war plans describing, in florid detail, a Mahanian battle against the U.S. Navy in the Caribbean. The variance in historians' stories is also due to the fact that they ask different questions. The questions that German historians have asked about Wilhelmine expansionism have been framed by Fischer; these historians are investigating the breadth of the German expansionist impulse. Seeking German imperialism, they find it in the Western Hemisphere.

Certainly one can find evidence of expansionist urges in the reams of data on Germany in Latin America—in German, American, and British archives, the press, the Reichstag debates, pamphlets, and literature. But one cannot easily move from this to the assertion that Germany posed a threat to the Monroe Doctrine. It is important not to conflate policy and dreams, the official and the personal; it is important not to emphasize rhetoric while downplaying the record of what was actually done. Otherwise one risks cajoling historians of U.S. imperialism into believing that there was indeed a German threat, when one finds merely evidence of an expansionist urge. This matters because it bears the weight of the American recourse to the Monroe Doctrine—the claim that the region required protection. The question for a historian of U.S. foreign policy, therefore, is: Did these expansionist urges amount to a threat to the Monroe Doctrine? Did the region need protection?

To answer this question I investigate the international dynamics of Latin America during this time of flux, when England was retreating and Germany and the United States were rising rapidly. I look closely at German actions—at what Berlin actually did in the hemisphere—and at the perception of this policy in the United States, in all its fuguelike complexity, for the perceptions of the state department, the president, the navy, and the press always differed. The analysis of the press poses a special challenge because even if it were possible to read more than a small fraction of it (and it is not), one could still not determine its relationship to public opinion. Nevertheless, the press, especially in the United States, was an important player in this story, fanning the flames of jingoist fears of Germany. Therefore, I use the press, knowing full well that it can provide only an oblique and imprecise reflection of the popular mood.

I begin by setting the scene, describing U.S.-German political and economic relations at the turn of the century and comparing the German war plans against the United States with the U.S. plans against Germany. Germany's participation in the 1902–3 blockade of Venezuela has been considered the clearest evidence of Berlin's designs on the hemisphere by Americans from Teddy Roosevelt to Holger Herwig, and Roosevelt's claim that the Germans agreed to arbitration only after he had softly threatened them with the big stick of the U.S. Navy has lent credence to the notion. I look closely at the record and question the standard explanation of Germany's motivation for participating in the blockade. I move to an examination of the German threat to southern Brazil, a region that had attracted close to half a million German emigrants and that German jingoes had loudly proclaimed would become part of a New Germany. The Zimmermann telegram seems to cap the indictment of Germany's sinister intentions, but placing the telegram in the context of Germany's policy toward Mexico before the outbreak of World War I, when Berlin struggled to accommodate Wilson's agonizingly slow determination of his Mexican policy, exposes the discontinuities caused by the war. Finally, I analyze the constants of Wilhelmine policy toward Latin America and the Monroe Doctrine, and I speculate on the patterned and consistent gap between this policy and the U.S. perception of it.

This investigation provides, therefore, a case study in threat perception, the study of the subtle tug-of-war waged between capabilities and desires. This is an inherently complicated subject that wrestles with the slippery, symbiotic relationship between perception and reality. The close analysis of German actions anchors it and helps to ward away the insidious assumption that U.S. perceptions were indeed reality; that is, that because the United States perceived a threat there was in fact a threat. It serves as a rigorous mirror to the patterned distortions—the exaggerations—of U.S. perception. Furthermore, German policy is part of the true picture. The Caribbean Sea and southwestern Atlantic were not U.S. waters. With the withdrawing British navy and the simultaneous growth of the German and American fleets, these were international waters, and the historian must have a firm grasp of the international dynamics of the region before understanding and judging U.S. policy.

When U.S. policy is seen in this international context, its fundamental lack of exceptionalism is revealed. The United States, like Germany, was an imperial power seeking as much hegemony as possible at the lowest cost. The Monroe Doctrine, the justification of expansionism in the hemisphere, was, like the rhetoric of the pan-Germans, the statement of a dream. The difference between it and the pan-German rhetoric was that, by the turn of the century, it was within grasp. In Latin America, the United States was the more successful imperialist not because it had more military power, and not even because of proximity, but because, unlike Germany, it was surrounded by weak neighbors and the rolling sea.

The German threat, bandied about by the U.S. press and naval officers and politicians at the time, and by historians to the present day, whether sincerely believed or not, was useful. The Germans, with their expansionist talk and their growing navy, provided the Americans with an opportunity. The depiction of Germany as a potential aggressor in the hemisphere helped to exonerate the interventionism of the United States. It distinguishes U.S. policy from European policy. This satisfies a deeply felt need, and it helps to explain the durability of the image. Therefore, it is necessary to examine German policy very closely, for there is resistance to dismissing the German threat. It is not so much, as some have argued, that we needed an enemy to justify naval expansion but to see ourselves as different, and better.

The Rise of German-American Antagonism

It was the beginning of the twentieth century. The German navy had drawn up plans to wage war against the United States. Although it had toyed with the idea of a direct assault on New York or Cape Cod, it favored the establishment first of a base in the Caribbean from which it would lure the U.S. fleet to its Waterloo. Predicting this strategy, the U.S. Navy's General Board was alarmed by any German activity in the Caribbean. Reports surfaced that the Germans were plotting to buy the Danish West Indies, that they were on the verge of prying the island of Margarita from the Venezuelans, and that they had sinister designs on Haiti. Therefore, the U.S. Navy devised detailed plans to counter a German attack in the Caribbean, plans that dovetailed with the German plans with eerie precision. After decades of friendly relations, how had it come to this? [1]

Background to Antagonism

At the end of the nineteenth century both Germany and the United States were rising powers; both were building strong navies; both were latecomers to the imperial scramble; both were nipping at England's heels. The tenor of the time was "expand or perish"; there were bound to be conflicts and jealousies, and the military establishments of both countries were bound to translate these tensions into contingency plans.

The United States emerged from Reconstruction in an explosion of productivity and change: Americans moved from farm to city, where they rubbed elbows with new immigrants, were dazzled by a torrent of inventions, and sought work in new industries. Washington was led by probusiness presidents, but the best-known names of this Gilded Age are those of the superstar businessmen: Carnegie, Mellon, Rockefeller. In the 1880s, Germany, too, seemed to be releasing long-pent-up energy after its unification in 1871. Germans, like Americans, moved to the cities, were dazzled by inventions, and took jobs in factories. The most famous name of the 1880s in Germany was not that of the kaiser but of his "iron chancellor," Otto von Bismarck. This "big, rumbling, heavy, fiery, minatory, objurgatory" man, as the U.S. minister described him, attempted to juggle the fractious interests of Germany's complex hybrid political system and to hold the dizzying array of competing forces of German society—the rulers of the various states, the large landowners, the industrialists, the urban workers, the Catholics, the socialists, the liberals, the conservatives—at bay, at least temporarily.[2]

The German states and the United States had enjoyed cordial, even warm, relations during the tumultuous mid-nineteenth century. There had been very few bones of contention between them. The German states had sympathized with the North in the U.S. Civil War, and the U.S. government, while officially neutral in the Franco-Prussian War of 1870–71, had been clearly sympathetic to Prussia, as had been the majority of the American people. But these ties had begun to fray by 1880, and by the turn of the century, the erstwhile friends were at swords' points. Andrew White was shocked by the transformation. American minister to Germany from 1879 to 1881, he returned as ambassador in 1897 to discover many changes. "On my settling down to the business of the embassy, it appeared that the changes in public sentiment since my former stay as minister, eighteen years before, were great indeed. At that time German feeling was decidedly friendly to the United States. . . . But all this was now changed. German feeling toward us had become generally adverse and, in some parts of the empire, bitterly hostile."[3] The souring of the relationship was due primarily to the interplay between the similarities and the differences of U.S. and German industrialization.

The fact that both Germany and the United States burst into the industrial revolution like roaring steam engines making up for lost time had many repercussions: agricultural and industrial production soared (steel production, for example, rose tenfold in Germany and twentyfold in the United States between 1880 and 1913), and the population skyrocketed—between 1870 and 1900, German population grew from 40 million to 56 million, while the United States grew from 40 million to 76 million.[4] The attendant shift in power from farm to city led to parallel political challenges: landowners grew anxious as the urban poor and the middle class swelled. Both Washington and Berlin struggled to satisfy the increasingly strident demands of these groups, and both turned to trade policy to do so. The parallels between the trade policies of the two countries at century's end are striking. Tariffs and import bans appeased farmers and heads of dynamic nascent industries while at the same time raising revenue for projects to placate the urban middle class. However, these barriers also carried high risks: they could alienate the urban poor, who would be forced to pay more for necessities, or they could precipitate a trade war, hurting exporters. Both Berlin and Washington feared that the world would be carved into closed trading areas, and neither wanted to be left out of the scramble. Thus anxiety seeped in, while the two governments embraced their own tariffs and denounced all others. The uneasiness was inflated by the absence of a bilateral trade agreement regulating German and American tariff rates. Berlin considered the Americans bound by an 1828 treaty that had granted Prussia most-favored-nation (MFN) status. The Americans, however, argued that since the 1828 treaty had been with Prussia rather than Germany it was defunct and that, in any case, it had not guaranteed MFN.[5] Further complicating tariff policy was the simple fact that the pace of industrial, social, and scientific change outstripped the ability of the U.S. Congress and the German Reichstag, both bogged down in debate, to respond coherently. The playing field kept changing.

Thus, in many ways, Germany and Washington were facing similar problems in the late nineteenth century. But there were also important differences. First, of course, was scale: America's raw material base and size gave it an almost unassailable advantage. Second was the nature of their exports: about 75 percent of all U.S. exports to Germany were agricultural, supplying either necessary food (particularly grain and meat) to the burgeoning population or raw materials (particularly raw cotton, also petroleum and copper) on which German industry depended; only about 25 percent of German exports to the United States, on the other hand, were raw materials for U.S. factories (pig iron and cement); the remainder consisted of finished goods such as chemicals, drugs, wine, manufactured fabrics, hides, and glassware, none of which was a necessity, and sugar, which could be supplied by other countries. Third, Prussian Junkers (conservative owners of large landed estates east of the Elbe) were closer to the center of power in Wilhelmine Germany than were American farmers, who struggled unsuccessfully on the periphery (in the defeated South and in the West) to create a viable populist movement in the final decades of the century.

The differences in scale and types of exports meant that American agricultural exports to Germany threatened to overwhelm German domestic produce and also that the United States could afford to slap higher tariffs on German imports than the Germans placed on U.S. imports. The impact of the greater political power of large landowners in Germany was that Berlin restricted some U.S. imports, even though this had a deleterious effect on U.S.-German relations. The antagonism centered on three products: sugar, pork, and beef.

"The race for commercial supremacy." Uncle Sam is jubilant that U.S. exports to Germany are increasingly outstripping German exports to the United States. The kaiser, on the other hand, shown in this 1900 cartoon in full military regalia with fist upraised in fury and frustration, is left in the dust. (*Harper's Weekly*, 2 June 1900, cover)

By 1880, German farmers felt squeezed by U.S. competition. In the preceding decade, Germany had had to feed an ever increasing population while it had suffered crop failures and a series of economic downturns; as a result it had changed from being a food exporter to being a food importer. During the same decade the United States had doubled its grain exports to Germany and replaced Germany as a grain supplier to England and France.[6] And in 1875,

Washington had dealt a serious blow to the largest single item Germany exported to the United States—sugar—by lifting all duties on Hawaiian sugar and raising the duty on all other imported sugar. (Germany was at the time the world's largest sugar producer.) The United States was the German beet sugar growers' second-largest market, absorbing about a quarter of their crop.[7] By the end of the decade large farmers, fearful of foreign competition and outraged by high foreign tariffs on their imports, turned to protectionism. In 1879 Bismarck reversed Germany's traditional free-trade policy and used protectionism to forge the crucial "rye and iron" coalition, appeasing the large landowners and key industrialists alike with protective tariffs. The collateral damage of the chancellor's shaky marriage of convenience was that relations with the United States, as well as European countries, were damaged. The American chargé declared Bismarck's policy to be "in reality a desperate attempt to resist the competition of the cheap produce and manufactures of the United States and Great Britain."[8]

The most famous incident to ignite the rivalry between the two rising powers was the Pork War, an incident that historian Louis Snyder aptly calls "a fascinating microcosm of conflicting economic nationalisms." Pork products were serious business: in 1880, the Americans exported approximately $100 million worth of pig; this was 10 percent of America's total exports. Most (60 percent) went to Britain; in continental Europe, Germany, at 10 percent, was the American pork exporter's best customer. And yet, on 25 June 1880 the German government banned U.S. chopped pork and sausages, and in 1883 it extended the ban to include all U.S. pork products. Berlin claimed that it was merely protecting its citizens from unclean American meat. While the fear of trichinosis was genuine (the scientific understanding of the parasite was in its infancy, and Germans, who ate pork raw or nearly raw, were particularly vulnerable to it), and although Italy, Portugal, Greece, and Spain had already banned U.S. pork on the same grounds, the explanation also provided a handy cover. The flood of U.S. pork in Europe undersold domestic pork; in Germany, U.S. ham cost 40 percent less than the local product. The Agrarians, emerging from the difficult 1870s, demanded protection, and a ban based on sanitary precautions sidestepped the wrath of the populace, who faced higher pork prices, by alleging that it was for their own good; furthermore, a sanitary ban, unlike a tariff, bypassed the exposure of a Reichstag debate.[9]

The German ban provoked an uproar in America: Germany was an important customer, and its trade policy was considered trendsetting on the Continent. "It is the German position which is fraught with the gravest dangers," an American analyst explained, "not only for the interests it directly affects, but also for the impetus it is likely to give to imitation by other nations which are

"We never speak as we pass by." The Pork War began in 1880 when Germany, here portrayed as Chancellor Bismarck, claimed that U.S. pork was unsanitary and banned it. Americans were outraged. (*Frank Leslie's Illustrated Newspaper*, 1 March 1884)

looking to her for a lead." Indeed, France, Austria-Hungary, Turkey, Romania, and Denmark did follow the German lead.[10] Not only were profits affected — the U.S. secretary of agriculture estimated that the ban cost the United States more than $260 million — so too was American honor.[11] Pig mavens on both sides of the Atlantic, all operating in scientific uncertainty, pontificated on the cleanliness, or lack thereof, of U.S. pork. The *New York Times* noted wryly, "Americans will be somewhat surprised to know that the same article of food which is consumed in such enormous quantities in this country becomes dangerous to health when it reaches German territory." One U.S. senator declared that the only difference between a protective tariff and a sanitary exclusion was "that the one is manly and direct, while the other is indirect and based on false pretenses." In 1888, President Grover Cleveland threatened retaliation.[12]

After a bruising decade of insults, accusations, and scathing cartoons, the Germans finally lifted the ban on American pork in 1891. While it is true that the United States had just passed a Meat Inspection Act, which alleviated some German anxiety about trichinosis, this was not what spurred the truce. Rather, it was fear of retaliation. The act granted the president the authority to strike back at any country that persisted in proscribing U.S. meat by banning the importation of any of its products whatsoever. As a French journalist declared, "This puts the knife at the throat of England, France, and Germany." Furthermore, the protectionist McKinley Tariff, which had been enacted in 1890, lifted the duty on sugar that had been in place since the Civil War. This pleased the Germans, but two other provisions of the law gave them pause: a surtax was levied on bountied sugar (which included all German sugar), and the president was granted the authority to reimpose the sugar duty on any country that "imposes duties or other exactions on . . . products of the United States, which . . . he may deem to be reciprocally unequal and unreasonable." Although this threat had been drafted with an eye to South American cane sugar producers, it alarmed German sugar beet growers, whose $36 million trade exports to the United States would disappear if saddled with a $20 a ton duty. This fear led to the resolution of the Pork War. "The German Government has really been forced to take the action it has," the *Chicago Tribune* explained, "to protect the great beet-sugar industry." On 22 August 1891, the Saratoga Agreement, stipulating that the United States would not use the provisions of the McKinley Tariff to reimpose the duty on German sugar if Germany would lift the ban on U.S. pork, was brokered, and on 3 September the pork ban was repealed.[13]

The Saratoga Agreement and the truce were ephemeral. Until the First World War, the "guerilla warfare," (as the *Kölnische Zeitung* deemed it) between the two countries persisted.[14] In the 1890s, U.S. tariff policy was buffeted by the vicissitudes of domestic politics (particularly the Republican attempt to woo farmers from the Democratic Party) and the severe depression of 1893–97. In 1894 the Wilson-Gorman Tariff replaced the McKinley Tariff and therefore, according to Washington but not Berlin, abrogated the Saratoga Agreement. Under Wilson-Gorman, duties on most imports were lowered, but the sugar tariff was reimposed and the surtax on bountied sugar maintained.[15] Three years later the Dingley Tariff, and its associated surtax on bountied sugar, almost doubled the rate imposed on German sugar. Washington was not deaf to Berlin's protests but overruled them because of the importance of the sugar tariff in raising revenue and, perhaps, because German sugar exports to the United States continued to increase throughout the decade despite the higher tariffs.[16] Further, Americans were indignant over continuing German restrictions on U.S. meat. Their demands for retaliation (against adulterated German wines or toys painted with toxic substances) escalated.[17] Fears of a tariff war rumbled through the decade. In the *New York Times* in the 1890s, the lion's share of articles about both Germany and trade disputes concerned U.S.-German tariff wrangles. In contrast, the other major European powers—even France, which imposed higher duties on U.S. imports than did Germany but was a less important customer and considered less influential—got off lightly.[18]

The German reaction was tortured. On the one hand, stung by the futility of its violent tariff war with Russia of 1893–94 and by the rising protectionist walls in Europe and eager not to invite U.S. retaliation, Berlin bent over backward to accommodate the unaccommodating Americans.[19] Despite a tumultuous decade in which two chancellors, General Leo von Caprivi and Prince Chlodwig zu Hohenlohe-Schillingsfürst, failed to create either calm or order in the wake of Bismarck's dismissal, Berlin doggedly respected Bismarck's interpretation of the (in the *Kölnische Zeitung*'s words) "venerable, somewhat mythical" treaty of 1828 and granted the United States MFN status.[20] Determined to restructure Germany's foreign trade, Caprivi earned the hatred of the Agrarians by launching a series of trade treaties in 1892 that lowered tariffs with European states; in accordance with MFN principles, he extended the lower tariff to the United States.[21] Washington did not reciprocate. In 1897, the state secretary for foreign affairs asserted that the average U.S. duty on German exports to the United States was 50 percent; on U.S. exports to Germany, 9 percent. Although the State Department quibbled with the figures, it did not deny their essential correctness. "The result," the second secretary of the U.S. embassy in Berlin, who was a commercial specialist, wrote, "is that she [Germany] now [1902] buys about 100 per cent more goods from the United States than she sells to the American republic."[22]

On the other hand, in order to maintain the rye and iron coalition, Berlin bowed to the wishes of the Agrarians, who were incensed by the deluge of cheap American foodstuffs and the American restrictions on German sugar. They complained that in the five years following the resolution of the Pork War the United States had erected tariff barriers against German imports while U.S. exports of meat to Germany had increased sixfold, despite the fact that local German municipalities continued to restrict U.S. pork imports. "We are flooded with American wheat, yet America closes its doors to our sugar," an Agrarian leader complained in the Reichstag.[23] In October 1894, two months after the Wilson-Gorman Tariff reimposed the sugar duty, Germany banned U.S. beef imports and, as it had with pork, justified the ban on

"In bad form for good shooting." Uncle Sam, peeking out from behind the tariff wall, is delighted to see Germany sweat. As frustrated as Berlin was with U.S. tariff barriers, it did not dare retaliate for fear of starting a trade war that would hurt it much more than the United States. (*Butte Inter Mountain*; reprinted in *Literary Digest* [3 March 1906])

health grounds, specifically the risk of infection of German cattle with Texas fever. The United States had supplied about half of Germany's meat imports in 1891; by the end of 1904, it supplied only about 15 percent. The beef ban hurt American beef exports to Germany, caused a prolonged meat shortage in Germany, and raised American hackles. The ban was "all the more irritating," President Grover Cleveland declared in his 1895 Annual Message to Congress, because of the "excellence and wholesomeness of [our] . . . exported food supplies."[24] In 1898 Prussia banned American fruits, citing fears of the spread of San José scale. ("The real bug," the *New York Evening Post* explained, "is the Dingley tariff.")[25]

The government in Berlin was uneasy with the bans, in part because they hurt German-American relations and in part because they hurt its relations with the working class, industrialists, and progressives, who faced meat and fruit shortages and higher prices. But the Agrarians lobbied relentlessly, and the conservative German press lambasted the government for its alleged weakness toward American outrages.[26] By the end of the decade the Agrarians went for the jugular: they refused to support Kaiser Wilhelm's pet project, the building of a great navy, unless the ban on American meat was maintained. The *New York Times* commented, "In order to secure support for his naval programme he [Wilhelm II] will do anything, in or out of reason." The U.S. ambassador, whose correspondence to the State Department had dealt with the sanitary bans more than any other issue and who had been optimistic that the ban would be moderated, accepted political reality in March 1900. "The heart of the Emperor is set on passing the navy bill," he wrote, "and without the support of the main body of those demanding this meat inspection bill . . . the navy bill can not be made a law." It was an unequal contest, and despite the government's qualms, on 3 June 1900 it passed an "exceedingly drastic" meat inspection bill that broadened the ban on American meat. Nine days later, the Reichstag passed the naval bill.[27]

Thus, in the final quarter of the nineteenth century, the friendly ties that had connected Germany and the United States were strained. The increasing trade between the two countries led to genuine conflicts of interest. Nevertheless, this trade also bound the two countries closer together. By 1890, the United States was Germany's second most important customer and fourth most important supplier; Germany was the United States' second most important customer and supplier. More than 10 percent of each nation's total foreign trade was with the other. By 1898, the United States had become Germany's most important supplier.[28]

The problems between them arose from several factors. First, trade policy in both countries was highly politicized. Once the U.S. Congress and the German Reichstag had processed them, these policies were compromises that reflected the fleeting partisan balances of power at the time. Their impact on actual foreign trade was frequently lost in the process. Thus the U.S. sugar tariff that so incensed the Germans was in fact a revenue and trust-busting measure, and the German Meat Inspection Law that enraged the Americans was the price the Agrarians extracted for Wilhelm's fleet. Second, not only did trade policy reflect domestic concerns, but it also was frequently directed toward a state other than Germany or the United States, and the impact on them was, so to speak, "collateral damage." Thus, Bismarck placed a tariff on wheat in 1879 with Russia foremost in mind, but U.S. wheat exporters also paid; likewise, the U.S. sugar duty was written with the Latin American cane sugar producers in mind, but Germany suffered. Third, the U.S. juggernaut threatened to overwhelm Germany. In the 1880s the bilateral balance of trade favored the Germans, but by 1890 this had begun to change, and by the end of the decade—the pork and beef bans notwithstanding—the balance had swung strongly in the United States' favor. In the 1890s, the value of U.S. exports to Germany increased 133 percent, while U.S. imports from Germany rose only 12 percent.[29] Fourth, there were genuine fears about the spread of contagious diseases.[30] Finally, as the century closed, both countries were also beset with growing anxieties about sharpening competition for the Chinese and, especially, the Latin American markets. The Americans had been usurping German markets in Europe for twenty years, but the competition was still largely theoretical in the relatively untapped markets outside Europe. Yet in the final decades of the century, both Germany and the United States had steadily increased their participation in foreign trade, and in some important products, notably iron and steel, they were in direct competition. By 1900, Germany had doubled its share of foreign trade and surpassed France. In the same period, the United States had nearly doubled its imports and tripled its exports, leaving it second only to the United Kingdom. Many Europeans, including many in Germany, feared that the Monroe Doctrine and the high American tariffs of the 1890s cloaked the intention of the United States to squeeze Europe out of Latin American markets.[31] As the twentieth century began, fears of the impending contest were in the air.

The third of these five factors—that the balance of trade was shifting in the United States' favor—merits some attention. To the constant irritation of the Germans, the United States held better cards. America had a vast and expanding market with an abundant supply of raw materials, and the Germans, who imported difficult-to-replace necessities from the United States, were more dependent on the United States, which imported easy-to-replace luxuries from Germany, than vice versa. Even the U.S. ambassador noted in 1899, "There is undoubtedly among Germans of all classes a feeling very deep and widespread that our country has dealt very harshly with them from a commercial point of view." [32] But there was little Germany could do. The pork and beef bans only made the Americans swarm; they did not slow them down. They were, as the German American scholar Wolf von Schierbrand wrote, "but needle-pricks, irritating." [33] Some "Agrarian hot-heads" (in the *Kölnische Zeitung*'s words) asserted that the fatherland's honor and security demanded a tariff war, but most industrialists and government officials demurred, asserting that Germany would suffer most in such a contest.[34] In 1898, Sartorius von Waltershausen, a well-known and respected professor specializing in German-U.S.

economic relations, analyzed the impact of a tariff war and asserted that Berlin would have to target U.S. cotton exports, which constituted one-third of all U.S. exports to Germany and had always been admitted duty-free. However, to penalize U.S. cotton (or, for that matter, U.S. copper and petroleum) would be to cut off one's nose to spite one's face. It would raise the price of German textiles and render them less competitive abroad. Further, Sartorius argued, U.S. retaliatory tariffs on German exports would hurt Germany but not the United States. "England would gladly take our place in supplying cotton, woolen, and leather goods; Belgium and France in furnishing increasing amounts of sugar, and Austria, clothing and linen." Finally, a tariff war would seriously hurt German shipping agencies. "To summarize: it would be the worst possible commercial policy."[35] Dissuaded from a tariff war, disgruntled Germans dreamed of a European coalition, a customs union, against the United States. The Conservative and Agrarian leader, Hans Wilhelm von Kanitz-Podangen, declared in the Reichstag in 1898 that there was in Europe a "certain readiness to make common cause" against the United States.[36] However, instructed by the State Department to report "any serious movement in favor of a combination so gravely affecting the interests of the United States," Ambassador White dismissed the notion: "[I do] not look upon a coalition against our interests as at present at all likely to be made. The interests of all European nations are so diverse and indeed in many respects so hostile to each other that any union against us would be extremely difficult, especially in view of the fact that the questions which divide many of them excite deeper feelings than those which at present separate us from Europe."[37] As the *New-Yorker Staats-Zeitung* observed dryly, "The battle cry of 'All Europe against all America' is more easily raised than carried into action." The prominent liberal daily, the *Berliner Tageblatt*, agreed: "This idea [of a European customs union] is not possible now, or even, to be more truthful, in the foreseeable future."[38] For there was never any chance that Britain, with its almost religious dedication to free trade and its growing ties to the United States, would join. Without England, a European *Zollverein* would only irritate the United States and reveal its own impotence. The idea came to nought. The scale and geographical isolation of the United States made it a more resilient country.

While this imbalance galled the Germans, it gave the Americans a certain swagger. They could afford to demand low tariffs from Germany while slapping the McKinley, Wilson-Gorman, and Dingley tariffs on them. As the *New York Times* editorialized in 1900, "A total cessation of commercial intercourse would directly damage Germany twice as much as it would damage the United States."[39]

By the end of the century, both countries were annoyed with each other, but the causes were slightly different: Germany feared the effect of America's boundless potential and resented its protectionist policy that indiscriminately swept German imports into its web; the United States had several specific grievances against German exclusions of particular U.S. exports, especially pork and beef. These tensions over trade practices predated and exacerbated the growing tensions between the two powers about each other's imperial policies at the century's end.

On 1 January 1898, the German ambassador in Washington, Theodor von Holleben, reported that Germany had become "the most hated land" in the United States because of anger and frustration over trade.[40] Six months later Ambassador White wrote a long report analyzing the seven causes of German ill will toward the United States. "The first of these is, no doubt, what the Germans consider as the extreme protective policy of the United States. This, of course, alienates to a considerable extent the manufacturing classes," he explained. "As a second cause I shall name the great productivity of the United States. . . . This naturally alienates the land-owning interest." White listed his third reason as the antipathy of German reactionaries, the fourth as the disappointment of German liberals with some aspects of American life (particularly lynching); fifth was American arrogance toward Europe and fears that the United States was trying to impose its view of international law on the system; sixth was resentment at America's sometimes cavalier treatment of Germany; and finally, White mentioned (perhaps with a grain of self-interest) the German sense of resentment that the U.S. embassy in Berlin was spartan compared with the embassies of other countries, seeming to imply a lack of respect for the German nation.[41] This list, written in August 1898, provides a snapshot of Germany's view of America at the very moment that the relationship was changing. White stressed the impact of trade disputes; he then cited a number of grievances stemming from U.S. arrogance and perceived slights. With the exception of the reference to German anxieties about U.S. international law, political and imperial concerns did not appear in this thorough discussion of German complaints about the United States. This was about to change.

1898: The Perception Is Formed

Before 1898, trade disputes occupied center stage in the tensions between Germany and the United States. Two major events in April 1898—the passing of the First Fleet Bill in Germany and the outbreak of the Spanish-American War—made the situation more complicated. Germany continued to be alarmed by U.S. growth and economic competition, and concern about American arrogance imposing its views on the international system was exacerbated by the U.S. imperial surge. American anxieties about Germany, on the other hand, shifted dramatically from trade to another sphere: the possibility of a German challenge to the Monroe Doctrine.

Kaiser Wilhelm II's decision to build a great fleet was both logical and insane. His Germany was complex and idiosyncratic. How could it have been otherwise, given the kaiser's character, Bismarck's legacy, and Germany's position in the center of Europe? German emperor from 1888 to 1918, Wilhelm was vindictive, petty, and unbalanced and also energetic, willful, and gifted. It was widely remarked at the time that he was a disturbed man, a man of bizarre and alarming personality quirks. "Their [the Germans'] surprising sovereign," the *New York Times* remarked in 1897, "will sooner or later 'go queer' altogether."[42] Wilhelm's instability has contributed to a tendency among historians to airbrush him out of history. But the kaiser mattered. Ambassador White, who had once been president of Cornell University, understood this in 1898:

> As to the Sovereign himself, it is a great mistake to consider him merely a fitful and versatile man, "everything by turns and nothing long." He is, indeed, a man of remarkably varied abilities—an orator, a poet, an artist, and much else, but, with this, a man of convictions, of ideas, of real force, of character, successful in devising plans and managing men, and deeply impressed with the . . . ambition of extending the power of . . . Germany. His utterances at times have doubtless seemed, to many, careless and ill-considered, but it may well be questioned whether he has not understood his audiences and the effect that he has wished to produce better than his critics have done. . . . It would be a serious mistake to suppose that he has not the respect or love of his subjects.[43]

Wilhelm was the hub for his dozens of splintered advisers, whose careers depended on their sage handling of him. His whims and worldview trickled down through the court, the diplomatic corps, and the bureaucracy. Like the defining fractal of a crystal, the kaiser's personality was stamped on every aspect of the German government. There was order in the apparent chaos: his harried court followed his every move like starlings alighting and swerving over a field. This was Wilhelm's system of "personal rule," in which he controlled all appointments, in which he determined even the weddings of the court, in which his amusement meant promotion and his displeasure dismissal. Personal rule may have been invisible, but it was as real as a straitjacket. It meant that Wilhelm's worldview was replicated by those around him. By the turn of the century he had surrounded himself with men who either thought as he thought—about Germany's role in the world, about Social

Democrats, about Jews—or were spineless or cynical. This cabal was accountable only to the kaiser, and the kaiser was accountable to no one. Wilhelm
was a disaster for Germany, but it was the system of government in Wilhelmine Germany that allowed him to impose his stamp for so long. The power
of the kaiser dwarfed that of the Reichstag, which, curbed by the conservative
civil service and the Prussian-dominated Bundesrat (upper house), provided
only a fragile facade of democracy. Perhaps Bismarck, who had designed the
system, could have tempered the kaiser, but one of the young sovereign's first
acts had been to fire the "iron chancellor." Wilhelm proceeded to go through
three chancellors in less than a decade. He was a man of strong, if unpredictable, will.[44]

In 1897 Kaiser Wilhelm II launched his world policy, Weltpolitik. This signaled a fundamental change in German foreign policy. Wilhelm II rejected
Bismarck's contention that Germany should concentrate on its position as a
great Continental power. Except for his brief, and aberrant, foray into colonization, Bismarck had argued that German diplomacy had to focus on de-
fusing the threat of a two-front war. Facing an implacably hostile France after
the Franco-Prussian War and the drama of Alsace-Lorraine, Germany had to
secure its southern and eastern fronts. To this end, Bismarck concluded an alliance with Austria-Hungary and strove to maintain good relations with Russia.
Bismarck's vision was of a Germany that, by dint of its great army and subtle
diplomacy, would be secure in its role as the leading power of the European
continent; this was his *Grossmachtpolitik*. Wilhelm II's Weltpolitik was far
more ambitious: Germany's domain was no longer Europe; it was the world.
Wilhelm was too restless to play the frustrating game of the European balance
of power. The constraints of Germany's geographical position irritated him.
His vision was of a Germany that, by dint of its great navy and aggressive diplomacy, would be secure in its role as a great Continental *and* world power.
Weltpolitik was therefore, first and foremost, a naval policy. As the motto
adorning one of the German buildings at the Paris Exposition of 1900 stated,
"Our future lies on the sea." Wilhelm had signaled this as early as 1890 when
he had proclaimed to the naval officer corps, "As my late grandfather [Kaiser
Wilhelm I] once said, 'My last thought will be of my Army'—So I promise you
now, 'My last thought will be of my Navy.'" Through Weltpolitik, Germany
would leapfrog over its Continental borders and be shoved onto the high seas.
Germany, under Wilhelm II, would pretend it was an island nation.[45]

Why did the kaiser launch Weltpolitik? The answers range from an infantile
obsession with ships, to an Oedipal hatred of England, to a sage assessment
of the unifying power of the fleet domestically, to the restlessness of a rising
power that was hemmed in on all sides.[46] German records are incomplete,

because of the nature of records, subsequent wars, and the character of the Wilhelmine bureaucracy. The purpose of government policy more often than not remained hidden in the kaiser's inscrutable mind; it was not committed to paper; it was not debated in the Reichstag. It is, therefore, ripe material for the debate of historians. To complicate further the interpretation of Weltpolitik, the two men whom the kaiser appointed in 1897 to push his program through the Reichstag—Rear Admiral Alfred Tirpitz, to oversee the navy, and Bernhard von Bülow, to oversee foreign policy—construed it in different ways.

The bureaucratic vicissitudes of the German navy in this period are dizzying. Buffeted by the need to professionalize, personal rivalries, and the kaiser's desire for absolute control, the structure of the navy was overhauled time and time again. Tirpitz did not head the German navy—he was appointed secretary of state of the Reichsmarineamt, one of the navy's three branches, each of which was directly responsible to the kaiser, the commander in chief. Tirpitz was able to use the confusion in the naval bureaucracy to his advantage. He made himself the most powerful and enduring figure in the navy. Equally adept at handling the kaiser and the Reichstag, he was ruthless in disposing of his enemies. Because of his stubbornness, his political agility, and his thoroughness, he exercised de facto control of the whole navy. His interpretation of Weltpolitik was simple and unwavering: Germany needed a world-class navy as soon as possible. To this end he steered two major fleet bills through the Reichstag. The first, passed in April 1898, launched Weltpolitik. By mandating the construction of seven battleships and nine cruisers in six years, this bill signaled that Wilhelm's Germany had turned toward the sea. The Second Fleet Bill, passed in 1900, dramatically accelerated the pace and dimension of the change by adding nineteen more battleships (totaling thirty-eight) and twenty-three new cruisers by 1916. The two bills, by doubling the fleet and undermining the power of the Reichstag to micromanage the naval budget on an annual basis, were essential to Tirpitz's plan, but they carried a very high price abroad. Tirpitz recognized this and urged the Wilhelmstrasse to be cautious during the "danger zone" while the fleet was being built, but nothing—not the rising alarm of England, not the growing isolation of Germany, not the development of dreadnoughts or of submarines—made him question his plan. He would, in his dogged, ambitious, politically savvy, and strategically inept fashion, insist on building a big ship navy until he retired, with the rank of grand admiral, in 1916.[47]

Bülow was appointed secretary of state for foreign affairs in 1897, rising to Reich chancellor in 1900, a post he held until 1909. A polished and cunning man, whose main characteristic was, in the estimation of the U.S. ambassador, "sweet reasonableness," Bülow knew that he had been appointed to create the political conditions that would allow the fleet to be built: "When I was called from Rome to Berlin [to be secretary of state]," he wrote in his memoirs, "the job I was given was to facilitate the strengthening of the fleet." Weltpolitik was initially popular at home, and Bülow used it to dampen domestic dissent and to build political coalitions, but its high financial cost and minimal successes eventually caused it to complicate Bülow's tasks at home, just as it did abroad. Bülow had to keep Germany at peace while the fleet was being built. To this end, he continued Bismarck's reliance on the alliance with Austria-Hungary and sought to improve relations with Russia, while seeking to avoid the constraint of a formal alliance. He wanted a "free hand." As the fleet grew and the aggressive, expansionist rhetoric of the pan-Germans escalated, Bülow's free hand came back to haunt him: freedom on the world stage is perilously close to isolation.[48]

Weltpolitik was Wilhelm's impatient throw of the dice. It was his gamble that he could defy history and geography. Tirpitz egged him on, and if Bülow had doubts, he did not share them with the autocratic ruler on whose pleasure his job depended. And so Germany lurched onto the seas, hoping on the one hand that enhanced naval power would give its potential enemies reason to retreat and its potential friends reason to approach and, on the other hand, that England would not respond to the threat during the twenty years it would take to build the fleet to full strength. Anxiety about this danger zone coupled with the kaiser's braggadocio caused Berlin's policy to veer between caution and abandon. Lumbering and uncoordinated, Germany was, as Tirpitz said, "dancing on eggs."[49]

Underlying Weltpolitik were real strategic concerns. As a German naval enthusiast, Hans Hartmann, wrote in 1900, Weltpolitik was the "natural result of the historical, social, and industrial development of Germany."[50] Germany's overseas interests were growing; in the 1890s a strong navy was considered crucial to the protection of international trade. In 1894, while he was chief of staff of the Oberkommando (High Command) of the navy, Tirpitz had written, "Any state with global interests must be able to make its power felt beyond its territorial waters. Global trade, industry . . . transportation, and colonies are impossible without a fleet capable of taking the offensive."[51] This reflected the new thinking about the navy that had been given voice in 1890 by Alfred Thayer Mahan's *The Influence of Sea Power upon History*. Like other important statements of strategy, such as George Kennan's long telegram of 1946, *The Influence* was influential because it was a perfectly timed, coherent explanation of the impact of the profound changes that had occurred in geopolitics and technology. The paradigm shift Mahan advocated was fundamental: a modern navy was not defensive but offensive. According to Mahan, conflict was inevitable, trade rivalry would be its primary cause, and history showed that the navy would provide the key to success. Power was defined as control of the sea. This control would be won either in head-to-head clashes of concentrated fleets or through deterrence—persuading one's adversary that it risked destruction if it dared launch a war. From control of the sea, all good things would flow. Without control of the sea, everything else (raids on shipping, coastal defense) would be ephemeral. In 1894, Wilhelm announced that he was "not reading, but devouring Captain Mahan's book." Two thousand copies of it were distributed by the Imperial Naval Office prior to the debate on the First Fleet Bill.[52] Weltpolitik was Germany's embodiment of Mahanian thinking: states must seize greatness on the high seas.

In the summer of 1898, the Spanish-American War confirmed the importance of naval power. In the story of the souring of U.S.-German relations, this war plays a decisive role. In the months preceding the war, Berlin, hoping to uphold the principle of monarchy and to keep the United States from accruing too much power, was openly sympathetic to Spain. The Germans participated in, and occasionally led, European efforts to organize a coalition to stay Washington's hand. They approached the British; they approached the French; they approached the Austrians; they approached the Vatican. They were willing to follow anybody's lead—but they were not willing to take the lead themselves, and they were not prepared to participate in a European démarche unless it was unanimous. Bülow reminded the kaiser of the importance of the U.S. market for Germany's economy, and in April 1898, just two weeks before the war broke out, he warned, "We must avoid everything . . . that could possibly be construed as against the United States." Since no other power was willing to lead, the rather unseemly scrambling came to nought. Europe was unable to unite versus the United States, and Germany was unwilling to go it alone. Rather than revealing that Germany posed any danger to the United States, its maneuvering before the war exposed its weakness in dealing with Washington.[53]

One of the most famous incidents of the Spanish-American War involved the scuffle between U.S. admiral George Dewey and German admiral Otto von Diederichs in Manila Bay. All hopes of an anti-American coalition having collapsed and war having broken out, Germany expected to capitalize on its reluctant neutrality by gaining something—at least a few naval bases—from the dissolution of the Spanish empire. In an era of coal-burning navies, overseas bases were essential to the assertion of sea power. Mahan emphasized the importance of a global network of secure coaling and repair facilities from which one could wage, or credibly threaten to wage, distant wars. In the spring of 1898, Tirpitz believed that Germany required a base in the West Indies, and he thought that the war, by distracting the Americans, could provide an excellent opportunity for Germany to buy Curaçao from Holland and St. Thomas from Denmark. The Wilhelmstrasse, however, was more interested in the Pacific. Its acting head, Oswald von Richthofen, told Ambassador White that Germany wanted Samoa, the Caroline Islands, and the Sulu Archipelago of the Philippines. To explain the situation to Washington, White described a political cartoon: "It represents Admiral von Diederichs in the foreground and an English representative in the background lying with their mouths open awaiting the chance that they will thus catch some of the roast pigeons flying about their heads, one of them being labelled 'Philippines.' The legend above the caricature reads 'Who gets the Philippines?' and that below . . . 'See the roast pigeons flying about. Perhaps one of them will fly into my mouth!'"

To Washington's dismay, White considered these German hopes reasonable and told Richthofen as much. Meanwhile, in London, Ambassador John Hay was receiving a barrage of letters from his friend at the British embassy in Berlin, Cecil Spring-Rice, warning him about German designs on the Pacific islands. "Germany . . . will be certain to intervene with success," Spring-Rice cautioned Hay on 7 May, "and get something out of the scramble." Just a day later, Bülow wrote the German ambassador in London, "There should be no doubt that the German government expects . . . not to go empty-handed in any new division of the globe."[54]

The Germans saw an opportunity in the Americans' apparent lack of interest in annexing the Philippines, even after Dewey's defeat of the Spanish fleet in Manila Bay on 1 May 1898. They hoped to gain a foothold there either through an amicable agreement among the great powers or, perhaps, by the Filipinos asking Berlin for protection. Prince Heinrich, the kaiser's brother and commander of the Asiatic squadron's Second Division, had cabled Bülow, "The natives would gladly place themselves under the protection of a European power, especially Germany." But Bülow questioned the report. The Filipinos showed "scant disposition to exchange the Spanish yoke for another direct and effective domination," he wrote the kaiser. "To subject the Tagalogs against their will to such foreign rule would probably be no easy task."[55] He cabled the German consul in Manila "to maintain therefore a negative attitude towards any soundings or approaches in this direction. Observe unobtrusively and report any signs that may indicate that one or another power, for example England or America, is attempting to establish itself permanently through negotiations with the insurgents." He advised the kaiser against any "imprudent move." He remained hopeful, however, that Germany would succeed in gaining several potential bases through diplomatic means, and he actively pursued this avenue before, during, and after the war.[56]

"Who gets the Philippines?" "The German Admiral in East Asia: See the roast pigeons flying around? Maybe one will land in my mouth!" Admiral Diederichs, in the foreground, and an Englishman in the background lie with their mouths open wide, hoping to catch some of the spoils of the U.S. defeat of Spain. Americans were outraged by reports that Diederichs had obstructed the U.S. fleet in Manila. After the encounter, Admiral George Dewey declared, "Our next war will be with Germany." (*Lustige Blätter* [27 July 1898])

On 2 June Diederichs, the commander of the Asiatic cruiser squadron, was ordered to Manila, where Dewey was awaiting reinforcements before attacking the Spanish, who still controlled the capital.[57] Like the French, English, and Japanese, who also sent squadrons, the Germans wanted to observe Dewey's blockade, to be in position to take advantage of any opportunities, and to be able to evacuate their nationals if necessary. Dewey, a veteran of the blockades of the Civil War, was unflustered by the foreign ships. The Germans, however, riled him: Diederichs, who arrived on 12 June, outranked him (the German was a vice admiral; Dewey had been promoted from commodore to rear admiral after the battle of Manila Bay), for several weeks the German fleet was larger than the American, and reports flew that the Germans were fraternizing with the Spanish on shore, presumably encouraging them to hold out by dint of their preponderant fleet and their words. Furthermore, Dewey alleged that Diederichs obstructed his enforcement of the blockade. The navy's official report on the campaign accused the Germans of either "an intentionally offensive policy or . . . a simple lack of . . . sea-manners."[58]

In fact, the disputes between the two squadrons had much more to do with Dewey's "almost pathological," in William Langer's words, distrust of the Germans than with actual German actions. As Diederichs himself wrote, "The tension between Admiral Dewey and myself is not due to the actions of my ships but rather to the Americans' mistrust of Germany."[59] Despite his unexpectedly easy victory over the small Spanish fleet, Dewey considered his position vulnerable. As he anxiously awaited the arrival both of reinforcements and of another Spanish squadron, he was edgy. And it was clear that Berlin wanted some of the spoils. As Ambassador White had written in June: "Germany is at present in a state of elation over the rapid and vigorous strokes which have given her an important foothold in China; . . . she is realizing more and more the importance of new territories in Africa; . . . she has begun the acquisition of a considerable navy; . . . her Minister of Foreign Affairs has publicly announced her intention to take part in a competition for the commerce of the world; and . . . the old aspirations toward a colonial dominion are evidently cherished more and more, especially by the Emperor and his trusted advisers."[60] Given this backdrop, Dewey interpreted every German move in the worst possible light. Furthermore, unlike the other foreign observers, Diederichs observed strict neutrality and did not defer to the American, who, he alleged disapprovingly, "regarded himself as the absolute ruler over land and sea." This earned Diederichs the sobriquet of "mischief maker."[61] He refused to accept Dewey's interpretation of the international law governing blockades (Dewey claimed the right to board neutral ships to establish their identity; Diederichs objected), and he went about his business, scouting out possible bases on the archipelago. This unnerved Dewey, but it was within Diederichs's rights, and, given the expectation that the United States was not going to annex the Philippines, it made good sense. Stirring up the tension between the two admirals was the British press, which controlled the cable link to the United States and delighted in maligning the Germans.

By the first week of August, Dewey's squadron had been reinforced, and on 13 August Manila surrendered. Three days later, Diederichs received orders to depart. (The armistice had been signed on 12 August.) On 21 August the Germans withdrew from Manila Bay. Upon being congratulated by the departing French admiral for blockading the port without "a single mistake," Dewey fumed, "Oh, yes . . . I made one—I should have sunk that squadron over there." And he pointed to the German fleet.[62]

Dewey dramatically amplified his complaints about the Germans once he returned to Washington. From Manila, his cables had hardly mentioned German misdeeds, and his logbooks do not record them. It seems that it was the usefulness of a German bogey, as much as any actual German misbehavior, that really got his dander up.[63]

While Cuba, Puerto Rico, the Philippines (including the Sulus), and Guam fell into America's lap, Berlin, which had hoped for so much from the dissolution of the Spanish empire, was reduced to secret and delicate maneuvering with Madrid to purchase any of the remaining spoils. The Germans resented the Americans' good fortune, but the kaiser himself urged caution. "It is now the task of diplomacy," he scribbled in the margin of a report, "to avoid difficulties with the United States so long as that is compatible with the dignity of the Empire." The former state secretary for foreign affairs, Herbert Bismarck, assured Spring-Rice—who immediately reported to Hay—"that Germany had never any intention of going to war with America and that the chief object of German policy had been to withdraw from a false position with as little dishonour as possible." Spring-Rice then asked Bismarck, "Was Germany prepared to face the consequences and had the Gov't counted the cost? . . . He [Bismarck] said . . . that it was unfortunate that the ships had been sent [to Manila]. . . . On the whole," Spring-Rice concluded, "these two things seem pretty plain—that Germany wishes a coaling station but will on no account hazard the possibility of a war." Thus Berlin ended up buying the Carolines, the Palaus, and the Marianas (without Guam)—"scattered islands in the Pacific that were no longer of any use to Spain and that the United States did not care to acquire"—for $4.2 million.[64] Germany got the leftovers, while the United States got the jewels: Cuba and Puerto Rico would guard two deepwater passages leading to the planned isthmian canal.

Berlin paid more than money for these disappointing acquisitions. Despite the fact that the German government's behavior during the war had been, in White's estimation, "everything we could wish, in the spirit as well as in the letter," the encounter in Manila Bay confirmed emerging American suspicions in a dramatic and memorable way; nothing the Germans did in the years before the outbreak of the First World War succeeded in shaking the conviction of the American press—and of many U.S. political leaders—that Germany was a marauding bully.[65] The Reich's behavior seemed all the more egregious given the docility of the other great powers, particularly England, to the dramatic U.S. expansion. Britain had actively appeased the United States, offering its nearby bases and cable lines. Two weeks after Dewey's victory at Manila Bay, the powerful colonial secretary Joseph Chamberlain (considered second in power only to the prime minister) had declared, "Terrible as war may be, even war itself would be cheaply purchased if in a great and noble cause the Stars and Stripes and the Union Jack should wave together over an Anglo-Saxon alliance."[66]

In contrast, German protestations of correctness were lame. In the Reichstag, Bülow tried to explain his government's policy by asserting that Diederichs had been sent to the Philippines solely to protect German citizens and trade, that he had dealt with Dewey in "a spirit of mutual courtesy," and that all rumors to the contrary were "the most bare-faced falsehoods."[67] In response, the *London Daily News* commented rather uncharitably, "It would be more honest to admit that the German public backed the wrong horse."[68] The truth was even more basic: Germany did not have the power in 1898 to stop the Americans. While the United States asserted its primacy in the hemisphere, Wilhelm's Germany dreamed of a different world, indulged in careless rhetoric, and watched in frustration. A U.S. naval intelligence officer reported, "The attitude of high German officials as to the war with Spain, was one of regret that we [the United States] were to be the country to be under the tree when the colonial plums fell from the old Spanish tree. Our war with Spain was in fact a sad blow to Germany. . . . It was the irony of fate that we got colonies we were not trying to get, and Germany lost the chance." As Tirpitz himself admitted, "The Spanish American conflict came politically too early."[69] Not only did Germany fail to reap the rewards it had expected from the demise of Spain, but the war enhanced the status of the United States and increased German fears of U.S. competition. The sentiment was reciprocated.

The war also led many American naval officers to be profoundly shocked by their navy's lack of preparedness. They may have won what one senior officer called a "pseudo-war," but they were sorely unprepared for a real war, "only less unprepared than Spain." Victory had led to an awareness of weakness among those officers who had faced this truth.[70] "What if . . . ?" they asked.

"What if Spain had been a great power? What if Spain had been England, or Germany?" As Roosevelt wrote Captain William Kimball in January 1900, "You make me rather uneasy about the German war! I have always regarded Germany while the present Kaiser lives as our most probable serious opponent, and we are capable of such infinite folly in this country that we may not prepare as we should. I do hope that neither the nation nor the navy accepts the war with Spain as anything but a warning. If we permit ourselves to relax in our exertions to bring the navy higher and higher, and if we do not build up the army and the forts, we should have a terrible time against Germany."[71]

The Growth of the U.S. Navy

The end of the nineteenth century was a time of dramatic change in the U.S. Navy. The spotlight that naval officers such as Commodore Robert Shufeldt cast on the connection between a country's fleet and its commercial success led to increasingly widespread concern about the fact that the U.S. fleet was, in the words of the *Army and Navy Journal* in 1880, a "heterogenous collection of naval trash."[72] The establishment of the Naval War College in 1884; the passage of the Naval Act of 1890, which authorized the construction of first-class battleships for the high seas; and the publication of Mahan's *The Influence of Sea Power* in the same year were clear signs of change. The exact source of this desire to expand and professionalize the navy is impossible to pinpoint; with the frontier closing, prospects of international trade beckoning, and technological breakthroughs in steam and communications occurring rapidly, it was time to turn outward. These changes not only increased the potential power of the navy but also put a premium on readiness. To shoulder this burden, the U.S. Navy, refuge of Episcopalian gentlemen from the East Coast, had to change. It had to become professional. The Naval War College would be part of the process. It had been difficult to convince the Congress in the late 1880s and early 1890s to fund the college because of the pervasive skepticism, in Congress and U.S. society at large, about the notion of "teaching war." Only a small, but vocal, slice of the navy had promoted the idea behind the college. Most officers had believed, along with the public, that war was neither inevitable nor subject to study: if it did break out, then the country would deal with it as it always had—a leader would emerge, the people would rally, and the vast potential resources of the country would be harnessed to the effort. In the House of Representatives, the expansionist William McAdoo had declared that there was no way a group of men sitting in Newport, Rhode Island—of all places!—with its "giddy maidens who disport themselves on the rocks in sunbonnets," could prepare for war.[73]

But this worldview was shifting. Mahan, who served as the professor of naval history at the Naval War College from 1886 to 1894, was not only a scholar; he was also a great publicist, writing prolifically in popular magazines and stressing the same themes from 1880 until his death in 1916. He and his followers gained sympathetic ears in Washington and in the press.

In *The Influence of Sea Power*, Mahan had emphasized the importance of the Pacific for the United States, and in early 1897, he wrote Theodore Roosevelt, who had just been appointed assistant secretary of the navy, "We have much more likelihood of trouble on that side [the Pacific] of the ocean." But just a few months later, even before the Spanish-American War, he had changed his mind. "At the present time," he opined, "Germany represents the probable element of future trouble for us." [74] From that point on, part of Mahan's credo was that control of the Caribbean was essential for U.S. security and prosperity. "The Caribbean Sea is one of the most interesting and vital regions in the world to the United States, considered from the point of view of commerce and war; not that most of our commerce passes there, or even will pass there, but because our interests may be most seriously interrupted, by hostile navies, in time of war," he wrote before the peace treaty with Spain had been signed. Part of his message was that Germany posed the most likely threat to this control. [75] The incident in Manila confirmed these fears.

Just as suspicions of the United States were growing in Germany, so too were suspicions of German intentions growing in the United States. In part these derived simply from the widespread belief that Germany, an overpopulated rising power, had to expand. Like the United States, Germany had come late to the imperial scramble; unlike the United States, it was hemmed in on every side. Between 1883 and 1885, Bismarck had seized several tracts in Africa (South West Africa, Cameroon, Togo, and German East Africa) and in the Pacific (northeast New Guinea, Palau, the Marshall Islands, the Brown Islands, part of the Solomon Islands, and the Bismarck Archipelago). These colonies were disappointing economically and strategic liabilities. By the end of his time as Reich chancellor, Bismarck had announced, "I am sick and tired of colonies." But Bismarck was fired in 1890, and by 1897 it was clear that the kaiser had changed course. "That Germany, under the present regime, is anxious to increase her colonial possessions, is a well known fact," the U.S. ambassador to Berlin wrote the State Department in 1897. [76]

The Reich's occupation of the Chinese port of Kiaochow in 1897 was a clear example of this new course. It was straightforward imperialism: many Germans believed a base in China was essential to the successful implementation of Weltpolitik. At the turn of the century, when the U.S. Navy was growing increasingly worried about Berlin's designs on the West, Germany was, in fact, preoccupied with the East. Nevertheless, not all Germans were enthused about the imperial grab. Tirpitz was acutely aware that Germany would be in a danger zone until roughly 1920, when the fleet would be complete: a keynote of the diplomacy of Weltpolitik was the futile desire to avoid raising suspicions and riling potential adversaries before the great fleet was ready. He therefore warned against premature adventures, and the Wilhelmstrasse and large export firms of Hamburg and Bremen worried about possible complications with Russia, England, and Japan. Few noticed that the Reich's adventure in China fueled the rising alarm felt in U.S. naval circles.[77]

Weltpolitik was more than the policy to build a navy; it was the response of a dissatisfied, ambitious power to a world in which it felt its position did not correspond to its power and significance. Too late on the imperial scene, Germany was not content with the scraps from England's and France's table. A few unpromising tracts in Africa were not enough, in material or symbolic terms. Germany had to expand, and where could it go? Adventures in Africa, the Middle East, and China could bring it into direct conflict with its powerful European neighbors. Latin America, on the other hand, was protected only by the Monroe Doctrine. "For what is South America?" a British journalist asked provocatively. "It is the last and most tempting field for the reception of overcrowded Europe—colossal, sparcely populated, much of it almost unexplored, inhabitable by Caucasians, its interior easily accessible by water, its soil of seemingly endless fertility, its mineral wealth barely tapped. Such is the prize that is dangled before the world. . . . It seems part of the inevitable evolution of things that a congested Europe should one day fling itself upon South America."[78]

American anxieties about a potential German attack on the Monroe Doctrine were heightened by the shifting balance of power in the Western Hemisphere. The turn of the century was a time of flux, of definition, in the region. England, with its superior fleet, was still the kingmaker, but in the Venezuela boundary dispute of 1895–96 London had sent the first signal that it might withdraw from the region. Aware of its imperial overextension, Britain had deferred to strident U.S. demands in the settlement of the boundary dispute between its colony of British Guiana and Venezuela. In the process, England had implicitly accepted the Monroe Doctrine. Under the pressure of the rising German fleet and the Boer War, the Royal Navy began to reduce its presence in the Western Hemisphere. As a U.S. naval officer observed, rather uncharitably, "England . . . withdrew her naval forces from North America and left us with the Monroe doctrine to protect her American colonial possessions. . . . We have therefore been holding the bag for her."[79] At the same time, the U.S. Navy was growing, and the United States could finally foresee a time when it would be able to enforce the Monroe Doctrine. However, Kaiser Wilhelm's Germany, propelled by Weltpolitik, could challenge the United States for the prize. No other country posed a threat: Spain was defeated; France was satisfied with its American colonies and was not building an offensive fleet; Russia was not interested; Japan was not ready. Only the United States and Germany could contemplate filling England's shoes in the hemisphere, if indeed England did withdraw. Yet in the final years of the nineteenth century, neither had sufficient power to do so. It was therefore a time of preparation, of testing, of tension.

There had been a precursor to this testing on the other side of the world: the opéra bouffe played out in Samoa in the 1880s and 1890s. Here, England, Germany, and the United States wrangled—at times perilously close to war— for more than a decade about the partition of a country of no economic or sentimental significance. The "Samoan tangle," as Paul Kennedy has aptly called it, was not about Samoa. It was about the balance of power between the three powers; it was a test, the first dress rehearsal, played against the backdrop of economic and strategic competition. Mahan recognized at least two-thirds of this: "The affair of the Samoan islands, trivial apparently, was nevertheless suggestive of European ambitions." In one sense, over and above whatever economic benefits a colony (formal or informal) could bestow, the motivation was simply to deprive the rival on principle.[80]

Germany's attitude toward the Monroe Doctrine ignited American fears. Germany alone among the European nations refused to bow to the doctrine. Germans, already aggrieved by America's tariff policies, began to speak openly against the doctrine, both in official circles and in the press. They chafed against U.S. pretensions in Latin America; the United States had "dibsed" the region eighty years ago and still lacked the power to stake its claim. Why should Germany, or any power, defer to it? This aggressive rhetoric was, in part, a consequence of Tirpitz's propaganda machine. The German fleet enthusiasts found it useful to emphasize the broad utility of the fleet—to cast a wide net—in order to lure traders, jingoistic expansionists, and businessmen into the fold of the naval enthusiasts. This included arguing that the fleet would be useful vis-à-vis the United States, both to protect Germany's trade and to counter a rival and a potential enemy.

The kaiser himself joined the chorus. Although it is unlikely that he had entertained even a passing thought about Latin America until the 1890s, with the pursuit of Weltpolitik everywhere in the world was suddenly relevant, and Wilhelm himself occasionally gave vent to his exasperation with U.S. pretensions. His marginalia on German actions in the region were cheerfully aggressive: "Bravo Panther!" he crowed when the German gunboat *Panther* sank a

"Does Germany aim to control the Caribbean Sea?" By 1900 the United States had the upper hand in the trade wars with Germany. It was less confident that its navy could defeat the German navy. One of its perennial fears was that Germany would seize a base in the Caribbean. (*Harper's Weekly*, 22 November 1902)

Haitian vessel; "South America is our aim, old boy!" he scrawled on an officer's report about a visit to the continent; "Fleet! Fleet! Fleet!" was his punctuation to a report about the need to show the flag in Latin America.[81] These pithy exclamations were leaked to foreign diplomats or to the press, already replete with the rabble-rousing rhetoric of the ultranationalists. American diplomats, consuls, and military and naval attachés reported rumors, stray remarks, and theories about German designs on the hemisphere. Not one of these reports fell on deaf ears. They fit right into the preconception of German policy, and they cumulatively provided the evidence.

The innumerable reports that the Germans were angling to acquire a base in the West Indies confirmed the suspicions. German interest in Samoa, the Carolines, and the Philippines signaled that they, too, were following Mahanian logic and trying to grab strategically located bases around the globe before all the "uninhabited" lands were taken. The U.S. Navy suspected that the German navy was also scouting out the Caribbean. There were reports of the Germans trying to get hold of the Danish West Indies and of German ships casing out Martinique and Margarita (off Venezuela); there was concern about the large German community in southern Brazil; there were rumors of German designs on Haiti. Dewey put it bluntly in a letter to the secretary of the navy in November 1901: "We [the General Board] find Germany deeply interested in Haiti, and undoubtedly she would be equally interested in . . . St. Thomas if opportunity were ripe." *Harper's Weekly* stated the problem succinctly in 1900, "Germany is alleged to want certain things that it is our duty not to let her have, even if we do not want them ourselves." [82]

And yet, at the turn of the century, certainly not all Americans were worried about Germany. Most significantly, the State Department was not alarmed. This was demonstrated in its calm response to a German show of force in Haiti.

In the fall of 1897, the Germans responded to a petty episode in Haiti with classic gunboat diplomacy. The Haitians had jailed Emíl Lüders, whom they considered a Haitian citizen (he had been born in Haiti to a Haitian mother), for resisting arrest and assaulting a policeman.[83] German businessmen in Haiti seized on the incident to embarrass the Haitian government of President Augustin Simon Sam, which, they claimed, had been recalcitrant in loan and treaty negotiations. Loudly proclaiming that Lüders was a German citizen because his father had been German and he had served one year in the German army and that he had done nothing wrong—only ordered a policeman, who had tried to arrest one of his employees without proper warrant, to leave his premises—they berated the Wilhelmstrasse for not protecting its own. Even after the U.S. minister in Haiti, fearing that "the slightest indiscretion [would] engender bloodshed," had secured the release of Lüders, the nationalistic press in Germany demanded retribution for the affront.[84] The Wilhelmstrasse, eager to garner votes for the First Fleet Bill, protested to the Haitian government, demanded an indemnity of thirty thousand dollars and an official apology, sent two school ships to the region in early December, and threatened to bombard the Haitian coast if its demands were not met in four hours. "We hope to induce the [German] government to energetically demand the necessary satisfaction, in the shape of damages, and to enforce this by proper means," Bismarck announced in the *Hamburger Nachrichten*. The U.S. minister was appalled: "To require an indemnity . . . for an alleged insult that was not given should not be entertained, and would not be required if these people were in a position to defend themselves." The Haitian newspaper *Impartiel* declared: "Let them, the Germans, now come! We are ready to die and to kill!" Andrew White, in Berlin, was amused. In his autobiography he regales his readers with "a bit of international comedy" consisting of the Haitian chargé ("Parisian to the tips of his fingers . . . whose government . . . after a joyous career of proclamations, revolutions, throat-cutting, confiscation, paper money, and loans, public and private, had at last met a check") pointing out "the duty of the United States to oblige Germany to desist." White continues, "I assured him that neither the President, whose name the famous 'Doctrine' bears, nor the Secretary of State who devised it, nor the American people behind them, had any idea of protecting our sister republics in such conduct as that in which the Germans complained." The government of President Sam, chastened by the silence of the international community—particularly the United States—capitulated. On 7 December, Haitian admiral Killick, aboard the flagship *Crête-à-Pierrot*, formally dipped his country's flag to the standard of Germany as the Haitian navy played the German national anthem and fired a twenty-one-gun salute. "Hayti was Cowed by German Guns," blared the pronaval *New York Herald*'s headline. "Hayti's Humiliation Complete," added the *World*. [85] The McKinley administration stood aloof from Haiti's humiliation for several reasons: as White indicated, it sympathized with Germany's position; it wanted to avoid the possible embarrassment of Germany rebuffing its offer to mediate; and it did not foresee a German attempt to seize Haitian territory.[86] Racism also played a part, as the French *Le Temps* understood: "President Sam . . . imagined that the convenient and elastic Monroe Doctrine would apply to the situation. This little calculation was wrong. The United States was not eager to extend its hand to help a negro state." [87]

The gap between the responses of Washington and of the American press to the Lüders incident is striking and indicative of the pattern that would be repeated time and time again. While the State Department instructed its minister to observe the strictest neutrality, Pulitzer's *New York World* warned ominously that Germany had taken "a first step toward aggression and the acquisition of territory on this side of the ocean," and even the more staid *New York Times* and the *New York Herald* were berating German militarism and the U.S. government's spinelessness. "America has lost much influence and prestige through allowing the Germans to do as they wished," the *Herald* opined.[88]

The fear that "America's hemisphere" was threatened was articulated clearly in an 1897 article in the *North American Review*: "We must not suppose that the German government is seeking to spend more money upon its fleet merely for the pleasure of seeing a large number of warships together in Kiel. . . . It should not surprise us if we read some morning the news that the German flag had been hoisted on St. Thomas or Curaçao."[89] And in February 1898, for example, a navy captain, Arendt S. Crowninshield, expressed his anxieties forthrightly in a letter to the secretary of the navy: "Before many years have passed, Germany will succeed in acquiring one or more territorial possessions in the Western Hemisphere. . . . The present temper of the German government is so aggressive that it is not unreasonable to expect her to take such action at a time not far distant."[90]

Only a handful of naval activists, however, were concerned about the German challenge before the First Fleet Bill, and even after it only a small minority of professional naval experts expressed alarm about the threat. The U.S. press barely commented on the bill. The *New York Times* observed calmly:

> The peculiarity of the case of Germany is that there is in the increase of the fleet no question of national defense. . . . A great navy is a vital necessity to Great Britain. . . . With us, a navy is also a necessity of defense. . . . But Germany neither imports the greater part of her food supplies, like England, nor has she a long and vulnerable coast line, like ourselves. . . . The use of a navy for Germany is simply to maintain and extend her foreign trade and her outlying possessions in case of war. The present German navy seems to be ample for the present uses of the empire. Consequently a proposed enlargement implies a general policy of expansion. . . . It is clear that Germany means to be much more of a world power than she has been heretofore.[91]

A naval intelligence officer noted, "The extensive program for the increase of Germany's naval strength is one of the most important steps taken by any of the European countries to augment sea power," but he did not stress any danger to the United States.[92] It was the 1900 Second Fleet Bill, with its acceleration of the rate of growth and its emphasis on battleships, that confirmed the fears of the suspicious and convinced the doubters. The significance of this bill can hardly be overstated. It was the alarm, the tocsin. "Germany has settled upon a definite and far reaching program of construction," Walter Meriwether wrote in the popular *Munsey's Magazine*. "[Its navy will be] second only to that of Great Britain." [93] It meant that a heavy shadow of suspicion fell on each and every German action in the hemisphere. Henceforth every stray comment of the kaiser—and with Wilhelm there were many stray comments—and every pan-German tract were seen as clues to the menacing German plot. Officers of all ranks, led by Mahan and Dewey, joined the fray. Captain Charles Sperry wrote his wife in 1901 that Germany would, "sooner or later . . . rise up in arms to protect and extend her interests." [94] The image that Germany was a threat to the hemisphere resonated with the American public, not just because whatever the navy said was ipso facto believed or because of social Darwinism or shifts in the balance of power but because the words and actions of the Germans themselves seemed to confirm it.

Particularly after the Second Fleet Bill, the rumors of plotting reached the highest levels of the U.S. government. Secretary of War Elihu Root delivered a muscular speech at a dinner in April 1900 honoring Ulysses S. Grant in which he declared that the United States would soon be called on to forcibly uphold the Monroe Doctrine: "No man who carefully watches the signs of the times can fail to see that the American people will within a few years have to either abandon the Monroe Doctrine or fight for it, and we are not going to abandon it. If necessary we will fight for it." This was widely interpreted to be a scarcely veiled reference to the German threat. The *Berliner Neueste Nachrichten* countered, "The assumption that Germany would seize territory from existing South American states for the establishment of colonies is simply nonsense." Cooler heads noted that the 1900 presidential race was in full swing. The *Herald* quoted a "high official in the German foreign office" saying, " 'Nobody in Germany contemplates annexations in South America. This . . . seems to be . . . a campaign utterance.' " The *Buffalo Courier* explained, "The eloquent Elihu must again take up the cudgels for the Monroe doctrine and 'sound the alarm' against Germany. It helps keep Root before the public." The *Herald* concurred, chastising Root for playing "the Monroe-doctrine-versus-Germany card." [95]

A month later, Senator Henry Cabot Lodge (R-Mass.), enthusiastic leader of the expansionists, gave a "warlike" speech in the Senate during a debate on the naval appropriations bill. "Hands Off! Says Lodge to Germany" was the *Herald*'s banner headline reporting the speech. "I am by no means convinced that some European power, perhaps one of those whose navy is just now receiving such a rapid increase, may want to test that [Monroe] doctrine and that we may find ourselves called upon to protect Brazil or some other South American state from invasion. . . . I am not conjuring up imaginary dangers,"

Lodge warned. "I think that they exist, and are very real." [96] The speech generated much press comment: the *Philadelphia Times* editors noted, "We have had these warnings from England before now, but the American eagle has remained unruffled. Senator Lodge, following Secretary Root, thinks it time for the eagle to scream," and the *Denver Republican* commented wryly, "The Kaiser claims that the reason why his mustache has lost its fierce, upturned points is because he discharged his barber, but Henry Cabot Lodge is convinced that his Monroe Doctrine speech in the Senate did it." [97] On the Senate floor, John W. Daniel (D-Va.) opined, "This suggestion of war . . . has had its echoes. Those echoes have reverberated on the continent of Europe. They are being circulated around the throne of the warlord of Germany, who . . . now is reflecting over . . . the idea that at some day or other we are to have a war with them." Indeed, Ambassador Holleben reported the "fiery speech" and the reaction to it fully to Chancellor Bülow, and the British *Spectator* warned, "The doctrine cannot be supported on tall talk. . . . If America should wish to enforce the Monroe Doctrine she must be able to destroy the German fleet," while the *National Review* summed up the situation plainly, "Just now Germany is the bogey." [98]

Roosevelt himself, then governor of New York and about to be the Republican vice presidential candidate, was alarmed. As early as May 1897, he had written to Mahan, "We should . . . serve notice that no strong European power, and especially not Germany, should be allowed to gain a foothold [in the West Indies] by supplanting some weak European power." [99] In 1901, Roosevelt and Lodge, who were close friends, exchanged an interesting series of letters about the German threat. The vice president wrote,

> I find that the Germans regard our failure to go forward in building up the navy this year as a sign that our spasm of preparation, as they think it, has come to an end; that we shall sink back, so that in a few years they will be in a position to take some step in the West Indies or South America which will make us either put up or shut up on the Monroe Doctrine; they are counting upon their ability to trounce us if we try the former horn of the dilemma. They . . . count upon England standing to one side if the fight occurs. . . . The only power which may be a menace to us in anything like the immediate future is Germany. [100]

Lodge responded that the German threat, while probably not immediate, was indeed a reality.

> As to Germany, I have heard the same reports that you have; in fact that sort of rumor has been in the air for a good while. I have myself very grave

doubts as to their undertaking to attack us. It would be a pretty dangerous undertaking in any circumstances, but at the same time it is well within
the range of possibilities, and the German Emperor has moments when he
is wild enough to do anything. . . . Our only safety is in being thoroughly
prepared. . . . The Navy is the vital point. We must . . . build up the navy as
rapidly as possible. . . . If we have a strong and well equipped navy I do not
believe Germany will attack us.

The senator then linked the strategic danger with the commercial competition
with Germany: "At the same time there is a fundamental danger which arises
from our rapid growth economically. We are putting a terrible pressure on
Europe, and this situation may produce war at any time. The economic forces
will not be the ostensible cause of trouble, but they will be the real cause,
and no one can tell where the break will come."[101] Admiral Dewey voiced
the fears most succinctly: after the Spanish American War, he declared, "Our
next war will be with Germany."[102]

Rival Fleets

From 1898 to the First World War, the American rivalry with Germany was
played out, at least from the American point of view, on the high seas. The
Germans continued complaining about tariffs and trade, but the Americans
focused on the rapidly expanding German fleet. American anxiety was based
on a simple fact: the German navy was stronger than the U.S. Navy; by both
American and German reckoning, the United States would lose a naval war.[103]
   It is very difficult to compare military strength: the tangible factors are
unequal, and the intangible factors are, needless to say, intangible. Charge
the equation through with time, with ships planned and under construction, and the tidy tables buckle under the weight. Different analysts compare
different factors. However, all—American and German, contemporary and
current—agreed on one thing: the German fleet was superior. U.S. statistics
from 1900 emphasizing tonnage indicate that Germany had the edge in ships
most relevant to a German-American war in the Caribbean: in battleships,
the Germans boasted 44,400 tons, with 111,000 under construction, to the
United States' 12,300 tons, with 36,900 under construction; in cruisers, the
German advantage was less dramatic but still significant—it had 15,300 tons
already built, with 32,500 under way, whereas the United States had 12,800
tons, with 19,200 tons on the way.[104] German comparisons emphasizing numbers of ships conclude that in 1902 the German navy boasted nineteen first-
class battleships to the Americans' nine; eight second-class battleships to the

Americans' one; and six armored cruisers to the Americans' two.[105] This in-feriority in numbers and tonnage, however, was not considered the decisive factor by the German and the American analysts. Indeed, given the assump-tion that a German-American war would be fought in the western Atlantic or Caribbean, most analysts agreed that the Americans could afford to have a smaller fleet than the Germans. The factor that ensured German victory was the superiority of German training and readiness.

For the U.S. Navy, the German fleet—not the British—was the bench-mark and German training the model. In 1905, the *New York Times* reflected, "Ever since the international friction in Apia Harbor [Samoa] seventeen years ago . . . the question asked by Americans about their own navy has been how it compared with that of the Germans." [106] Again and again in the records of the General Board of the Navy, that body of the most illustrious Americans charged in March 1900 with the development and coordination of strategy and war plans, there are envious and respectful reports of the precision of German gunnery and target practice, of the rigor of German fleet maneuvers, of the discipline of the German crews. A U.S. naval officer, for example, noted, "I was impressed with the splendid discipline . . . by the thoroughly military bearing of [the German] officers and men. . . . In this respect the [German] en-listed personnel seems in marked contrast to ours." [107] No other navy is held up so regularly as the standard against which the U.S. fleet must be measured. The General Board listened to reports about every aspect of German naval practice and considered emulating every German innovation. The extent of the admi-ration for all things German can be gleaned from the fact that when the Office of Naval Intelligence (ONI) reported that the Germans were considering sub-stituting "right" and "left" for "starboard" and "port," the General Board im-mediately debated the merits of a like change in the U.S. Navy.[108] It is almost endearing to read the minutes of the board and to grasp the extent to which its members were awed by German professionalism and militarism. These senti-ments reflected and shaped public opinion. They were repeated in the popular press. An article in *Harper's Monthly*, for example, stated in 1901: "Unless her rivals copy or improve upon Germany's organization, they are likely to ex-perience some unpleasant surprises in war. . . . If there is anything in Pericles's famous saying, 'Naval science is not a thing to be cultivated at chance mo-ments or odd times; it is a mistress jealous of every other pursuit,' then, indeed, Germany has a signal advantage over us, which she will use to the utmost." [109]

The Germans also considered the American fleet inferior to their own, par-ticularly in the composition of its personnel and the quality of its training. The German navy, however, had a different obsession and a different bench-mark—the Royal Navy. German naval officers rarely compared their fleet with the U.S. Navy, and when they did, it was generally to heap scorn on the poorly trained and ill-prepared American crews.[110]

The reasons for American inferiority are not hard to find. First, the German navy had Wilhelm II, an emperor who had decided to do for the navy what his grandfather had done for the army. Wilhelm was mercurial and impulsive, but after 1897 he consistently, even doggedly and blindly, followed the constellation composed of Weltpolitik and naval power. But Wilhelm alone, despite his vast powers, could not achieve his dream. He needed Tirpitz. Tirpitz was the German navy's second great pillar. He molded the navy from 1897 to 1914; in the crucial early years he had the political skill, the brilliance, and the power to pry a long-term commitment from the Reichstag to fund the steady expansion of the fleet. This largely freed the German navy from the vagaries of the political process, and it enabled Tirpitz to make deals with German shipyards.[111]

The U.S. Navy had no comparable leaders. It is tempting to draw parallels between Theodore Roosevelt and Wilhelm II, but the similarities are superficial. Born just three months apart, both were physically weak children (Roosevelt suffered from asthma; the kaiser was born with a withered arm) who matured into extroverted, occasionally flamboyant men who relished situations in which they could prove their virility. Woodrow Wilson's aide, Colonel Edward House, reported that the British undersecretary of the Foreign Office, Sir William Tyrrell, drew the parallel at a dinner in 1913: "He said the Kaiser was a spectacular individual and partook more of French qualities than he did of German. He likened him to Roosevelt." After meeting the kaiser, House agreed: "I found he had all the versatility of Roosevelt with something more of charm, something less of force." Each developed the enduring conviction, shaped by Mahan, that his own country's greatness would depend in part on the strength of its navy. After reading *The Influence of Sea Power*, Roosevelt had written the author, "It is a *very* good book—admirable; and I am greatly in error if it does not become a naval classic." A few years later, he wrote his German friend Hermann Speck von Sternburg (who would become the ambassador in Washington in 1903), "I am glad Mahan is having such influence with your people, but I wish he had more influence with his own. It is very difficult to make this nation wake up."[112] Appointed assistant secretary of the navy in April 1897 by President William McKinley, Roosevelt became convinced that the U.S. fleet's ability to enforce the Monroe Doctrine was crucial. At a public meeting in 1900, Roosevelt, then governor of New York, shared the dais with Mahan and declared, "I want to assert right here . . . that I stand by the Monroe Doctrine and all that it implies. We must either stand by that doctrine with all emphasis in our power or let it go altogether."[113] Like the kaiser, Roosevelt rose to great power at a young age.

After serving less than a year as vice president, he became America's youngest president upon McKinley's assassination in September 1901. He fascinated the public, this novel mix of eccentricity, impetuosity, vigor, and charm. Surrounded by his boisterous children, confident, brash, and youthful, Roosevelt symbolized the new century. The president was certain—as were most Americans—that it would be a century in which the United States would assume new international rights and responsibilities. And he was convinced, as a good Mahanian, that the navy would be the key to success.

There are similarities between Roosevelt and Wilhelm II, but there are also stark differences. Theodore Roosevelt was president, not emperor. Elected for a limited term, responsible to the electorate, challenged by Congress, he could not promote the U.S. Navy as Wilhelm promoted his. Nor would he have wanted to: once he became president, his dedication to the navy was one aspect of a crowded agenda. It was not his polestar.

Just as the U.S. Navy had no Wilhelm, so too it lacked a Tirpitz. Mahan was an intellectual leader, not a political dynamo, and he retired in 1896 (leaving all official duties in 1912). While continuing to proffer technical advice from retirement, he was reluctant to comment on current events. "I become continually more and more convinced," he wrote Roosevelt in 1901, "that the average man can't tell—as years advance—when he has really got out of touch with the times, & becomes a mere 'wind-jammer'—to use a naval expression for useless talk." [114] After Manila Bay, George Dewey was enormously popular, but following an unpopular marriage to a wealthy Catholic and a bumbling, belated presidential bid in 1900, he was tinged with controversy.[115] His foray into politics particularly damaged his relationship with Roosevelt. "What a perfectly extraordinary affair this Dewey outburst is!" Roosevelt wrote after Dewey declared his candidacy. "It cannot help but alter my views of him." [116] Thus his influence with the Congress, and on the General Board, was diminished. And during the time that Tirpitz alone was at the helm of the German navy, the U.S. Navy had to adjust to eight different secretaries. (During the Roosevelt administration, Dewey bemoaned the fact that the "kaleidoscopic post" boasted seven incumbents.) The U.S. Navy had to stumble through annual naval budget debates in Congress; this restricted the growth of the fleet and hamstrung planning. After 1903, the General Board consistently called for a forty-eight-battleship navy built at a rate of four per year, but the Congress balked, funding only one in 1904 and two in 1905.[117] Not only could the navy not be certain of any fleet increases, but it also could not assure the shipyards of future contracts. A consequence was a constant battle against labor troubles and inefficiencies at the yards. This did not go unnoticed by the Germans. A German naval officer assured his superiors in 1902 that despite the

U.S. plans for ship construction, "Germany would be superior for the foreseeable future . . . especially since U.S. shipyards [were] so slow." [118]

In 1901, a book by Baron Franz von Edelsheim, an officer in the German army, described a war in which the Germany navy defeated the U.S. Navy, paving the way for a German army invasion of the continental United States. Edelsheim confirmed what U.S. officials had suspected—that Germany had developed war plans against the United States. Although this meant that the Germans had done no more than the Americans, and no more than the U.S. Navy already feared, it nevertheless caused a stir. The *New York Times* editorialized that this "cautious theorist['s] . . . novel suggestion . . . [was] 'mighty interestin' reading.'" [119] In December, the German ambassador in Washington reported to Berlin that Admiral Dewey expected Germany to attack the Danish West Indian islands of St. Thomas or St. John. A year later, the suspected German target was Washington itself.[120] Further reports of German war planning surfaced in attaché reports, and the kaiser himself blurted out stray remarks to his family, to journalists, and to diplomats about the danger of a war with the United States.[121]

The plans themselves, however, remained hidden until 1971, when Holger Herwig unearthed them in the archives, and the story hit the *New York Times*. "Reading about Kaiser Wilhelm's secret plan to invade the United States back before World War I," a columnist wrote, "could make your hair stand on end." [122] Only three scholars have plumbed the primary sources on the story of the development of the war plans. Herwig and David Trask wrote the standard account, which asserts that the war plans provide not only dramatic but also significant evidence of German imperial aims in America. All scholars who refer to the war plans rely on Herwig's and Trask's research and analysis. Ragnhild Fiebig–von Hase adds detail and nuance to their account but follows their basic interpretation. My research indicates, on the other hand, that the war plans were minor, hollow, and defensive. It is therefore necessary to retell the story briefly to put it in its proper context.[123]

The Development of German War Plans against the United States

After a cursory study in Berlin of a German-American war during the Samoa crisis of 1889, which stressed that war against the United States was unimaginable, no war plans against the United States were discussed until early 1898, when the First Fleet Bill was being debated. Then, in the winter of 1897–98, the strategic study of war against the United States was, for the first time, one of twenty-nine possible topics assigned to junior officers as *Winterarbeiten*, or strategic problems. Lieutenant Eberhard von Mantey alone chose this topic. His paper—a purely theoretical, student exercise—was a brash call for a combined navy and army assault on the key cities of the U.S. eastern seaboard.[124] In the ensuing months, trade tensions escalated, the First Fleet Bill was passed, and the Spanish-American War erupted.

In January 1899, Ambassador Holleben set the keynote for the year to come: "Only once before," he reminded the aged Chancellor Hohenlohe, "on the occasion of the first Samoan conflict, has there been serious talk of a war between Germany and the United States. Today, the possibility of such a war lies much nearer." [125] The ambassador was referring particularly to the recrudescence of friction over the partition of Samoa, but U.S. and German concerns about the growth of each other's navy, festering trade tensions, and the messy aftereffects of the encounter in Manila fanned the fear of war between the two countries. It was in these first months of 1899 that the German navy set to work on an operations plan against the United States. Whether based on Mantey's study or not, it came to a similar conclusion: Germany could launch and win a war against the United States. The war would destroy the U.S. fleet and, by extension, the Monroe Doctrine. The only significant difference of opinion among the men drawing up the war plans concerned strategy: should the German fleet attack a Caribbean outpost or an east coast city? An attack on a Caribbean island would be less costly than an assault on the U.S. mainland, but it might not draw the U.S. fleet to battle. To ensure that the Americans would expose their fleet, the Germans targeted Puerto Rico, which, although less strategically located than Haiti, would compel the Americans to come to the defense of territory they controlled. The purpose of the war plan was to lure the U.S. fleet to a Mahanian battle to claim control of the seas, not the occupation of the Caribbean base or the east coast of the United States.[126]

Later in 1899, Tirpitz asked the navy for a position paper he could use in the Reichstag "clearly describing the course of a war against the United States . . . and explaining in language the Budget Committee can understand how difficult, even hopeless, our situation in such a war would be . . . since the Americans could paralyze our merchant marine with virtually no effort." [127] On 20 January 1900, the paper, which argued that thirty-eight ships of the line, twelve large cruisers, and thirty-two small cruisers would be needed to ensure victory in a war against the United States, was presented to the Budget Committee.[128]

On the same day, the kaiser called for a "joint navy-army report" concerning the war plan against the United States, but it was not until May that the navy finally got around to asking the head of the General Staff of the Army, General Alfred Count von Schlieffen, for his input.[129] Schlieffen did not respond. Six months later, on 28 November 1900, the navy reiterated the request.[130] Finally, on 9 December, Admiral Diederichs, Dewey's nemesis, who was now head of the war-planning branch of the navy, had an *Immediatvortrag* (formal audience with the kaiser) on war plans against the United States, which Schlieffen attended. Schlieffen deemed the navy's plan foolhardy, a costly, impractical, and unnecessary adventure. The kaiser sent the admiral back to the drawing board.[131] After a year of aborted communications with Schlieffen, Diederichs decided that conferring with the army about the plan was "hopeless."[132] He continued to tinker with the plan, but he never troubled the army again, and the kaiser maintained a "hands off" policy.

In 1903, Wilhelm Büchsel, who had replaced Diederichs, wrote, "There can only be *one* aim for Germany's strategy: direct pressure on the American east coast and its most populous regions, above all New York City; that is, a ruthless assault that through the use of terror and the destruction of trade and property would create an unbearable situation for the American people. . . . Thus will the Monroe Doctrine be broken." He admitted, "The natural advantage lies with the United States, with its very advantageous geographical position and total independence from the rest of the world. . . . Nevertheless, we still have the offensive advantage, but probably only for three to five years. Germany could bear such a war for a very limited time. A quick and decisive battle is essential." He added, however, "For Germany to wage war against the United States there would have to be a political situation in Europe that gave us an entirely free hand abroad."[133] In 1903, Germany's hand in Europe was far from free. Despite German hopes and overtures, Russia had strengthened its alliance with France, forged in 1892–94. Moreover, England had become increasingly antagonistic because of German sympathy with the Boers in their war against the British in South Africa, tensions over the handling of the second Venezuela crisis, and, above all, the ominous growth of the German fleet. England's alliance with Japan in 1902 deepened Germany's isolation. Germany was, in sum, facing hostility to its east, to its west, and across the English Channel. Nevertheless, Büchsel did not shelve the war plans against the United States. He added a note of caution to his apparent recklessness, writing a captain who was reconnoitering ports in Puerto Rico and Florida, for example, "It is well known that the United States is suspicious of such missions. Avoid giving the U.S. press any opportunities to publish anti-German articles. If suspicions are raised, postpone your mission for a while."[134]

Büchsel polished his plan, which was known as Operations Plan III, for two years, shifting his emphasis from an attack on a Caribbean island to a direct assault on the east coast.[135] By 1906, however, the severity of the con-

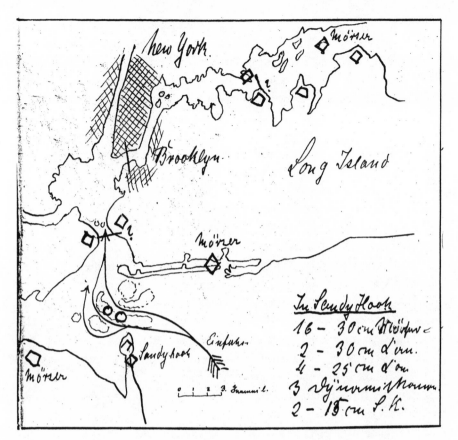

"Assault on New York." This dramatic map from the German naval archives
depicts one of the German navy's boldest plans: an assault on New York City. The
plan, however, was as sketchy as this picture. It never won the support of Admiral
Tirpitz, General Schlieffen, or the kaiser. (Bundesarchiv-Militärarchiv, Freiburg
[RM5/v.5964])

straints imposed by Germany's position in Europe was finally fully accepted.
England's entente with France in 1904 had dealt a devastating blow to the
Wilhelmstrasse's foreign policy, and tensions with Britain had intensified as
a result of the continuing naval arms race and London's heightened fears of
a German threat to France. The Algeciras Conference, held in early 1906
to resolve the first Morocco crisis, confirmed Germany's isolation. All the
participants except Austria-Hungary — including, most significantly, England,
Russia, Italy, the United States, Spain, and Portugal — supported France, and
Italy's defection exposed the weakness of the southern flank of the Triple Alliance. Furthermore, the new liberal government in London revived fears of

British protectionism, a tariff war, and an accelerated arms race. Facing these facts, on 9 May 1906, Büchsel ordered that "detailed preparatory works for a war against the United States be terminated."[136]

The mere existence of these war plans can strike an American reader as alarming. Büchsel's reference to a "ruthless assault" and statements such as one admiral's comment in 1899 — "Every astute German naval officer is concerned with the consequences of war between Germany and the United States" — are eminently quotable.[137] They are, however, misleading. While it is possible to select juicy quotations and to isolate the plans against the United States — and the allusions to plans and the references to plans — and in so doing give the impression that war against the United States was indeed uppermost on every German officer's mind, the truth is that the war plans against the United States were toothless.

They were a low priority for the navy. How could it have been otherwise for a nation threatened by closer and more powerful countries? The Germans had been devising naval operations plans since 1882. They had plans against Russia, France, Denmark, and England and permutations of them all. The plans against the United States were a sideshow, an appendix. (In *The Navy and German Power Politics*, Ivo Lambi devotes less than ten pages of his careful and detailed [429-page] analysis of German naval war planning to plans against the United States.)[138] To put these plans in context, in September 1899, for example, the navy was ordered to work on a plan against America, and five months later orders were sent to overseas cruisers about war plans against the United States. This can appear ominous — and has been made to do so — but the truth is that in both cases the United States was just one of many countries mentioned; the navy and the captains were also told to plan against France, Russia, and England. This perspective must be borne in mind if one wants a true picture of the importance of the United States in German naval planning.[139] Furthermore, it was the business of the German naval officers to plan for all possible eventualities. That does not mean that they were seriously intending to launch a war.

Although it may appear impressive in a brief summary, the attention devoted to the plan against America was in fact sporadic and superficial. For example, even in 1899, when work on the plan was at its most intense, no action was taken on it from April to September, and attention to it fell off dramatically after the navy had delivered its memo to the Reichstag in January 1900. This is not because the Reichstag quashed it. It is because after this memo, which Tirpitz had requested, the admiral himself was averse to the plans.

The memo was an anomaly. It was the sole instance of communication between the navy and the Reichstag about operations against the United States.

And it was the sole instance of Tirpitz expressing any interest in the issue. His sudden espousal of the cause and equally sudden abandonment of it are easily explained: his interest in the United States was pure domestic politics; he wanted to get the Second Fleet Bill, doubling the fleet, through the Reichstag, and so he positioned himself downdraft of the anti-American sentiment in the land. The war plan against the United States served its purpose as soon as the Reichstag voted for the increase to a thirty-eight-ship navy, and immediately thereafter it become a liability, for if the navy was able to draw up plans to wage war against the United States relying on the navy at hand, how could the admiral justify the increases he sought in the fleet without arguing that his true target was the British navy—an admission he dearly sought to avoid during the danger zone?

From the moment that Tirpitz distanced himself from the plans, they were bound to founder. Instead of becoming coherent plans coordinated at the highest level, they became a hodgepodge of studies, of data, of stabs at a plan. Tirpitz's refusal to support them condemned them to marginal status.

As it was, the plans were a grand overture to silence. From Mantey's 1898 exercise through Büchsel's 1903 Operations Plan III, none dealt with the thorny problems of supply, and all assumed that the naval assault would be followed by army operations on land. And yet, two years elapsed before the navy even sat down with the army to discuss them. And when it did—in the *Immediatvortrag* of 1900—General Schlieffen refused to cooperate. His attitude is evident in a memorandum he sent Diederichs in March 1901. Responding to the admiral's queries about landing places, he dismissed Cape Cod—Diederichs's first choice—because it could easily become a bottleneck. In response to Diederichs's query about the number of German troops required to attack the east coast, he remarked that that would depend on the number of U.S. troops they faced. (This led a frustrated naval officer to write in the margin, "Brilliant.") Schlieffen estimated that to take Boston alone, Germany would need 100,000 men. Taking New York would require, of course, a much larger force. Schlieffen devoted little attention to Cuba and Puerto Rico; he expected the Cubans to side with the United States and estimated that Germany would need 50,000 men to capture it and 100,000 more to attack the mainland from a base in Cuba.[140] Herwig and Trask comment that this exchange

marked a return to sober military strategy and a turning away from what can only be termed the reckless offensive oriented thinking that had characterized the Admiralty Staff thinking ever since Mantey's first *Winterarbeit* of 1898. . . . And finally, the letter shows quite clearly that a German-American conflict was a distinct possibility, that serious planning was underway among Germany's highest naval as well as military planners, and that . . . one did not shrink back from contemplating and planning a war 3000 miles away from one's own shores for stakes . . . that can at best be described as mediocre.[141]

This misleads the reader. Only the war-planning branch of the navy was returning to sober military strategy: Tirpitz, Schlieffen, and the kaiser had never strayed from it. Further, Schlieffen's letter does not show that a German-American conflict was a distinct possibility or that "serious planning was underway among Germany's highest naval as well as military planners": it merely shows that the war-planning branch of the German navy had contemplated the strategic requirements of such a war. More significant is that with this letter Schlieffen effectively killed the operations plan. Germany had recently sent thirty thousand men to China to take Kiaochow, and this had been difficult. One hundred thousand was out of the question. Far from revealing the seriousness of the German threat, the letter announced the general's emphatic, if nonconfrontational, refusal to play ball.

The kaiser could have ordered Schlieffen to cooperate with the navy. He did not. Perhaps he had been influenced by Schlieffen, or perhaps by Tirpitz, neither of whom wanted to divert attention to a costly, improbable, and nonessential scheme. Or perhaps he himself, the leader who is generally portrayed as an erratic firebrand held in check by his subordinates, recognized that Diederichs's plan was unworkable. Without Tirpitz, Schlieffen, or the kaiser, the war plan against the United States was nothing more than a flamboyant overture to silence.

Finally, the line between offense and defense is never as clear as it may appear. It is true that the plans imagined a German fleet attacking the United States or its possessions. But why did the Germans contemplate going to war against the United States? In general, the naval officers refrained from speculation as to the causes of war and the aims of it. There are, however, a few revealing exceptions.

In the January 1900 memorandum that the Admiralstab, the war-planning branch of the navy, sent to the Reichstag at Tirpitz's request, the navy offered a glimpse into its notion of the causes of a German-American war. Such a war, the memo stated, would be a response first to the heightening trade tensions between the two countries—tensions that were bound to deepen with the increasing industrialization of both countries—and, second, to the imperial ambitions of the United States. As Büchsel wrote, "Such a war will not be sought by us, but it can be forced upon us."[142] The Germans envisioned a defensive war, and their only means of defense was to attack. They had to capitalize on the advantages they had, and—particularly given the American slowness to mobilize—their advantage lay in the offense. The U.S. fleet was not going to attack them: U.S. trade and imperial policy were.

Thus, the German war plans are not such hard evidence of German aggressiveness as they might at first appear: they were marginal compared with the elaborate plans against nearer enemies; they were the brainchild of the inferior wing of the navy, unsupported by the rest of the navy, the army, and the kaiser; and they were conceived as defensive in nature.

The Development of the U.S. War Plans against Germany

The American war plans against Germany echo the German plans against the United States. Both began in 1897 as school exercises, both saw the Germans launching naval operations against the United States in the Caribbean, both offered a similar variation of a landing on the east coast, and both saw the Germans as having the edge.

Suspicion of German intentions in the hemisphere had deep roots. After the Franco-Prussian War, surprise was expressed in U.S. naval circles that Germany had not pressed for the cession of Martinique, and, during the flare-up over Samoa in 1889, there was talk of Germany as a possible enemy. There was no formal war planning, however, until Weltpolitik.[143] All the early exercises of the Naval War College, which was the branch of the navy most concerned with war planning at the time, had been directed against England.[144] The ONI also occasionally drafted war plans, but its importance waned as the Naval War College's grew. The first time either the war college or the ONI turned its thoughts to fighting a war against Germany was in 1897, and it occurred in the context of an academic war-gaming exercise.[145]

Beginning in 1894, the core academic exercise at the college—and its chief innovation—was the solution of the "annual problem," a war game. The idea was of German origin. (A widely repeated apocryphal story described the reaction of the chief of the Prussian general staff upon being awakened at midnight with the news that the war with France had broken out. "Get the portfolio of plans in the third left-hand drawer of the second case," he is said to have stated, calmly. "It's all there." He then, according to legend, went back to sleep.)[146] The games served several purposes simultaneously: they confronted officers with specific problems; they revealed weaknesses in the fleet; they were good public relations tools. The press, particularly the *New York Herald*, reported the games extensively. The public could understand them, and they helped rally support for the fleet.[147]

Germany first appeared in a problem involving German intervention in

Haiti to settle outstanding German claims and protect German citizens. Unlike the German navy, which had rejected an attack on Haiti for fear the United States would not bother to defend it, the U.S. Navy considered it the likely target because it had a deep natural harbor at Môle St. Nicholas, because it could muster no significant local resistance, because studies indicated that German ships could steam no farther without recoaling, and, most important, because of its strategic location guarding the Windward passage, which controlled access to the future canal zone. "The Windward passage," Dewey wrote, "is the main doorway of the Caribbean. Who holds that passage has the key to the defense of the canal." [148]

The Naval War College held classes only four months a year. It could not make policy; it could only make recommendations, and it was not clear to whom: there was neither an individual nor an agency charged with the development of naval strategy. The reformers in the navy worked tirelessly to remedy this situation. After much dissension and infighting, the General Board of the Navy was created in 1900. It was a compromise body, neither the full-blown Prussian general staff that some wanted nor the spineless committee that others espoused. Although the war college continued to work on its annual problems, the General Board assumed the primary role in the development of war plans.

The head of the General Board was George Dewey, now admiral of the U.S. Navy. (Indeed, one compelling reason to create the board had been to manufacture a suitable position to take the decorated admiral from the political arena after his presidential bid.) Dewey was chair until 1917, but Admiral Henry C. Taylor, a former president of the war college, actually dominated the board until his death in 1904. There were ten other members, including the chief of naval intelligence, the president of the Naval War College, and the commandant of the U.S. Marine Corps. Many of these men had been with Dewey in the Philippines, and in a startling reprise, they were now shadowboxing with their old nemesis, Otto von Diederichs, head of the Admiralstab. The board met weekly—dividing its time between Newport and Washington—and reported to the secretary of the navy. It was strictly an advisory body, but because of the seniority of its members and its direct access to the secretary, it carried significant clout. Josephus Daniels, secretary of the navy in the Wilson administration, deemed it "the Supreme Court of Naval policy." [149]

As the members of the General Board realized, it was useful to have a specific situation, and a specific enemy, in mind when trying to determine future requirements. As the General Board was being set up, the Second German Fleet Bill was being debated. Although the board was officially charged with the responsibility to "explore all eventualities," its true mission had been articulated before its first meeting by Admiral Taylor; its "first aim," he announced, should be to investigate German attempts to seize land in Latin America.[150] And at the board's second meeting, in May 1900, it recommended that war plans specify that a "campaign be prepared for some definite theatre of action and against a definite enemy and it is further suggested that the conditions of such a possible war be laid down as follows: — An attempt by Germany to occupy a portion of the South American continent south of Rio [de] Janeiro in 1905. A declaration of war by the United States. Possession of the Cape de Verde [sic] islands by Germany. Advance of the Germans upon Porto Rico and Hayti and a consequent centering of the theatre of action in those Islands."[151] Variations on this "war situation in the Caribbean" obsessed the board for the next five years and were revived a decade later. A reader perusing the proceedings for 1900 and 1901 could believe that an actual war was raging in the Caribbean. The premise was that in an attempt to destroy the Monroe Doctrine Germany would seize a base on the island of Hispaniola (Haiti and the Dominican Republic) and challenge the U.S. fleet to a decisive battle in the Caribbean. A second version of the plan, which vied with the first for prominence, had the Germans attacking the east coast of the United States.[152] After 1903, however, interest in the plan dropped off as the General Board turned its attention to recommending specific technical improvements and, more important, as the threat was perceived as less acute. "In considering possible wars with the great nations of the world," Mahan wrote in December 1903, "it seems to me inconceivable that any one of them should expect seriously to modify, or weaken, our position in this hemisphere. Naval success of a moment there might be; but our position, numbers and wealth, etc., etc., must forbid to any European state the hope of permanent assertion against us on this side of the Atlantic. Great Britain has abandoned the idea; who better than she could maintain it? . . . In brief, the American question, the Monroe principle, though not formally accepted, is as nearly established as is given to international questions to be."[153]

In attempting to analyze the earliest versions of the plan against Germany, the historian faces two dilemmas. First, none of these early versions exists in pure form. The General Board discarded, or "expunged," portions of a war plan as soon as they were updated; most of these expunged papers are no longer available. The portfolios, which were unbound sheaves in large paper envelopes until 1906, were constantly updated. As the board commented in a 1904 critique of the war plans, "At present . . . there is no system in the arrangement [of the war portfolios], and no two Portfolios are arranged in the same order. There are a number of papers now in the Portfolios which are no longer necessary."[154] Evidence about the earliest drafts is therefore oblique.

The historian is confronted with the last version and with references to earlier plans in the General Board files. It is clear in all these files that the plan against Germany was the key preoccupation of the board in its first three years. It was constantly discussed and fine-tuned. It structured the discussions of force requirements and fleet concentration. However, no version of the plan that is clearly dated earlier than 1910 has survived.

Second, the General Board saw war plans as manuals that commanding officers would keep with them at all times. They were, as one scholar has said, "like Baedekers"; they were not analytical; they had no political content: they simply told the commanding officer what to do if war was declared. In 1904, the General Board reported, "Nearly all, if not all, the plans are lacking in some points; . . . [many] are of a sketchy nature." [155] In his memoirs, Admiral Bradley Fiske, who was in charge of the board's war plans, recalled his dismay at discovering that the plans were "so general in character as barely to be war plans at all." Dewey explained: "A naval war portfolio is a concrete work for a specific practical purpose and brevity and clearness demand the elimination of all matter which does not bear directly on the purpose in view." [156] Therefore, the plans are stripped of politics, history, and analysis.

The files in the General Board war plan portfolios are of very unequal substance. Several are simply collections of data on ports and sample letters that the U.S. naval officer would present to the resident authorities in the event of occupation: Nicaragua, Rio de Janeiro, Puerto Rico, and Haiti/Santo Domingo. Two are more substantial plans of war against, on the one hand, Germany and, on the other, Japan. Finally, there is a file entitled "General Considerations." [157]

Of the plans detailing the occupation of particular countries, the Haiti/ Santo Domingo (or Hi-Sd) Plan is by far the most detailed. The General Board called it "the key plan for the Caribbean." [158] It is officially dated July 1915, but work must have started on it in 1900, when it was mentioned at more General Board meetings than not. A hodgepodge of a plan with its roots in the war college games of the last years of the century, the Hi-Sd Plan, which posited an attack on Hispaniola, was the most plausible war scenario of an implausible lot, and it was also the most manageable—no alliances, only one front, waged in America's backyard, and in support of a sacred principle, the Monroe Doctrine. Furthermore, it was a useful analytical tool. But it is a dry affair: a sheaf of detailed plans for the attack and occupation of the island's coastal towns. It includes data about Haitian and Dominican harbors, fortifications, topography, and local militia, and it contains sample letters that the occupying officer would deliver to the island's authorities. The plan includes not a word about strategy, and the details of coordination with the army were left vague.[159] Nor were the problems of supply resolved. For example, the General Board realized in 1903 that the plan called for 173 mines but that the navy had only 100 mines in total.[160] Finally, the plan was silent as to why such an occupation might be necessary, and it did not even specify who the enemy might be. For this, one must look back to the proceedings of the board, which identified the enemy and explained the war's rationale: Germany did not accept the Monroe Doctrine, was building a formidable fleet, and was expected to challenge the doctrine by seizing a base. "From a general conception of German aims, her policy might seem to be as follows," chief intelligence officer Captain Charles Dwight Sigsbee reported to the General Board in May 1900. "First.—Her Diplomatic or Political Motive: To force an initial rupture of the Monroe Doctrine with a view to colonization in South America and the extension of her foreign market. Second.—Her Strategic Scheme: To obtain a permanent intermediate base in the West Indies with a view to protection of her commerce and colonization near or remote in the Americas."[161]

The ulterior motives are made even clearer in the war plan against Germany. Called the Black Plan, this was the navy's most detailed war plan of the prewar years. ("Black" was the code name for Germany; "Blue" was the United States.) In fact, its only competition was War Plan Orange, a plan against Japan that originated in 1907 and was much less detailed than the Black Plan. Unlike the portfolios about the occupation of particular countries, the Black Plan explains the causes of the presumed war.[162] It was submitted to the Navy Department in 1913 (appendixes date from 1910 to 1917), but it is misleading to think of it being devised then. It is clearly the sedimentary accretion of the previous thirteen years. "These problems," a note in the war portfolios explains, "embrace studies of the War College for the last twelve years."[163] This is an important point because the date of 1913 on the Black Plan has thrown researchers off the scent. The assumptions underlying the Black Plan do not make sense in 1913—when Germany was clearly preoccupied in Europe—and this lack of fit has made the Black Plan seem fantastic and bizarre. As a result, several historians have dismissed it utterly. Alfred Vagts, for example, considered it incomprehensible; Richard Challener said it "bordered on fantasy"; Holger Herwig deemed it "surrealistic"; Ivo Lambi called it "another expression . . . of a naïve zeal"; Thomas Baecker considered it the result of "a gross failure in judgement."[164] When the Black Plan is seen as a product of 1913, it is either ludicrous or cynical.

However, when the Black Plan is correctly dated—when its roots in 1900 are acknowledged—it begins to make sense. Part of its value is lost if it is simply dismissed as a historical oddity; it should be viewed instead as a geological outcropping that sheds light on the board's earlier thinking. The

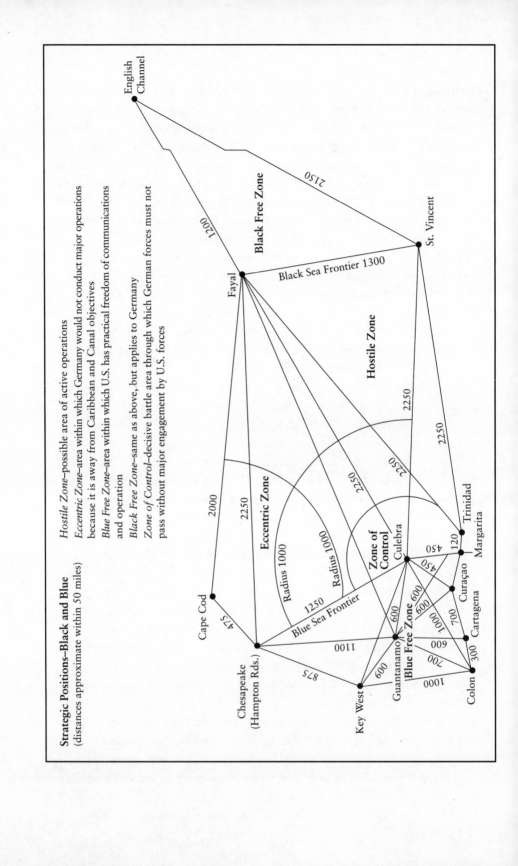

Strategic Positions–Black and Blue
(distances approximate within 50 miles)

Hostile Zone–possible area of active operations

Eccentric Zone–area within which Germany would not conduct major operations because it is away from Caribbean and Canal objectives

Blue Free Zone–area within which U.S. has practical freedom of communications and operation

Black Free Zone–same as above, but applies to Germany

Zone of Control–decisive battle area through which German forces must not pass without major engagement by U.S. forces

Haiti–Santo Domingo Plan was, according to the General Board in 1905, "the key plan for the Caribbean," and the Black Plan provides the rationale behind it. The Black Plan's basic premise, its view of Germany, and its sense of threat date from the turn of the century. It stands on four basic assumptions.

First, there is the Darwinian assumption that Germany had to expand. "Germany is the uneasy state of Europe. . . . Since 1870 the population has increased at an average rate of 1.14% and it is not a matter of many years before she will have outgrown her borders. Expansion is therefore a necessity that becomes more pressing with every year that passes and it is evident that the German government is fully alive to the situation."

Second—in an assumption that was reasonable in 1900 but bizarre in 1913 —South America beckons. "Thus far Germany has not been fortunate with her colonies and the temperate regions of the world that are feebly held have now been preempted. In South America there are rich localities in a temperate climate that might be seized from the holding nations were they the only obstacles, and in southern Brazil there is already a large community of Germans."

Third, the Monroe Doctrine is threatened—another assumption that made more sense in 1900 than in 1913. "But the Monroe Doctrine stands in the way of such an enterprise which may not unreasonably be assumed to be unfair in the German mind in view of their problem of over-population. It also stands in the way of their getting a foothold in the Caribbean which would be desirable for trade reasons if for no other."

Fourth, Germany is the United States' most likely opponent. "When in addition it is recalled that the United States was largely instrumental in preventing the partition of China, it is seen that there are latent causes that render a break with Germany more probable than with either of the other two great maritime powers, and more probable moreover than with any other European power." [165]

These four assumptions are stated succinctly: "the steady increase of Black [German] population . . . must find a *protected* market abroad; . . . when conditions at home are no longer considered bearable and Black is strong enough,

"The Black Plan." How could the United States defend its interests against a German attack in the Caribbean? This was the question that consumed the general board of the U.S. Navy from its first meeting in 1900. This diagram charts zones of control between the English Channel and Culebra, the U.S. Navy's forward base in Puerto Rico. The German fleet was larger than the U.S. fleet, and it mobilized much faster. The U.S. Navy was not optimistic that it could defeat it, even in America's backyard. (Based on War Portfolios of the General Board of the U.S. Navy [box 10, GBW])

Black will insist on the occupation of Western Hemisphere territory . . . and Blue will then have to defend her policy by force, or acquiesce in the occupation."[166] The plan added the observation that it was likely that Blue could count on no ally, while Black could count on the active support of Austria and the tacit support of England and all Europe. Although it is possible that the United States would have had no allies in a war to defend the Monroe Doctrine, it strains credulity to imagine that in 1913 England would have tacitly supported German aggression in Latin America, and it contradicts what George Dewey himself had observed as early as 1906. "One can reasonably expect passive, if not active, assistance from Great Britain should it become necessary to prevent German acquisitions of territory in this hemisphere. . . . The relations of the United States with England have never been better than at the present time and the relations between England and Germany are never good, so that in the event of war with Germany, it is not at all unlikely that the United States will be able to secure the passive friendship of England, and, probably, if necessary, a treaty of mutual support and protection."[167]

The Black Plan fleshes out the Hi-Sd Plan; while it has a thin gloss of relevance to events after 1903 (referring, for example, to the impact on U.S.-Japanese relations of the 1906 San Francisco school board decision to segregate Asian children), it is in fact a graft onto the thinking that informed the earliest war plan of the General Board. It sheds light on the analysis of the threat to the Monroe Doctrine posed by the new German fleet in the first years of this century that underlay, but was not made explicit in, the Hi-Sd Plan.

The board's analysis of the probable development of a German-American war revealed serious weaknesses of the U.S. Navy. In the calculations of the war college and of the General Board at the turn of the century, the United States invariably lost the naval war. Indeed, Admiral Taylor commented that a 1900 Naval War College study that concluded that the United States could defeat Germany was "a fairy tale."[168]

The central dilemma for the United States was its slowness to mobilize. This negated the advantage of proximity. The General Board put it succinctly to the secretary of the navy in 1901: "In case of sudden hostilities [in South and Central American waters] . . . we should find ourselves at great disadvantage." In the thirty days that it would take the United States to mobilize in the best circumstances (if the fleet was divided or entirely in the Pacific, it would take much longer), the German navy, with a mobilization time of a bare nine days, could have steamed across the sea and seized a base in the Caribbean. From its first meetings, the General Board (and the Army War College, to which it sent problems and studies) tried to resolve the problems of mobilization in several ways. It promoted the concept of advanced bases, settling finally on Culebra, off the easternmost point of Puerto Rico, as the most advantageous spot for such a base. Dewey presented the board's reasoning in an August 1901 letter to the secretary of the navy:

1. In considering the plans for a possible war in the Atlantic, the General Board has arrived at the conclusion that a probable theater of action will be in the West Indies, for it is in South and Central American waters that the conflicts between the political and commercial policies of our own and European nations seem to be most pronounced.

2. In that region, our facilities for successfully carrying on a war are almost entirely wanting. . . .

3. If time permit after a threat of hostilities, preparations can be made, but with some European nations there is a constant state of preparedness. . . .

4. The General Board believes that a naval stronghold should be established in the northeastern Caribbean . . . [and] Culebra . . . presents the greatest advantages for use as a base.[169]

The board ran into pork barrel politics in its effort to get congressional funding: Congress was loath to vote funds away from bases on the continental United States and grant them to a "foreign" outpost. The General Board's plans for Culebra stalled. In the meantime, it organized improved training exercises that would allow the fleet to practice mobilizing, finding the enemy, and attacking; indeed, the fleet had engaged in no war games prior to the establishment of the board, and no station had ever practiced rendezvousing with any other. The board debated—and debated—the question of where to station the fleet in peacetime. Finally, the board worried that the American public's attitude toward war, its alleged pacifism as opposed to Germany's alleged militarism, put the United States at a disadvantage. By releasing certain studies and by holding well-publicized exercises, it hoped to do more than rally support for the navy; it hoped to prepare the people for war. By 1913, because the U.S. Navy had managed to mobilize somewhat faster and was considered roughly equivalent in size to the German navy, the Black Plan was more optimistic than the early General Board had been about U.S. chances of success in defeating, and deterring, a German assault on the Monroe Doctrine.[170]

Vagts argued that the navy's emphasis on the German threat was a gimmick to pry money from Congress.[171] Certainly, much of the publicity about the German threat was written with an eye to increasing public and congressional support for large naval increases. This cynicism, however, ignores the classified record of the General Board that makes it abundantly clear that this highest body of the U.S. Navy considered the German navy the most serious threat to the United States. Furthermore, the U.S. Navy put its fleet where its mouth was: from the Spanish-American War to the First World War, the fleet was stationed in the Atlantic (except for the cruise around the world in 1907). A token force patrolled the Pacific, but, despite growing fears of Japan and an acute sensitivity to the vulnerability of the United States in the Pacific, the arguments in favor of concentration and the threat posed by Germany consistently held sway, and the fleet remained in the Atlantic, facing its most formidable foe.[172]

The idea that Germany posed a threat to Latin America went unchallenged by the rest of the U.S. government—at least in public—and by the press. This was, in part, due to the weakness and lack of professionalism of the State Department at the turn of the century. In dire need of professionalization, the department was the degenerate heir to the spoils system. It was, in part, due to lack of communication between departments—for example, the General Board did not forward its war plans to any civilian department for comment. It was, in part, due to the fact that the navy was the best organized of the relevant departments, and naval officers tended to file the most interesting and complete reports on activities in Latin America. (The State Department representatives in the small Latin American countries, particularly the consuls, were not impressive; theirs were not prestigious posts.)

But more than any of these deficiencies, the image of an untrustworthy Germany, prowling around the hemisphere sniffing out opportunities, was provoked and reinforced by the Germans themselves. Their unexplained emphasis on building a great navy, their flights of anti-American—and anti–Monroe Doctrine—rhetoric, their loud complaints about American trade practices: all this gave credence to the navy's fears.

And these fears seem to get solid confirmation with the discovery of the German war plans. But the plans against the United States were not nearly as important in German planning as the American plans countering them were in American planning, and the battleships Germany was building were suited to wage war in the North Sea, not in the Caribbean. Furthermore, the U.S. plans against Germany were the obsession of the most illustrious planning body of the U.S. Navy, headed by its highest-ranking officer.

Rather than revealing the aggression of Germany and the defensive reaction of the United States, the plans reveal the symmetry of German and American development and the subtle interplay of fears and dreams and real clashes of interest. For example—a single example—both navies were convinced in 1898 that they were in dire need of overseas bases. How else would they maintain their soon-to-be far-flung interests? However, by 1902, both navies had cooled on the idea of a necklace of bases around the globe. Both gradually realized— independently—that too many bases would weaken their defense by scattering vulnerable outposts in indefensible places. "The General Board," Dewey wrote the secretary of the navy in 1904, "has repeatedly advised against the acquisition of small outlying islands or harbors for coal depots."[173] It is striking when looking at both plans, and the navies that produced them, to realize how parallel were the tracks on which they were traveling.

The interesting point, other than the elegance of the symmetry, is that the United States—which feared the German drive for bases because it presumed that several would be in Latin America—failed to imagine that the German navy might have also concluded that bases were impractical. Long after the General Board had thought better of its desire for bases—and long after Tirpitz had done the same—the U.S. Navy continued to fear German intentions. The idea that the Germans sought a base in the region was impossible to quash.

In part, this was due to the eruptions of florid rhetoric that flowed from Berlin. The kaiser's asides and the jingoes' diatribes reflected the Germans' sense of grievance and their dreams.

They also reflected real conflicts of interest between the two countries. Both were on the threshold of world power. Latin America was the power vacuum. It presented attractive trade prospects, and, as the Black Plan noted in its explanation of why Germany would challenge the Monroe Doctrine, "Trade competition is . . . becoming exceedingly keen. A battle is on throughout the world for commercial supremacy. . . . There is constant irritation over Blue tariff charges and regulations . . . [and] retaliatory measures put in force by Black."[174] Germany had the strength to challenge the United States, and the United States knew it. America, at the time, could not shake its sense of vulnerability, its sense of grievance. Thus, with the burgeoning German navy as a backdrop, it saw German behavior in "its" sphere—in Venezuela and Brazil and Mexico—as inexcusably aggressive and threatening. Only a careful examination of Berlin's behavior can uncover the seriousness, the depth, and the immediacy of the German challenge.

2

The Height of
the German
Challenge

The Venezuela Blockade,
1902–1903

In 1906, Captain Georg Hebbinghaus, a German naval officer who had worked on the German war plan against the United States, wrote, "A German declaration of war against the United States is possible only if we are allied with England."[1] The improbability of such an alliance, however, had been revealed more than three years earlier, during the Anglo-German blockade of Venezuela.

The basic story is mundane. Battered by years of revolution and saddled with a fiery dictator, Venezuela was neither paying its bills nor compensating foreigners for damages suffered as a result of domestic turmoil. Numerous countries were aggrieved—about debt default, unsettled claims, and the blustering of the Venezuelan president, Cipriano Castro. "You owe money," the American minister to Caracas told Castro bluntly, "and sooner or later you will have to pay."[2] In December 1902, Germany, England, and Italy imposed a naval blockade on Venezuela to force Castro to address their grievances. It was standard operating procedure, classic gunboat diplomacy, a little arm-twisting that led to arbitration and the settlement of the claims.

Beneath the banality of the adventure lie fascinating hints of the balance of power in the Caribbean basin at the time. It was a time of definition in the region: England was retreating, Germany was waiting in the wings, the United States was hovering, and the Latin American countries were trying to hold on to independence. Thus there was a subtle system, a jockeying for position, a simultaneous probing of England's intentions, of Germany's intentions, and of the United States' intentions. This was a time when the German fleet was stronger than the American fleet, and yet neither country had sufficient power to assert hegemony confidently; England was still the kingmaker.

The Venezuela blockade was Berlin's most aggressive action in the hemisphere. Here, it is said, Berlin revealed its true aggressive and opportunistic colors, manipulating England, viciously bombing Venezuelan ports, and risking war with the United States. What made it particularly troubling to Americans was that the Reich was acting with the kingmaker in tow. It was the best possible situation for Germany, the worst imaginable for the United States. This was the height of the German challenge.[3]

President Theodore Roosevelt later claimed that it was only his big stick (wielded quietly) that stayed the kaiser's hand. An analysis of German aims and ambitions in Venezuela, however, does not support this interpretation. It indicates that it was the withdrawal of British support, not Roosevelt's stick, that convinced the Germans to end the blockade. It also reveals that, U.S. fears and allegations to the contrary, Germany was exceedingly cautious before, during, and after the blockade. Its policy was far from recklessly aggressive. It was timid.

Bülow's Gambit

German traders were well ensconced in Venezuela by the turn of the century. German middlemen dominated the import/export sector and the informal banking system. But these Germans were not the favored sons of the pan-Germans: frequently they had gone disturbingly native, and they did not always bring business back to the fatherland. Rather, it was the industrialists and the bankers who sought to establish subsidiaries and railroads in Venezuela—men with their feet firmly on German soil—who wielded influence in Berlin.[4]

A decade of revolution had brought hardship to these merchants and firms. A stream of complaints about the treatment of German nationals and entreaties for protection flowed back to the Wilhelmstrasse. The Reich's response was unfocused. In 1898 and 1900, the continuing complaints from Venezuela were used as fodder for the first and second fleet bills, but there was a paucity of will—and ships—to mount a show of force. In 1900, action was rendered impossible by the diversion of ships to the Boxer Rebellion.[5] But by the summer of 1901, Chancellor Bülow decided that Germany should respond. German businessmen, imperialists, exporters, and right-wingers called for intervention to collect the outstanding claims. The government faced the prospect of significant protest if it remained passive in the face of this outcry,

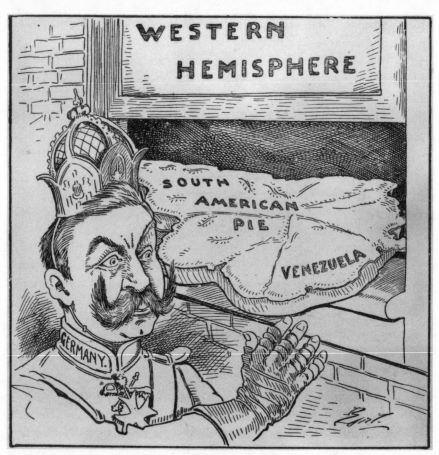

"He may not be hungry, but he has a hungry look." The kaiser is tempted by the Latin American market. (*Minneapolis Journal*, 26 January 1903)

and Bülow could ill afford this at a time when he needed to build support for the major tariff bill that was pending in the Reichstag. Furthermore, Bülow hoped that successful coercion of Castro would strengthen the Reich in the Latin American market. He saw no danger of the United States objecting, no danger of failure; he saw only a clear victory, a cheap ticket to enhanced status. It was this boon to German prestige that he stressed to the kaiser, the navy, and the Reichstag.[6]

Bülow's primary motivation was, as always, to please the kaiser. This was the chancellor's great skill: he was an almost flawless sycophant. And in the summer of 1901, some strain having intruded into his hitherto well-oiled relationship with the kaiser, Bülow was particularly eager to find something to boost his currency.[7] But it is perilous to determine motivation—of countries or of individuals. There is a point at which the original aims become somewhat irrelevant, when a project simply becomes one's own, when one's own prestige is at stake. This occurred with Bülow and Venezuela.

In mid-August, he sounded out the Admiralstab about the feasibility of a blockade of Venezuela. Admiral Diederichs, who was in charge of war planning, was enthusiastic, even reckless: despite the fact that he did not share Bülow's confidence that the United States would remain neutral, he endorsed the plan and recommended the occupation of Caracas if a blockade proved insufficient.[8]

But no blockade was mounted in 1901. Bülow did not even formally discuss his plan with the kaiser until December. And when he did, the result was not what he had anticipated. The kaiser did not approve.[9] That Wilhelm should display such caution turns preconceptions on their head. Two considerations were uppermost in his mind.

The first concerned a disagreement between Bülow, Diederichs, and Tirpitz about the blockade. The dispute revolved around the question of whether Germany should mount a war blockade or a pacific blockade. The essential difference was that neutral ships running a pacific blockade would be turned away while those running a war blockade would be sequestered; furthermore, the Reichstag would have to declare war only if a war blockade was imposed, and a declaration of war would give Venezuela belligerent rights. Bülow consistently recommended a pacific blockade. Diederichs, on the other hand, doubted that a pacific blockade would be sufficient and recommended a war blockade. He estimated that a cruiser division would be required to mount the blockade and seize the customhouses, and six thousand men would be needed to occupy the Venezuelan town of Puerto Cabello. Tirpitz, whose Second Naval Law had passed in 1900, wanted to avoid returning to the Reichstag for more funds; he may also have been concerned that gunboat diplomacy— in which fast, shallow-draft cruisers would be most useful—would reveal the weakness of his big ship plan; and he wanted to avoid conflict until the fleet was built (that is, during the danger zone). Moreover, the Reichs Marine Amt (RMA, Imperial Naval Office), which he headed, had no interest in a base in the Caribbean. Its desire for overseas bases, which peaked immediately after the Spanish-American War, had abated by 1901 with the realization that far-flung bases would be vulnerable and thus weaken the nation's defense; the Second Fleet Bill's emphasis on battleships indicated this shift. Nevertheless, rumors were rampant in the United States and in England that Germany was interested in the Venezuelan island of Margarita, fueled by hints that Castro was considering selling and by a visit of the German cruiser *Vineta* to the island in May 1900. The *Vineta*'s assessment of the island, however, had been clear: because it did not have a port large enough to accommodate a war fleet, it would be a liability.[10] Although the Admiralstab, Diederichs's branch of the navy, maintained an interest in overseas bases (logically, as its mission was to devise workable war plans), Tirpitz was consistently able to overrule it. In April 1900, Tirpitz's deputy informed the Budget Committee of the Reichstag that Germany had no further interest in overseas bases. For Tirpitz, who wanted Germany to conserve its fleet until it was built to full strength, a blockade of Venezuela meant squandering resources in a marginal theater.[11]

"In some ways I feel sorry for Bülow," the éminence grise of the Wilhelmstrasse, Friedrich von Holstein, wrote in his diary.

> He is not a strong character, and up till now has achieved everything by amiability and his cleverness. . . . The other day the Chancellor proposed that, should the Government of Venezuela fail to meet certain fairly large German claims, action should be taken against it—blockade, occupation of customs-houses in the ports, etc. The Kaiser kept the Chancellor's report to himself for quite a while; finally, two days ago, he got the Commanding Admiral, Diederichs, to write to the state secretary in the foreign ministry [Oswald von Richthofen]—not the Chancellor—that he regarded the use of force by naval vessels as inappropriate and unnecessary. H. M. decided on refusal after hearing a report from the Commanding Admiral. . . . But the chief opponent was Tirpitz. The Commanding Admiral thinks that he had previously talked to the Kaiser. Tirpitz has no stomach for a fight.[12]

Beyond the reservations of his most influential military adviser, Wilhelm had a sentimental reason to dislike Bülow's idea. In a flourish of naive and narcissistic diplomacy, the kaiser put on hold any action that could have antagonized the United States while, in February and March 1902, he dispatched his only brother, Prince Heinrich of Prussia, on a goodwill mission to the United States.[13] The visit, despite its serious side—the kaiser wanted to flatter the Americans with royalty and to rally the straying community of German Americans to their patriotic duties—was largely fluff. "The aim is merely that you . . . make the Americans happy and win them over. . . . Do not speak about Central and South America," Bülow told the prince. But even before His Imperial Highness had landed in New York, his visit had given rise to an unseemly scrap in the press about Germany's and England's purported intrigues against the United States in the Spanish-American War. "Uncle Sam is not unhappy," the Paris *Revue Bleue* observed, "to see the Greats of all the World bowing and scraping in front of him." Nevertheless, there was some optimism about the visit: "Confidence is felt," the American chargé in Berlin wrote, "that it will bear beautiful flowers if not fruit."[14] The view from London was less rosy: "The political aims of Germany and the United States in

South America are too vitally divergent to be reconciled by royal politeness," the *Saturday Review* stated. A gift expressed the gulf. In thanks for the warm reception given his brother, the kaiser offered a statue of Frederick the Great "to President Roosevelt, who could not help it," the Paris *Temps* observed dryly, "and to the American people, who did not want it." [15]

In early February, Germany had tried to exert mild pressure on Castro by sending three cruisers to La Guayra. This was a harmless probe, and when Castro got wind of it, he ratcheted up the provocation: "Germany is mistaken if she imagines that a few men-of-war in the harbor will settle her claims. Venezuela is a sovereign Power, independent of and equal to other powers in dignity. . . . She can make her enemies suffer and give tit for tat." He mocked the show and crowed as the German cruisers departed, "The Germans are welcome to come! We have enough ammunition and enough blood!" The British minister in Caracas described the effect of the German display well, if graphically: "An eye witness told me that the other day in the public room of the chief Hotel here someone made a remark to the Minister of Arts and Public Instruction about what the Germans might do. 'The Germans,' replied his Excellency. 'I will show you how we treat them'—and he jumped on a chair and—well broke wind—as I see the dictionary politely calls it." [16]

Any further action in Venezuela was delayed until autumn at the earliest: the summer was deemed unhealthy, and the winter was the export season, when an effective blockade could be mounted. The Admiralstab advised the Wilhelmstrasse that "only pressing political needs could justify mounting a blockade of the Venezuelan coast after April." [17]

Meanwhile, civil war raged, Castro remained defiant, and the German chargé d'affaires, Gisbert von Pilgrim-Baltazzi, was frustrated. He expressed to his friend, the British minister William Haggard, "his astonishment—not to say his disgust—at the action of his Government in, as he put it, leading him on to the very point of action and then letting him drop." In May, he told Haggard that he had considered suggesting to Berlin that Germany "seize his [Castro's] ships and blockade the ports," but, stung once, he had decided against it "as he feared that his government might not be disposed to follow." The Foreign Office was not alarmed. "The German chargé d'affaires is again vapouring about warlike measures," was the flippant minute on the dispatch. [18]

Bülow, meanwhile, was regrouping. Appointed to implement Weltpolitik, he was to garner support for the kaiser's program by patching together workable coalitions from the increasingly fractious groups that vied for power and influence in Wilhelmine Germany. At the same time, he had to protect Germany during the danger zone when the fleet was strong enough to agitate the Reich's enemies but not yet strong enough to repel them. It was the Second Fleet Bill, passed by the Reichstag in 1900, that made Bülow's task well nigh impossible: the prospect of Germany, already the strongest land power, doubling its fleet was profoundly destabilizing. England was bound to respond. Initially, however, Bülow was not worried: England was not central to his strategy because he was confident that the colonial conflicts that had dominated politics in the nineteenth century would continue to prevent Britain from allying with either France or Russia. Bülow, like Bismarck before him, saw Germany's peril on the Continent to be a two-front war. Facing an inevitably hostile France, he shored up Germany's southern flank by relying on Bismarck's alliance with Austria-Hungary (and, to a much lesser extent, Italy). To protect the eastern border, he persistently sought to improve relations with Russia. As long as Russia focused on expanding to the east and not the Balkans, which would bring it into conflict with Germany's ally, Austria-Hungary, Bülow could be optimistic about improving relations with St. Petersburg. The chancellor, however, had to be a deft and lucky juggler to ensure Germany's position on the Continent at the same time that he was implementing Weltpolitik: the fleet raised hackles abroad and at home. Garnering support for it was challenging.

Anglophobia—common ground between Agrarians and pan-Germans— helped Bülow; a keystone of his foreign policy strategy was faith in its beneficent powers. It was, as historian Lawrence Sondhaus has written, "the yeast that caused German navalism to rise."[19] Hatred of England would nurture love of Germany. Furthermore, any move toward Britain could alienate Russia, which Bülow still had hopes of wooing. Thus he consistently belittled, discouraged, and undermined the talks about talks that took place from 1897 to 1901 about a possible Anglo-German alliance, or at least a warming in relations. These putative alliance talks were plagued by hesitation and indecision. After Germany gained a foothold in China in 1897, some British politicians, notably the influential colonial secretary Joseph Chamberlain, thought some sort of entente could be useful, and the outbreak of the Boer War in October 1899 heightened their desire to improve Anglo-German relations in order to avert an anti-English Continental coalition. However, the Conservative prime minister, Lord Salisbury, judging the likelihood of such a coalition to be very remote, was consistently averse to forging any alliance with Germany. In Berlin, by contrast, Wilhelm, who was drawn almost inexorably to England, found the idea quite attractive, but he faced Bülow's stout and persuasive opposition to any overtures.

In January 1902, the chancellor took on Chamberlain. The anti-English tone of the German press coverage of the Boer War had outraged the British, and an exasperated Chamberlain had finally retaliated by casting aspersions on the

German army. Bülow rose in righteous indignation in the Reichstag and thundered the words of Frederick the Great, "Let the man do as he likes, and do not worry about it: he bites on granite." [20] It is testimony to the complexity and fluidity of European politics at the time that the chancellor's bête noire salvaged his scheme for decisive action in Venezuela, for at that very moment, Bülow, not nicknamed "the Eel" without reason, was slithering toward the English.[21]

The "Iron-Clad" Agreement

The debate as to who first concocted the scheme of Anglo-German cooperation in Venezuela began in 1902 on the front pages of German, English, and American dailies and, albeit in less prominent places, continues to this day. "There is no question then that Germany first conceived of the idea of using force against Venezuela," pens Warren Kneer, who has focused on the English side of the story. "It seems clear" to Holger Herwig, who has looked primarily at the German side, "that the government in London in fact seized the lead." [22]

The only thing that seems clear is that this was a case of dovetailing interests gelling at the same time. The British sounded out the Germans; the Germans sounded out the British. To assert that either party took the initiative and to dig feverishly through the archives for proof ignores the subtlety of life. In this decision, the question of who took the initiative is buried forever in innuendo, in inference, in the tone of voice, the raised eyebrow that leaves no paper trail.

London's grievances against Caracas paralleled those of Berlin, Rome, Washington, and Paris. "A feeling of regret and disappointment exists among the British inhabitants here at not receiving any effective protection for their lives and property," a British consul in Ciudad Bolívar reported in 1902. British citizens sought damages against the Venezuelan government for injuries incurred during the revolutions (particularly the seizure of British boats), the English backers of the railroad were owed $1.3 million, and England held most of the almost $15 million debt that Venezuela had negotiated in 1881 and defaulted on twenty years later. "The amount of these claims is no doubt comparatively insignificant," the Foreign Office conceded, "but the principle at stake is of the first importance." England's complaints were exacerbated by a disagreement over the sovereignty of the island of Patos and by simmering disputes between Venezuela and the nearby British colony of Trinidad. (The Venezuelan government believed that ships registered in Trinidad [that is, British ships] were smuggling arms to its opponents.) Haggard sent Castro seventeen notes about these grievances between February and June 1902, none of which was graced with a reply. London was annoyed.[23]

In late 1901, Britain was concerned that Germany would embarrass it in

Venezuela. It would look bad if Germany defended its citizens' rights while Whitehall idled. Thus, the British Foreign Office began to toy with various approaches to Venezuela. In early January 1902, while the kaiser was sitting on Bülow's proposal, the British undersecretary of state in charge of the American Department, Francis Villiers, was sounding out the German chargé in London about the possibility of "common action." The Anglophobic chancellor was not enthusiastic; in early January he still concurred with State Secretary Oswald von Richthofen, who wrote in the margins of the report of the probe, "We'll go our own way." British foreign secretary Lord Lansdowne was not deterred; a fortnight later he wrote that England was "awaiting a favorable opportunity for further action [in Venezuela], which may possibly take the form of joint action with one or several of the Powers interested." [24] Lansdowne later explained his interest in cooperation with the Germans as simple practicality, that he wanted to avoid the confusion of two different blockading fleets patrolling the Venezuelan waters at the same time, but he had been interested in improving relations with Germany for some time. In April, he told his ambassador in Berlin to sound out the Wilhelmstrasse about its intentions in Venezuela. The kaiser, awaiting his brother's return from the United States, did not respond.[25]

There the matter rested until June. There were two parallel tracks to the Venezuela story: despite the fact that the sophisticated professionals in Berlin and London believed that they were giving the orders, the record indicates the subtle influence of the persistent reporting of their representatives in Caracas. In Venezuela, German chargé Pilgrim-Baltazzi and British minister Haggard conferred often and acted in concert, and they excluded the American minister, Herbert Bowen.[26] Throughout the late spring and early summer, Haggard relentlessly whined and nagged the Foreign Office. The cumulative effect, not so much of the gravity of the affronts to British property in Venezuela but of Castro's utter stonewalling, convinced London that something had to be done, and the case of the *Queen*, a British ship that was seized by Castro on suspicion of aiding the rebels, provided the final impetus. "It appears to be what was lacking before," the assistant legal counsel opined, "clear proof of an outrage that justifies, and . . . requires reprisals." The senior legal counsel raised the temperature: "We are in some danger of carrying the forbearance of a great power towards a petty statelet unduly far, if we suffer this gladly." And the foreign secretary capped the minutes with: "We cannot let this pass." [27] There were dissenting voices, led by Chamberlain. Although he had earlier championed a rapprochement with Germany, the colonial secretary's public feud with Bülow and his growing suspicion of German goals had made him wary of cooperation with Berlin. His dissent was muted, however, by his absence from England during the crucial winter months of 1902 and 1903. Furthermore, the new Conservative prime minister, Arthur Balfour, was more favorably disposed toward cooperation with the Germans than his uncle and predecessor, Lord Salisbury, had been. In Venezuela, meanwhile, Castro seemed to be on the verge of losing the civil war to the rebels, who had sworn they would not honor the dictator's debts.[28] All the ingredients were ready.

In July, Germany revived the discussions of cooperation. The Wilhelmstrasse informed its ambassador to Britain, Count Paul von Wolff-Metternich, that it "thoroughly favored" a joint pacific blockade of Venezuela. Its reasons for welcoming British partnership were straightforward: "1. It would probably mean swifter Venezuelan compliance; 2. Germany would have to send significantly fewer ships, thus eliminating the navy's financial objections to the action; 3. We would probably have to share the rewards with England even if she did not participate."[29] Metternich talked to Lansdowne, and Lansdowne agreed "in principle" to the joint blockade.[30]

The British Admiralty had no hesitation in approving a blockade of the Venezuelan coast; its decision was made simple by the fact that the ships already in Western Hemisphere waters would suffice, thereby reducing the cost of the operation. On 14 August, it recommended that the action commence in November. Five days later, Lansdowne and Metternich agreed that the joint blockade should go ahead.[31] But in October Villiers wrote Lansdowne, "Time is running on, and I do not think we ought to delay any longer. . . . If the Germans want to associate themselves with us in this preliminary step [delivering the ultimatum], they can do so."[32]

In November, Lansdowne took two draft telegrams—one to Haggard requesting that he deliver the ultimatum to Castro, and the other to Michael Herbert, the British ambassador in Washington, requesting that he inform U.S. secretary of state John Hay of the ultimatum—with him to the royal estate at Sandringham, where the kaiser was visiting his uncle, King Edward VII, on a partridge-shooting holiday. The foreign secretary saw the king and Count Metternich on 10 November. Later that day, he telegraphed the Foreign Office from Sandringham that both telegrams should be sent. Neither telegram breathed a word of the Germans.[33]

The Germans then jumped hastily on board. On 11 November, the "iron-clad" agreement was forged at Sandringham.[34] The agreement stipulated only the first step—the seizure of the Venezuelan gunboats. After that, there was disagreement about the nature of the blockade and about the ranking of the claims. But one agreement was indeed iron-clad: neither ally could back out unilaterally. "The two claims [Germany's and England's] ought to stand or fall together," Lansdowne wrote after talking to Metternich. "We ought to exclude the possibility of a settlement between Venezuela and one of the two Powers without an equally satisfactory settlement in the case of the other. . . . Neither Government should be at liberty to recede except by mutual agreement. . . . The German Government evidently desired that once embarked we should travel with them to the end of the voyage." [35]

British journalists covered the kaiser's trip to Sandringham as a social and familial affair, but later, when they found out about the pledge that had been made during the visit, they were irate, incredulous, and contemptuous. "An itinerant and energetic Emperor has stolen our independence in the intervals of partridge shooting at Sandringham. A saloon carriage full of Ministers was taken to Sandringham to listen to Emperor William's marching orders," the London *Daily News* exclaimed. "This barbed hook Lord Lansdowne cheerfully bolted," the *Daily Mail* sneered, "so that England is bound by a pledge to follow Germany in any wild enterprise which the German Government may think it proper to undertake." [36] After swallowing the hook, Lansdowne immediately changed his orders to Haggard: "If you have not yet delivered the ultimatum," he cabled, "confer first with Pilgrim-Baltazzi." Bülow took it well: "We [in the Wilhelmstrasse] value cooperation with England in Venezuela very highly, and we welcome it wholeheartedly, even though our position has been made somewhat more difficult by the recent unilateral step of England [Lansdowne's first cables to Haggard and Herbert]," he reported gamely.[37]

"It is now too painfully clear that in this miserable Venezuela business the British nation has fallen into a trap laid by Germany," the *Daily Mail* concluded, with hindsight, after the blockade had begun. This gives Germany too much credit: Britain willfully sauntered into a buzzsaw. Lansdowne "was caught napping." [38]

American Signals

That Lansdowne miscalculated the British reaction is, frankly, astonishing. In hindsight, it seems obvious that the British public, still smarting from German behavior during the Boer War and in Shanghai (the Germans had tried to negotiate a separate deal with the Chinese behind Britain's back during the evacuation of Shanghai in November 1901), would be outraged by collaboration with Berlin. "The very notion of a Germanized foreign policy is utterly hateful to the British people," the archimperialist *National Review* opined in November, while the London *Spectator* was warning Whitehall "against playing the part of tail to the Hohenzollern kite." [39]

That Lansdowne miscalculated the American reaction, on the other hand, is completely understandable. He would have had to have been a seer and a psychic to have predicted the uproar in the United States.

Scholars frequently credit Theodore Roosevelt with masterful and subtle diplomacy in the affair. The president, they assert, was sending signals to the Europeans to fence off the American sphere, to define exactly what was meant by the Monroe Doctrine.[40] But if Roosevelt was being subtle, only he—and scholars sympathetic to him—was in on the game. The English, the Germans, and the Italians saw no subtlety in his signals. On the contrary, for them, Roosevelt's signals were as loud and clear as the Rough Rider himself.

First there were the words: the president's first message to Congress, in December 1901, explicitly stated, "We do not guarantee any [American] state against punishment if it misconducts itself, provided that punishment does not take the form of the acquisition of territory by any non-American power."[41] These words were backed up by actions. Washington's response to European activity in the hemisphere in 1901 and 1902 was remarkably calm.

This is true despite Roosevelt's eminently quotable outbursts against Germany before he became president: "Germany is the Power with which we may very possibly have ultimately to come into hostile contact";[42] "Germany is the power with whom I look forward to serious difficulty";[43] "Germany is by far the most hostile to us[;] . . . with Germany, under the Kaiser, we may at any time have trouble if she seeks to acquire territory in South America";[44] "Germany . . . is much more bitterly and outspokenly hostile to us than is England";[45] "if we fail to do so [prepare], it may well be that, a few years hence, should Germany try to establish herself in South America, we shall have to learn a bitter lesson";[46] "I absolutely agree with you about . . . the extreme desirability of keeping Germany out of this hemisphere. It seems to me that Germany's attitude toward us makes her the only power with which there is any reasonable likelihood or possibility of our clashing within the future. . . . Germany is the great growing power, and both her faults and her virtues . . . are so different from ours, and her ambitions in extra-European matters are so great, that she may clash with us."[47]

When he became vice president, however, Roosevelt began to change his tune. His insistence on the German threat had been the refrain to his exhortations on the naval expansion. As vice president, his responsibilities broadened, and his voice modulated. Predictions of the German threat diminished, and sober reflections on the proper interpretation of the Monroe Doctrine increased. In June 1901, he wrote Senator Lodge,

> I told him [the German consul general in New York] . . . that . . . I have a hearty and genuine liking for the Germans both individually and as a

nation; . . . that I was delighted to see South America kept open commercially to Germany and to the United States on an equal footing; that if a big German-speaking community in a South American state could not stand misgovernment, and set up for itself, there would be in that fact by itself nothing to which I should object; but that I did not desire to see the United States gain any territory in South America itself, and that . . . I would do all in my power to have the United States take the attitude that no European nation, Germany or any other, should gain a foot of soil in any shape or way in South America.[48]

As president, Roosevelt's attitude toward the German threat and the Monroe Doctrine continued to evolve. Despite the continued alarums of the naval men, President Roosevelt looked with a cool eye on the possibility of a German challenge to the Monroe Doctrine. Less than a month after McKinley's assassination, he wrote his friend German diplomat Speck von Sternburg, "I most earnestly desire to have Germany and the United States work hand in hand." And his actions in the first year of his presidency were absolutely consistent with the remarks he had written Sternburg in July: "If any South American State misbehaves towards any European country, let the European country spank it; but I do not wish the United States or any other country to get additional territory in South America."[49]

In September 1901, for example, days after Roosevelt took the oath of office, England, Germany, Italy, France, and Belgium delivered a joint protest to Guatemala to collect the debts they were owed. The Roosevelt administration smiled benignly. In April 1902, the British minister to Guatemala threatened that England would seize the country's customhouses and implied that the British would be joined by the Germans if the Guatemalans continued to dally. The Guatemalan president blinked and agreed to pay.[50]

The interesting points in this case are two. First, Britain did not consider notifying the United States before it made its threats. Second, Hay expressed serene indifference when the American minister to Guatemala informed him of the impending European pressure on the country. "It is within the right of the creditor nations to require payment of debts due to their nationals," he remarked. And when Germany approached Washington to see if it would be interested in joining the Europeans, the response was aloof: "The United States is indisposed to join in any collective act, with foreign powers, which might have the aspect of coercive pressure upon . . . Guatemala."[51]

And in June 1902, the French provided Roosevelt with another opportunity to display his interpretation of the Monroe Doctrine. Aggrieved by the Venezuelans' imprisonment of seven French merchants, the commander of the French cruiser *Suchet* seized a Venezuelan gunboat and, according to a German captain on the scene, "informed the Venezuelan captain that he could not leave, and that he—the French captain—reserved the right to confiscate the Venezuelan ship." The British minister, whose report corroborates the German's, mentions that the French captain "significantly add[ed] . . . that he [the Venezuelan] had better remember that he was under the guns of the *Suchet*."[52] President Castro was indignant, saying that the French had insulted the Venezuelan flag; nevertheless, the seven Frenchmen were freed in "less than an hour," and a public apology was offered France.[53] The French government "highly approved of the energy displayed by the captain," but the American on the spot, Minister Bowen, considered the episode "irregular and reprehensible." In Washington, Assistant Secretary Alvey Adee jotted on Bowen's report, "Concur in this view although regarding incident as closed so far as we are concerned," and the State Department expressed not a whisper of displeasure to France.[54]

In the autumn, it was the Germans' turn. When, in September, Haitian rebels on the gunboat *Crête-à-Pierrot* boarded a German steamship on the high seas and forced it, in what the U.S. minister called "a high-handed proceeding," to hand over weapons destined for the Haitian government, Wilhelm decided to dispatch the gunboat *Panther* to Haiti.[55] The German boat fired a shot across the *Crête*'s bow and announced that it was going to sink the ship. The rebel captain, Admiral Killick, was ashore at the time, sick in bed, but he arose, rowed out to his vessel, ordered his officers and crew to leave, and, according to the U.S. minister, W. F. Powell, placed "three kegs of powder, some large cartridges and a can of kerosene oil" in his room. "The last thing he was seen to do was to light a cigar, fire this train, take a seat in a chair, dressed in his uniform." The ensuing explosion was coupled with the fire from the *Panther*. "The next day," Powell added, "the blackened corpse of Killick was found floating near the 'Crete.' "[56] The kaiser was gleeful: "Bravo *Panther*!" he dashed in the margins of the report of the incident. The American chargé d'affaires in Berlin wrote to Hay, "Several colleagues in the Diplomatic Corps were inquisitive as to the attitude which would be taken by the United States in the matter. . . . The opinion is general [in the German press] . . . that the incident shows that the Monroe Doctrine does not mean that the United States will object to the proper protection of its commercial interests by a European Power." The State Department's legal adviser, John Bassett Moore, labeled the sinking "illegal and excessive," but Acting Secretary of State Adee declared that the "destruction of . . . the Crête-à-Pierrot [would] probably re-

"Hayti: 'Hoch der Kaiser!'" In 1902, a German gunboat sank a Haitian ship in retaliation for an alleged assault. The Haitian captain went down with his ship. Washington was not alarmed. (*Philadelphia North American*, 9 Sept. 1902)

lieve the [disturbed political] situation." The *New York Times* told its readers, "Germany was quite within her rights in doing a little housecleaning on her own account."[57]

Nor had a ripple of alarm spread through the U.S. government or press when, in the summer of 1902, the British had hoisted the Union Jack on the island of Patos, between Trinidad and the Venezuelan coast. As real estate, the island was of questionable value. "I know the island personally," the hydrographer attached to the Foreign Office reported. "It is little better than a mass of rock. It is difficult to see what use it is or can be to England." The Admiralty consistently dismissed the island's usefulness, but Minister Haggard, convinced that its location at the mouth of the Orinoco gave it strategic significance, relentlessly argued the opposite.[58] The critical point, one that was not lost on the British authorities, was that this was a territorial claim and therefore skirted dangerously close to challenging the Monroe Doctrine. The Colonial Office recommended that Washington be consulted before any action was taken, and the Foreign Office researched American interest in the island. But Lansdowne and Villiers decided that the British claim was sound and that there was "no more reason to communicate with the United States about Patos than to ask their leave to stay in Trinidad." They expected no trouble from Washington, and none was forthcoming.[59] Bowen's was, not for the first time, a voice in the wilderness: "In my opinion Great Britain's title to Patos has not yet been sufficiently proved," he wrote to Hay. "Would it not be very proper for our Government to suggest to Great Britain that if she is not disposed to relinquish her claim, she should propose to Venezuela to submit the controversy to the Tribunal at the Hague?"[60] His query was never answered.

Finally, Washington had ample opportunity to express displeasure at the impending collective blockade of Venezuela. It seized not one of these opportunities. In June 1901, the U.S. chargé in Caracas informed the State Department that Germany was contemplating applying pressure on Venezuela and wondered if Washington might be interested in joining a concert of powers. Secretary of State John Hay's response echoed his reply to the similar inquiry about the Guatemalan incident: it was not U.S. practice, he explained, to join other powers in claims protests.[61] On 13 December (ten days after Roosevelt's first message to Congress), Ambassador Holleben delivered a memorandum to the State Department stating that the Reich was contemplating blockading Venezuela's ports or temporarily occupying its customhouses in order to collect its debts. "Under no circumstances," Holleben hastened to add, "do we consider in our proceedings the acquisition or the permanent occupation of Venezuelan territory." In reply, Hay merely noted the president's address to Congress and expressed the expectation that Germany would keep its promises.[62]

The Italians, ever scrambling, were not far behind. Italy had a small but significant interest in Venezuela—about four thousand Italians lived there, and there were diverse trade links between the two countries. Italian claims against Venezuela amounted to $145,000. The Italian press reported the indignities to which the Italians were subjected during the incessant civil wars and pointed to the lackluster performance of the Italian government in protecting its citizens. In February 1902, the Italian ambassador to the United States was instructed to get an assurance that Washington would not object to Italy taking coercive measures against Venezuela. Secretary Hay, the ambassador reported in March, had told him "that the United States appreciates our consideration and that we are free to exert our rights whenever and however we see fit, as long as we seize no territory."[63]

By October 1902, when the British cabinet took up the coercion of Venezuela, Lansdowne was convinced that Britain could "assume the acquiescence of the United States." And in November, when England officially notified the United States of its imminent action in Venezuela, Hay's response was predictably low-key: "The United States government viewed [it] with regret . . . but they could not object . . . provided [it] . . . did not contemplate any territorial acquisition."[64]

This was American diplomacy at its most straightforward. Words and actions coincided. The light was green. The Europeans had every reason to believe that they fully understood Roosevelt's definition of the elastic Monroe Doctrine. The United States would oppose the acquisition of territory, but none was planned. "The United States government knew very well that we did not wish to establish ourselves in Venezuela," Metternich asserted, "and we had received a free hand from them to move against the reprobate debtor." Lansdowne later echoed these sentiments in the House of Lords: "My Lords, the German Government dotted the i's, because they explained . . . not only that coercion was intended, but that that coercion should take a particular shape. . . . With so plain an indication as that of the policy of the United States Government, there was no reason why we should have had any misgiving." The only anxiety the Foreign Office expressed about the Americans concerned their reaction to a pacific blockade—a legalistic qualm, not anxiety about the Monroe Doctrine.[65]

What is striking in reading the British records of the Venezuela affair is how utterly marginal the United States was in the Foreign Office's conception of the operation. It is indicative of this lack of concern that, immediately before the matter was discussed by the cabinet, Lansdowne asked Villiers, "Am I right in believing that the U.S. have publicly announced that they do not intend to raise objections?" In reply, Villiers referred not to any British correspondence with Washington (because there was none) but to the American response to the German probe of the previous December. Lansdowne then assured the cabinet, "It will not be necessary to say anything as to our intention of doing this [allying with Germany to coerce Venezuela] to the U.S. government, until we see the effect of our ultimatum." And this is exactly what they did: the British did not inform the Americans until 11 November (with the dispatch of the telegram Lansdowne took to Sandringham), and they included not a whisper about Germany.[66]

Why this reticence, despite Anglo-American friendship? It is not that the idea of consulting Washington never occurred to the Foreign Office. On the original Admiralty go-ahead to the blockade Lansdowne jotted, "We ought to give the U.S. timely warning of our intention." In August, he had even floated the idea to Metternich of inviting the United States to participate in the coercion of Venezuela. Germany did not object; it was Lansdowne himself who vetoed the idea.[67]

The basic reason was that the British sincerely and understandably did not expect the Americans to object to their actions, which they thought would render swift results. They were confident that British-American relations were sound after a string of conciliatory gestures in Latin America—their capitulation in the first Venezuela crisis, their support for the United States in the War of 1898, and their signing of the 1901 Hay-Pauncefote Treaty, which gave the United States a unilateral right to the isthmian canal. Perhaps the seasoned British ambassador, Julian Pauncefote, would have warned the Foreign Office about the folly of their ways, but he died in May 1902, and his replacement did not arrive until October.[68] But there were two further reasons for British silence. Lansdowne had been warned strongly and explicitly by the Admiralty that absolute secrecy would be the key to the successful seizure of the Venezuelan navy because any warning would give the Venezuelans time to move their fleet up the Orinoco to shallow waters inaccessible to the British ships. In the words of the first lord of the Admiralty, "This proposal must be kept a very dead secret as these gunboats may be put away somewhere." At the same time, Haggard had been battering the Foreign Office with vituperative reports of the unreliability of Bowen, whom he thought had been intriguing against Britain and currying favor with the Venezuelans. "The greatest danger of this [a leak] would be if United States Minister were to know exactly what is intended," Haggard warned from Caracas. The minute of Undersecretary Villiers was terse: "We have been careful not to tell the Americans (or anyone else) what we and the Germans intend to do." If the Americans knew, Bowen would know; if Bowen knew, Castro would know.[69]

Second, there is in the Foreign Office minutes a tone of bitter resignation about the growing U.S. hegemony in the Caribbean.[70] The communications with Washington were perfunctory. The situation after 1895 was galling for the British. This emerges clearly in the discussion of Patos. Since the British expected no objection from the United States to their coercion of Venezuela, they decided not to spend any of their dignity unnecessarily.

The Germans proved more savvy about American sensibilities than did the British. True, they refused to recognize the Monroe Doctrine; they saw U.S. pretensions in the hemisphere as unjustified, impertinent, insolent, and unenforceable. "It is generally assumed that the object of our government," the U.S. chargé in Berlin wrote in 1901, "is to acquire international recognition as the predominant power on the American continent, and to force the other States to accept us as a kind of guardian and arbitrator. Our purpose, it is said, is to remodel the phrase 'America for the Americans' so as to make it 'America for the North Americans.' "[71]

Nevertheless, the Germans were exceedingly cautious. In marked contrast to the Foreign Office, the Wilhelmstrasse referred to the expected reaction of the United States in virtually every major piece of correspondence on the Venezuela affair. When it first sounded out the navy in the summer of 1901, it addressed the American response directly. There was no danger of U.S. involvement, the Wilhelmstrasse asserted—trying to allay fears before they were even voiced—because Germany had no desire to acquire territory and would so inform Washington. When Roosevelt became president a few months later, Bülow was heartened by his apparently pro-German outlook and was convinced that debt collection in Venezuela would not violate his interpretation of the Monroe Doctrine. Holstein and Albert von Quadt, the chargé in Washington, agreed with Bülow. They were also reassured by the attitude of the U.S. press. "The American papers almost unanimously have declared that Germany has the full right to protect her interests in Venezuela with force if necessary. This would not be a threat to the Monroe Doctrine," Quadt wrote from the United States in August 1902. But Ambassador Holleben, although he stopped short of contradicting the chancellor, expressed doubt and called for delays.[72]

Nor were the navy and the kaiser convinced by Bülow's assurances. Diederichs, who feared that time was not on Germany's side, was in favor of the scheme, while continuing to work on the war plans against the United States. Tirpitz and Wilhelm, who believed that time was on Germany's side, were reluctant to volunteer for any unnecessary adventure before the fleet had been built to full strength. This was the "danger zone," when Germany had to be particularly careful not to provoke its enemies. To overcome the kaiser's doubts, Bülow reversed his prior stance against cooperation, stressing instead that the English were firmly committed to the undertaking and also, embroidering the truth, that it had been their idea. It was still difficult for Bülow to assuage all the kaiser's doubts. Wilhelm was worried that the British would not be reliable allies. In January 1902, he scrawled permission for Bülow to explore joint action with the British only "if we can be sure that they would not take advantage of these approaches in order to place us in a suspicious position with the Americans." Wilhelm feared that the British would leak information to the Yankees, and he feared that they might leave the Germans high and dry in the middle of the operation. These qualms were finally allayed just before the coercion began, when the "iron-clad" agreement was forged at Sandringham.[73]

Once he was certain that the alliance was firm, the kaiser welcomed it. Partnership with England would reassure Washington and deflect any criticism that the Americans might hurl Germany's way. It would reduce any risk to the German fleet both because the costs would be shared and because Germany could use British ports in the region for resupplying and recoaling. It would also strengthen Berlin by nudging it closer to London.[74]

Germany sheltered in England's lee. This proud nation took extraordinary measures to avoid incurring the displeasure of both Washington and London. It did not take the lead in determining the participants, the timing, or the strategy of the blockade. The acceptance of Italian participation in the blockade was British policy, not German. Although Italy was a member of the Triple Alliance (and Bülow, who was married to an Italian, was an ardent Italophile), Berlin treated Rome with contempt. Italy did not presume to ask for a voice in the planning of any proposed action against Castro, but it did expect Berlin to keep it informed and to allow it to participate as a very junior partner. Throughout 1901 and 1902, when the Italians suspected that something was afoot, the Wilhelmstrasse was tight lipped. Britain's ambassador in Rome reported that the Italian foreign minister felt he had "not been kept well informed, especially by his agent in Venezuela." This was no wonder, "the Italian Minister [in Caracas] and the German Chargé d'Affaires not being on speaking terms."[75] As late as 27 November 1902, the Germans were assuring Rome that no decision had been made about action in Venezuela, and on 2 December, the undersecretary of state for foreign affairs, Otto von Mühlberg, "threw cold water on the idea" of Italian participation. The Italians, stonewalled by their ally, turned to the British, only to be rebuffed again. "I told him [the Italian ambassador] as little as possible," Villiers wrote. "[Italian] cooperation," the head of the American division of the Foreign Office remarked on 2 December, "would be the reverse of an assistance." The foreign secretary capped it with: "[We] could not allow other powers to 'cut in' at this stage."[76]

On 5 December, Lansdowne told the Italian ambassador that Britain would have welcomed the participation of Italy, but, unfortunately, it was too late:

the ships were on their way. He reversed himself two days later, however, after the Italians shrewdly pointed out that they could be helpful to the British in Somalia. "You showed, I thought, no little dexterity in running the Somaliland and Venezuelan cases together," he later wrote to his ambassador in Rome.[77]

Bülow was not delighted. "Politically, I consider any increase in the blockading fleet troublesome because the mood in the United States, which until now has shown no excitement, could change if additional naval units were to be sent," he told the kaiser. But on 9 December, Germany yielded to the British request, and Italy was accepted as a partner. "The day before yesterday—China," the Rome daily *Il Mattino* crowed. "Yesterday—the Red Sea. Today—Venezuela!"[78]

The British designed the operation. In September, the British commander in chief of the North Atlantic station, Vice Admiral Archibald Douglas, recommended, "as an alternative scheme to the Blockade, that all the Venezuelan Gunboats should be seized and retained until our demands are met." Douglas thought that this would be more effective than a blockade because the Venezuelan fleet, motley as it was, was crucial to Castro's ability to defend the coast from the armed rebels.[79] In October, Lansdowne suggested, "We should . . . in the first instance, address a final warning to the Venezuelans, and . . . if it is disregarded [inform them that] we are prepared to join with them [the Germans] in measures of coercion . . . [that is,] the seizure of the gun boats." This was followed to the letter: "Overall," Bülow declared in early November, "we can declare ourselves in agreement with these proposals." He went on to comment, "We should urge the British government to specify which further measures should be resorted to if the confiscation of the warships, contrary to the expectation of the British Admiralty, does not lead to any results." Wilhelm concurred emphatically: "This statement must *eo ipso* be received before we take any step."[80]

But it was not received. As late as 25 November, Villiers wrote the Admiralty: "There are still a few points of detail which we have to settle with the Germans." And on 7 December, both England and Germany sent ultimatums to Venezuela before there was any agreement about further measures.[81]

The main sticking point was whether the allies would impose a peace blockade, as Germany, at Bülow's urging, insisted, or a war blockade, as England wanted. Bülow thought a pacific blockade would interfere less with neutral (that is, American) vessels, but the British were characteristically concerned with international law and saw no precedent for a peace blockade. Germany yielded to the English demand. "Since it seems highly desirable," Bülow wrote Wilhelm, "to convince the English that we go with them without reservation—hand-in-hand—I ask you to approve the English proposal."[82]

"Italy: 'I'm the Kaiser's monkey: whose monkey are you?'" A worried England is depicted as dancing to Germany's tune during the Anglo-German-Italian blockade of Venezuela. (*Tacoma Daily Ledger*, 10 February 1903)

Even on details, the Germans bowed to the English. The Foreign Office wanted both the English and the German representatives in Caracas to leave immediately after delivering the ultimatums. However, the German chargé preferred to remain in Caracas with his pregnant wife, who had been advised not to travel. "I don't think we can allow Madame Pilgrim's inopportune indisposition to upset all our plans," Lansdowne wrote. Pilgrim-Baltazzi left the capital, with Haggard and without his wife, as soon as the ultimatums were delivered.[83]

On 9 December, receiving no response to their ultimatums, England and Germany imposed an unofficial blockade and began to seize the vessels of the Venezuelan navy. Virtually all—"a few antiquated old tubs" crewed by men "who were more fishermen than sailors"—were captured in two days. On land, however, the operation met resistance: in what the London *Times* deemed "the bravado of burlesque," Castro arrested more than two hundred German and English residents of Caracas, thundered nationalistic speeches, and called his citizens to arms. Fearing that their citizens were at risk ashore, the allies landed troops to evacuate refugees.[84]

At sea as well, the operation did not proceed as smoothly as the allies had expected. The Germans, unable to spare a ship to tow two captured and un-seaworthy Venezuelan vessels to Curaçao, unceremoniously sank them.

On the 13th, Commodore R. A. Montgomerie, the British senior naval offi-cer, "demanded apology for insult to British flag." (A British steamer had been boarded at La Guayra, the crew had been treated disrespectfully and briefly held under arrest, and the Union Jack had been lowered.) The apology not arriving within the hour, "the [English cruiser] *Charybdis* and the [Ger-man cruiser] *Vineta* shelled Forts Libertador and Vigia [at Puerto Cabello]."[85] Castro leaped to his soapbox: "This is no longer an assault on the govern-ment and people of Venezuela—it is an assault on civilization itself! The souls of our illustrious forefathers are assuredly rising from their graves, imposing and severe, to inflame the patriotism of all Venezuelans at this solemn hour when their legacy is being challenged!" Castro's government also lodged a formal protest to the bombing: "Contrary to the universal custom in cases of bombardment, no time was given in which to take defensive measures, and, as a result, in addition to the victims in the prison and in the Fort Solano, innocent persons, old and young, male and female, suffered from this unlooked-for bombardment." Montgomerie was unrepentant. "When boys are naughty," he explained to the American consul at Puerto Cabello, "they should be spanked."[86]

The British directed the bombing of Puerto Cabello. Montgomerie praised his German colleague: "German commodore backed me up most loyally." This was to be expected: although the English and German operations in Venezuelan waters were geographically separate, the Germans took their lead from the British. Orders were sent to the German senior naval officer in Vene-zuelan waters to do only as the English did. The German traveled to Trinidad to confer with the English admiral—not vice versa. Germany sent only four ships to Britain's eight, and in terms of total tonnage, the German contribution was even less than the Italian (which arrived on 16 December). Wilhelm com-mented: "The more ships the British send the better. The more our action fades into the background and theirs takes the foreground, the better. Of course we will follow the British program. I am against sending more of our ships to Venezuelan waters. Our flag is represented. Let's leave the British up front."[87]

Castro continued to surprise the Europeans, who had expected him to capitulate abjectly. Instead, he sent Washington an offer to submit the dispute to arbitration. The State Department forwarded the request without comment to London and Berlin; it was received on 13 December, the day Puerto Cabello was bombed. Neither London nor Berlin relished the prospect of protracted negotiations with the dictator; both worried about the enforceability of a negotiated settlement. Spurred by the threat of arbitration, England hastened to move to the next stage: the official blockade. A comedy of errors ensued. "The admiral has once more ignored his instructions," Villiers complained, learning of the first delay, caused by a minor mechanical problem on the flagship *Charybdis*. Three days later—when the blockade was to have begun—Lansdowne scrawled, "The delay [caused this time by the lag-time in communicating with ships in Venezuelan waters, particularly after the cable station at Puerto Cabello was no longer available] is unfortunate." On the 17th, while the Foreign Office was absorbed in the discussion of Castro's arbitration offer, Montgomerie asked for a delay until the 24th. Lansdowne was obdurate: "We have now settled for the 20th," and on the 20th, the official notice of the blockade was published in the *London Gazette*. But the Germans were left to scramble: Commodore Scheder had sailed to Trinidad to confer with Montgomerie, and he was unable to return to Puerto Cabello in time to impose the blockade on the 20th. After all Britain's fuss about a simultaneous blockade ("It is clearly absurd to commence a blockade without the cooperation of the Germans," Villiers had written on 13 December), the Germans were unable to mount their blockade on Puerto Cabello before 22 December, and that on Maracaibo had to wait until the 24th. Whitehall had difficulty communicating with the British admiral, while the Germans were left in the dark. Meanwhile, on 18 December, both England and Germany had officially informed the United States that they would accept arbitration.[88]

Roosevelt's Black Hole

Much has been written about Germany's decision to accept arbitration. Theodore Roosevelt bequeathed this black hole of scholarship to future researchers when he claimed, almost fourteen years after the fact, that he had delivered a secret ultimatum to the Germans that had brought them to the bargaining table. The former president asserted that he had informed the hapless German ambassador that, if Berlin proved recalcitrant, he would unleash Admiral George Dewey's fleet (which at that moment was massed in unprecedented strength at Puerto Rico) on the Reich's ships in Venezuelan waters.[89]

These U.S. naval exercises had been planned well in advance and were known to the Germans and the English before the blockade began, yet not one document has been found to confirm the president's assertion—not in the United States, not in Germany, and not in England. Not to worry, according to historian Frederick Marks, who turns the absence of evidence into a virtue: there must have been a gentlemanly conspiracy to destroy all documents pertaining to the kaiser's humiliation! Marks's thesis is unlikely, not only on the face of it but also according to the hard evidence. The persuasiveness of the alleged ultimatum was equivalent to the persuasiveness of Dewey's fleet. Let us suppose that every reference to the purported ultimatum and to Dewey's fleet was removed from the Wilhelmstrasse and Foreign Office records. Not only is the alleged ultimatum not mentioned, the sole reference to the American admiral in the British Foreign Office and Admiralty archives is the following terse telegram: "The United States squadron . . . arrived on 21st and 23d Dec., and left again on 27th and 28th Dec. The visit was apparently merely for purpose of giving leave to the men, and had no political significance." There remains a further source—the huge, bound Admiralty ledgers. Into these tomes a minion in the British Admiralty laboriously penned every reference to every ship and every seaman that appeared in every item of Admiralty correspondence as it passed through the department. (For example, the *Crête-à-Pierrot* is listed and cross-referenced.) In the volumes for 1902, no mention is made of either Dewey or his ship. Is it credible that in deference to the kaiser's ego the ledgers for 1902 were totally rewritten? Furthermore, immediately after accepting arbitration, the Germans asked Roosevelt to serve as arbitrator (which he declined), hardly a likely request if the president had just threatened them with war. And yet Roosevelt's claim sits, sucking scholar after scholar into convoluted, circumstantial arguments about the president's credibility: Did he or didn't he?[90]

The question can be recast: Why did the Germans accept arbitration? The simple answer is that Berlin accepted arbitration because the costs of the intervention were much higher than it had anticipated. Castro was not groveling, and the operation was precipitating a wave of anti-German vitriol in the British and American press. This reaction swelled to a crescendo during the days that Berlin was considering Castro's offer. For the Germans, Britain's press was particularly important. Since one of the primary goals of cooperation had been to improve Anglo-German relations, and since the Germans wanted to follow England's lead, the British press was an important weathervane for Berlin, signaling the stresses on the Balfour government. The Wilhelmstrasse followed it closely; Metternich was a virtual clipping service.[91] And the onslaught of anti-German sentiment in the British press as soon as the blockade began gave the kaiser pause. His perennial fear that England would leave Germany out in the cold, smoothed over at Sandringham, resurfaced. "The German Government . . . have been frightened by the tone of the English press," the British ambassador in Berlin explained. "They certainly do not wish to increase our difficulties with public opinion in England. The idea of arbitration did not smile on them, but they accepted it at once because we had proposed it. . . . The Germans are very sensitive about our Press which they believe has far more influence than it really has." [92]

Uproar in the Press

The announcement of the cooperation in Venezuelan waters caused barely a ripple of alarm or dissent in the British press.[93] Britons were happy to see Castro brought to heel. "It would be difficult anywhere to find a Government more dishonest, more corrupt, more incapable of maintaining order or realizing the elementary demands which civilization makes upon every community. Law and order are words without meaning in Venezuela," the conservative *Daily Mail* proclaimed, while the *Times* condemned "the ridiculous arrogance that animates [the Venezuelans] . . . as it does the half-educated politicians of many other South American states." The *Daily News* noted simply, "Castro has the insolence of infinite littleness." [94]

Furthermore, the press was confident that the Foreign Office had sounded out the Americans and that Roosevelt, true to his 1901 Annual Message (which was frequently cited), had no objection to the exercise. The British press was relentlessly pro-American, and particularly pro-Roosevelt. No paper even intimated that the young president could do any wrong. Even the *Saturday Review*, which the *New York Times* labeled "one of the most spiteful of the few journals that systematically deride and misrepresent the United States," never questioned the importance or correctness of England's friendship with the United States; it merely expressed its irritation with the moralism of U.S. foreign policy and cast a cold eye on the returns Britain got for its support of Washington.[95] The *Pall Mall Gazette*, an upscale conservative paper with close links to Parliament, expressed the confidence shared by all the British papers: "It is absolutely certain that the United States will offer no sort of opposition to the just and necessary vindication of British and German rights." Their assuredness was bolstered by Roosevelt's second message to Congress, delivered on 5 December, which repeated the first's definition of the Monroe Doctrine virtually verbatim. The *Times* even opined that London's cooperation with Berlin would, by tempering the Germans, soothe and please the United States.[96]

Only the *Daily News* betrayed any anxiety. "The Venezuelan question is not likely to be such plain sailing as the *Times* seems to imagine," it editorialized on 1 December. The *News*, considered the leading Liberal newspaper and therefore a critic of the Conservative Balfour government, was worried that the operation might not be as swift as everyone anticipated, and it wondered how England and Germany could strong-arm Castro while managing to stay within the bounds of the Monroe Doctrine.[97] But it was on its own for more than a week.

Then, one by one, the papers fell.

On 9 December, the conservative *Morning Post* stumbled. Although it continued to believe that Washington would raise no objections and it did not anticipate vigorous opposition from Castro, this stuffy "greybeard of London dailies" regretted England's cozying up to Germany, particularly so soon after the disclosures about German double-dealing in Shanghai and Bülow's anti-English tirade in the Reichstag. "The transition from that speech [the "granite" speech] . . . to yesterday's announcement is a little abrupt." The *Post* called on the Foreign Office to explain itself. This was the first criticism of the alliance with Germany in the eleven papers examined, and its appearance in a conservative paper, the Balfour government's natural ally, indicates the difficulty the prime minister faced in building support for his Venezuela policy. The conservative press was more anti-German and pro-American than the liberal press. Thus, the government's Venezuela policy eventually managed to raise the hackles of virtually every editor.[98]

On 12 December, the wide-circulation *Daily Mail* and three influential liberal papers—the *Manchester Guardian*, the *Westminster Gazette*, and the *Daily Chronicle*—joined, with varying vigor, the ranks of the critics.[99] On that day, articles appeared about the seizure of the Venezuelan navy, the imminent blockade, and Castro's arrest of the British and German residents. These stories changed the situation: the press had assumed that the English and German forces would temporarily occupy the customhouses and so recoup their citizens' debts. Short and sweet. Seizing the Venezuelan navy and imposing a blockade was another matter: it looked belligerent, and its effectiveness was by no means guaranteed. It could take a long time, it could irritate the United States, and it would empty the coffers that would repay the debts. The *Manchester Guardian*, voice of liberal intellectuals, instructed the Foreign Office: "The immediate task before the Government is to get hold of money by threats. It must be money because the Monroe Doctrine makes any other form of compensation impossible."[100]

In the meantime, Castro was more belligerent than anyone had anticipated. As the *Westminster Gazette* commented ruefully, "Even wicked and corrupt races are capable at times of formidable resistance to invaders."[101] Had Castro collapsed like a punctured balloon (as everyone expected), there would have been no problem. It was Castro's resistance—not the U.S. fleet—that made the British press bemoan the Foreign Office's lack of forethought. What could England do if Castro refused to bow to the blockade? It could not seize territory—the Monroe Doctrine prohibited that—and so it could do no more than loiter in Venezuelan waters, the victim of Castro's whims, all the while irritating the United States. The *Morning Post* put it dryly: "The interesting point about this war or coercion is in the problem which it sets of how to coerce a State which the coercing Powers are not prepared to crush or conquer." This "interesting point" quickly became the focus of increasingly shrill concern among Britain's editorial writers.[102]

The complaint was simple: the Foreign Office had carelessly risked American goodwill. The "heavyweight liberal paper," the *Westminster Gazette*, after grousing about "the habit of the Government to risk great dangers for trivial causes," laid out the indictment most clearly: "The seizure of territory and the administration of the country in the interest of the creditors is barred to us by the Monroe Doctrine. The *ultima ratio*, therefore, is denied to us from the beginning. . . . The danger in this case is that the Government should be going down a blind alley which is blocked at the far end by the Monroe Doctrine." America's goodwill was the most solid currency in British foreign relations; it was the steady point, the issue about which all shades of opinion agreed; it was, as the *Manchester Guardian* stated, "one of the cardinal principles of our national policy." It was clearly ludicrous to risk even a fraction of it to recover a paltry debt in Venezuela! "Any claim that either Great Britain or Germany have against Venezuela are trifles light as air in the great balance of national policy," the *Morning Post* explained.[103]

The press was not worried about the response of the Roosevelt administration to the operation. It agreed with the Foreign Office that official opinion in Washington was not alarmed by England's activities in Venezuelan waters. But the British press, unlike the Foreign Office, did not consider this the sum total of American goodwill: there was also public opinion as expressed in the papers. And the American papers were rapidly turning against the adventure.

Most newspapers in the United States focused on the Venezuela story for only a few days, but they were the crucial days when Germany and England were mulling over Castro's offer to submit the claims to arbitration.[104] Initially, the U.S. papers had not been alarmed by the joint coercion of Venezuela. Their mood had been one of alert complacency: the Monroe Doctrine was not threatened, yet the situation bore watching.[105] Mahan himself was sober: "The action of the two powers [Britain and Germany] does not contravene the Monroe Doctrine," he wrote the editor of the British *National*

"Uncle Sam: 'That's a live wire, gentlemen!'" During the Venezuela crisis, Uncle Sam and the Monroe Doctrine were frequently depicted as holding England and Germany at bay. (*New York Herald*, 16 December 1902)

Review, "but I fear the *joint* action will excite a popular sentiment here injurious to both. . . . It is illogical to object to two Powers doing jointly what there is no objection to either doing singly; but feelings take little heed of logic." And indeed, from 13 to 14 December—with the sinking of the ships, the arrest of the Germans and English in Caracas, the bombing of Puerto Cabello, and Castro's spirited refusal to bow—feeling did overwhelm logic. The situation looked like it was getting out of control, America's control: the Monroe Doctrine could be threatened.[106] There were two basic reasons for concern: Castro's pig-headedness and German impulsiveness. Editorials and banner headlines grew strident, blaming Germany and seeking solace in the presence of Dewey's fleet. The exact purpose of the fleet was not stated, but it was taken for granted that it greatly increased America's (unspecified) options.[107]

Although British papers carefully reported the rising concern evidenced in the American press, their absence of interest in Dewey's fleet is striking. The fleet was not mentioned once by the *Pall Mall Gazette*, the *Daily Chronicle*, the *Observer*, or the *Spectator*. The *Westminster Gazette* and the *Morning Post* each had a single deadpan reference to it.[108] The *Manchester Guardian* referred to it twice: once, obliquely, simply to report that no U.S. warship would be sent to Venezuela, and once to quash any rumors ("The fact that American warships have been ordered to Venezuelan waters is taken in some quarters as indicating the purpose of this Government [Washington] to interfere. All such rumours are wide of the truth.") The *Daily News* echoed the *Guardian* in its two news stories that mentioned the fleet in passing. The *Daily Mail* toed a similar line.[109] The *Times* brushed aside any rumors about the fleet early and utterly. "[The U.S.] yellow press . . . [is] attempting to prove that the presence of strong squadrons of United States warships in the Caribbean Sea for manoeuvres is something more than a coincidence. As a matter of fact, the manoeuvres were arranged months ago, and unless the State Department is credited with the power of prophecy it is impossible to suppose any connexion between the presence of the British and German and of the American warships in the same region." [110] And that was all there was. If there is a story in the British press's handling of the Dewey fleet, it is that it was a nonstory; it was not considered newsworthy. Nor was Dewey's fleet mentioned once in any of the numerous scathing attacks on the government's policy delivered in the British Parliament.[111]

This is, frankly, startling. It flies in the face of the common American supposition that Dewey's fleet was a powerful, nay decisive, prophylactic. Unless one extends the Marks thesis (the bleaching of the diplomatic record) to the English press and Parliament, one is forced to conclude that the British were not interested in the perambulations of the American admiral and his largest ever U.S. fleet. The notion of the United States Navy intervening in — or contemplating war against England and Germany over — Venezuela was so ludicrous, so unbelievable, that it could not be sold to any shade of the British public. One would not even have to mention such an unlikely scenario except that Roosevelt's alleged threat, coupled with American ethnocentrism, has given it a certain respectability.[112] The major British dailies were expressing their anxiety about something more subtle. Basically theirs was a cost-benefit analysis: the operation, which all had expected to be swift and uncomplicated, suddenly looked messy and costly.[113]

It was Castro's behavior that first gave birth to these anxieties. It was German behavior that ripened them. In the early days of the operation, the British press was uniformly blasé about the German role. This was due, in part, to ignorance of the extent of England's commitment to Germany and in part to a widespread desire to avoid knee-jerk Germanophobia.[114] Thus, there was not one word of criticism of the fact that England was acting in concert with Germany until 9 December. One could be forgiven for thinking that somehow, miraculously, the British journalists had forgotten Berlin's transgressions. By 15 December, however, several stories coalesced in rapid succession. First, there were increasingly frequent reports that the Americans were getting restless. Second, the news came that the Germans had sunk two Venezuelan ships. Third, there were rumors about the bombing of Puerto Cabello.

The upshot of these events was irreversible. Once released, the British public's distrust of Germany could not be assuaged. It was foolhardy, the *Daily News* complained, to be yoked to Germany ("the American bête noire") in America's backyard. "Germany's designs in South America are well known," the *News* observed. The *Pall Mall Gazette* agreed: "Germany is a young power with a teeming population, a vast and increasing trade, and ambitions in the direction of expansion and *welt-politik* which are now backed by the powerful argument of a navy which is already strong, and which will soon be much stronger. . . . We cannot afford to endanger the good understanding between the two branches of the Anglo-Saxon race in order to chastise Don Cipriano Castro, and thereby to extract chestnuts for the mailed fist. . . . Germany desires nothing more earnestly than to see England and the United States at loggerheads." The *Daily Chronicle* concurred: "We do not . . . complain of the Government's determination to protect British subjects in this case. But we do complain of the way in which the Government has set to work, and of the undertaking towards another Government, into which it appears to have entered with an inadequate appreciation of the risks involved. We are taking joint action in a case where . . . the larger political interests behind are certainly not in all respects the same." [115] This crescendo of criticism of the government crested with the release of the White Paper, a collection of Foreign Office documents related to the crisis.

Nothing is bound to so irritate all shades of press opinion as the government's simple and persistent failure to inform. Friends and critics alike of the Balfour government expressed surprise that the Germans should be better informed about their government's claims and procedure in Venezuela than were the British. Surprise soon gave way to exasperation. "How much longer are we to remain in the dark about Venezuela?" exclaimed the *Daily Chronicle*. "That is the question which rises from the whole country. . . . It is nothing but blind confidence that is asked of us." [116] The press demanded the release of a White Paper, which the Foreign Office had provided in other crises in a more timely fashion.

When the White Paper finally came, on 15 December, it was worse than too late; it, more than any other single factor, fanned the flames of criticism of the government. The "meager handful of papers" revealed what no one had suspected, not even the government's harshest critics: England, as Sir Henry Campbell-Bannerman, the Liberal leader, exclaimed in Parliament, "was bound hand and foot" to Germany.[117] "That terrific creature the British lion," the *St. James Gazette* bemoaned, has "become the German tame cat."

ON THE VENEZUELAN PATH.

GOING BLIND AGAIN.

"On the Venezuelan path—going blind again." A typical British cartoon expressing outrage at the government's Venezuela policy, which bound England hand and foot to Germany and risked offending the United States. (*Westminster Gazette*, 6 January 1903)

Furthermore, the claims were even more insignificant than expected, and there had not been close consultation with the Americans. Wemyss Reid, in the *Nineteenth Century and After*, exclaimed, "That Ministers took this step before they had consulted with the Cabinet at Washington is not to be believed." The *Manchester Guardian* summed up the dismay: the White Paper "confirms the apprehensions and brings the danger of international complications . . . into the very forefront." [118]

The alliance with Germany was so shocking for two reasons: it was unnecessary, and it was dangerous.

It was unnecessary because the Royal Navy did not need the kaiser's boats to collect a debt in the Caribbean. "Have we come to this under our glorious Government—that we cannot face even a South American Republic without the help of our Teutonic cousins?" the *Daily News* thundered.[119]

It was dangerous because, as the *Daily News* explained, "behind all these considerations loom[ed] the figure of the United States." England and Germany did not have the same attitude toward the Monroe Doctrine. This was not soft and sentimental blather about the special relationship or blood or language or culture. In fact, the British press expressed considerable irritation with the United States, with its assumption of the benefits but not the responsibilities of the Monroe Doctrine. But the bottom line was that U.S. goodwill was useful to England, and the Monroe Doctrine was in England's interest. It suited England that the hemisphere be roped off to European colonization. It did not suit Germany. As the *Westminster Gazette* stated clearly: "We have reasons for respecting the susceptibilities of the United States which Germany may not have, and we cannot be led blindfold by even the friendliest of allies. . . . It is for the United States a game of 'Heads I win, tails you lose.' " [120] The *Fortnightly Review* concluded: "An agreement with Germany is no longer possible as a basis for British policy abroad; . . . what Germany wants is what England now possesses. . . . The countries, in short, are natural rivals, and not natural allies." When Metternich sent Bülow the clipping, he highlighted that passage.[121]

By the time the White Paper was issued, only the *Times* (of the newspapers here surveyed) supported the Balfour government. The venerable *Times*, considered an anti-German paper, was saturated with the Foreign Office point of view: it was within Britain's rights to enforce its claims on the tawdry republic, and the United States government would not—and had no right to—object. The press would not determine the resolute Roosevelt's policy. Besides, the *Times* explained, the Americans considered the Germans to be "the wicked partner in this affair." And, although it considered the White Paper "meager," it remained steadfast. When it heard of Castro's offer to submit the claims to arbitration, the *Times* was contemptuous. "President Castro's sudden readiness for arbitration is only the last throw of the gambler," it explained.[122]

Not one of the other papers agreed. On 12 December—that is, before the report that Castro had proposed arbitration—the liberal *Daily Chronicle* suggested that arbitration, if guaranteed, might pose the best way out. On the following day, the conservative *Morning Post* and the liberal *Daily News* endorsed the idea. On the 16th, the conservative *Daily Mail* fell in line. "The conduct of the government has shattered its prestige and shaken its position in the country," the *Mail* declared. "The sooner it recognises the folly of its action the better." [123]

The British Parliament was forced to rely on the press for information about Venezuela, and it was not happy about this state of affairs. It repeatedly complained about the government's failure to provide it with thorough and timely information, but a full debate had to await the tabling of the White Paper on 15 December. Then, members of Parliament complained about the alliance with Germany, the straining of Anglo-American friendship, and the government's behaving like a debt collector; the tone of the debate the day the White Paper was issued was alarmed, sarcastic, and incredulous. There was strong support for arbitration. Luckily for Balfour and Lansdowne, Parliament (perhaps not coincidentally) went into recess the next day.[124]

Fallout

This outcry had several repercussions: not only did it mean that Anglo-German relations, far from being improved by the adventure, would be damaged, it also meant that England, in all likelihood, would accept arbitration. "I have learned," Metternich reported from London, "that in political circles here the fear is growing that the German/British action against Venezuela might lead to a cooling of relations with the United States, and I have also heard in strict confidence that the King views the action against Venezuela unfavorably." The next day, he cabled: "If the British government were supported in our joint action by British public opinion, the Parliament and the press, then we could look forward to the further unfolding of the action, without concerning ourselves with excessive American demands. Unfortunately this is not the case. . . . Reluctantly, I must therefore express my opinion that the sooner we get out of this business with honor, together with England, the better." Bülow might not have liked England's "inevitable bow to the United States," but he harbored no illusion as to its significance. "Tell Lansdowne," he wrote in reply, "that our basic consideration in Venezuela will be to avoid providing ammunition to those elements in England who oppose the government and oppose cooperation with Germany." [125]

This submission to England was not merely to preserve the semblance of cooperation between the two governments. It was also to reduce the risk of the Conservative government falling—which could happen, Metternich would write, "in the flick of a wrist"—and being replaced by the Liberals under Lord Rosebery, who would, Bülow posited, "be far more dangerous than Balfour." [126]

Moreover, Bülow was worried about the durability of the "iron-clad" agreement. There were rumors that England might withdraw, leaving Germany exposed. "England . . . may easily . . . shake America's hand behind our back," was the warning from Ambassador Holleben in Washington. This was the eventuality that had haunted Tirpitz and the kaiser from the first discussions of cooperation, the misfortune against which they had sought to iron-clad themselves. Bülow's minute on this report sums up German policy: "His Majesty in the case of Venezuela will in no way go one step beyond England and will not take any step beyond England." [127]

Not only was the Wilhelmstrasse edgy about its ally across the Channel, it was also worried about Washington. It did not take remarkable prescience to imagine that the increasingly strident and anti-German tone of the press would percolate through the government if the operation dragged on, particularly if Germany had lost its shield.

And so, on 13 December when the Wilhelmstrasse received Castro's offer, what were its options? It could be obdurate, scoff at the arbitration proposal, and wait until the dictator agreed to satisfy the German demands without any unseemly and slow bargaining. But at what cost? First, at the simplest level, there was no guarantee that Venezuela, even if willing, would be able to pay its debts. But much more important was the prospect of the humiliation, cost, and danger of losing the alliance with Britain—either in fact or in spirit—if it rejected arbitration. Furthermore, it risked antagonizing the United States. This risk was heightened when, on 17 December, Washington again forwarded Castro's request for arbitration to the powers, this time with a strong endorsement.[128] If, on the other hand, Germany accepted arbitration, it could avoid an unseemly and undesirable schism with England and an unpleasant incident with the United States, and it could bargain hard to recoup everything Castro owed it. It was not the outcome Berlin had dreamed of, but it was the best possible outcome under the circumstances.

Weltpolitik

By choosing to deal with Roosevelt's alleged threat and at the same time not dealing with German aims in Venezuela, some historians have given the impression that accepting arbitration was a stunning concession on Berlin's part. It is assumed that German aims were larger than the mere collection of debts, that by accepting arbitration the Germans were giving up more than the other powers, and therefore that they had to have a stronger reason to do so. Roosevelt himself was explicit in 1916 about the breadth and danger of German aims in 1902: "Germany intended to seize some Venezuelan harbor and turn it into a strongly fortified place of arms . . . with a view to some measure of control over the future Isthmian Canal, and over South American affairs generally." [129]

Every scholar who looks closely at the Venezuela crisis is familiar with the report of the British minister to Caracas that the German chargé had visions of an intervention that would establish "something of a permanent administrative nature which would go far beyond the occupation of one or more Customs Houses . . . [an intervention] as had taken place in Egypt." Here, some argue, is the proof. Indeed, three separate reports of German naval captains confirm that in late 1901 Pilgrim-Baltazzi was dreaming of the establishment of German financial control over Venezuela. But so what? After commenting on Pilgrim-Baltazzi's rhetoric, the British minister, William Haggard, assessed the situation clearly: "The [German] Foreign Office has no desire for a Venezuela condominium." There is no evidence that Bülow or any other German official (and certainly not the kaiser) shared Pilgrim-Baltazzi's dream. Furthermore, given the evidence that does exist, this notion of German ulterior motives does not make sense.[130]

Although the direct motivation for the blockade was clearly to collect debts, the claims per se were of little importance to the Reich. The kaiser blithely postponed the adventure for almost a year. Pressure on Castro should begin, he wrote, "only after the end of Heinrich's trip, because whether the recovery of the sums happens a few weeks sooner or later does not make any difference."[131]

It was what the claims represented—the insult to German prestige—that spurred Bülow to action. He considered Castro the puffed-up tyrant of a statelet, but this made the dictator's effrontery all the more intolerable. "This treatment, if it remains unpunished, would create the impression that Germans in Venezuela are abandoned without protection to the arbitrary whims of foreigners. This will damage the prestige of the Empire in Central and South America," Bülow explained to the kaiser.[132] Bülow also had personal reasons for promoting the intervention—he needed a success. The kaiser would be pleased with its success, and the public (except the Social Democrats) delighted.

Significantly, the kaiser—and Tirpitz behind him—did not share the chancellor's optimism about the low costs, material and diplomatic, of the adventure. It would strain both the naval budget, he feared, and good relations with the United States. Nor was Wilhelm excited about the potential benefits of intervention. Contrary to the popular image of him, the kaiser expressed no interest in seizing the opportunity to grab a base or coaling station in the region. Ambassador Metternich expressed the emperor's thoughts well: "We are not interested in a couple more palm trees in the Tropics!"[133]

Wilhelm agreed to the operation only after he was convinced that England would be the senior partner in a hard and fast alliance. "I am very glad that His Majesty [Edward VII] is in agreement about our joint action in Venezuela," he told the chancellor. Bülow responded dutifully, "Following the wishes of Your Majesty, I will take great care that we in the Wilhelmstrasse cooperate with England as long as possible." Undersecretary Mühlberg considered the partnership the key to the emperor's support. "It is not certain that Wilhelm II . . . would agree to the action against Venezuela without the participation of England," he told Metternich.[134]

At this point, what had been for Bülow a means to persuade the kaiser to agree to Germany's coercion of Venezuela became for the kaiser a means to a much more important end—the improvement of Germany's relationship with England, frayed by the Boer War and the second naval bill. Yet as important as this goal was, it was not to be pursued at all costs. Musing about a worst-case scenario, Wilhelm calculated that the exercise could cost fifty to sixty million marks. "I am unable to say whether the aim justifies these expenses. In the difficult financial condition of the Reich, it would be very troublesome."[135] And it was not worth irritating the United States. The fleet was not ready, and time was on Germany's side. The impetuous kaiser was, in this instance, a patient and cautious man. Although he was reassured by Roosevelt's words and actions, he nevertheless did everything he could to ensure that, if the United States did object, England would bear the brunt of its displeasure.

Was Germany testing the Monroe Doctrine? In a way, of course it was—but gingerly, hiding behind the broad shoulders of the favored son. Testing, yes, but not provoking. As Ambassador White wrote, "The Monroe Doctrine was no more concerned in the matter than was the doctrine of the Perseverance of the Saints; but there was enough to start an outcry against Germany, and so it began to spread. The Germans were careful to observe the best precedents of international law, yet every step they took was exhibited in sundry American papers as a menace to the United States. There was no more menace to the United States than to the planet Saturn."[136] The blockade of Venezuela was not the wily Germans' first step toward the conquest of South America. The empire was not to be built on the Venezuelan customhouses. The Reich sent only four ships and deferred to the English in the planning and execution of the operation. "Taking into account the American government, it is better for us not to be more severe than England, but rather to follow exactly the same line as Britain," Bülow wrote Wilhelm. "Yes," the kaiser answered laconically.[137]

What of the kaiser's oft rabble-rousing marginalia? What of his "Bravo Panther!" and his "South America is our aim, old boy!"[138] These are not insignificant; even if just passing rantings, they are the rantings of the kaiser. They set the tone of the court and the courtiers, including Bülow and the Wilhelmstrasse. They jangled the nerves. They kept the court on edge. They have power, these brief volcanic eruptions that spill into the stiff diplomatic record. And they are especially tortured here, in the Venezuela incident, when Mother England is involved. But they did not determine policy. At the end of January 1903, for example, Metternich wrote, "King Edward . . . expressed his desire to conclude [the Venezuelan incident] as soon as possible. It is more important, he said, to end the incident than to satisfy the demands of the two countries." The kaiser spewed: "The Serenissimus 'Most Peaceful' loses his nerve. Grandmama [Queen Victoria] would never have said this." A compelling bit of raw passion—but what did Wilhelm do? He did exactly what the king wanted. "We are firmly decided to hold together with England," Bülow cabled Metternich less than a week later. As Wilhelm himself told Tirpitz, "One should not tie me down to my marginalia." [139]

Germany's acceptance of arbitration represented a shift in tactics but not in aims. It was seen as a way—the way—to maintain solidarity with England, to avoid provoking the United States, and to make the Venezuelans pay. It was neither a tremendous concession nor a miserable capitulation. As a German official quoted in the *Herald* stated, "It is not a question of the imaginary defects and weaknesses of German statesmanship, but of fixed immutable facts, ignoring which would have created a German-American complication in place of the German-Venezuelan incident." As Bülow said in the Reichstag debate following the blockade, "We attained what we wanted and what under the circumstances was attainable." [140]

Berlin's behavior in the months that followed the blockade showed that the Reich was far from cowed. At the Venezuela claims negotiations in Washington, the German representative was demanding, obstinate, and successful. "My chief difficulty at the moment," Roosevelt wrote his eldest son on 9 February 1903, "is the Venezuela matter in which Germany takes an impossible stand." [141] When the Washington Protocols were signed four days later, each of the three blockading powers received $27,500, and the Germans were guaranteed $340,000 more within three months. "Great Britain Apparently Outwitted" was a typical headline in the American press.[142] Furthermore, in late January, the German navy shelled Fort San Carlos in the most aggressive and controversial operation of the entire intervention.

The blockade remained in force for the duration of the Washington talks, and at San Carlos the German gunboat *Panther* attempted to enter the large, pendant-shaped lagoon of Maracaibo, to the west of Caracas. The waters were shallow and tidal, and treacherous to the large foreign blockading vessels, particularly after the Venezuelans had removed all buoys. The last Venezuelan gunboat—which was the navy's finest—had eluded the Germans by entering the lagoon.[143] (Fear of this simple tactic had prompted the British Admiralty to recommend strict secrecy for the operation.) Perhaps the *Panther* intended to seize this vessel, or perhaps it wanted to tighten the blockade, or perhaps it was merely seeking shelter. Its motives are unknown. The Venezuelans alleged that its intent was aggressive and that the *Panther* fired the first shot.[144] The Germans maintained that the gunboat had been "surprised by lively fire from the fort of San Carlos." The British agreed that the fort fired the first shot, but they considered the German bombardment "unfortunate and inopportune" nevertheless.[145] Unable to defend itself with its short-range cannon, the *Pan-*

ther retreated. (The *New York Times* reported that the *Panther* had signaled "Peace" with a red flag but that the Venezuelans in the fort, having no signal book, had not understood. "Perhaps," the *New York Times* commented, "that was not a judicious color to run up in sight of a commander belonging to the bull-fighting race.") The American consul in Maracaibo was sympathetic to the Germans. In a lyrical, if idiosyncratic, account, written "under the stupifying [*sic*] influence of the blockade," he described the impact of the *Panther*'s retreat: "It was . . . stated that the *Panther* had received much damage and been obliged to retire;—this, of course, flattering the public sentiments, helped much to humor the people."[146]

Castro was indeed jubilant. "Preparations for a victory celebration in Caracas are underway," the German commodore reported. "I was convinced . . . that German honor had in no way been hurt by the behavior of the *Panther*. However, given that the Venezuelans were boasting and construing it a victory, I thought it necessary to teach them a lesson and, as punishment for the attack, to make them feel our clear military superiority. And so . . . I gave the order for the bombardment of San Carlos."[147]

The fort was flattened. The Wilhelmstrasse was unrepentant. "No American or English admiral would have behaved differently," Richthofen asserted.[148] Be that as it may, it was a public relations disaster. The Wilhelmstrasse had hoped to mend the alliance with England and reassure the edgy Americans with its acceptance of arbitration and its clear deference to the British. It was not enough. German obstinacy was what was noticed and remembered.

The Venezuela story had moved to the back pages of the American press, but the German "attack upon a mud fort and a collection of naked fishermen," as the *Nation* described the bombing of Fort San Carlos, rekindled the anti-German flames in all their fury. The opprobrium was occasionally laced with sarcasm: the Germans, *Harper's Weekly* imagined, must have been "acting on the general neo-Teutonic principle, 'Whenever you see a fort, shoot at it.'" The *New York Times* railed against Berlin ("Worse international manners than Germany has exhibited from the beginning of this wretched Venezuela business have rarely come under observation of civilized men") and absolved the English ("The British Government is in the dark about this bombardment, and the English people regard it as they have regarded the entire transaction in which Germany has entangled them—with disgust"). Several papers once again heralded Dewey (who had in fact returned to Washington) as the great protector, and for a brief week there were rumors of war in some quarters. In the 29 January meeting of the General Board, an intelligence officer noted that "in the event of a war between the United States and any stronger naval power, the national capital [would] again be the objective of attack."[149]

The scare was given a second wind in March when Dewey cast aspersions on the German navy and asserted that the U.S. fleet had had a salutary influence on the kaiser during the Venezuela crisis. The German press immediately countered by belittling the U.S. fleet. These hints of war have given some credence to Roosevelt's later claim that he threatened the kaiser. But exactly what war was being contemplated? The entire U.S. Navy descending on four German ships in Venezuelan waters? Germany was certainly not on war footing. Its war plans against the United States were based on the ability of its navy to mobilize rapidly and seize a base before the Americans could respond, but it had sent only four ships to Venezuela, and it had been public knowledge since January 1902 that the Americans were planning an unprecedented massing of their fleet in November of that year. Short of canceling the operation, despite Washington's green light, or capitulating to the first terms that Castro offered, the Germans could not have done more to avoid war. This brief war scare was an American tempest, the American navy and American press chasing each other like a cat after its tail, spinning into an absurd frenzy. It was not a huge war scare (there is no record of Hay crossing the Potomac thinking he might never see it again). The General Board itself was blasé: after hearing the intelligence officer's report, it "decided that consideration of this subject be laid over till the next monthly meeting." [150] And by no means were all American papers swept up in it. The *Detroit Journal*, for example, pierced through the hoopla: "All this would make good material for a comic opera, except for one thing—that the correspondents . . . attribut[e] the activity they find—and which does not exist outside their imaginations—. . . always to Germany. . . . And this though the German Government has not made a move in the Venezuela matter without consulting the wishes of this Government, and being guided by them. . . . It is because prejudices die hard that it is greatly to be regretted that a systematic and persistent effort is being made to discredit the good faith of Germany." [151]

While the war scare was fleeting, it was nonetheless significant in its impact and in its revelation of American fears and prejudices. It led the newly appointed German ambassador in Washington, Speck von Sternburg, to declare forthrightly to the *New York Herald*, "We have no more intention of violating the Monroe Doctrine than we do of colonizing the moon." Yet not even Sternburg, whom Kaiser Wilhelm had dispatched as ambassador to repair the frayed fabric of U.S.-German relations, could defuse the situation. The German chargé summed up the situation accurately when he wrote to Bülow, "At no moment since the beginning of the operation has the mood in the press been so excited against us." Even though the Germans cleared their policy with the Americans, deferred to the British, and accepted arbitration, they were seen as aggressors. The sinking of the two Venezuelan ships, the shelling of Fort San Carlos (not the British assault on Puerto Cabello, which was forgotten), and the "foot-dragging" on accepting arbitration confirmed the image. The Germans had no margin for error.[152]

The Venezuela crisis clarified the balance of power in the Caribbean. Ever since England had deferred to the United States in 1896 and the Americans had ousted the Spanish in 1898, the rules of the game in the Caribbean had been unclear. The powers—as well as the powerless countries of Central America and the Caribbean—were groping to determine what was and was not permissible in the region. Germany was hungry and powerful, but how much would the Reich risk for the prizes Latin America could offer? England had renounced its potential claim, but how thoroughly? Where would the swing vote—the British navy—go? The United States had laid claim to the region, but it was difficult to evaluate the strength of the claim. In 1823 the Monroe Doctrine had been blithely arrogant rhetoric, but by 1902 the United States had staked out Cuba and Puerto Rico, and its navy was substantial and growing. Furthermore, geography (not proximity but the happy absence of powerful neighbors) smiled on American preeminence in the region. Germany, by contrast, would face the nightmare of the Anglo-French entente in 1904, and the noose would tighten three years later with the Anglo-Russian agreement; the Reich was distracted by its powerful neighbors. Nevertheless, in 1902, the United States did not yet have the raw power—military, economic, or diplomatic—to enforce the Monroe Doctrine, and it was not clear how much relative or intangible power it had.

This uncertainty led Theodore Roosevelt to give the wrong signal to the Europeans before the Venezuela crisis. In December 1901 he grappled with the question in a letter to Pastor Edward Everett Hale, "In South America it is positively difficult to know just how far it is best to leave the nations alone and how far there must be interference, and also how far we can with justice prevent interference by others."[153] Before Venezuela, he had thought that Europeans forcibly collecting debts in the hemisphere would help keep the irksome republics in line, but during the crisis he realized that debt collection could arouse the U.S. public and lead to complications that the United States could not yet control. Like Dean Acheson and Korea, James Baker and Kuwait, Roosevelt defined the national interest only to realize that, as soon as the crisis broke, his definition had been wrong.

Thus the European powers were essentially in the dark about U.S. policy; they had to guess how the Americans would react to any action they took in the region. In one way, their situation during the Venezuela crisis was similar to that they would face a decade later during the first year of Woodrow Wilson's presidency, when American policy toward Mexico was a mystery. Yet in an important way, it was entirely different. Wilson was presumptuous; he was arrogant. He had the power to call the shots in Mexico—and he knew it—and the Europeans would have to await his pleasure.[154] Roosevelt, on the other hand, was uncertain—of England's stance in the region, of Germany's will, and of America's power.

In Venezuela, Berlin had hoped that a little cooperative gunboat diplomacy would forge a significant bond with England, as though the English would not notice the threat posed by the burgeoning navy across the Channel. And the kaiser had hoped that the formal notification of plans and the deference to England and the small number of German ships involved in the blockade would reassure Washington. As Bülow declared, "Nobody can reproach us for acting without dignity and calmness."[155] But the Americans did reproach the Germans; they saw in Venezuela proof of German aggressiveness, impulsiveness, scheming, and unreliability.

German policy was naive. Germany failed to understand how threatening the growth of its fleet and of its industrial power was. This reality could not be wished away with tactics and flattery. Both the Americans and the British— press and politicians—profoundly distrusted the Germans. If England wanted to maintain friendly relations with the Americans, it could not enter any alliance, however temporary, however practical, with the Germans in the Western Hemisphere.

American policy was also naive. The United States failed to understand how privileged its position in the hemisphere was. The Spanish-American War had given Washington a new and unfamiliar coat; it took a while to get accustomed to it. During the Venezuela blockade, Roosevelt realized that the United States neither needed nor wanted European help in its backyard. In June 1904, he wrote Secretary of War Elihu Root, "If we intend to say 'Hands off' to the powers of Europe, then sooner or later we must keep order ourselves."[156] That December, he announced the Roosevelt Corollary, which declared the right of the United States to intervene "to punish chronic wrongdoing" in the Western Hemisphere.[157] Yet the Venezuela crisis did not merely put more swagger in the American step. It simultaneously led to increased anxiety. The prize was great, it was within reach, and it could be snatched away.

It was not groundless in 1902 to perceive a German threat, but after the Venezuela crisis the American navy should have breathed easier: English friendship and German timidity had been confirmed. As Roosevelt wrote former president Grover Cleveland, "We have succeeded in . . . getting England and Germany explicitly to recognize the Monroe Doctrine."[158] After the crisis, the idea of a German threat should have faded from the pro-naval

"Never again! Brother Jonathan: 'I guess, Brother John, next time you'll find it better to paddle your own canoe.' John Bull (to himself): 'I will.' " After the Venezuela debacle, England determined never again to cooperate with Germany in the Western Hemisphere. (*Punch*, 4 February 1903)

press, not because of the new assertiveness of Washington but because of the increasing isolation of Germany in Europe. The General Board of the Navy implicitly recognized this, dropping its interest in war planning against Germany in 1903. Roosevelt, who had not been concerned about German intentions toward Venezuela, learned about the power of the press's image of Germany and gained confidence from America's clear leverage in the situation. He went on to take Panama and quell disturbances in the Dominican Republic with newfound assurance.

And yet, the image of a marauding Germany persisted. It was an image that may have spurred the Roosevelt administration to seize its prize more quickly than it might otherwise have done. It did not, however, determine U.S. actions. These actions—the taking of Cuba, Puerto Rico, Panama, Haiti, and the Danish West Indies and the interventions in the Dominican Republic and throughout Central America—were the clear and simple assertion of hegemony. The United States was not the smug protector of the status quo in Latin America. It, like Germany, was a fledgling imperial power, and Latin America at the turn of the century was the arena in which the two potential rivals were sizing each other up, eyeing each other suspiciously, full of bravado and fear.

3

The Reach of the Monroe Doctrine

The Germanization
of Brazil

It was in Brazil that the Germans had the best opportunity to expose the conceit of the Monroe Doctrine, and Washington and Berlin knew it. In its three southernmost states—Paraná, Santa Catarina, and Rio Grande do Sul—clones of German hamlets had sprung up. Emigrants from Germany, the first of whom had arrived in 1824, were cushioned from the full rigors of exile there because they lived in isolated pockets of *Deutschtum*, places where the German way of life was maintained, free from the harassment of officials from Rio. Numbering from a quarter million to half a million souls, the German community was the largest immigrant group in southern Brazil at the turn of the century and the largest German settlement in Latin America. German culture there was, in the words of a Frenchman who traveled through the region, "cohesive and pure," or, as one U.S. intelligence officer described it, "very clannish." The German community dominated the local trade in southern Brazil, importing more German goods than British and using German ships for their exports. Thus the region offered unique opportunities to the Reich. Pan-Germans were vocal about their hope that a New Germany would flower there, and they seemed to be supported by their government.[1]

Some American naval officers had been wary of German immigration to Brazil as early as 1830, but their suspicions did not acquire any intensity until the 1890s. The tocsin was struck with growing fervor in 1900 when the Second Fleet Bill was being debated. If, as the naval officers at the war college and on the General Board had predicted, the German navy could prevail in the Caribbean, the U.S. Navy's task would have been well nigh impossible in southern Brazil, some four thousand miles farther south. Brazil's ports were roughly equidistant from Germany and the main U.S. ports and much closer to German ports in west Africa than to U.S. ports. The conclusion of the General Board was succinct: "Should the war in which the United States becomes engaged have its theater in South America, the difficulties for this country would be greatly increased and the fleets would be on a practical par as regards distance from home bases. Should Germany be the enemy she will have a harbor to base her fleet upon [in southern Brazil] and friendly population on shore." [2]

Many U.S. politicians, naval officers, and journalists assumed that the Reich would make its move in Brazil. Perceptions of the German threat to Brazil differed, however, among individuals and groups and at different times. Thus, for example, at the turn of the century the U.S. Navy, the pro-naval press, and some politicians were alarmed by German activity in Brazil. Senator Lodge, for instance, in one of his fiery anti-German speeches, declared in 1900, "We may find ourselves called upon to protect Brazil." At the same time, however, the U.S. minister in Rio was assuring the State Department that the Germans posed no threat to U.S. interests in the region. And in 1914, Wilson's aide, Colonel Edward House, declared, "The Kaiser was trying hard to curry favor with the South American peoples. The Germans are assuming the attitude of being their friends. . . . The Kaiser is desirous of forming a European coalition for the purpose of insulating the influence of the U.S. in South America. . . . His purpose is not to go to the extent of war but to do everything he can within the bounds of international law." [3]

A study of German policy in Brazil broadens the scope of the analysis of U.S. perceptions of a German threat to the Monroe Doctrine. Unlike the Venezuela crisis, which concerned a brief moment of high politics, German penetration of Brazil—or at least U.S. fears of it—ranged over time and embraced not just diplomats and officers but also strident pan-Germans, struggling immigrants, and hardworking German salesmen plying their wares in the Brazilian hinterlands. It is a study of the possibility of both formal and informal imperialism.

It also presents a limiting case of German policy in the hemisphere. In southern Brazil, geography, demographics, and politics favored Berlin. An examination of how Germany took advantage of these opportunities, or failed to do so, should help to reveal whether the Reich did, in fact, have designs on the hemisphere.

The Fifth Column

Germans had been immigrating to southern Brazil since the early 1800s. They had gone seeking the usual things: opportunity, escape from the past and from poverty, adventure. The Brazilian government recruited immigrants, luring

"And nations rested 'neath its grateful shade." President Monroe intervenes to protect the Western Hemisphere, especially Brazil, from becoming Germany's next place in the sun. (*New York Herald*, 12 May 1900)

them with free or subsidized land in isolated settlements, and various societies in the German states encouraged emigration, as a safety valve to the pressures (real and perceived) of overpopulation and inadequate opportunity at home.

By the midcentury, however, Prussia grew concerned that German immigrants, particularly Protestants, were being treated harshly in Catholic Brazil, a concern exacerbated by Rio's policy of declaring all persons born in Brazil to be Brazilian citizens, which greatly complicated the German consuls' ability to protect the descendants of German settlers. Anxiety increased with the cessation of the slave trade to Brazil in the 1850s, which caused a labor shortage, alleviated, it was feared, by the hapless immigrants. One critic of the recruiters charged that the immigrant was "caught like a fly by a pretty paper, hallucinated with visions of an earthly Paradise; and thus, addleheaded, dumb-cattle like, reliant on others, helpless and exacting, he is shipped off to the Eldorado to be *sold*."[4]

As a consequence, the Prussian minister of trade, August von der Heydt, proposed a law that, while not forbidding Prussian citizens from immigrating to Brazil, did prohibit all promotional efforts encouraging them to do so. In

1859, the Prussian government passed the *Heydt'sche Reskript*. Other German governments rapidly followed suit.

Twenty years later—after the unification of the country and during the economic turbulence of the 1870s—there was growing sentiment in Germany for the lifting of the *Heydt'sche Reskript*. The government was slow to respond. For Chancellor Bismarck, neither Brazil nor the *Reskript* was a burning issue. Bismarck had contempt for Germans who emigrated: they were cowards evading military service. Moreover, in Bismarck's opinion, Brazil was a particularly undesirable destination, because of the continuing horror stories about the conditions among the Germans who lived there and because it fell within the United States' sphere of influence. In the margin of an 1880 report from his minister in Rio enthusiastically predicting that Germany could assume control of the seceding southern provinces, Bismarck jotted derisively: "Those people will be . . . no more friendly toward their fatherland than the Yankees are toward England." [5]

Several events in the 1890s would change Berlin's stance on the *Reskript*. First, Bismarck's dismissal in 1890 paved the way for Wilhelm II to consolidate his power, and he looked favorably on the expansion of German influence in Brazil, as his comments—scrawled characteristically in the margins of his ministers' reports—indicate. [6] Second, political instability in Brazil following the fall of the monarchy in 1889 led Berlin to hope that the federal government in Rio de Janeiro would be unable to hold the country together and the southern states would break away and turn to Germany for protection. These hopes were boosted in 1893 by a naval mutiny in Rio and a simultaneous revolt in southern Brazil. Berlin, sympathetic to the mutineers and the secessionists, was alone among the European great powers in refusing to join the United States in sending warships to Rio, whose port had been blockaded by the rebels, to assert the rights of neutral shipping and, in so doing, help defeat the rebellion. The Wilhelmstrasse, however, was cautious, in a pattern that would be repeated almost a decade later during the Venezuela blockade: it would not support the rebels unless England did so first. "The decision," as historian Gerhard Brunn states, "was in London." When the British Foreign Office demurred, the Germans sat back quietly, hoping the rebels would emerge victorious but doing nothing to help them. Lacking foreign support and exhausted, the rebels surrendered in March 1894, but hopes persisted in Germany that they might one day rise again. [7]

Less than a year later, in 1895, the new German minister in Rio, Richard Krauel, who was the first German diplomat to visit the German settlements in the south, began to send enthusiastic reports to Berlin about how well the Germans were being treated and how exciting the trade prospects were. Never-

Map 2. Southern Brazil

theless, the flow of German emigrants was drying up—better economic times in Germany had led to a fall in the number of Germans immigrating to all destinations. Krauel's reports conveyed the frustration of the settlers at Berlin's apparent indifference to them. "The German colonies in southern Brazil are a rich treasure that has been overlooked until now due to prejudice and fear," he wrote.[8] Based on Krauel's accounts, *Export*, the weekly publication of the Central Association for Trade, Geography, and the Development of German Inter-

ests Abroad, asserted, "Nowhere in the world offers . . . comparable opportunities."[9] This opinion was shared by Karl Kaerger, a German agricultural
expert traveling through Brazil and Argentina, who suggested that Germany
follow what he called the "English model" and prepare for political annexation by promoting emigration that would establish economic penetration.[10]

Dreams

The final factor influencing Berlin's stance on the *Reskript* was the gathering
momentum of the pan-German movement, or, as historian Roger Chickering calls it, "national religion," in the late 1880s and early 1890s. "There
is nothing in all the Bismarckian period to compare with this exaggeration
of national egotism, with this hot passion for expansion," William Langer
writes. The creation of the Pan-German League and the Colonial Association
reflected this rise in the salience of German jingoism.[11] Although the Pan-
German League would focus eventually, and notoriously, on Europe—on the
irredentist dream of gathering all Germans into a greater Germany in Middle
Europe—it began by promoting the idea of a New Germany flowering in a
remote land. When pan-Germans, whether officially members of the league
or not, scanned the globe for places to build a New Germany, southern Brazil beckoned. There, the climate was pleasant, the land fertile, the natives
friendly, and thousands of Germans already lived there. Moreover, the three
southern states, particularly Rio Grande do Sul, were demographically congenial to the pan-Germans, imbued as their worldview was with racism: few
indigenous people remained, few Africans had been brought there, whites
were dominant, and among the whites, the Germans were preeminent. "Brazil is a distant, chaotic country of 16,000,000 people," an ultranationalist
wrote at the turn of the century, "but it controls a rich and fertile empire . . .
that could become as important as the United States if only people of German rather than Latin stock were to rule it." The German jingoes dreamed of
these seeds flowering into a thoroughly Germanized southern Brazil.[12]

The pan-German movement's views of Germany's future were shared by a
large section of German society. Foreign markets were closing, and overpopulation was believed to be looming. Emigration and expansion seemed to be the
logical solution, but only if the emigrants were not, in the words of the U.S.
ambassador to Germany, a "stream" flowing away from the fatherland but
rather an offshore "reservoir." The overwhelming majority of Germans who
emigrated went to the United States, "the grave," according to a speaker at
a pan-German congress, "of *Deutschthum*."[13] Of the 626,000 Germans who
emigrated during the 1870s, 556,000 went to the United States, while 21,000

went to Brazil; in the 1880s, of the 1,342,000 who emigrated, 1,237,000 went to the United States, while 19,000 went to Brazil; in the 1890s, of the 530,000 who emigrated, 479,000 went to the United States, while 12,000 went to Brazil.[14] As early as 1864, a German pamphleteer was touting the benefits of Brazil over the United States as a destination for emigrants: "A German emigrant who comes to southern Brazil is more valuable to Germany than twenty who go to North America."[15] Germans in Brazil bought manufactured goods from Germany and exported produce to Germany that was not grown there, whereas Germans in the United States bought American manufactured goods and exported produce to Germany that competed with the local product. "Any German who goes to South America . . . and starts working there," a prominent pan-German wrote, "is a more effective propagandist for German products than the best trader can be."[16] At the German Colonial Congress in 1902 the head of the Colonial Geographical Society, Dr. R. Jannasch, contrasted the Germans who went to the United States with those who went to Brazil: "We bear the cost of educating our future competitors [in the United States], we strengthen [its] . . . economical power. . . . The only countries in which . . . the German people have retained their fatherland culture is [sic] in sub-tropical South America, and very especially in Southern Brazil." The congress adopted a resolution encouraging emigrants to go to Brazil. Five years later, the German consul in Curitiba in Paraná echoed the point: "The best way to serve German interests [in Brazil] . . . is with massive emigration. German immigrants here . . . are good customers for our products and . . . help to turn the natives and other immigrant groups into buyers of German products. In North America, German immigrants are lost." These sentiments were shared in the Wilhelmstrasse: "In southern Brazil, German emigrants remain consumers of German products, while their produce does not compete with ours."[17]

The pan-Germans were joined in their pleas for change in the government's policy on immigration to Brazil by the powerful shipping company the North German Lloyd, whose profits were suffering because of the decrease in emigration in the 1890s. (In 1899, the directors of the Hamburg American Line and the North German Lloyd became founding members of the German-Brazilian Society, which was established to promote trade with southern Brazil and to steer emigrants to it.)[18] Furthermore, as anti-American sentiment rose in Germany after the McKinley Tariff of 1890, many Germans were ever more eager to direct their emigrants away from the United States. Brazil looked increasingly attractive.

In 1896 Berlin lifted the *Heydt'sche Reskript*.[19] Wilhelm II had been persuaded by Krauel's portrait of the opportunities being lost in southern Brazil.

"The oyster and the shell." Americans feared that the kaiser would take the offer of friendship from South America in order to claim the juicy oyster of its commerce for himself. (*Minneapolis Journal*, 22 November 1906)

"Ways must be found as quickly as possible to strengthen *Deutschtum* there," he commented in the margin of one of his minister's reports.[20] What had been a passive, if not overtly obstructionist, stance became active and interventionist as Berlin sought to direct German emigrants toward specific locations in which they would remain tied, culturally or economically, to the fatherland. Southern Brazil was the destination of choice. The preamble to an 1897 law directing emigration stated, "[In Brazil] not only will the German preserve his nationality, but he will find . . . all the conditions favorable to a prosperous existence. He will, moreover, become a consumer of the products of German industry."[21]

The German jingoes were predictably heartened. "In a few years a German

Colonial Empire will grow up there [in Brazil] as mighty as, if not mightier than, any other that ever emanated from Europe," one wrote at the turn of the century. It was only justice, another declared: "[Germany] cannot allow herself to be simply dispossessed of her inheritance in one of the most thinly peopled and richest quarters of the world."[22] All that was needed was more and more emigrants pouring from the homeland into the ports of Brazil. As the German Colonial Congress resolved in 1902, "It is in the interest of German emigration, trade and industry to direct emigrants to a country with a moderate climate in South America, and especially to southern Brazil. We must encourage the settlement of Germans there through the German spirit of enterprise, German capital investment, and German commercial policy."[23] Two years later an enthusiast in southern Brazil wrote, "Nowhere are our colonies, those loyal offshoots from the mother root, so promising as here. . . . Surely to us belongs the future of this part of the world."[24]

For the ultranationalists, this was straight arithmetic: start with a few Germans, add more, and eventually—empire. The British *Spectator* explained the pan-German viewpoint well: "The idea is that if concentrated in Brazil the emigrants might in the end be numerous enough to set up a separate State, which would either declare itself a German colony or a Republic in strict alliance with the motherland." And, of course, there did not have to be as many Germans as Brazilians in the region. The cream would rise: German culture would naturally predominate. A critical mass would suffice.[25]

The dream would be fulfilled through a combination of strong German influence and weak Brazilian government. The southern states would secede and turn to Berlin for protection. By "protection," the expansionists meant anything from friendly interest to annexation. An eminent political economist at the University of Berlin, Gustav Schmoller, wrote, "We must at all costs try to create in southern Brazil a Germanic country. . . . It is not important whether it remains part of Brazil, becomes an independent state, or has a close association with the German empire." In 1895, a writer in *Export* had noted, "Rio Grande do Sul is the problem child of the government in Rio. There is no doubt that during the last insurrection the question of secession was real: it was the ghost looming in the background."[26] Four years later, the conservative *Kreuz Zeitung* bemoaned the German government's "incomprehensible" failure to take advantage of the "very brilliant colonial prospects" in southern Brazil. "The critical time is approaching," it warned, "when Germany will have to decide whether to forcibly protect its interests in Brazil or to surrender them entirely." In 1901, the *Deutsche Post*, a German-language paper published in São Leopoldo, still held out hope: "We should not wonder if, especially in consequence of maladministration at Rio de Janeiro . . .

the states of Paraná, Santa Catarina and Rio Grande do Sul at least some day should declare for secession and independence. Then a new outlook would be open to Germany."[27]

The relationship between the pan-Germans and their government is a fascinating, elusive, and hotly contested question. The Pan-German League and the Colonial Association—both interested in immigration to Brazil—were not official groups that spoke for the government. While they were symptoms of growing agitation of the middle class to have a political voice, they were not political parties. They were associations, clubs, substitutes, perhaps, for the old camaraderie of the guilds. The Pan-German League was small and politically marginal—unlike the Navy League, which enjoyed "intimate relations" with the Navy Department and with the kaiser.[28]

The perception of this relationship, however, is not disputed. Pan-German rhetoric and dreams were infused with significance across the North Sea and the Atlantic. "This mission of culture," the president of the Society for the Perpetuation of the German Language Abroad wrote in 1903, "is to weld together and consolidate Germans in Europe and across the seas, ethnologically, economically, and therefore politically; so that where the German language is spoken there too may German interests and authority be paramount." The pan-Germans were the " 'enfant terrible' of German chauvinism," according to the London *Times*. "One of the fundamental errors," Roland Usher warned in 1913, "is to treat this vast project as an unreality."[29]

Certainly the Germans had no monopoly on jingoism. Racism and imperialism combined to produce a particularly potent strain of triumphalist nationalism at the turn of the century. The pan-German program, however, was infused with particular significance, in part because of the natural flow of information to a vacuum. The German government after Bismarck was bewildering to many in England and the United States. The kaiser was outspoken, temperamental, and ambitious, and, especially after the fleet bills, the world craved clues, explanations of Germany's intentions. The rhetoric of the pan-Germans provided the clearest and simplest answer: Germany was engaged on a crusade of expansion and empire. "To Germany a [fleet] is merely a means to an end, and that end," observed a British journalist at the turn of the century, "is the . . . domination of the world."[30] This was Mahanian thinking of the purest kind. The pan-Germans were seen to be speaking this truth—unadulterated and unobfuscated. They were believed to have influence, and to be dangerous. As the editor of the London *Spectator* said in 1903, "Each grain of gunpowder [referring to the pan-German pamphleteers] by itself is small, smutty, and so contemptible, but in the mass how dangerous!"[31]

By the turn of the century, the Wilhelmstrasse was aware of the fears about

German aims in southern Brazil, and it wanted to assuage them, but it failed to distance itself persuasively from the pan-German program. It would have taken a dramatic event—not simply the persistent failure to seize opportunities—to have changed the perception that was forming in the United States as the twentieth century began. "Although the German Government is careful to dissociate itself officially from the German 'invasion' of Brazil," a journalist wrote in 1903, "it stands godmother to its promoters and has never yet censured . . . [the pan-Germans] who openly advocated such a policy." [32]

Berlin's ambivalence sprang from two facts. First, the progovernment coalition in the Reichstag was delicate, and those who sympathized with the pan-German viewpoint were an important constituency, particularly because of their support for the financial sacrifices demanded by the rapid growth of the navy. [33] Second, many powerful Germans in business and in government, including the kaiser, shared their dreams. It was not the Pan-German League that mattered but what it espoused. Like many fringe groups, its power derived not from its numbers or connections but from its willingness to express sentiments that were widely shared but unacceptable, in some quarters, to state aloud. While the German government did not officially support the recommendations—or the dreams—of the pan-Germans, Weltpolitik embodied their basic premise that Germany had to look beyond the sea, that Germans should feel at home in every continent. In the margin of a report written in 1905 in which Chancellor Bülow described the hopes of Captain Behnke of the German navy that southern Brazil would fall under Germany's sway, Wilhelm II wrote, "We certainly hope that Behnke's predictions come true." [34] A prominent pan-German wrote, "The pan-German conception . . . is no fantastic idea confined to a small class of Jingo politicians, but is the avowed aim of modern German economists who make the music for the politicians. . . . A greater Germany across the seas . . . is the dream, the *telos* of German policy." [35]

In his thoughtful study, Chickering concludes that while the government used the league for its own ends, the league sometimes turned against the government. "The documents do not . . . substantiate the charge . . . that the Pan-German League was the inspiring force behind German foreign policy. Officials hoped to use the league to promote policies they themselves had chosen. Their tactic would, to be sure, have made no sense but for a degree of consonance between these policies and the league's program." [36] The government's stance toward the pan-Germans was deeply ambivalent and deliberately ambiguous: the pan-Germans did not speak for the government, but they did embody some of its deepest desires. The occasional comments from the government dissociating itself from the expansionist schemes of the pan-Germans were meek and unpersuasive. For example, in 1901, Bülow granted a long, exclusive interview to the *New York Herald* in which he declared that he was baffled by Dewey's remark that America's next war would be against Germany. "I really cannot possibly understand it. . . . Germany has not the least desire to quarrel with the United States."[37] And two years later he declared to a Brazilian paper: "In this matter, truth is intertwined with falsehood: it is not true that we are stimulating emigration to southern Brazil. . . . There have existed, however, in Brazil for decades large German colonies . . . and it is only in virtue of the physical law of attraction that relatives or friends of colonists . . . direct their steps thither. . . . In Brazil . . . we are not trying to form any State within a State. . . . It is nevertheless just . . . that the Germans in Brazil . . . do not forget their maternal tongue nor lose their affection for their country of birth."[38]

It was insufficient. As the well-informed journalist George Chamberlain observed, "This declaration is apt to suggest to the reader an urchin looking up at a very green apple just out of reach. . . . Who will vouch for persistent abnegation?" Against the backdrop of rumor, suspicion, and a rapidly growing navy, Bülow's words swayed no one: the skeptical remained convinced that the pan-Germans were voicing the unstated hopes and plans of the German government. As the Chicago paper the *German Democrat* reported, "The Government pretends that the vigorous agitation of the German Brazilian Society in favor of annexation of Brazilian territory is causing the Imperial authorities embarrassment. Yet through the Colonial Office these same authorities continue to pat that body and to invite it to all colonial conferences. They also permit it to remain a member of the Central Bureau of Emigration which is subsidized by the government."[39]

The Fourth Estate

In this era of the telegraph, stories in Berlin affected those in New York, London, and Rio. Expansionist rhetoric in pan-German papers fueled anti-German tirades in the U.S. and British press, which spurred the pan-Germans to greater heights, and so on, in waves and crescendos. The press was the medium that amplified, and sometimes distorted, the waves created by the pan-Germans. As it shaped and reflected public opinion, it at times provoked and at times inhibited the politicians.

In Germany, not only the *Alldeutsche Blätter*, the official organ of the Pan-German League, but also the mainstream press toed the pan-German line often enough to give pause to commentators on both sides of the Atlantic. "In order to attain decisive political action in southern Brazil," the influential, pro-imperialist *Grenzboten* wrote in 1898, "we need a large infusion of

German blood, but we must understand that colonization on this scale can only sustain itself if one creates an independent German republic in Brazil." [40] Three years later it proclaimed, "Undoubtedly, excellent German colonists in southern Brazil will be able to establish the solid racial roots for a political community of a completely modern nature." [41] These dreams reached a crescendo in 1903, first in an article:

> We should draft laws that levy penalties on those Germans who emigrate anywhere other than Brazil. Once we have completely enclosed southern Brazil in our sphere of influence we will be able to assure the colonists a safe future, particularly since this will also lead to much greater interest on the part of German capital. . . . We must be careful not to act as though such a state could be created overnight. It should be as autonomous as possible with native officials and a colonial army in which everyone could fulfill their military service without having to come back to Germany. . . . In a few years we could see the creation of a strong German colonial empire on the other shore of the Atlantic that would be the most beautiful and lasting colonial enterprise that all Europe has ever achieved. [42]

And then in an editorial:

> Can the German Empire, which wants to be—and will always be—a world power, remain a spectator to the passage of one South American Republic after another into political and commercial dependence on the United States of America? . . . To formulate the question is to answer it! The complete exclusion of Germany from all America would be equivalent to our economic and political death. . . . We cannot tolerate and we will not tolerate being excluded from that part of the world which is as yet not apportioned. . . . It is inconceivable that the mixed races of South America will be able much longer to call their own those lands so prodigally dowried by nature. [43]

The impact of statements such as these was clear. As early as 1895, Krauel was complaining from Rio about the "tactless" articles in the German press that fueled rumors about German intrigue in southern Brazil. And an official at the Wilhelmstrasse scrawled in the margin of one such article, "This can only make trouble." In 1903, David Thompson, the new U.S. minister in Rio, sent the State Department a clipping from a Brazilian paper about an article that had recently appeared in the *Grenzboten*. "This article is being copied in nearly the whole Brazilian press," he observed. A few years later, A. W. Sellin, a German who had significant interests in southern Brazil, wrote, "Lately, the fairy tales that have been published in the German press have become stereotypes and are very common. . . . Even the leading papers, from whom we might have expected a certain degree of sophistication, have lent themselves to the dissemination of the most stupid rumors and groundless fears. . . . Even official declarations have not helped in the least to diminish these rumors."[44]

Throughout the period framed by the Spanish-American War and World War I, the saber rattling of the pan-Germans was amplified by the anti-German British papers and then picked up by the imperialist, pro-naval U.S. papers. As a naval intelligence officer reported in 1911, "These [pan-German] articles are invariably calculated to engender mistrust and hatred of anything and anyone not German; they are, necessarily, overdrawn and often quite false in their assertions, yet they represent a force not to be disregarded."[45] Even the *New York Herald*, which had correspondents on the scene, frequently followed the lead of the British press, particularly the *Spectator*. In January 1900, the *Spectator* published an article entitled "Germany and the Monroe Doctrine," which proclaimed, "He [Kaiser Wilhelm II] wants a fleet in order that when he puts his South American policy into operation he will not be made ridiculous by an order from Washington. Mark, he does not want to attack America in the very least, but merely to have the proper physical backing when he asks the United States not to play dog in the manger any longer in regard to Spanish and Portuguese America." Despite the immediate protests and refutations of the German ambassador in Washington, the story was picked up by the *New York Times* and the *Herald*.[46] Likewise, a story that appeared in 1901 in the British weekly the *Saturday Review* alleging that the German navy's goal was expansion in South America was quickly picked up not just by the *Herald* but also by the staid *New York Times*.[47]

Predictably, the stories made their way to Brazil, where they graced the pages of Rio's dailies. The possibility that they could damage the Brazilian public's generally positive attitude toward the Germans, and thereby limit the goodwill of Brazilian politicians, worried some Germans both in Brazil and in Berlin. "Unfortunately," a German businessman in Brazil wrote the Wilhelm-strasse, "part of the Brazilian press is picking up these attacks [on German policy in Brazil that appeared in the U.S. and British press], and they have created hostility in Brazilian public opinion. I am convinced that the Brazilian politicians don't believe the reports, but public opinion could force them to refrain from showing the German settlement the goodwill it needs."[48] *Export* editorialized in 1896, "Just as it is right to ask that German culture in southern Brazil, which is a half century old, be maintained . . . so it is wrong to try to take advantage of these cultural ties for the Reich's political benefit. Ideas like this must be attacked sharply."[49]

What Is a German?

This distinction that *Export* drew between culture and politics lies at the heart of the matter. By the turn of the century, estimates of the number of Germans in southern Brazil ranged from two hundred thousand to five hundred thousand. The disparity in the figures reflects not only the imperfect record keeping of the time but also the problems of definition. Most second-, third-, and fourth-generation Germans—and even many recent arrivals—became Brazilian citizens. Some estimates, therefore, do not include them as German, while other estimates include all German speakers. This difference of definition points to the complexity of determining how German these expatriates really were.[50]

There were three categories of Germans in Brazil: those living in the cities, in the well-established German towns, and in remote settlements in the Brazilian forest, or *Urwald*. The Germans living in the cities were the object of neither pan-German dreams nor American fears. Their numbers were small—only four thousand Germans lived in Rio—and they tended to retain their German citizenship because they planned to return to the homeland. Middle-class businessmen looking for profit, they treated Brazilian society with open contempt, had no contact with their compatriots in the *Urwald*, and no sense of shared identity with them.[51]

It was the Germans in southern Brazil—in the remote settlements and in towns like Joinville and Blumenau in Santa Catarina—who were the object of the pan-German dreams. Most had been agricultural workers in Germany. In Brazil, they were small coffee, tobacco, and potato farmers. In the early days, their life was hard, and in the most inaccessible regions many perished. A commentator in the 1870s wrote, "Contracts proved false, authorities partial, soils barren, climates lethal, measurements faulty, payments slack, sympathies scanty, laws and religion alien . . . but German . . . industry and German frugality survived this and more; until at last, for weal or woe, this race seems to have really won a footing in the country."[52] By the end of the century, life was more comfortable in the relatively prosperous German towns in the south, where the settlers lived in simple houses with basic amenities. A German navy captain reported in 1904 that the Germans in the capital of Paraná, Curitiba, "belong[ed] mainly to the middle class . . . and [made] overall a good impression. In general they live[d] well." He was even more impressed with the larger town of Joinville. "It has the character of a village, but it is the seat of active and diversified small industry and small import houses. The people seem law abiding and hard working, and they seem to live well."[53]

A U.S. naval intelligence officer was captivated by the German settlement of Jaguary in 1903: "German women in short skirts, coarse white stockings and wooden heelless shoes carried water and did their shopping about the town, hatless, sometimes with a broad kerchief knotted about their heads under their chins. White haired children were everywhere visable [*sic*]. The men sat in front of their houses and talked to each other, with bottles of beer sitting on the ground beside them. The colony is new . . . but very, very German." [54] In the more remote settlements, however, life remained difficult. The colonists lacked the tools and infrastructure to practice agriculture according to modern German methods, so they adopted Brazilian methods that quickly exhausted the soil. Lack of basic communication and transportation facilities isolated them. The same German naval captain observed, "The colonists in the interior suffer greatly due to the difficulty, or more accurately, the impossibility, of exporting their produce." [55]

And yet, by all accounts, they were happy to have left Germany. Here's the rub: this purported vanguard of the fatherland in the Southern Hemisphere had no desire to return, was in fact averse to returning, to its protection. These Germans had left their crowded land to start afresh in an exotic setting. They were risk takers. They were culturally German, happy to retain their language and customs, comfortable with one another, but they had left Germany, decisively. As the *Nation* noted in 1897, "German colonization has to contend against the growing desire of mankind to manage their own affairs, vote their own taxes, and arrange their own lives." [56] The Germans in Brazil accepted any help the German consuls could give them and appreciated any financial support they received from Germany, but they gave their allegiance to their new country. Albert Shaw proclaimed, "They [the Germans in Brazil] are the last people in the world upon whom the German imperial government should rely for assistance in the carrying out of its supposed South American ambitions." [57] A song that the German community in the Santa Catarina port of Florianópolis sang during the visit of a German cruiser is revealing:

> You fight for your Fatherland
> And we for the German customs
> That have grown strong roots
> In the midst of the tropical forest.
>
> You fight for the Emperor, honor, and glory
> For the glorious future of Germany;
> But we fight for the sanctity of
> Our German mother tongue. [58]

Culturally and linguistically, these rural Germans in Brazil were German. Unlike the émigrés in the United States or Argentina, they lived in pockets of replicated Germany where, owing to Rio's policy of recruiting immigrants with promises of free or subsidized land in isolated settlements, the German language and many German customs were maintained for a longer time. "We have the curious phenomenon of the foundation of a colony in the midst of another nation," the *Review of Reviews* remarked in 1905.[59]

To the pan-Germans back home, to the press sympathetic to them, and, tellingly, to Wilhelm II, questioning the Germanness of the Germans in Brazil was absurd. It was inconceivable to them that the Germans in Brazil were not aching to strengthen their ties to the fatherland. Likewise, those Americans who were alarmed by the dreams of the pan-Germans overlooked the subtleties of nationalism. They did not consider the differences between the immigration policies of the United States and Brazil—one encouraging assimilation while the other fostered separation. "These people [the Germans in Brazil] are naturalized Brazilians, but scraps of paper do not count when it comes to patriotism," a journalist cautioned. "The German is a German, all and every time, and no oath or promise can make him anything else."[60]

But those on the scene, those in a position to know, whether German, Brazilian, or American, considered the Germans in the settlements to be loyal citizens of Brazil. The reports of both German and American ministers reveal a striking consensus on this point.[61] As early as 1885, an expert in the Wilhelmstrasse wrote that the colonists in Brazil "like to proclaim their *Deutschtum* when it is convenient for them. . . . They prefer to become Brazilian citizens, and then they boast about how things are good for them because there are no German authorities around."[62] Twenty years later, reporting to the Wilhelmstrasse that the Germans in southern Brazil had not celebrated the kaiser's birthday, the German minister in Rio, Mr. Treutler, wrote, "It is not surprising. . . . From the political point of view, these people [the Germans in Brazil] with few exceptions are ONLY Brazilian and are often more chauvinistic than their Portuguese-Brazilian countrymen."[63]

Most Brazilians expressed no anxiety about the Germans in their midst. Charles Bryan, the U.S. minister in Rio, informed the State Department of this fact in 1900 when the department, responding to Henry Cabot Lodge's fiery anti-German speech, asked all its representatives in South America to assess German influence there. "Regarding Germany's alleged desire to obtain a foothold in southern Brazil, I have the honor to report that little apprehension on this score is manifested by Brazilian public men," Bryan wrote. "Confidence in the adherence to the Brazilian Government by the Germans in southern Brazil seems to be justified by the constancy with which they have striven to uphold the Republic against revolution." A year later, the *New York Times*, quoting the soothing words of the Brazilian press that the Germans in Brazil "are good and loyal citizens, and consider themselves Brazilians," editorialized that the presence of four hundred thousand Germans in Brazil should not "alarm even the most vigilant American."[64] And in 1903, the officers at the Naval War College remarked, "There is at present no opposition by the Brazilian Government to the immigration of Black's [Germany's] subjects."[65] There was a small group of xenophobic ultranationalists in Brazil who wrote lurid anti-German (and anti-French and anti-American, and so on) tracts. Foreign journalists of the day were adept at presenting this group's views as the mainstream.[66] In fact, however, the Brazilians wanted more Germans to join them. One German journalist mused that there seemed to be "a platonic love affair between the Brazilians and the Germans living in their midst."[67] The Brazilian government recruited emigrants from Germany even more vigorously and successfully than did the Colonial Association, offering German emigrants free passage, free seed, free animals, and loans at favorable rates. As Bryan's successor noted in 1903, "The Brazilian Government is deeply disappointed over the decline in German immigration into Brazil that has taken place in the last ten years." The Brazilians sought workers, a middle class, and a "whitener."[68]

Nor were American officials in Brazil alarmed. After touring the German settlements in Rio Grande do Sul in 1901, Minister Bryan wrote Andrew White, the U.S. ambassador in Berlin, "The German-born inhabitants . . . everywhere joined in the acclaim that welcomed each reference to the Monroe Doctrine."[69] It is worth quoting a report that his successor wrote in 1903 at some length:

> All immigrants undergo a change of views and convictions after long residence in a foreign country and the Germans who emigrate to Brazil are no exception to the rule. . . . The class among whom these latter are recruited in Germany is the lowest in the economic scale and as they prosper in the new country and enjoy local self-government and freedom, . . . they naturally become deeply attached to their locality and to the nation they have adopted as their home. When removed from the larger commercial centers they may retain their own language and customs for a generation or two but no such communities have had any share of influence on commerce or politics. They have remained agricultural and unprogressive. Upon being brought into contact with the larger outside world of commerce and modern thought by means of railway facilities they will be moulded in a short time into the uniform Brazilian mould as has regularly been the case in the

past. In other words, only in isolated rural communities of the states of Santa Catarina and Rio Grande do Sul have the Germans retained any large measure of German characteristics. . . . If one listens to the talk of children at play in even German private schools here, he is left in no doubt that Portuguese is the language of the country.

I have talked with Brazilians of German origin from Rio de Janeiro, State and City, and I have talked with some from the South, I have personal knowledge of the Germans in this region . . . and I have noted the activities in Brazilian politics of men of German birth or descent from the Southern States, and I have yet to learn of a sentiment among them that would admit of any construction that excludes the idea that Brazil is their country, first, last and always.[70]

The *Deutsche Zeitung*, the official German-language paper of Rio Grande do Sul, inquired the same year, "Because we speak German in intimate circles . . . because we hold aloft German honesty and truth, because we inspire ourselves from German literature and history and learn to be good burghers and men, for these reasons are we a danger to the land?"[71]

The U.S. Navy's Opinion

In 1895, after the failed naval revolt in Rio, the High Command of the German navy drew up a war plan against Brazil. It was based on a scenario in which Berlin would be forced to issue an ultimatum to Brazil that would lead to war. After explaining that the plan assumed peace in Europe, its author, Captain Schröder, zeroed in on Rio, stressing that a landing there would be difficult both because it would be impossible to bring heavy equipment and artillery ashore and because "rich Americans" and Europeans would come to Brazil's aid, possibly mining the harbors. (This was the only reference to America in the report.) Nevertheless, Schröder, who contributed other war plans historian Jonathan Steinberg has deemed "worthy of Jules Verne," emphasized that it was imperative that Germany occupy the capital city. The plan did not capitalize on Brazil's German population; Schröder explicitly excluded consideration of what should be done with them. It was simply a straightforward, if far-fetched, plan of how to respond to a provocation from Rio.[72]

A second plan was drafted two years later, and only a rough copy, with a lengthy appended comment expressing disapproval of the whole idea of attacking Brazil, remains. The plan called for the takeover of the southern provinces, hoping to avoid bloodshed by coming to a prior agreement with the government in Rio. A year later, a war game against Brazil was analyzed. The war would begin in 1901, when German ships, with British support, gathered outside Rio to collect claims. The author proceeded to specify the ships and supplies that would be needed, but he neither predicted an outcome nor mentioned the Germans living in Brazil. Like the first war plan, this was conventional gunboat diplomacy.[73]

It would be wrong to read too much into these three plans. The German navy was churning out war plans to meet every conceivable—and inconceivable—eventuality, and the idea of war against Brazil was never developed beyond the first, hypothetical stage.

These plans would not have surprised the U.S. Navy. At the turn of the century, naval strategists considered the possibility of a German assault on Brazil, and the prospect alarmed them. In 1901, a lecturer at the Naval War College predicted that "German overproduction would have to lead to colonization, probably in south Brazil, thus a challenge to the Monroe Doctrine." And later that year, the assistant secretary of state, Francis B. Loomis, told the assembled officers:

> Personal conversations with, and observations on the part of divers European statesmen . . . lead me to believe that the question of acquiring some sort of definite foot-hold in South America has not been wholly excluded from the thought of certain governments in connection with their plans for commercial political expansion. . . . This is a contingency which offers one of the most intricate and delicate problems that can be suggested by our future relations in Latin-America. The ultimate fate, declaration, scope and interpretation of the Monroe Doctrine is indissolubly connected with it.[74]

These fears were reflected in the Black Plan. "There is one contingency to be borne in mind," it warned,

> the possibility that the enemy's objective may be in South America. . . . In southern Brazil there are many Germans. The latter are the only probable cause of any trouble. The German emigrant is usually noteworthy for the ease with which he assimilates himself to his new surroundings, losing even his language. In Brazil this does not seem to be the case, the Germans there retaining their language and customs and forming an alien body politic within the state. The likelihood of trouble does not seem to be acute just now, but the germs are present. Should any trouble arise, and should Germany come to the aid of her sons in Brazil, or should she attempt the establishment of a German colony politically connected with the empire, the United States would almost certainly become involved in view of the present day acceptation of what the Monroe Doctrine means. . . . There are plans in the portfolio for the occupation and defense of Bahia and Rio [de] Janeiro.[75]

In 1901, the General Board, realistic about the United States' inability to project power south of the Amazon, discussed limiting the Monroe Doctrine to territory north of the great river. Rear Admiral Henry Taylor read a paper "which had as its foundation the idea of putting a southern boundary to the application of the Monroe Doctrine." The minutes noted that it "was received with great interest and excited considerable discussion." Dewey wrote the secretary of the navy, John D. Long, "Beyond the Amazon, we cannot control the naval situation in war against any probable European enemy. . . . South of the Amazon, we have no advantage of position over Western Europe. . . . Whether the principle of the Monroe Doctrine . . . covers all South America . . . is not for the consideration of the General Board, but only the fact that the principles of strategy and the defects in our geographical position make it impracticable successfully to maintain naval control by armed force beyond the Amazon." Long forwarded the report to McKinley. That the administration decided not to tamper with the doctrine did not change the reality that its ability to enforce it faded as it stretched to the south.[76] The pan-Germans were well aware of this. "South of the Isthmus of Panama the Yankees count for little or nothing," one of them declared.[77] The renowned Harvard professor Hugo Münsterberg, in the most widely read book on the United States published in Germany around the turn of the century, observed,

> [The Monroe Doctrine] is to-day entirely without value. . . . The antiquated Monroe Doctrine . . . must and will succumb. . . . So long as the United States were small and weak, this exaggerated fear of unknown developments was intelligible; but now that the country is large and strong, and the supposed contrast between the Old and New Worlds no longer exists . . . any argument for the Monroe Doctrine on the ground of misgivings or fear comes to be downright hysterical. . . . If the Monroe Doctrine were to-day to be applied no farther than Central America, and South America were to be exempted, the possibilities of a conflict with European powers would be considerably decreased.[78]

In 1903, the Naval War College estimated that the German population in southern Brazil was about 300,000 and "constantly increasing." In the "Solution of the Problem" of the Black Plan, the General Board asserted that "more than half of the total population of 1,800,000 [of Rio Grande do Sul and Santa Catarina] [was] of Black's race." At another point, the plan lowers its estimate to "not less than 600,000." The board considered these Germans in Brazil to be a fifth column, a potential source of succor to an invading German fleet. In the summer of 1903, these fears were most graphically expressed in the navy's war-gaming exercises. They were also heightened by Lieutenant

Cassius Barnes, a naval intelligence officer who spent three months reconnoitering southern Brazil. Barnes claimed that there were 1 million Germans in southern Brazil, and he lambasted the complacency of the Brazilians. "When the bolt drops," he wrote, "the most surprised men of all nations will be the Brazilians of the three southern states whose first warning will be finding themselves fast in the clutches of their own townspeople."[79]

Barnes's tour was the longest and most exhaustive investigation of southern Brazil by a German or an American. It was extraordinary: the Office of Naval Intelligence did not post a permanent attaché to Latin America until 1910. Posing as an English lawyer seeking to find a German Brazilian to inform him of an inheritance, Barnes ventured into the remote German enclaves. His lengthy (fifty-six-page), often entertaining report is noteworthy both for its observations and for its conclusion, which are fundamentally at odds with each other. Barnes's conclusion is straightforward: "They [the Germans in southern Brazil] constitute a menace to the Brazilian government and to the Monroe Doctrine." The lieutenant's own report, however, undermines this bold assertion. It is a superb example of the truism that one finds what one seeks: Barnes sought pan-German skulduggery, and that was what he saw, despite the evidence he himself cites to the contrary. He expected to find it in the shooting clubs (the armed vanguard of the movement), but by his own description they turned out to be haphazard drinking groups, and the weapons the men sported were an old and motley assortment. Nevertheless, Barnes assured himself, "It is my opinion that they [the Germans in Brazil] are providing themselves with the means of carrying out their purpose." Barnes's evidence from Blumenau is typical. At a dinner at which all were "freely partaking of Rhein [sic] wine" (a staple at all events he attended), Barnes announced that if he were a German born in Brazil and the kaiser arrived and asked for help, he would answer the call. The intelligence officer faithfully recorded his German Brazilian host's response: "I think [I would] not. All my interests are here and those of my family." Undeterred, Barnes pressed him: "But . . . you would certainly retain all your property . . . and the whole country would attain that prosperity to which it . . . certainly is entitled." Turning to the others, he asked, "What do you gentlemen think?" Prodded and besotted, they "arose from their chairs and declared themselves in loud tones and with violent gestures as ready and willing to assist the German Emperor in such an undertaking at any time he saw fit to begin it." Voilà!

Similarly, at a shooting club in the German settlement of Villa Germania, where all the members were "in various stages of intoxication," Barnes dutifully reported that someone complained when the president of the club delivered a speech in German, "saying that they were not German." Another member then stood up, unsteadily, and delivered an address "sometimes in German, sometimes in Brazilian." This led Barnes to conclude, "They are Germans in thought, speech and manner of living, and they could not deny it." When he later asked his hosts why the Germans did not participate in Brazilian politics, he was told that "opposition to the government was not organized." Nevertheless, he cabled Washington: "Aspect of affairs appears to be serious [in] southern Brazil. . . . Daily they discuss the matter [of] change of authority." When, even with such prompting, he failed to hear of pan-German plots, he attributed it to the possibility that "the plans of the German government are not yet thoroughly disseminated among them, or . . . they are silent through fear of detection," and he asserted confidently,

> If . . . the Germans there have not yet thought of appeal to the fatherland, they soon will accept that idea as the only means of bettering their governmental conditions. . . . If the German Emperor had never coveted this territory, even if he had coveted it and given up all hope of ever realizing his dream; when confronted with the facts that the majority of the population in these states are citizens of the German confederation [this statement was false] . . . and these subjects of his are milched as monkeys, trodden down, cast aside, even murdered and granted no appeal, all done by a weak government under the hated form of a Republican constitution—when these facts are brought before him, laying aside his known desire for territorial aggrandizement, his craving for military honors and the desire to establish before the eyes of his merchants the efficacy of the German fleet, his own creation, he is bound . . . to interfere for the protection of his subjects. But signs are not wanting to show that the Emperor has not given up on his desire to establish a dependency to the German Confederation in Southern Brazil. . . . The establishment of so many consulates . . . the presentation of his portrait to the burghers of Blumenau are but loud assertions of his purpose—to protect the rights of German citizens. He certainly will not be able to remain obdurate when the outspoken desire for his authority and the offer of their assistance in establishing it is heard from Santa Catharina and Parana together with the appeal for succor from the robbed and beaten of Rio Grande. . . . South America, . . . thinly settled by weaker peoples, affords a much easier problem to Germany than Asia to Russia.

Beyond the gap between the evidence and the conclusion, Barnes's report is noteworthy for the stark contrast it depicts between German and Brazilian civilization. "The German end of this street [in Cachoeira] presents much the same appearance as that of an Arkansas cotton town on a fall day, literally packed with farmers' wagons—the Brazilian end is like a dog kennel with the dog astray. . . . They [the Brazilians] are like a pack of wolves . . . but they are without even the cleanly personal habits of those animals." This creates an ethical dilemma for Barnes: purging Brazil of the Germans, he argues, would condemn the country to backwardness unless the United States was prepared to take their place. And, finally, Barnes's painstaking description of the difficulties he encountered traveling to most of the German towns underlines their acute isolation. "The difficulties to which one is subjected in traveling in this country are," he wrote with exasperation, "beyond description." [80]

While Barnes was struggling through the mud and corruption of Brazil, the young officers at the Naval War College were handed their annual war-gaming exercise: it was a scenario based on a German takeover of southern Brazil. The problem began: Black [Germany] occupies Rio Grande do Sul "with or without the tacit consent of that country, in opposition to Blue's [the United States'] fixed policy." Black's fleet, carrying four thousand men, "sails from Wilhelmshaven, destination unknown. . . . Blue declares war on Black." [81] The solution, which the General Board declared "a very confidential document," [82] noted:

It is probably true that in the Brazilian provinces adjoining the ports of Rio Grande do Sul and Santa Catarina . . . all male adults of that [German] origin possess rifles, that in their various benevolent societies and shooting clubs they possess a practically perfect militia organization and that among them will be found many officers of the Black regular army and others who are in fact imperial agents engaged in the Black propaganda. It is evident that should Black control the sea the provinces referred to would probably be able to declare their independence and accept a Black protectorate, even if they did not become an integral part of the Empire.[83]

This scenario reflected the fears that had been bandied about in the American press and in U.S. naval circles for years. While it was clear that Wilhelm II intended to do for the navy what his grandfather had done for the army, it was not clear what the mercurial kaiser's ultimate intentions were. As the German navy grew, so too did the debate as to its target.[84]

The summer exercise of 1903 was, therefore, a test of the Monroe Doctrine: Given a frontal assault on it in Brazil, what could the United States do? The answer of the junior officers at the Naval War College was pessimistic: "The chances of a successful campaign by Blue [the United States] . . . are very limited and will depend upon some unexpected accident to Black [Germany]." [85]

The vulnerability of the Monroe Doctrine—one of the few articulated mainstays of U.S. foreign policy—heightened the navy's fears of German intentions in Brazil. As the General Board concluded dryly, "The Doctrine is just as strong as the armed and organized forces maintained to enforce it." [86] Add to this the backdrop of tension in German-American relations, particularly in the naval and trade spheres, the belief that Germany was overcrowded and had to find somewhere to expand, and the Mahanian mind-set of the navy, and the summer 1903 war game begins to look reasonable.

Realities

This is the kernel of truth around which the perception grew. It is understandable. What is less easy to understand is the durability of the perception, for several reasons.

First, Germany's increasing isolation on the Continent, and therefore its constricting options abroad, were readily apparent. The pillars of Bismarck's foreign policy were crumbling: France and England forged their entente in April 1904, and London announced that it was reconfiguring its fleet to strengthen its North Sea (that is, anti-German) defenses. Two years later it would launch its first dreadnought. Defying all Germany's expectations, in August 1907 England and Russia drew closer together. The vise tightened. Germany's isolation was made painfully obvious to all at Algeciras, where both Britain and Russia supported French claims on Morocco and even Italy—its purported ally—left Germany twisting in the wind. Upon shelving the war plans against the United States in 1906, Captain Hebbinghaus had added to his caution that Germany could contemplate such a war only if it was allied with England the proviso "and if our flank is protected against France by Austria, Italy and possibly Russia." [87] By the end of 1907, Russia was aligned with France and England, Italy's deficiencies were obvious, and Germany was encircled. Whatever freedom of maneuver Berlin may have had outside Europe in 1900 had vaporized by 1907.

Teddy Roosevelt understood this. If he had entertained any lingering fears of a German challenge to the Monroe Doctrine, by 1903 they had receded utterly. The absence of any record of a discussion in Washington—at the White House or at the State Department—about a German threat to Brazil is absolute. Alarmist press clippings, naval reports, and private letters fell on deaf ears. In 1907, for example, Andrew Carnegie informed Roosevelt that a British cabinet member had told him that the kaiser had told the British ambassador in Berlin that Germany was building its navy against America. When the kaiser heard the rumor, he immediately cabled the president: "All Mr. Carnegie has heard in London are foul and filthy lies." Roosevelt grabbed his pen. "I never gave the matter a second thought," he assured Wilhelm. "I have no time to devote to thinking of fables of this kind. I am far too much occupied with real affairs. . . . Your Majesty may rest assured that no such tale as this of your building your fleet 'against America' will ever cause me more than good-natured amusement." [88]

The president apparently never did give the matter a second thought, and the historian is left, therefore, to interpret silence. Why was Roosevelt not concerned about the German threat? Even before the Venezuela crisis, he had been unruffled by the prospect of German ambitions in the hemisphere, and after the crisis he certainly grasped the impact of Germany's deteriorating international position. Throughout his life Roosevelt sought out, befriended, and corresponded at length with foreigners, such as "Springy" (Spring-Rice) and "Specky" (Speck von Sternburg). His letters convey his curiosity, his hunger to understand, and his thrill at being in a position to control some events. Thus Roosevelt understood that Germany's encirclement in Europe hog-tied it in Latin America. To the dismay of his old friends, he did not push Congress for the full naval increases the navy requested. He advocated keeping the fleet in the Atlantic not because he was panic-stricken about the German threat but because he was convinced that concentration was essential ("Don't you know me well enough to believe that I am quite incapable of such an act of utter folly as dividing our fighting fleet?" he asked Mahan in 1907).[89] Until the end of his presidency, Roosevelt succeeded in dealing with Wilhelm on respectful and friendly, if not warm, terms, swapping compliments and co-operating, edgily, in the Far East.

Tariffs, the kaiser's character, and fundamental disagreements, however, eroded this tentative and superficial friendliness. The tariff issue, never dead, resurfaced as both countries adjusted their trade regimes. Like part two of a Hollywood blockbuster, the story remained the same, but staler. The Germans wanted a fair deal, and the Americans had even less reason to give them one. Frustration in Berlin; satisfaction in Washington.[90]

Throughout his presidency, Roosevelt grew increasingly wary of the kaiser's temperament. In 1905, he considered Wilhelm's "violent and wholy irrational zigzags" a double-edged sword, rendering him "too jumpy" to be trusted but also "too erratic" to be capable of concocting "any long-settled and well-thought-out plans of attack upon England." [91] Three years later, after the kaiser gave disturbingly undiplomatic interviews to the *New York Times* and *Daily Telegraph*, "in language," Roosevelt wrote Root, "which would invite an international explosion if made public," Wilhelm's jumpiness took on more serious overtones.[92]

Now I do not for a moment believe that the utterances of the Emperor in-dicated a settled purpose; but they did make me feel that he indulged in red

"Dot iss der last time vot I puy sometings here yet, if I haf to climb me dose stairs up. Vat?" Uncle Sam stands triumphantly looking down from his high tariff walls as Germany sweats. The door to reciprocity is locked. (*Ohio State Journal*, 6 May 1905)

dreams of glory now and then, and that if he was indiscreet enough to talk to a strange newspaperman in such a fashion it would be barely possible that sometime he would be indiscreet enough to act on impulse in a way that would jeopardize the peace. . . . I am now striving to have us build up our fleet because I think its mere existence will be the most potent factor in keeping the peace between Japan and ourselves and in preventing any possible outbreak thru disregard of the Monroe Doctrine in America.[93]

As the unsound foundations of Weltpolitik shifted with the changing European alliances, Roosevelt remained calm. He did not underestimate the danger of Wilhelm's "brain storms," but he was confident that if the kaiser posed a threat, it was not to the United States.[94] One month before he left office, Roosevelt wrote to the incoming secretary of state, Philander Knox, "I do not believe that Germany has any designs that would bring her in conflict with the

Monroe Doctrine. The last seven years have tended steadily toward a better understanding of Germany on our part, and a more thoro [sic] understanding on the part of Germany that she must not expect colonial expansion in South America." [95]

Roosevelt's assessment of German intentions toward Latin America was based on his analysis of the balance of power in Europe and on his knowledge of German policy toward the region. As he himself had declared, he had no time to waste on fables, and the reality was that Germany seized none of the opportunities that presented themselves in Latin America. Roosevelt and the State Department were aware of this reality.

It was particularly striking in Brazil, where the opportunities were thought to be greatest. The kaiser's occasional saber rattling and his government's failure to distance itself from the pan-Germans were not the tip of an iceberg of plots to snatch southern Brazil. The grandiosity of pan-German rhetoric about Brazil and the strength of the German navy blinded many Americans to the frailty of the so-called fifth column and the absence of any coherent German policy toward Brazil. Three events show this. First, the Wilhelmstrasse and the German banks failed to help the Hansa, the foremost German settlement in southern Brazil, to survive, while at the same time the U.S. press was reporting the opposite. Second, in sharp contrast to the United States, which started negotiating trade treaties with Rio early in the 1890s, Germany did not develop a trade policy with Brazil. Third, during the most heated diplomatic exchange of the period between Brazil and Germany, the *Panther* incident of 1905, Wilhelm II displayed the opposite of the aggressive stance that many Americans expected; he acceded to Rio's wishes and publicly apologized for his navy's behavior. Brazil and the United States, on the other hand, used the incident to forge a closer relationship.

The Hansa

The sorry tale of the Hansa colony shows clearly that despite the lifting of the *Heydt'sche Reskript*, the Wilhelmstrasse remained reluctant to promote immigration to Brazil. A consortium of large German export and shipping firms, including the North German Lloyd and the Hamburg American Line, agreed in 1896 to set up the Hanseatic Colonization Society (HKG) to buy a large tract of land in Santa Catarina and attract German colonists to it. The society was incorporated on 30 March 1897 with a capital outlay of 1,150,000 marks. The purchase of the land was negotiated with Santa Catarina on 28 May 1897, and work began in September 1897, but only in earnest after Berlin had granted permission to recruit emigrants. The society's plan was to begin with

1,000 immigrants per year, increase this quota annually by 500 for eleven years, and maintain an influx of 6,000 emigrants per year until 50,000 Germans had settled in the colony.[96] The *New York Times* reported on the ambitious plan: "The abrogation of the Prussian Rescript . . . has already produced an effect. It is announced that three large Hamburg companies . . . have acquired a large tract of territory in the Brazilian province of Santa Catharina with the object of founding a German colony. It remains to be seen, however, . . . whether the United States will consider the planting of a German colony in South America to be compatible with the Monroe Doctrine."[97]

The syndicate's request to the German government for permission to form the society, however, provoked strenuous debate. The Agrarians, who were averse to all emigration, criticized the scheme. "It is doubtful," the imperial secretary of the interior, Arthur von Posadowsky-Wehner, declared in a meeting of the Prussian Ministry of State in June 1898, "that it is wise . . . to grant a concession to an emigration society for the *Urwald* in Brazil when we are suffering from a shortage of agricultural laborers at home and relying on Russian and Polish workers. Moreover, southern Brazil is of little significance as a market for German products." The Prussian minister of agriculture supported Posadowsky, but Bülow, then foreign secretary, disagreed adamantly. Although Germany was experiencing an economic upswing and needed agricultural workers, he argued, "the day may come when we will want more people to emigrate. It makes sense, therefore, to start now to direct them away from the United States and toward southern Brazil. We have big interests in southern Brazil. If we encourage this very modest level of emigration, and if we surround it with the necessary precautions, we will safeguard the future without threatening our interests at home. . . . Furthermore," he added weightily, "the Kaiser and the chancellor are in favor of it." The ministers of justice and of trade agreed with Bülow, as did Tirpitz, while the powerful finance minister, Johannes Miquel, expressed only minor reservations.

The Brazilians are half savages . . . and so we must ask the government in Rio to guarantee the autonomy of the German settlements. We should also determine whether our fleet could respond effectively to any mismanagement on the part of the Brazilian government. . . . Considering the severe shortage of workers at home, this enterprise seems untimely, but since the Kaiser is in favor of it, all we can do is grant the concession, with the requisite restrictions attached. . . . The attempt to send people where they can maintain their *Deutschtum* and form, in a sense, a state within a state is the right idea, and it should be approved despite the current scarcity of workers.

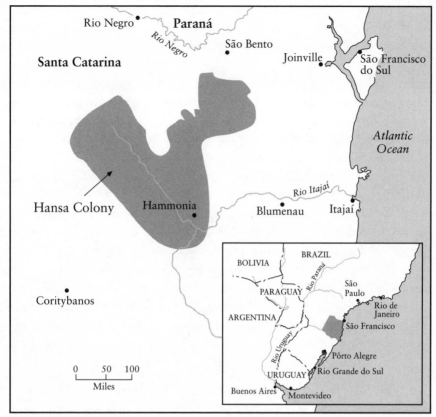

Map 3. The Hansa Colony

On 13 November 1898, after a delay of several months, the concession was finally granted.[98]

The land was a tract of some 1.6 million acres (roughly the size of Delaware) 75 miles west of Blumenau.[99] In 1898 the German newspapers were blanketed with advertisements to attract emigrants to it. Pan-Germans extolled the vigorous life of the colonists. "Here the brawny German settler, with wife and bairns," one rhapsodized, "swings of a Sunday afternoon into his favourite tavern, and empties many a pot of beer to his German Fatherland." To no avail. The land, chosen for the HKG by the Brazilian government, was isolated, perhaps to gerrymander the region so that the German community was unable to obtain political clout. The HKG mounted a vigorous campaign to attract colonists, which led the *Illinois Staats Zeitung* to comment: "The imbecilic outcry over 'the German danger in Brazil' can be traced . . . to the imprudent agitation of a German land speculation company which under the title 'Hansa' owns millions [*sic*] of acres in Santa Catarina, for which they can create hardly any market and therefore, as a last resort, call upon German nationalism and try to present the purchase of a homestead in the Brazilian far south as a patriotic duty." [100] The Germans who were persuaded to give the colony a chance were unhappy and dissatisfied. Rather than living in congenial villages, immigrants to the Hansa lived on primitive farms surrounded by *Urwald*. They needed at least six months to grow crops, and, in the meantime, they depleted their savings or accrued crippling debts. In the first ten years of the colony, more than half of the newcomers left. German consuls blamed the initial screening process: some emigrants were doomed to fail, either because they lacked the skills to make a living in Brazil or because they were Social Democrats—a comment revealing the prejudices of German officials. An employee of the Central Bureau for Emigration who did the screening explained, "I did not advise them [a couple who were not farmers] to go . . . and I warned them about the difficulties. . . . But many hear only what they want to hear and forget everything else." [101]

The difficulties the emigrants faced were no surprise to the businessmen at the head of the Hansa colonization scheme. They had not underestimated the task facing them, and they had spelled out the support they would require from the government. One of the directors wrote to Bülow in 1898,

> The HKG faces a very difficult challenge. . . . [It] must counter the negative image of Brazil as a tropical, disease ridden country, an image that is true of only a small region and that is a result of the decades-long effort of the German government to prevent emigration to Brazil. . . . If my fear is correct [that the government is considering capping the number of emigrants to Brazil at 1,000 per year], it would be better to forgo all thought of increasing *Deutschtum* in southern Brazil because this can only be successful with the emigration of tens of thousands every year. Despite all the care the HKG will exert in the selection of the land and emigrants, it is inevitable that many will be disappointed and will complain, but any large scale emigration scheme is impossible unless one has the courage to accept these risks. [102]

The main problem with the colony was obvious. The Hansa was inland, and it had no link to any town or port. The settlers, isolated on an impoverished island, could not prosper, psychologically or financially. Slick middlemen preyed on their need for transport, and the inflated transportation charges made the goods they produced uncompetitive outside the colony and the goods they brought in prohibitively expensive. Land prices were thereby depressed. From the moment the colony was established, there were plans to build a railway from its principal town, Hammonia, to Blumenau. "The building of this railway cannot be separated from the cultural task of maintaining *Deutschtum* in southern Brazil," the semiofficial *Kölnische Zeitung* declared at the end of the century. "Soon, a cultural street will be laid through the heart of South America that will be a major artery for the spread of German activity." [103] The railway was not just of practical, but also of symbolic value. A French analyst noted, "This [decision about the railway] is a very important moment for the spread of German influence outside Europe." [104]

But a railway required capital, estimated at five million marks. "If we do not get the necessary financial support, our successful settlement work may . . . have to end," the directors of the HKG threatened. They warned Bülow in 1903: "Our initial capital is almost exhausted. Your response will be of decisive importance. We do not need to explain the significance for Germany of our endeavor to you, nor do we need to remind you of the negative consequences for the prestige of Germany in Brazil should our society fail. . . . Therefore we humbly request that the society receive at least 300,000 marks from the group of banks under control of the government." As the head of the North German Lloyd informed the Wilhelmstrasse, "This capital cannot be raised without the active participation of the government." [105]

By 1903, the annual report of the HKG betrayed exasperation: "The railway should have been built first, before we even thought about colonization. That is how the United States always does it. Instead, in southern Brazil, we have done the opposite. This is why most of the colonists are still poor. They almost never see cash, and they have no hope of a future without worries. If a railway were close by, the middlemen would not be able to engage in their usual bloodsucking because there would be competition. As it is, the colonists are at their mercy." [106] In 1904, a German naval captain touring Brazil reminded Berlin that Santa Catarina "lacks good natural harbors . . . and navigable rivers. This makes it all the more striking that the whole state has only one short stretch of railway. . . . It is said that the HKG . . . will collapse soon. That would be a great pity for Germany. . . . It would be of greatest significance if the railway to Blumenau were to be funded with German capital." In the same year, the German consul in Santa Catarina echoed the claim: "For the Hansa, this railway is . . . a matter of life or death." [107]

The Wilhelmstrasse, which knew that the railway was key to the colony's success, quietly urged the banks to put up the capital. But they refused. A director of the HKG wrote in disgust, "The Berlin banks paid no attention to the chancellor's suggestions." [108] The two leading German banks had divided up South America to reduce competition: Diskonto had taken Venezuela and Brazil; Deutsche Bank had taken Peru, Chile, and Argentina. Diskonto had negotiated two loans in 1887 for a Brazilian railway that had failed two years later; the German lenders had lost their investment. And in 1902, the Brazilian state of Minas revoked a German railroad concession. German bankers lost any enthusiasm they might have had for Brazilian railways.[109]

German banks entered the South American market late, after the British had established a broad and well-respected network. This was due to Germany's relatively late industrialization, the chronic scarcity of capital in Germany, and more attractive investment opportunities at home and in the Middle East. Furthermore, unlike the German traders who took risks to increase their market share, the German bankers who did venture to Brazil preferred to establish a reputation for reliability. They were cautious, frequently spreading risks through partnerships with other foreign, particularly British, banks.

The bankers' caution occasionally dismayed German officials and businessmen interested in trade with South America, who bemoaned the fact that the Germans "stood by and watched with their arms crossed while other nations fought for capital investment opportunities." At the 1902 Colonial Congress, Jannasch exclaimed, "Let us work methodically to win this remunerative market [in southern Brazil]! Let us induce our great moneyed institutions to establish affiliated banks there. Let us press our insurance companies to form branches there! Let us persuade everyone in Berlin that the railroads in southern Brazil should be held by German shareholders! . . . In short, let us cultivate the far west of southern Brazil just like North America has cultivated its west!" The financiers, however, were obdurate. Their raison d'être was profit, they were loath to invest in risky ventures, and Brazilian railways were notoriously risky. The same prudence applied to German participation in Brazilian government loans.[110]

The Wilhelmstrasse could have done more than urge the bankers to increase their exposure in South America. It could have lobbied the Reichstag to change the stock market legislation that restricted a bank's freedom to raise capital for foreign ventures, legislation particularly crippling in Germany, where capital was in short supply. German traders and businessmen in Brazil were disgruntled. They complained, according to a German naval report, "that German initiative and German capital remained aloof from Brazil."[111]

Berlin, however, was unwilling to risk a confrontation with the domestic groups who opposed overseas investment. The Wilhelmstrasse explained its stance in an interesting exchange in 1907 with the German minister in Rio, Franz von Reichenau. Frustrated by the lack of German capital investment in Brazil, Reichenau sought the views of his consuls and sent Berlin a long letter expressing their shared opinions: "Ever since I became minister, I have observed . . . that with rare exceptions German capital is very passive about the economic development of Brazil. . . . I asked all the career consuls for their expert opinions about this, and their responses confirmed my observation. Almost all said that over the last decade they had repeatedly stressed the importance and profitability of economic endeavors in Brazil, but to no avail. . . . In terms of capital investment in this country, Germany is in last place." [112] The Wilhelmstrasse's reply is a clear explanation of its ambivalence toward overseas investment.

> It is true that German capital frequently eschews investment overseas. The nature of our laws [restricts] such participation . . . and a significant change in them is unlikely in the foreseeable future. Moreover, it is probable that money will continue to be tight and that it will be more profitable to invest at home than abroad. Furthermore . . . our large financial institutions have acquired the international reputation they now enjoy because of their great reliability. . . . It is well known that some foreign, especially US, institutions are less exacting. . . . What these banks and firms like to call generosity and daring is often simply a lack of scruples. . . . Moreover, our capital wealth, while increasing at a satisfactory pace, is still considerably less than that of other countries and it is still needed for important tasks at home. . . . For the foreseeable future . . . we will have to make sure that German capital concentrates as much as possible in countries where there are either very important political considerations or where the venture is particularly rewarding financially and not overly exposed to risk. . . . Brazil can be counted among the latter countries only with very severe limitations. . . . This does not mean that Germany should renounce all financial activity in Brazil . . . but that the Wilhelmstrasse must be very careful before it uses its influence with German businessmen to promote a Brazilian venture. Political considerations are not relevant because we cannot realistically hope to supplant American interests in the near future. Therefore, we are forced to look at investment in Brazil in economic terms—the return and safety of capital. [113]

Accordingly, the Wilhelmstrasse did no more than inform the bankers of the Hansa's need for capital and gently ask them to consider providing it. It professed support for the colony, but it did little.

Nevertheless, the rumor mill ground on. Even responsible American journals printed exaggerated reports about the influence of German capital in Brazil. The *Review of Reviews*, for example, claimed in 1906: "The policy of the [German] empire was obviously directed toward the acquisition of colonies, and the eyes of its statesmen were at first turned toward Brazil, almost the whole industry of which had been capitalized by German bankers." The truth of the matter was that the German banks balked at financing the railway that would have been the lifeblood of the Hansa colony, and, despite a

vigorous campaign to attract colonists, by 1906 the Hansa stood on the verge
of collapse. The German consul in Florianópolis had thrown down the gauntlet a year earlier: "It is not a question of the profitability of a small local rail
line of a few kilometers, but of our national purpose. Will Germany, in view
of the threatening U.S. invasion which is already at the door, . . . maintain its
present interest in Santa Catarina or will we surrender it?" [114]

This U.S. invasion had been foreseen by the Blumenau newspaper *Der Urwaldsbote* as early as 1900: "The ambitious Yankees were already directing
their greedy looks here [southern Brazil]. They would love to skim the cream
from the milk." In 1906, as foreseen, a U.S. company bought a controlling
interest in the São Paulo and Rio Grande Railroad. (This was a line related
to the stretch that would connect Hammonia to Blumenau.) "This purchase
is of very great political and commercial interest to the United States," the
U.S. minister in Rio, Lloyd Griscom, explained to the State Department. "[It]
runs through the heart of the great district in southern Brazil inhabited by
German colonists. I feel confident that when it is made public that this purchase has been made and that it is an American owned railway which will in
future form the backbone of the German colony, an end will be put to all the
absurd supposition that Germany has political ambitions in Southern Brazil."
Reichenau agreed, "One thing is clear: with this railway business, the Americans have assured themselves a very strong position in southern Brazil that
will not only threaten and hurt the first place that we have heretofore enjoyed
but also damage the future development of our interests in the region." Only
after the Americans expressed interest in the southern Brazilian railway did
the German banks finally raise the capital for the Hansa line. [115]

On 26 February 1906, the Santa Catarina Joint Stock Company was created
with a capital investment of four hundred thousand marks to build a railway
from Blumenau to Hammonia. It took a year, however, for the company to
be officially registered in Berlin. [116] In the course of that year, the pressure on
Berlin intensified. An editorial in *Der Urwaldsbote* in May expressed the colonists' growing despair:

> Once again, deafening silence is all we hear about the railway for which
> we have harbored such high hopes. Even diehard optimists—among whom
> we count ourselves—are overcome with pessimism. When the conversation
> turns to the railway, people say, "Once again, nothing has happened." It
> seems to be terribly difficult for German businessmen to make a decision:
> they would like to support the railway, but they don't dare. We receive
> neither a clear yes nor a frank no but are given a run-around that tries our
> patience. . . . [The men] in whose hands the future of the railway lies abide

by the motto ... "Inch by inch." We suggest they adopt instead: "It is better to do something than to contemplate doing it forever." [117]

In August, the directors of the HKG threatened to dissolve the society and hand the concession to the Americans if the railway was not financed by January 1907.

The construction of this railway is fundamental to the success of our undertaking, as we stressed from the beginning. We believe that the liquidation of our society is inevitable [if the railway is not built]. The failure to build it has had a devastating impact on the morale of the colonists. Bitterly disappointed, many families have left. . . . The resulting loss is all the more significant because we had given many of these families substantial cash advances. I believe that we will have to . . . transfer our concession and all the relevant contracts to a U.S. society. . . . We were recently approached by a middleman, apparently with U.S. backers, interested in building the Santa Catarina railway. It is no secret that the United States has recently . . . made a concerted effort to achieve commercial and political hegemony in Brazil by pushing out European, and particularly German, trade.[118]

And in December, Sellin published an article in *Amerika* that emphasized the same point: "If this railway is not built, then we should give up all hope that Santa Catarina—which for eighty years has been colonized by Germany—will be German in the future. . . . We will lose more and more ground to the United States in southern Brazil. The North Americans are only waiting to settle into the warm nest that the German colonists have been preparing for years." [119]

Registered on 2 February 1907, the company finally opened the railway in October 1909. It was too late to help the ill-fated colony. Although Wilhelm minuted "Bravo!" while reading a report on the railway in 1911, the colony, which had hoped by then to have attracted 50,000 German emigrants, boasted a population of a bare 2,478 souls in 1912, only 400 of whom were German citizens, and the railway was reporting—as the wary bankers had always predicted—a loss.[120]

Deutschtum

If the German government's support for the Hansa colony, the most serious of Germany's attempts to plant settlers in southern Brazil, was tepid apart from the occasional flight of rhetoric, its backing for other measures to bolster the *Deutschtum* in the region was even more lackluster. The government did subsidize German schools, but the sums involved were risible. In 1902, for example, the Reich sent forty-two thousand marks to German schools in southern Brazil, roughly 5 percent of the total it spent on all schools abroad. "Schools could have spread German culture," Ernest Tonnelat wrote in 1908, "but lack of money made the rural schools miserable. There was often a single teacher in a shack for several communities, and the teachers, who were poorly paid, were those who were incapable of doing anything else." These schools were funded by a special tax that the Brazilian government allowed to be levied locally and by private contributions gathered in Germany. Most of the costs were offset by tuition, which, according to a German naval officer visiting the German settlement of Joinville, "was quite high by local standards." "Therefore," the officer remarked, "the less well-off German families have to send their children to the State school. . . . One must really hope for a rise in the German subsidy. . . . The most important requirement to maintain *Deutschtum* is to give more support for German schools." [121]

The extent of the Reich's support for German schools was exaggerated in reputable U.S. papers, just as the significance of German banking in Brazil had been. These stories were often based on other press reports, particularly British, or on the hearsay of naval experts, or on the occasional U.S. journalist who ventured to Brazil and relied on sources in the cities. Although the *New York Times* usually—but not always—reflected the State Department's position that the German settlements in Brazil did not threaten the United States, its reports got less play than the more colorful ones. The *Atlantic Monthly*, for example, claimed blithely, "These regions [in southern Brazil] have German schools and clergymen under the pay of the German Emperor." [122]

Echoing those writers of the day who were alarmed by German intrusions into Brazil, most scholars have assumed that the Reich pursued an expansionist policy in Brazil. For example, Jürgen Hell, an East German scholar who had extensive access to the Potsdam archives, argued that Wilhelmine Germany had pursued an imperial policy of "peaceful penetration" in Brazil. Hell claimed, for example, that the Reich sought to unite the German churches in Brazil. In fact, however, the churches were acting on their own initiative. Hell mentioned a press fund of two thousand marks to "encourage" the Brazilian papers to publish pro-German articles. The paltry sum, however, was rarely used. He mentioned the attempt to encourage the construction of a cable line to Brazil. The effort, however, failed. He noted the changes in citizenship regulations to make it easier for Germans in Brazil to remain German citizens. These changes, however, were few and late. Even after the Delbrück law, which allowed Germans to hold dual citizenship, was passed in 1913, Germans abroad still had to register regularly with the consular office; for the hard-pressed farmers in the hinterlands, this was an onerous burden. Germans in Brazil, therefore, continued to renounce their German citizenship and become Brazilian citizens.[123]

The German government did contribute to *Deutschtum* in southern Brazil by enlarging its consular representation there. In 1897, Germany opened consulates in Santa Catarina and Rio Grande do Sul. Eventually there were as many professional consuls in Brazil as in the rest of South America. But the consuls were hamstrung by the fact that most émigrés had renounced their German citizenship. "The consuls, when we have foolishly gone to them," the German-language paper in Pôrto Alegre lamented, "have told us in no uncertain terms that they can do nothing for us, nothing at all."[124] When the German minister in Rio, Baron von Treutler, asked the Wilhelmstrasse in 1903 to create a post of agricultural attaché for southern Brazil—to collect information for potential emigrants and advise the Germans immigrants about the latest agricultural techniques—nothing was done.[125]

Treutler lamented in 1906, "The longer I am here, the more I see, the more I am convinced that the sacrifices we make for them [the Germans in Brazil] are deserved only in a very few cases. Therefore, I increasingly ask myself whether it is right to continue—or even increase—our sacrifices and efforts on their behalf." He concluded that the efforts were worthwhile for a very unsentimental reason: they would help boost German trade. "Our actions are absolutely necessary given the situation," Treutler explained. "Without our assistance, these elements—already lost to us politically—would also be lost to us economically. We must—by all available means—preserve the German language because it will give us an advantage over our most dangerous competitor. We must face the fact that the United States is becoming very active here."[126]

Trade

It was not until the second half of the nineteenth century that the German states had begun to look with interest at trade with South America. This dearth of interest is reflected in the fact that no minister from any German state was sent to Brazil until 1851, whereas one had been sent to Mexico twenty years earlier. With industrialization, the development of the banking system, and the growth of shipping companies, however, the South American market began to beckon. By 1890, Brazil was Germany's main supplier of coffee. This is indicative of the pattern: Brazil—and South America in general—was a source of supply for Germany but, despite high hopes, not of markets. One reason was the meagerness of Brazil's purchasing power. As the U.S.

minister in Rio, David Thompson, reported in 1903, "The total consuming capacity of Brazil has in fact remained nearly stationary since [around 1890]. This is due to the fall in price of her great product, coffee." [127]

Germans, and not just the pan-Germans, expected the German settlements in southern Brazil to boost trade with Brazil as a whole. But although the immigrants did tend to buy German goods, they were not wealthy, they were a small percentage of the Brazilian population, and they had virtually no "shirt-tails." This was acknowledged in 1905 at the Second German Colonial Congress, where, as the U.S. chargé in Berlin, H. Percival Dodge, reported, "Great interest was . . . shown as to German commercial relations with South America." Dodge delineated the key conclusions of one speaker at the congress:

> The mere number of Germans in a South American country did not necessarily increase the commercial importance of that country to Germany. Nor was it an advantage to Germans if they kept themselves apart from the general population. On the contrary the important point for increasing German trade in South America was that the Germans there should mingle freely with the population, making their habits and customs known and appreciated, while at the same time preserving their German character and spirit. He cited Argentina as an example of this. Here the German population was . . . about three or four times less numerous than the German population in Brazil where the Germans to a great extent shut themselves off entirely from the general population, and yet German imports from and exports to Argentina . . . were now more important than those to or from any South American country. [128]

A careful examination of trade patterns by an Australian scholar, Ian Forbes, confirms these observations. Forbes shows that it was not the presence of German colonists in a country that determined the expansion of trade between it and Germany but rather the internal conditions in the country itself. The South American states, he writes, "constituted no virgin ledger sheet awaiting merely the skill or clumsiness of German trade accountants." Thus, although more Germans lived in Brazil than in Argentina, German trade with the latter outstripped the former because of the growth of Argentina's economy and the diversification of its trade. Brazil, on the other hand, was engulfed in civil war in the 1890s, and afterward its economy was sluggish compared with that of Argentina. [129]

German middlemen were notoriously ambitious. Every commentator agreed that the German businessmen in Brazil were more numerous, more aggressive, and smarter than their American and British counterparts. U.S. consuls bemoaned the American traders' insensitivity to the local market and ignorance of the hinterlands; they drew a sharp contrast between the creative, adaptable German entrepreneur and the rigid, unadventurous American. "Germany has for a long time worked steadily to monopolize the South American markets and German drummers are very active and numerous in Brazil," Thompson reported in 1903.[130]

Unlike the American traders, the Germans published catalogs in Portuguese, used local weights and currency, worked for smaller profits, offered long-term credit, made frequent visits to the customers, spoke their language, took note of their habits, were willing to accept small orders, and packaged their products attractively and well. "Into this fertile territory [southern Brazil] Germany is pushing her interests with an aggressive spirit and a thought to detail," a captain at the Army Staff College noted in 1910, before drawing the conclusion: "which presumes a well digested plan." In 1912, a U.S. military intelligence officer predicted, "Someday the commercial supremacy of South America will be their's [sic]. For they are a plodding, frugal, conservative race, mutually aiding one another. . . . Behind all this is the constant support of the German Government." Furthermore, Germany's shipping lines were booming: much Brazilian trade—including that with the United States—was carried in German bottoms. These German strengths led to widespread fears among American consuls and businessmen that the United States would be bested by Germany in the Brazilian (and South American) market.[131]

Cold trade statistics reveal, however, that the opposite was happening. As the *Berliner Neueste Nachrichten* noted in 1899, "The 'imaginary danger' is that . . . Germany may endeavor to annex it [south Brazil]. The 'real danger,' however, is the designs of the United States upon the whole of South America." Brazil's trade with the United States grew between 1890 and 1913 at a faster rate than did its trade with Germany. By 1905, the liberal *National Zeitung* (Berlin) was bemoaning the fact that "sad though it is, it is quite likely that Rio Grande do Sul is lost to us. The United States will succeed in pushing the Germans out of Brazil." [132]

The reason was simple: the U.S. government was ahead of its traders, urging them to do more in Latin America; the German government lagged behind its traders, who were habitually urging their government to do more. The United States, acting, to use Emily Rosenberg's term, as "the promotional state," abolished import duties on coffee as early as 1870 and negotiated its first commercial treaty with Brazil in 1891: Brazilian coffee, sugar, rubber, and hides would enter the United States duty-free, and duties on all other Brazilian exports would be reduced by 25 percent. This led to reciprocal concessions for U.S. exports (machinery, wheat, and flour) to the Brazilian market and solidified the U.S. position as the leading importer of Brazilian goods, primarily coffee, rubber, and cocoa. Although the economic benefits of the treaty accrued more to the Brazilians than to the Americans, it was, as Walter LaFeber comments, "one of the most important reciprocity treaties signed under the McKinley tariff." [133]

Despite Berlin's envy of U.S. trading privileges, the Wilhelmstrasse refused to lower duties on Brazilian goods. This was particularly harmful to Brazilian-German trade because, like Brazilian-U.S. trade, the Germans wanted coffee and rubber in exchange for manufactured goods. After reporting on the 1891 U.S.-Brazilian trade treaty, the German minister in Rio warned the Wilhelmstrasse: "It is obvious that European influence is slowly being displaced by the Americans." Berlin increasingly worried and complained that Washington was roping off Latin American trade by means of reciprocity treaties. Just a month after he became president, Roosevelt wrote Sternburg, "I regard the Monroe Doctrine as being equivalent to the open door in South America," but he added, tellingly, "save as individual countries enter into individual treaties with one another." Washington pursued these bilateral treaties with vigor, and from 1901 to 1912, the German share of Brazilian trade fell.[134]

Berlin was not indifferent to the expansion of German trade with South America. It was involved in the details of marketing—circulating reports about local conditions and charging its consuls to intervene on German traders' behalf—to a degree that surpassed the Americans and would have been considered improper by the British Foreign Office. But, as Forbes concludes, German officials, constrained by domestic politics, "made little effort to woo producers in the ABC states [Argentina, Brazil, Chile]." The German tariff on coffee was the government's second most important source of revenue. (The tariff on grain was the first.) Thus, for fiscal reasons, Berlin raised the tariff on coffee in July 1909 despite the obvious impact this would have on trade with Brazil.[135]

This points to the heart of the matter: Berlin would have welcomed the expansion of German trade with Brazil, just as it would have welcomed trade expansion anywhere. Unlike the United States, however, it had no policy toward Brazil. German traders there might have been more competent and energetic than their American counterparts, but they were not supported by their government. If this was economic imperialism, it was economic imperialism of a singularly inept variety.

An exception is sometimes made for the armaments industry. Holger Herwig, for example, argues that here one finds German economic imperialism, as the Reich aggressively promoted the German armaments manufacturer Krupp and curried favor with South American armies in order to increase the sales of German weapons.[136] There is some truth to these allegations, both in Latin America as a whole and in Brazil. The Reich did intervene more often and more aggressively to help Krupp than any other German company operating in Brazil, and it did allow Brazilian officers to train with the German military. German arms dealers in Brazil did manage to edge out their competition more successfully than did the merchants of any other commodity. By 1912, Captain Levert Coleman, the U.S. military attaché in Rio, who was alarmed about German penetration of the arms market and who had been pressing Washington for more than a year to seize the opportunity to sell Brazil U.S. coastal defense systems, lamented, "I have very strong reasons for feeling sure that the German minister and his assistants including the Military Attaché are acting in concert with . . . the Krupp agent here in systematically gaining every possible advantage for forcing the adoption of Krupp coast defense materiel throughout Brazil. . . . In all things military she [Germany] is arbiter of Brazil's destiny."[137]

To understand this success, however, the role of the arms dealer and of the Brazilian authorities must be considered. German arms traders in South America were a skilled, organized, and aggressive lot. They had been plying their wares in Brazil since the 1860s. During the Brazilian civil war of 1893–95, their share of the trade increased. It grew steadily, if gradually, until 1908, when it began to increase more rapidly. The reasons were many. German arms had an excellent and well-deserved reputation, and their salesmen were second to none. This was a highly lucrative trade: the Germans sold the Brazilians outmoded equipment and used the proceeds to finance development and research at home. And they sometimes had help from the government. In 1902 and 1903, for example, the Wilhelmstrasse threw its weight behind Krupp in order to wrest a Brazilian government arms order away from the French and British competition.[138]

Captain Coleman was worried that Germany would try to penetrate the arms market by insinuating itself into the training of the Brazilian army. "I feel it my duty to lay great stress upon this," he wrote in 1912. "Germany has systematically gained military and political influence by acquiring and utilizing the right to train the Military Forces of Chile and of Argentina. . . . She is preparing skillfully and systematically to complete her projects [by] acquiring similar control in Brazil. France has tried in vain to stop the progress of this most important movement. . . . England . . . is indifferent, but the United States is the Power most vitally concerned." Coleman's fears notwithstanding, the Reich did not increase its official contacts with the Brazilian military in order to promote the sale of German arms. The record points in the opposite direction: the Brazilians, not the Germans, took the lead. When they pressed Berlin for the opportunity to send their officers to Germany, the kaiser hesitated for more than a year before replying. He finally agreed in 1906 to take eight Brazilian army officers—not the ten Brazil had requested—and no naval officers, although Rio had asked that two be received.[139]

A similar picture emerges from the discussions of the proposed German military mission to Brazil. When the Brazilians—not the Germans—first asked for a mission in 1906, Wilhelm II considered the suggestion "absurd," in part because he thought German officers would have difficulty dealing "on an equal rung with black and colored" officers. Treutler agreed: "Miscegenation has caused such moral decay . . . that any attempt to improve . . . the [Brazilian] army is virtually hopeless."[140] The Germans feared that the difficulty of disciplining these Brazilian troops could cause a backlash against Germany. It was not until 1910, when Wilhelm II agreed to send twenty German officers to Brazil for three years, that the Germans changed their minds about the mission. Then they delivered their ultimatum to Rio: Germany would set up a military mission in Brazil if, and only if, the Reich was granted the exclusive right to train and advise the Brazilian army. While the Brazilian army signaled its readiness to accept the terms, there was an outcry in France, which was itself trying to corner the Brazilian arms market, and also in Brazil, where public opinion was divided in its preference for French or German military instructors. Two years later, Coleman wrote, "I am reliably informed that . . . the [German] Mission will surely come in the immediate future. This . . . will destroy the splendid opportunity we had of . . . gaining the political and military friendship which that would bring in its train and the consequent ability to enforce the Monroe Doctrine in this the most coveted of lands against the Pan Germanists." Coleman's reliable informant notwithstanding, the Brazilian legislature deadlocked, and the German mission was never established.[141]

A similar story can be told of military attachés. When France invited Brazil in 1909 to station a military attaché in Paris, the German minister in Rio, Count von Arco-Valley, advised the Wilhelmstrasse, "This is clearly a way to increase French exports. Germany should do the same." Berlin agreed, and an attaché was invited. The United States, however, was the only country to station a military attaché in Rio.[142]

These facts were ignored by those who feared the rise of German influence in Brazil. Once again, their reasoning led them back to Berlin: the German arms merchants were doing well in Brazil; ergo, they were tools of Berlin's imperialistic policy.[143]

The increase in German naval visits to Brazil fanned these flames. The navy considered its visits important contributions to the strengthening of *Deutschtum*. "The presence of a warship moves the national spirit of the *Deutschtum*," explained one officer.[144] In 1911, when the battle cruiser *Von der Tann* went around South America, its captain's report about his reception in southern Brazil was rapturous: "The colonists came in great streams from every direction to greet us. . . . No one wanted to miss seeing the train with the open car filled with the crew singing happy songs. Everyone wanted to show their joy. . . . The children were led by their teachers in singing 'Deutschland, Deutschland über Alles,' and several hundred people along the route spontaneously joined in with tears in their eyes. Old people exclaimed, 'How wonderful that I have lived to experience this!' . . . I am convinced that *Deutschtum* in Santa Catarina has received strong and healthy encouragement from this visit." The *Von der Tann*'s public relations coup spurred the U.S. Navy to send its newest dreadnaught immediately on a copycat cruise.[145]

The enthusiasm of the reports of visiting naval captains, however, contrasts markedly with the sober reports of the German ministers and consuls. Of course, the officers stayed only briefly and, after a long journey punctuated by visits to small, scattered German settlements, were dazzled by the large, welcoming German-speaking crowds that greeted them in southern Brazil. And the more one reads about the dreary lives of the colonists, the more understandable their reaction to the visits becomes. Everyone loves a parade.

The reports, therefore, were misleading. Germans living in Brazil were not a fifth column; although retaining their German culture, they had become Brazilian citizens and were loyal to Rio, not to Berlin. The garrulous German naval officers who broadcast optimistic assessments of the potential spread of German influence in Brazil failed to notice this. The U.S. minister in Rio reported in 1900, for example, "The Captain of a German man-of-war, recently in the harbor of Rio de Janeiro, volunteered the following remark . . . 'So far as we Germans are concerned you can have Amazonas but we intend to take Rio Grande do Sul.' "[146] Reports like this raised hopes among the pan-Germans and hackles in Washington. They alarmed politicians in Rio and irritated Germans living in Brazil, who had to extinguish the brushfires they ignited. Thus, while the visits of the warships gave little succor to the immigrants, they lent credibility to the allegations that Berlin had a nefarious plot up its sleeve. They fueled fears of the Reich's intentions—so much so that Treutler, who had asked in 1902 for more visits, pleaded four years later that they be curtailed. "The Admiralty would be making a big mistake," he wrote, "if it thought that it should show the flag in southern Brazil more often." The German ambassador in Washington, Herman Speck von Sternburg, echoed Treutler in a letter to the Wilhelmstrasse: "I would like to remind Berlin again of the advice that was given to me in 1903 when I took this job: As far as possible, keep German warships from [North and South] American waters." [147]

The diplomats need not have worried. Tirpitz was building a navy of battleships, not cruisers. The ships suited for service visiting American ports were few. The kaiser summed up the Reich's dilemma in the margin of a report asking for more naval visits. "If no have got," he scrawled in English, "how can do?" [148]

The *Panther* Incident

Nonetheless, the most serious diplomatic crisis between Germany and Brazil prior to the First World War occurred in 1905 after German sailors on the gunboat *Panther* called on a Brazilian port, sought a deserter ashore, and were angrily charged by Rio with violating Brazilian sovereignty. Despite the fact that Berlin vehemently denied the charge, Rio deftly obtained Washington's support and wrested an apology from Wilhelm II. This has led historians as eminent as E. Bradford Burns to label the episode a "German violation of Brazilian sovereignty." [149]

The incident reveals the international dynamics at the time. Brazil and the United States were drawing closer together, regardless of German dreams and desires. The United States had moved quickly to consolidate the advantage it had won from the Venezuela crisis. While Roosevelt vacillated in 1902—initially approving Germany's plan to blockade Venezuela and then objecting to it—in 1905 he was assertive. In the interim, he had proclaimed the Roosevelt Corollary, which was meant expressly to prevent future Venezuelas by placing the power of the U.S. Navy between financially delinquent Latin American states and their European creditors, and he had immediately put it into practice by taking control of the Dominican Republic's customhouses. In one of his more notorious acts, he had wrested Panama from Colombia and carved out the future canal zone for the United States. Roosevelt maintained his interest in naval affairs, and his administration also supported the growth of U.S. business in Latin America. Under his watch, the Monroe Doctrine, given substance by McKinley, moved more decisively from dream to reality.

It was a nuanced reality, meaning something quite different in the Caribbean than it did south of the Amazon. This was in part due to obvious geographical differences—it was easier for the still fledgling modern navy to assert hegemony closer to home—but it was also due to the greater power of the South American states. The United States could not treat Argentina, Chile, and Brazil with the same contempt it heaped on Haiti, the Dominican Republic, Panama, and the Central American states. The large South American countries had to be approached primarily through diplomatic rather than military channels; U.S. hegemony would not be asserted at the barrel of a naval cannon but through trade and the diplomatic nicety of "pan-Americanism."[150] In this effort, Brazil was key. Elihu Root, Hay's successor in 1905 as secretary of state, cognizant that the United States and Brazil shared an interest in stability in South America, decided that Washington should strengthen its relationship with Rio. Immediately before the *Panther* incident, he announced that he himself would attend the third Pan-American Conference, which was being held in Rio in 1906, the first time a sitting secretary of state visited South America. As the U.S. chargé in Rio noted, the decision marked "the predominance of Brazil among the nations of South America."[151] The *Panther* incident, as the Brazilian press noted, "hastened the moment when the Government of Washington will become in fact our Lord Protector," and was therefore well timed to further Root's agenda.

Friendship with the United States suited Brazil, whose foreign minister, Baron Rio-Branco—despite being an admirer of Europe—realigned Brazil's foreign policy toward the United States in 1902, in sober recognition of the facts that Washington's power over Latin America was increasing, that the United States could be a valuable ally in regional disputes, and that the United States was the chief consumer of Brazilian coffee and rubber.[152] Three years later, the two countries had upgraded their missions to embassies. "[Rio Branco's] desire is that Brazil should in a way dominate South America," Thompson wrote Hay, "and the move for the exchange of Embassies is a move . . . [toward] a closer friendship with the Washington Government." When Joaquim Nabuco took up the newly created post of ambassador to the United States in 1905, he wrote, "Obviously we are facing the dawn of a new era. . . . The Monroe Doctrine lays down a definite foreign policy for the United States which is now beginning to take shape, and it lays down a similar policy for us. Under such conditions, our diplomacy should receive its principal impetus from Washington. Such a policy would be better than the largest army or navy." Nabuco and Rio-Branco then masterfully used the *Panther* fracas to strengthen Brazil's ties with the United States.[153]

The rise of U.S. hegemony was possible because it was unchallenged. The Venezuela crisis marked a watershed in the balance of power in the Americas by clarifying that it was not in Britain's interest to risk even the appearance of questioning U.S. ascendancy in the Western Hemisphere. After Venezuela, if Germany wanted to challenge the Monroe Doctrine, it would have to do it alone, but as the Reich became ever more isolated on the Continent, such a prospect grew ever more unthinkable. The docility of all the Europeans in the face of the United States' ascent is evident in the striking lack of response to both the Roosevelt Corollary and the seizure of the Dominican finances. As historian Melvin Knight pointed out in 1928, "The European claimants [on the Dominican Republic] . . . merely wanted their money, while we wanted our money and our Monroe Doctrine."[154] Although some German papers denounced Roosevelt's extension of the Monroe Doctrine, the *Hamburger Nachrichten*, for example, calling it "a naked proclamation of the view that might makes right," the Wilhelmstrasse was quiescent. And when press reports later appeared alleging that Germany had aided Colombia during the Panamanian revolt, Richthofen immediately reassured U.S. ambassador Charlemagne Tower: "The question of an interference on the part of Germany in the revolution in Panama does not exist."[155] Berlin's submissiveness was also evident in the *Panther* affair; far from empire building, Wilhelm merely tried, unsuccessfully, to control the damage.

It was fitting that the *Panther* would be at the center of the controversy. The gunboat was the most notorious of the German ships prowling the American waters: it was the ship that had sunk the Haitian *Crête-à-Pierrot* in 1902, and, a year later, it had shelled the Venezuelan fort of San Carlos. In late 1905, it was paying courtesy calls on Brazilian ports. The visits were not proceeding smoothly. In Rio, Captain von Saurma-Jeltsch had quarreled with the head of the local German community, and the local German club had banned its members from any future contact with the ship's officers. "Everywhere I went I heard that the *Panther* was absolutely to blame for the problem," the German consul reported to the Wilhelmstrasse. "I hope that if the *Panther* ever has to return, that its visit will be as short as possible."[156]

Leaving that squabble in its wake, the gunboat pulled into the port of Itajaí, one of the most prosperous towns in Santa Catarina with a large German community. When the sailors disembarked on the evening of 26 November, a few hours of shore leave turned into an international incident with the flavor of comic opera, right down to the fact that something significant emerged from an utterly trivial event. Brazil charged the Germans with violating its sovereignty by arresting a man—Fritz Steinhoph—on Brazilian soil and forcibly taking him to their ship. Saurma countered that they had done no such thing. Assured beforehand of cooperation by Brazilian authorities, his men had searched the town "in a discreet way" for a sailor, Hasmann, who had not returned to the ship. Unable to find him, they had, regrettably, roughed up Mr. Steinhoph, a German citizen living in the town whom they believed had encouraged Hasmann to desert. They had arrested no one. They had gone back to the ship empty handed, Hasmann had returned the next day of his own volition, and the *Panther* had set sail for Argentina, "unconscious," as U.S. chargé Charles Richardson reported, "of the gravity of the situation, which was just beginning to be noised abroad." [157]

The Brazilian account was different. It insisted indignantly that the men from the *Panther* had goose-stepped through the sleepy town alarming its peace-loving inhabitants, that they had knocked loudly and rudely on door after door, and that when they had finally found their prey—or at least an acquaintance of his—they had beaten him up and whisked him off on the *Panther* to Argentina. Whatever was the truth of the matter, Steinhoph was nowhere to be found. The press was in an uproar, and on 7 December a member of the Brazilian parliament gave a speech denouncing the *Panther*'s willful attack on Brazilian sovereignty. On the 15th, the government demanded Steinhoph's return and an official apology from Wilhelm II.[158]

In Berlin, the head of the Admiralstab, Wilhelm Büchsel, believed the account of his officer and counseled the kaiser that no apology was necessary.[159] But the Brazilians were already taking advantage of the situation. Rio-Branco cabled Nabuco on the 11th denouncing the "violences [*sic*] practiced in our land in the silence of the night by foreign troops." There is no evidence that Rio-Branco, a first-class diplomat and politician, was ever swayed by the talk of German designs on Brazil. He was happy to see Germans there, and he encouraged more to come. A year after the *Panther* incident, he wrote John Bassett Moore that he was "well satisfied" with the German immigrants to Brazil. At the time, however, he told Nabuco: "Try to provoke energetic Monroeist articles against the insult." He hoped to use U.S. suspicions of German intentions in Latin America to extract concessions from the Germans and, more important, to forge closer links with the United States.[160]

Nabuco, who was well liked and respected in Washington, relayed the Brazilian foreign ministry's displeasure with Germany to the State Department and granted interviews to the U.S. press. Unconcerned, like Rio-Branco, with a German threat to Brazil, he nonetheless gave the opposite impression. The *Washington Evening Star*, the *Chicago Tribune*, the *Washington Post*, the *Baltimore Sun*, and the *New York Times* took the bait, ran the story, and expressed their sympathy for Brazil. "What confronts us now is the peril of Berlin's swagger in the Western hemisphere," the *Post* warned.[161]

On 11 December, Root saw Ambassador Sternburg and discussed the *Panther*. The U.S. government was at that moment renegotiating its commercial treaty with Germany, which was due to expire on 1 March 1906; it faced an uphill battle in the Senate. Fully cognizant of this, Sternburg assured the secretary of state that Germany would offer any and all appropriate reparations. On the same day, Root informed Nabuco that he believed the incident would be "resolved without problem." Sternburg, aware of the growing American friendship with Brazil, next did what Nabuco had hoped: he wrote the Wilhelmstrasse that if Steinhoph had been arrested on Brazilian soil, "US public opinion would demand that the Reich extend an apology to the Brazilians. . . . If Germany had purposefully set out to damage her reputation in Washington at the very moment she needs the wholehearted support of the president, the cabinet and the Congress to improve her trade relations with the United States, she could not have come up with a more effective scheme than the *Panther* incident." [162]

On the 15th, Brazil registered a formal protest with the Wilhelmstrasse. The Brazilian minister in Berlin discussed the incident with the state secretary, Oswald von Richthofen; the undersecretary for foreign affairs, Otto von Mühlberg; and Vice Admiral Büchsel.[163] In the background, the Brazilian press was alleging that the incident had been planned by Germany to test the sensitivity of U.S. public opinion to an infringement of the Monroe Doctrine. The German annexation of southern Brazil, it warned, would follow.[164]

The *Panther* incident may have been petty, but it placed Berlin in a very awkward position. Büchsel had told the kaiser that Captain Saurma had done nothing wrong: he had arrested no one, and surely a German officer should be believed rather than a Brazilian diplomat. Bülow, however, urged Wilhelm to offer an apology. After receiving a report from Saurma admitting that members of his crew had forced their way into Brazilian homes in search of the deserter (but had arrested no one), the navy added its voice to Bülow's. (At the very moment the incident was unfolding in Brazil, Tirpitz was in the Reichstag arguing for a new naval bill that would introduce six large cruisers, and the government was under fire from the socialists for its ineptitude in foreign policy, particularly in Morocco.) On the 17th, therefore, to extinguish a potentially costly fire, Wilhelm II offered an apology to the government of Brazil for an incident he did not believe had occurred. Richthofen explained the apology to U.S. chargé Dodge: "Richthofen . . . [said that] the facts had been ascertained after some delay . . . and had shown that the seamen had exceeded their orders by knocking at doors and making a disturbance. He believed that it was a general custom of all nations to send men on shore to trace deserters quietly and try to bring them back. . . . The regret which the Imperial government had expressed to the Brazilian Government he hoped would end the matter. . . . I believe that the German Government is seriously annoyed that this incident should ever have occurred." [165]

The totally unexpected ensued. The *Herald*'s headline blared the story: "Kaiser's Apology Not Enough." Indeed, Brazil declared that the apology was inadequate and demanded an admission that the captain's order had been irregular and an assurance that the perpetrators would be brought to justice. Treutler, who forwarded the demand, commented that "any unbiased individual would have accepted the Kaiser's apology as adequate," but he nonetheless recommended making the changes the Brazilians wanted, adding that Rio-Branco's "political survival and that of the President" were at stake.[166]

The kaiser balked, but Bülow's counsel prevailed: on the 31st, Wilhelm II assured the Brazilian government that the guilty parties would be punished by a military court. He refused, however, to concede that Saurma's order to search for the deserter had been unusual; he admitted only that the crew had overstepped its orders. The kaiser assured the Brazilians that Steinhoph could not be delivered to the port authority because he had never been arrested. He then explained that the captain of the *Panther* had not intended to violate Brazilian sovereignty but only to locate a deserter. "In so doing he had followed general naval custom. . . . As the Brazilian government has long known, the Imperial German government considers the maintenance of good relations with Brazil, to which it is tied by numerous economic interests, to be a matter of great importance. To avoid any alteration in these relations, to strengthen the existing friendly relations, and also because our investigation has shown that the crew overstepped its orders . . . the German government expresses to the Brazilian government its sincere regret about the incident. The guilty will be tried before a military court."[167]

The apology was grudgingly accepted by Rio-Branco on 6 January, although he denied that Saurma had "followed general naval custom." The Germans were left to mutter about "Baron Rio-Branco, who, despite all the goodwill we have shown—and he has acknowledged—creates one difficulty after another."[168]

In a footnote to the episode, Steinhoph surfaced in Buenos Aires a few months later, claiming that he had never been arrested. He had left Itajaí, he explained, to avoid paying his hotel bill.[169]

Ernest Tonnelat's verdict on the *Panther* imbroglio, written in 1908, is apt: "The German government does not waste a single opportunity to reassure the United States."[170] Faced with a minor fracas, the Reich folded without a whimper. Nevertheless, Germany's relations with both Brazil and the United States were damaged. A year after the incident, a director of the HKG wrote, "The Brazilians are making a mountain out of a molehill. They have refused to accept our clarification of this incident that was in itself so insignificant and instead have hurled the grossest insults at us in their press." [171] And in the spring of 1906, Sternburg strongly advised the Wilhelmstrasse not to send the *Panther* on a visit to the United States.

> That the commander [of the *Panther*] has been changed [in January 1906] is totally irrelevant. . . . Such a visit would represent a danger to our economic interests. . . . [It would be] a "red flag." . . . The *Panther* incident has damaged German interests both with Congress and the executive. This was particularly evident during the Moroccan crisis . . . when a *Dutch* [the Americans presumably confusing Dutch for Deutsch, or German] man was proposed as customs officer for the port of Casablanca. The Americans immediately suspected that this was in fact an attempt by Germany to acquire the port as a base of operations against Brazil. When I mentioned Casablanca to the president, he immediately retorted, "Is it on the Atlantic?" . . . This proposal created deep distrust in Congress and caused the Senate to call Roosevelt's attention to the hidden aggressive designs of Germany in South America. . . . The *Panther* incident has breathed new life into the deep mistrust here of German policy in Latin America. It will take a long time to heal this freshly opened wound. [172]

The Brazilians and the Americans did not let the incident die because it was useful to both countries to emphasize their common stand against the German marauder. Sternburg was well aware of this. "The Panther incident must not be unwelcome to Roosevelt and Root," he wrote the Wilhelmstrasse. "It will help them develop their new policy toward Central and South America. I have a hint from the Chilean envoy here that they will try to exploit the incident to this end. 'The United States,' he said, 'is trying to impose a protectorate over South America. We don't want it because we are convinced that we have nothing to fear from Europe, while we do have something to fear from the United States. The *Panther* incident is now being used by the United States to impress upon the Latin American republics again and again that they face a dangerous threat from Europe.' " [173]

The basis for the fears of a German challenge to the Monroe Doctrine can readily be seen in Brazil. Germany's policy there presents a limiting case because it was in Brazil that Germany had the best cards. Germans were already there in large numbers, the Brazilian state was weak, and the U.S. Navy was all but impotent so far south. Furthermore, a vocal section of the German public was firmly behind an aggressive policy, and these comments were spread by the British, American, and Brazilian press. This repetition reverberated against the growing fleet and gave these pan-German dreams weight. It was easy for anxious Americans to fear the worst.

And yet, nothing happened. The Reich launched no attack on Brazil; it did nothing to destabilize the wobbly regime. It kept the struggling Hansa colony at arm's length, watching it collapse rather than actively helping it. Berlin not only failed to negotiate a trade treaty with Rio, but it actually raised the tariff on Brazilian coffee. It was meek and submissive in its handling of the *Panther* affair. All of this could be attributed to prudence. But the Reich did not even make the simple, risk-free gestures that would have supported *Deutschtum* in southern Brazil.

Thus there was a glaring disjunction between the image of German policy and the policy itself. This was not because German policy in Brazil was particularly opaque: U.S. diplomats in Brazil were well aware of the timidity of the Reich's policy and consistently punctured any notion of a German threat to the country. In 1903, the U.S. minister in Rio had written, "It is clear to me . . . that whatever may be the occasional dreams or hopes of the German people or Government with regard to a German colony in South America, there are so many difficulties of a fundamental sort in the way of the realization of such a scheme in Brazil that all well informed persons, and the German Government may be expected to be well informed, must see the futility of any such plans." [174] And Berlin's difficulties only increased with its deepening isolation on the Continent. Even the German navy acknowledged the ramifications. On 9 May 1906, Büchsel ordered that "detailed preparatory works for a war against the United States not be continued." [175] Likewise, by 1905, the General Board of the U.S. Navy had stopped discussing the German threat. But the perception persisted.

Perhaps this was because the image was useful. Six months after the *Panther* incident Secretary of State Elihu Root gave a speech at the Pan-American Conference in Rio. "We wish for no victories but those of peace," he declared. "For no territory except our own; for no sovereignty except the sovereignty over ourselves. . . . We neither claim nor desire any rights, or privileges, or powers that we do not freely concede to every American Republic. We wish to increase our prosperity, to expand our trade, to grow in wealth, in wisdom and in spirit . . . to help all friends to a common prosperity and a common growth, that we may all become greater and stronger together." [176]

The idea of a German threat helped him to say this. This is why it has had remarkable staying power, why President Woodrow Wilson referred to it to justify his interventionist policies, and why it is a persistent refrain in the scholarly literature to this day.[177]

4

The Dominance of the United States

Huerta, Wilson,
and Wilhelm

After the blockade of Venezuela, after the shelving of the war plans, after the *Panther* imbroglio in Brazil, what did the Germans do in Latin America? The dramatic incident, the magnet toward which one gravitates for an answer, is the Zimmermann telegram. This cable, sent to Mexico by the German foreign secretary, Arthur Zimmermann, on 16 January 1917, proposed an astonishing scheme to bog the United States down in a war with Mexico. The British intercepted, decoded, and gave Washington the cable, in which Zimmermann suggested to the Mexicans that the Reich (and possibly Japan) would support them if they launched a war to reclaim Texas, New Mexico, and Arizona. This played into the old fears of German intrigue in the Americas. It was seen by many at the time and since as the smoking gun, the proof of German infamy. "Zimmermann's proposal," writes historian Michael Meyer, "was not a bold and newly devised scheme but rather the climax of several years of intrigue."[1]

Policy is, however, a hodgepodge of cables, letters, marginalia, reminiscences. One can pull juicy quotes from the record to support almost any point of view. Policy is rarely simple or truly consistent. This is certainly true in relation to German policy toward Mexico in the early years of this century, when the Wilhelmstrasse tried to sail between the oft alarmist cries of its minister in Mexico, Rear Admiral Paul von Hintze, and the clamorous marginalia of the kaiser. The historian Friedrich Katz, who has written the only thorough, and widely cited, examination of German policy toward Mexico, looked at the Zimmermann telegram and worked backward, amassing evidence that it was the culmination of German intrigue in Mexico. Katz argues that in the decade before the war the Reich had consistently been angling for a strategic maneuver to advance its geopolitical aims. "The protection of German interests in Mexico was less important for Germany," Katz asserts, "than the utilization of that Latin American country in an increasingly complex game of international diplomacy."[2]

Buttressing this point of view is the assertion that German policy occupied a central position in the international politics of the Mexican Revolution. Dana Munro proclaimed, for example, "One sinister aspect of the Mexican problem was the German effort to take advantage of the [Mexican] civil wars to make trouble for the United States." In a more recent book, Reinhard Doerries sums up the viewpoint well: "It is hardly surprising that it was particularly in Latin America where Berlin and Washington would collide. . . . America's pride was particularly vulnerable in all questions concerning Mexico. . . . Thus it was not without reason that Mexico should play a significant role in the German-American confrontation before and during the First World War." This is not only the view of many historians. Secretary of State Robert Lansing wrote in 1917 that there had been two reasons for Wilson's caution in Mexico: "military unpreparedness" and the fear of playing into Berlin's hands.[3]

It is an explanation that puts forth a pattern crystallized around three pillars: Diederichs in Manila, the blockade of Venezuela, and the infamous telegram. There were no dramatic countervailing examples—nothing to offset the image of Germany as the jackal—and so the image stuck.

The advocates of this interpretation are able to find quotations from the record before the outbreak of war in Europe—but not facts—to support their point of view. Berlin's policy was indeed opportunistic—in Manila, Brazil, and Venezuela—but when easy opportunity did not present itself, Berlin was cautious and deferential: hardly the stuff of imperialism on the march. Was it different in Mexico? In order to answer this question and assess whether the Zimmermann telegram was the culmination of years of intrigue or an opportunistic ploy of wartime, it is necessary to look at German policy in Mexico in the crucial years before the outbreak of the First World War.

The Reich began developing economic interests in Mexico in the late nineteenth century. Its trade with Mexico, including its arms trade, was modest in comparison with U.S. and English involvement. Strategically, Berlin—cognizant of U.S. hegemony in the region—pursued an even milder policy toward Mexico than it had earlier toward Venezuela and Brazil. In 1911, Secretary of State Alfred von Kiderlen-Wächter defined German policy in Mexico precisely: "to defend German interests energetically, but, aside from that, to do everything we can to keep a low profile."[4] The difficulty of maintaining this policy is shown in an analysis of the year and a half of General Victoriano

Huerta's rule in Mexico (February 1913 to July 1914). The central problem for the Europeans during the Huerta period was that the U.S. failure to recognize the de facto president undermined their attempt to protect their interests in Mexico. The Wilson administration gave the Europeans reason to be frustrated and hostile. Thus, in determining whether Berlin's policy toward Mexico was indeed part of an increasingly complex game of international anti-American intrigue, it is interesting to look at how it dealt with the slow, irritating evolution of Washington's policy toward Huerta.

Germans in Mexico

There were approximately four thousand Germans living in Mexico in 1913, more than half of whom lived in Mexico City. It was a community that had more than doubled since the turn of the century, and by 1913 it was the third-largest European group. As the U.S. ambassador, Henry Lane Wilson, was reported to have said, "The others [all foreign representatives other than the Americans, English, German, and, occasionally, the French] really did not matter." The German community was dwarfed, however, by the American community of about forty thousand.[5]

This overwhelming American presence colors any assessment of German economic ties with Mexico. Most of Germany's financial interest in Mexico was in trade and small businesses (breweries and coffee farms), not capital investment; the German community was neither financially significant nor politically powerful. Although Mexico was Germany's fourth-largest trading partner in Latin America, German-Mexican trade was minor compared with American-Mexican trade. For example, Germany supplied more than 12 percent of Mexico's imports (with a total value of forty-eight million Reichsmarks), a not insubstantial share. The United States, however, supplied 55 percent. German exports to Mexico were diversified; no sector of the German economy was dependent on the Mexican market. Mexico ranked a mere twentieth in the Reich's export markets, absorbing a bare 1 percent of Germany's exports. As for the purchasing of Mexican products, the dominance of the United States was even more pronounced: it took more than 75 percent of Mexico's total exports, and Germany took only 4 percent. One aspect of German trade with Mexico thrived at the turn of the century: the Hamburg American Shipping Line (Hapag) was the most frequent carrier to Mexican ports. The Mexican carrying trade, however, was not key to the huge company's financial well-being.[6]

Germany had a favorable balance of trade with Mexico: its imports were about half as valuable as its exports. These imports included nothing of strategic significance: the German navy avoided Mexican oil, realizing early that its supply could not be guaranteed in wartime.[7]

The arms trade, which was an important component of German trade with some Latin American countries (notably Argentina and Chile), was not a significant factor in Mexico; France had cornered that market. Berlin itself fumbled the opportunity to boost arms sales when it failed to respond positively to a Mexican request in 1906 for German military instructors to train the Mexican army. Berlin hesitated, fearful that such a policy would hurt its relationship with the United States and threaten civil peace in Mexico by strengthening the Mexican army and draining scarce resources from the treasury. In an attempt to keep French military instructors out, Germany advised the Mexicans to improve their army without any foreign help, and in 1908 Mexico withdrew the request for German training. This directly contradicts Doerries's assertion that "Germany, which had been trying for years to gain a larger share of military and economic influence in Mexico, also wanted to participate in Mexican affairs and at least be considered an equal partner among the big nations concerned."[8]

There is no evidence that Berlin was pursuing a policy—concerted or feeble—to expand its trade with Mexico. Even Katz admits that this trade did not present a challenge to American influence. He argues, however, that it did lay the foundation for such a challenge.[9] But was such a challenge planned? Several observations are relevant. First, as in Brazil (and elsewhere in Latin America), German trade with Mexico was the product of private enterprise, not of government schemes. Second, the Reich's attitude toward this trade was consistent: with the proviso that trade with Mexico was not of great importance to the men at the Wilhelmstrasse, the more the better, *if the political costs were low*. The Germans who traded with Mexico did not wield political influence in Berlin; the Wilhelmstrasse was not motivated to please them, and it was convinced that the expansion of trade with Mexico was not worth disturbing relations with the United States. This was the consistent message.[10]

The very same caution and absence of great concern are seen, as it was in Brazil, in the Reich's lack of support for German banks in Mexico. The first German bank in Mexico was established in the 1870s, but it was not until the turn of the century that the major German banks followed suit. The German bankers faced a market that was already serviced by American and English banks, and rather than trying to compete, they frequently entered on the backs of American banks, with which they tended to maintain close cooperation. The point is obvious: these bankers were capitalists. Their goals were economic, not political. Thus they would ally themselves with an American bank if it improved the bottom line. For the same reason, they would compete with or undermine German banks or traders in Mexico. The story of the Deutsche Bank is illustrative. In 1904, it joined the U.S. Speyer group to form a bank in which the latter was in control of management. The Deutsche Bank turned a deaf ear to the protestations of the Wilhelmstrasse. Further, it helped the Speyer group dislodge the venerable German Bleichröder Bank from the Mexican bond market. Two years later the German chargé in Mexico complained to the Wilhelmstrasse about the bankers' behavior. They should finance German businesses, he wrote. They should help German traders. They should get involved with Mexican government finances. But none of this was done. The chargé's suggestions received no response, and the bankers continued to wheel and deal independent of the influence or the desires of the Wilhelmstrasse.[11]

The same German laws that restricted capital investment in Brazil limited the Reich's banks from investing in Mexico. Furthermore, the competition in Mexico, where Germany was vying against well-established American, British, and (to a lesser extent) French banks, was much more rigorous. Germans did not invest in Mexican raw materials and had only a minor interest in Mexican railroads. Their investment in Mexico was concentrated in the public debt and constituted only 2–3 percent of total German capital investment abroad and no more than 6½ percent of total investment in Mexico; U.S. companies, on the other hand, controlled 70 percent.[12]

German interests in Mexico were therefore modest, in absolute and in relative terms. They were, in many ways, parallel to the Reich's interests in other Latin American countries, but with one major difference: in Mexico, U.S. hegemony was already established.

Furthermore, the customary lack of coordination between Wilhelm and his minions, between the Wilhelmstrasse and the banks, between the bankers and the traders, was exacerbated in Mexico by the chaos of revolution. The Germans in Mexico, as in Brazil, were not a monolithic group, pulling together for the old homeland. The bankers, the traders, and the Wilhelmstrasse were often at cross purposes, and their disagreements were exacerbated by the power of the German minister. Hintze was a commanding presence in Mexico City. In a bizarre twist of fate, he had been Admiral Diederichs's flag lieutenant at Manila. Although Hintze was deeply critical of U.S. policy, the wife of the American chargé sketched him in respectful tones: "The leit-motiv of his existence, the root of every thought and act, was love of country and of emperor. . . . He was entirely devoted to duty, of great industry. . . . As was inevitable, he had a profound contempt for Latin-American methods of procedure. . . . He had much personal dignity." A German captain reported from Veracruz, "He is respected and loved among the Germans [in Mexico], and he is appreciated by the Mexican authorities and the diplomatic community because of his talent, intelligence, and tact. He is one of the most important personalities in Mexico, one of the few who can wield influence over the present [Huerta] government." Hintze was a powerful voice in the formulation of German policy in Mexico, but in March 1913 he fell seriously ill, and the much less gifted chargé d'affaires, Rudolf Kardorff, stood in until late August. The Wilhelmstrasse frequently overrode the suggestions of both diplomats in the interest of maintaining harmony with the United States.[13]

The Rise of Huerta

In September 1910, the centenary of the Hidalgo Rebellion (considered the beginning of Mexico's independence from Spain) was celebrated with great fanfare. "Almost every government in the world was represented by delegates with sonorous titles who came thither with trains and suites and participated in the festivities for the better part of a month," the American ambassador recalled. "There were banquets and celebrations and balls and ceremonies in fatiguing succession." The United States sent a large delegation of senators, representatives, judges, and lawyers.[14] The kaiser's brother, Prince Heinrich, led the German delegation.

The pomp and fanfare, however, masked a crumbling regime. The long dictatorship of Porfirio Díaz was about to end. During his reign, rapid change had come to Mexico: railroads, oil, trade. By 1910 discontentment roiled in the provinces bordering the United States and around Mexico City, and on 14 May 1911, in a surprising display of people power, the dictator was ousted. The rebellion had crystallized around a most unlikely leader: Francisco I. Madero, an idealistic and dogged patriot from a wealthy family. In November, he became president of a country still riven with rebellion: Emiliano Zapata waving the banner of land reform in Morelos; Pancho Villa challenging the haciendas in the north; Victoriano Huerta leading men north of the capital. Thrust into the hot seat, Madero, a reformer and poet, compromised and hesitated. He appointed Huerta to lead an army division and urged Zapata and Villa to be patient. He was unable to unite the rebel factions and calm his country.[15]

Initially, foreign businessmen and diplomats in Mexico were sanguine about the rise of Madero. The new president came from a wealthy family; he would rule, presumably, like the dictators of old. Furthermore, the Germans were reassured by the fact that a German firm, the Deutsch-Südamerikanische Bank, enjoyed a close relationship with him.[16]

The foreigners' optimism, however, soon faded. As it became clear that Madero's victory had failed to quell the rebellions bubbling around the countryside, the foreign community was alarmed. One American diplomat described him as "a little man . . . overwhelmed by his troubles," while the U.S. Army chief of staff explained rather sardonically, "Madero was a dreamer, who now and then woke up to do some act of vigor, and then relapsed into his slumber." Hintze bluntly articulated the foreigners' position: "The cardinal error lies in his [Madero's] . . . belief that he can rule the Mexican people as one would rule one of the more advanced Germanic nations. This raw people of half savages without religion, with its small ruling stratum of superficially civilized mestizos can live with no regime other than enlightened despotism." (To which Wilhelm appended in the margin, "Right!") [17]

The foreigners in Mexico, therefore, were not displeased when, in February 1913, General Huerta—"a 'unique zoölogical type' . . . bronzed, flat-nosed . . . with restless eyes and big glasses," according to the wife of the American chargé [18]—unceremoniously removed Madero, forever. "A single bullet, in the back of the head, was his portion," Woodrow Wilson's special envoy wrote. "The hair was singed." [19]

Huerta declared himself provisional president and promised that presidential elections would be held in October. His time in office was marked by two unresolved crises that fed on each other: he could neither pacify Mexico nor placate the United States. German policy was buffeted by these twin failures. Germany was trying to dance in step with America, but it was tripped up by the fact that Woodrow Wilson was dancing a new, unpredictable, and, to Germany, utterly incomprehensible dance.

Recognition

The United States had been a firm supporter of Porfirio Díaz. Washington had appreciated his firm hand, his gracious welcome of U.S. companies, and the stability he had imposed on his vast country. In the early 1900s, however, Díaz had begun to look on Mexico's increasing dependence on the United States with a wary eye. He had turned to the French, English, and Germans to offset the growing influence of the United States. (After its defeat of Russia in 1905, Japan had been added to the list of possible counterweights.) [20] It was a complicated and dangerous game: it cost the old dictator the unconditional support of the United States and contributed to his downfall.

When Díaz sailed into exile, American policy toward Mexico, still gripped with revolution, became more tentative. President William Howard Taft recognized Madero but was increasingly disenchanted with him. "The Americans liked Madero as long as he did what they wanted," Hintze observed. "As soon as he expressed his independence, the American ambassador began to orchestrate the movement against him." Indeed, Lane Wilson was instrumental in the downfall of the "mystic revolutionary" and was midwife to the rise of Huerta. He urged on the plotters, openly assisted them during the confusing ten days of the coup, and promised U.S. recognition of their government. "I know—because I was there," Hintze wrote, "that Huerta would not have dared launch the coup without the encouragement and promises of [Lane] Wilson. . . . For a while, Huerta was just the tool of Ambassador Wilson, who was the real ruler of Mexico." Hintze, who supported the removal of Madero and was frequently at Lane Wilson's side as the American arranged the coup, urged the ambassador to extract a guarantee from Huerta for the safety of Madero and his family.[21]

Taft had been inclined to recognize Huerta as the de facto president of Mexico; the decision would be made, the secretary of state explained to Ambassador Wilson, "in light of the usual tests applied to such cases."[22] In the meantime, Huerta could be expected to be particularly eager to settle outstanding claims. Furthermore, when Huerta had launched his coup, Taft was a lame duck, and he took no action on the recognition question before Woodrow Wilson assumed the presidency on 4 March. "The country [the United States] is at present standing between two administrations, dissatisfied with the past and uncertain of the future," the British ambassador in Washington, Lord James Bryce, effused. "All eyes are turned away from the derelict hulk to the vessel bounding gaily over the billows with sails full set, of whose captain and crew little is yet known."[23]

Little was yet known, but there was no indication that the new administration would break with the American and European precedent of recognizing a ruler who appeared to be in charge. It was unlikely, Bryce assured London in February, "that the views of a Democratic Administration will differ materially from those of that now in office." Later that month Lane Wilson attended the first formal reception given by the Huerta government, an act that implied recognition. "The Government of the United States having originally set itself up by revolution has always acted upon the de facto principle," the counselor to the State Department wrote in May. "We regard governments as existing or as not existing. We do not require them to be chosen by popular vote. We look simply to the fact of the existence of the government and to its ability and inclination to discharge the national obligations."[24]

Woodrow Wilson came into office thoroughly ignorant of Mexico, and he compounded his difficulties by indiscriminately purging the State Department of its small band of Latin American experts.[25] His secretary of state, William Jennings Bryan, had been appointed to co-opt a powerful rival and appease his influential supporters; he had little knowledge of foreign affairs. "Mr. Bryan,

I incline to think," Bryce wrote soon after the inauguration, "culls his history from the morning papers, cursorily read over his coffee and rolls. . . . He is a rhetorician of a sentimental type, whose life has been spent on platforms and in addressing young mens' Christian associations." Months later, Bryce's successor commented that Bryan "thinks that he decided a matter whenever he has said something clever about it. . . . It is writing on ice to talk to him."[26]

Both the new president and the secretary of state seem to have been genuinely shocked by the assassination of Madero, an event that took place two days after Huerta's coup and less than a fortnight before Wilson's inauguration. The president had a visceral aversion to embracing a leader who had consolidated power through such unsavory—and un-American—means. "I will not recognize a nation of butchers," Wilson is reported to have exclaimed. Thus, when he received Huerta's traditional congratulatory letter upon his inauguration, he sidestepped the delicate problem of how to address him in his formal reply (calling him "President" would have implied recognition) by sending it simply to "General V. Huerta, Mexico City, Mexico."[27]

On 12 March Wilson issued a nebulous statement about the Americas and orderly government, but his assertion that "just governments always rest upon the consent of the governed" seemed at the time to be a rhetorical flourish, not a foreshadowing of his Mexico policy. U.S. policy toward Mexico was still unformulated on 13 March when German ambassador Count Johann von Bernstorff had his first official meeting with the new secretary of state. The subject arose at virtually every press conference in the spring of 1913. "What about the recognition of Mexico?" a journalist asked on 11 April. "Well, I don't know. We don't decide that—that is decided between brawls!" the president bantered. His first unsolicited utterance about recognition was delivered a day later, and it was of no help. The decision, he explained to the press, was "some way off. . . . The *de facto* Government of Mexico would be recognized as the Provisional Government when it had worked out the problem now before it—the establishment of peace—and demonstrated to the world that it is capable of running the republic."[28]

The failure of the United States either to extend recognition promptly or to explain its policy made what was ordinarily a simple proposition awkward for the Europeans. Peter Calvert, who has written a very careful examination of the issue, states, "A lead from Washington might have been ignored by the European powers, but it could not have been overlooked. But there was no lead; further official statements all gave the impression that the United States did intend to recognize Huerta, but not just yet." It was very difficult for the Europeans to protect their interests in Mexico without recognizing the de

"How about recognition? Mexico: 'Put 'er there, neighbor.'" General Huerta, depicted as the butcher of Mexico, begs Woodrow Wilson to recognize his government. (*New York Globe*; reprinted in *Literary Digest* [8 March 1913])

facto government. While the Mexicans might, albeit reluctantly, acknowledge the U.S. representative in Mexico City in the absence of U.S. recognition, the European governments could not count on such privileged treatment. In order to protect their interests in Mexico, they had to deal with a recognized government. Furthermore, until the new regime was recognized by the United States, its future would be uncertain. "It is general opinion here," the *New York Times* correspondent wrote from Mexico City, "that the fate of the existing administration hangs on American recognition." The European powers, who relied on Washington to help protect their citizens in Mexico, needed to avoid the exposure of having extended recognition to a doomed president.

On the other hand, prolonged stalling was uncomfortable as well, because business interests of all nationalities, including American, were clamoring for their governments to stabilize the situation by extending recognition.[29]

Most German businessmen in Mexico joined the chorus, and Chargé Kardorff immediately urged Berlin to recognize the general. "Huerta has done what no one else has managed to do for months: he has instilled confidence." These businessmen were convinced that Huerta was the only man who could restore order and that access to foreign loans—largely contingent on recognition—would greatly help him to do so.[30]

The Wilhelmstrasse turned a deaf ear to the entreaties of Kardorff and the German community. It was not sure immediately after the coup that Huerta had effectively consolidated power. Further, because of the American ambassador's prominent role in Huerta's rise, Berlin was initially worried that the general might turn out to be Washington's puppet. Soon these fears were compounded by worries that, without U.S. recognition, Huerta would be unable to quell the opposition that mushroomed almost immediately around him. Beyond customary diplomatic caution, however, the Wilhelmstrasse was stymied by its uncertainty about U.S. policy. Berlin wanted to avoid drawing attention to German policy; it wanted to avoid any appearance that an isolated Germany was backing Huerta.[31]

The Germans were not simply uninformed about U.S. policy: they were also irritated and confused. The clues they could glean about Wilson's likely policy were contradictory. On the one hand, there was every reason to expect that the United States would recognize the de facto president promptly. The U.S. ambassador was, after all, Huerta's biggest supporter. Furthermore, precedent demanded recognition, even Wilsonian precedent: in March 1913, Wilson had recognized the de facto Chinese government before the Europeans had done so. On the other hand, as the days passed, it was difficult not to wonder what was causing the delay.[32]

As in Venezuela, so in Mexico: it was the protective shield of England that enabled Berlin to dare to differ with the United States. Britain's substantial financial interests in Mexico had an important national security dimension. In the throes of the naval arms race, the British navy was converting from coal- to oil-fired engines, and British companies were developing the rich Mexican oil fields. Therefore, once its minister was confident that the Huerta government was stable, London decided that it could dally no longer, and on 1 April it announced that it would recognize Huerta as the provisional president. (Recognition was officially extended on 3 May 1913.)[33] The Foreign Office was concerned about U.S. policy but felt compelled to regularize its relations with Mexico. "Our interests in Mexico are so big that I think we should take our own line without making it dependent upon that of other Governments," Foreign Secretary Sir Edward Grey advised. "There could be no question of our intervening in Mexico," he later explained, "and we had therefore to recognise the only Government with which we could deal when it had any prospect of giving order and security." When informed of Britain's decision, Bryan merely commented that the United States "would at any rate wait some while longer before recognizing General Huerta's government." The president was even more deadpan. "Mr. President," a journalist asked at a press conference on 18 April, "is there any feeling because the British government has recognized the provisional government of Mexico?" The president replied laconically, "There is no feeling at all."[34]

This gave the other European governments heart: they would be buffered by England, and, in any case, the signs seemed to be pointing toward U.S. recognition of Mexico's de facto president. In May, a Mexican columnist wrote, "The United States *has* really recognized us. . . . It is merely that President Wilson is coy. . . . It is sufficient that the American ambassador remains at his post in this capital and that he has attended the official ceremonies . . . for it to be considered that, *de facto*, there has been the recognition . . . and that that recognition will be reinforced . . . by a more or less explicit declaration, when the occasion arises." Within weeks, Spain, France, Austria-Hungary, and Belgium followed England's lead.[35]

Finally, in mid-May, Berlin, hard pressed by the Germans in Mexico, recognized Huerta. The delay of almost three months, caused in part by uncertainty in Mexico and normal bureaucratic sluggishness, also reflects the Wilhelm-strasse's sensitivity to American opprobrium. Berlin was not sure that the United States would object—in fact, the signals were that it would not—but it was loath to take any risks; it waited until it was sure it would not be in the front line before making any move.[36] Although Wilson would later criticize the countries that recognized Huerta, the careful counselor to the State Department, John Bassett Moore, acknowledged, "There is nothing in the record to show that the governments that recognized the [Huerta] administration . . . in May, June, and July last felt that they were doing anything unusual, or that they were actuated by any other design than that of recognizing, in conformity with practice, what appeared to them to be the only governmental authority holding out the prospect of being able to re-establish order in the country. Nor had the United States said anything to indicate to them that it entertained a different view of their conduct."[37]

And Lane Wilson commented, after he had been recalled from Mexico City, "That Great Britain was moved to recognition by its desire to assist in the restoration of order is most likely true, and I believe that this factor

"His best platform manner. Secretary Bryan: 'I may say I am most annoyed, and if you do not immediately reform I hesitate to say what I may not be inclined to decide perhaps.'" Secretary of State William Jennings Bryan's inability to decide whether to recognize Huerta was amusing to some but irritating to European governments that had difficulty protecting their interests in Mexico while the Wilson administration dithered. (*Montreal Herald*; reprinted in *Literary Digest* [28 March 1914])

was the determining one with all Governments which followed the example of Great Britain. . . . The Governments of the other European powers recognized the Mexican Provisional Government . . . after waiting vainly for the recognition of the Government of the United States, which they universally thought should be accorded." [38]

President Wilson, however, kept his own counsel: his ambassador in Mexico was, the *Herald*'s correspondent in Mexico City wrote, "absolutely in the dark regarding Washington's policy." The question of recognition was discussed at length in a cabinet meeting on 23 May. According to the secretary of the navy, "the majority sentiment was against recognition," but no policy was announced. Nor was Congress consulted. Three days later the president quipped to a journalist who had inquired, once again, about recognition, "Oh, well, I don't permit myself fast to make up my mind about the changing scene."[39]

Midsummer Doldrums

European recognition of Huerta did not stabilize the turmoil in Mexico. Certainly a great deal of the unrest was attributable to strictly Mexican factors, but the continuing uncertainty about U.S. policy toward the country did not help.

The most serious repercussion for Huerta of Washington's lack of recognition was financial: it made it difficult for Mexico to negotiate international loans and, therefore, suppress the rebellion. Wilson had told Bryan to ask the French and British ambassadors to urge their governments not to give official approval to private loans made to Huerta by their subjects. Both governments assured the president that no such approval had been or would be given. "Mexico . . . is to-day not unlike a volcano," the *Herald* correspondent in Mexico City wrote, "which will remain inactive only as long as gold pours into the mouth of its consuming crater."[40]

In June 1913, French, British, American, and German bankers tried to forestall the eruption by financing a $100 million loan to the regime. American bankers carried the bulk of the loan, with three of the most important German banks—Deutsche, Bleichröder, and Dresdner—contributing 20 percent. All the bankers were motivated, unremarkably, by self-interest: Mexico was too big to fail. (There were reports that the Mexican National Railway, which was backed by a British, American, and German consortium, would go into receivership if it did not get funds to pay its creditors on 1 June.) Furthermore, as the *New York Times* observed, "The security will be of an exceptionally favorable character." Less than $30 million was actually disbursed, and most of it went to debt repayment, discounts, and charges. (Twenty-five million dollars was paid to Speyer & Company, $625,000 to Mexican banks, and $625,000 in discounts and charges.) As a German journalist commented, "In private life, we would call it extortion." Despite these favorable terms, the German bankers wanted to minimize their risk further by floating bond issues of the loan on the German stock exchange. The German government, however, prohibited the issuance of the bonds. "Now that the Mexican loan has been completed, largely through the exertions of American financiers," the *New York Times* editorialized, "the reproach cast upon this country and its people by many Mexicans and American citizens interested in Mexican business is removed."[41]

There was no response to the loan from Washington. The summer of 1913 was a period of stalling in America's Mexico policy. Wilson was convinced that an election would cure Mexico's ills, and he searched for a strategy to enable one to be held. On 14 June, he drafted a letter to Lane Wilson explaining that because of the Mexican people's "fundamental lack of confidence in the good faith of those in control at Mexico City," the U.S. government called for early, free elections in which Huerta would not be a candidate. But despite the repeated requests for edification from European capitals and from the U.S. embassy in Mexico, Wilson decided not to send the letter to anyone, not even Lane Wilson, who was left dangling in Mexico City. By midsummer, the administration's policy was still undefined, and President Wilson's most telling comment on the situation was, "The trouble is that we don't know what is going on in Mexico."[42]

Wilson did not know what was going on because he did not trust his sources. Much of the American business community in Mexico, while sympathetic to Huerta, had come to the conclusion that since Washington seemed unwilling to recognize him, Huerta would be unable to create the stability they sought and therefore U.S. intervention was necessary. Lane Wilson, on the other hand, who was in the awkward position of being ambassador to an unrecognized government, stood by Huerta, openly blamed the Democratic administration's failure to recognize him for his difficulties in establishing order throughout Mexico, and called for immediate recognition of the de facto president.[43] This led Secretary of the Navy Josephus Daniels to blast Lane Wilson as a "spokesman of exploiters." This was the red flag for the progressive Woodrow Wilson, whose campaign rhetoric had excoriated his Republican predecessor's Dollar Diplomacy as crass and sinister. Lane Wilson could not be trusted. Therefore, the president chose to rely primarily on his preferred method of dealing with trouble spots: personal agents. Lane Wilson was disgusted. "It may easily be imagined how embarrassing it was to me and how much it interfered with the usefulness of my work," he recalled, "to have two secret agents of my own government proclaiming up and down the highways of Mexico that they were political representatives of our government. . . . It well illustrates the loose and inadequate hands into which the conduct of our foreign affairs had fallen." Lane Wilson was right to be suspicious. One of the agents sent to Mexico, William Bayard Hale, was unstinting in his criticism of the ambassador and clearly played a key role in his recall. The personal agents kept control firmly in the president's hands. "There is only one person who knows what the policy of the United States is towards Mexico," the British ambassador in Washington wrote, "and that person is the President. He takes advice from no one."[44]

Lane Wilson was irritated and unrepentant. If the president continued to refuse to recognize Huerta, he told his British counterpart in May, "he [Lane Wilson] would put pressure on his own Government by sending in his resignation. They would be unwilling to leave the embassy in the hands of a chargé d'affaires, and it would be impossible, without recognition, for a new Ambassador to take up the post."[45]

The ambassador was right on the second count, wrong on the first. In mid-July he was recalled, as a result of revelations of his role in Madero's death and the president's growing distrust of his close ties to Huerta.[46] The upshot was that the administration's policy, which was already obscure, soon lacked all semblance of continuity.

Although Lane Wilson had been correct in assuming that Washington would not appoint a new ambassador to Mexico, he had been wrong in believing that the president would be unwilling to leave the embassy in the hands of Nelson O'Shaughnessy as chargé d'affaires. The president had barely more confidence in O'Shaughnessy, who had been first secretary for only four months and who was a strong supporter of Huerta, than he had had in Lane Wilson, but this was irrelevant given his continuing reliance on personal agents.

At the same time that Lane Wilson was recalled, several key German banks in Mexico decided that stability—which meant, for them, preventing the victory of the revolutionaries, who had declared that they would not honor Mexico's debts—was worth almost any cost. Thus, barely three months after they had urged the Reich to recognize Huerta, these German bankers told Gottlieb von Jagow, the minister of foreign affairs, that the "only practical solution" was U.S. intervention, even though this would surely increase the power of the United States.[47]

The European ministers in Mexico were also worried, in part about the security of their nationals in Mexico and in part about the security of the European banks that had participated in Mexican loans, but they sought a less drastic solution than the German bankers. They met at the British legation in July and decided to send their governments an identical note asking that they instruct their representatives in Washington to urge the United States to change its policy. "We believe that present situation is largely the result of reluctance of United States Government to recognise the present administration or to exercise any influence in the course of events in this country," they cabled.[48]

The Wilhelmstrasse's response was guarded. "German Government are anxious to make proposed representations at Washington *provided that Her Majesty's Government will do so*," the earl of Granville cabled from the British embassy in Berlin.[49] But Her Majesty's Government feared that "anything like joint European action would probably raise a storm" in the United States, and so Whitehall decided that it would be preferable for each of the European powers to talk informally to the U.S. ambassador posted to their country. Granville promptly wrote the Foreign Office: "Herr von Jagow asked me to report to you" that Arthur Zimmermann, undersecretary of state, "had taken the first opportunity of urging in an unofficial manner [to the U.S. ambassador in Berlin], the recognition by America of the Mexican government, in order to show how completely in accord he was with your views on the subject." [50]

Word of the European initiative leaked to the U.S. press, which reported that Britain, France, Italy, Spain, and Belgium had made informal inquiries of the United States. "The German diplomatic representative in Mexico City, it was learned," the *New York Times* reported, counterfactually, "declined to join in the representations of his European colleagues." The paper later restated its erroneous report: "The German Government has declined to use its influence at Washington to cause the United States to recognize Huerta. Neither has the Government submitted to the United States the plea of the German colony in Mexico for the recognition of the provisional Government." Foreign Secretary Grey, immediately suspecting that the Germans were manipulating the U.S. press, delivered a scarcely veiled threat. "If there is any attempt to make capital for Germany in the American press at our expense," he wrote the British ambassador in Washington, "you might tell [the] German ambassador . . . that I should have to make some statement to correct wrong impressions." [51]

The *Herald* urged that the initiative "be given the gravest consideration in Washington." The unflappable *New York Times*, however, said it was "not to be regarded as a very significant incident," and indeed, it was not: Washington did not budge. [52] The president dismissed the whole episode in a press conference on 17 July: "It has been said . . . that foreign governments are making representations which constitute a pressure on this government. Now, that isn't true. In the most informal way possible, they have conveyed to us the impressions as to the situation on the part of their representatives in the City of Mexico, which, you see, is a very different matter. And, if I may say so, in entire confidence, I think that one or two of their representatives in Mexico City are very excitable and unwise gentlemen." [53] And that was the end of it. Germany had followed England's lead, there had been a glimmer of European unity, and it had come crashing down: it had strained Anglo-German relations and had no visible impact on Washington.

The United States continued, doggedly, to pursue its vague and destabilizing policy in Mexico. But Washington had no intention of allowing the Europeans to police Mexico, and the Europeans knew it. Wilson's dallying left the Europeans frustrated and hamstrung: on the one hand, it fomented rebellion and threatened their interests, and on the other, it prevented them from protecting their interests themselves. Furthermore, no one could be sure what Washington's policy was. The administration's lack of response to the international loan to Huerta negotiated in June, and particularly to the participation of U.S. bankers in it, seemed to indicate a rather calm attitude. And the fact that Wilson did not break diplomatic relations with Mexico implied that he intended, ultimately, to recognize Huerta, for breaking diplomatic relations would have been the most acceptable way to have signaled strong displeasure. The president, however, was not sending signals; he was just keeping channels open so as to maintain control.

Lind's Mission

Control depends on information. For information about Mexico, Wilson relied on personal agents. His first emissary after the departure of Lane Wilson was John Lind, former governor of Minnesota and a personal friend of Bryan's, who left for Mexico in early August 1913. "Few envoys in history have ever undertaken a more quixotic mission or one more surely doomed to failure," Arthur Link has observed. Lind knew nothing of Mexico and spoke not a word of Spanish. "What peculiar qualifications Mr. Lind may possess for the duty intrusted [sic] to him it is not easy to determine from the record of his public service," the *New York Herald* noted dryly. "It would be difficult to imagine a more inept or unsuitable Envoy," the British chargé in Mexico City declared. "He was reared in the strictest tenets of the Calvinist faith, and regards the Catholic Church as the whore of Babylon. The ways and customs of the Mexicans, irregular and perhaps reprehensible as they may be, are to him anathema, and he looks for real American ideals, cleanliness, morality, and hygiene, in the success of . . . [the] revolution." Lind himself seemed to confirm this judgment. "I have only this to say that when you are dealing with a people whose actions are neither measured or controlled by the standards to which we are accustomed it is difficult to analyze a situation. . . . Politically, at least, the Mexicans have no standards. They seem more like children than men. The only motives that I can discern in their political action is [sic] *appetite* and *vanity*." Lind's only "praise" was revealing: "The potential capacity of development [of the Indians of southern Mexico] does not seem to be limited as is the case with the American Negro." [54]

In August, prior to Lind's departure—and prior to sending the powers any explanation of his policy toward Mexico—Wilson sent a circular note to the Europeans asking them to tell their representatives in Mexico to advise Huerta to give "very serious consideration to any suggestions this Government [represented by Lind] may make." Washington did not, however, grace the Europeans with a description of the suggestions. "The contents of this communication [that Lind would deliver to Huerta] will be made known to you when it is ready," the note informed the startled foreign ministers of the great powers.[55]

Besides the affront, the request put the Europeans in a bind. Sir Edward Grey said, with characteristic discretion, that he "had felt some delicacy when the United States had asked us . . . to use our influence with Huerta to smooth the path of Mr. Lind." And Sir Cecil Spring-Rice, the English ambassador in Washington, declared, clearly displaying some pique, "We cannot advise Huerta to quit because the President doesn't like him." The British, and the other Europeans, did not want Huerta to hold them responsible for proposals that might offend him.[56] Spain and Russia politely refused to do Washington's bidding, but Germany and England—revealing the distance they were willing to travel to accommodate America—decided to oblige. German foreign secretary Jagow instructed Kardorff to put in a good word with the general. The American chargé in Berlin expressed "his full appreciation" to the Wilhelmstrasse that Kardorff would be told "to confer with General Huerta and to urge upon the latter that he give very serious consideration to such suggestions as the Government of the United States might make towards bringing about a restoration of peace in Mexico." The touchiness of the kaiser on the point is evident in his marginal comment: the "very serious" in the letter is underlined in pencil and on the side is written, "Not quite so, only listen!"[57] The British also approached Huerta on Washington's behalf. "I explained that . . . [we] could . . . tell Huerta," Spring-Rice wrote Grey, "that it would be against his interest to be rude to the President's representative." The U.S. press gave the British credit for persuading Huerta to receive Lind and at no point mentioned the German role.[58]

When the Germans learned the content of Lind's proposals, leaked to the press on 10 August, they were alarmed. Lind called for an immediate ceasefire, followed by elections in which Huerta would not be a candidate, and an assurance that all parties would abide by the results of the election.[59] "In plain language, President Wilson asks the Mexican government to sign its own death warrant and Provisional President Huerta to decapitate himself," *Le Temps* of Paris asserted. The British Foreign Office considered Wilson's insistence on elections naive. "A dictatorship with a good man at the head would probably be the best thing for the country," an official noted. " 'Free elections' are pretty sure to be only a farce in Mexico." Therefore, it was thoroughly exasperated: "The U.S. Government's demand shows how little they understand the situation: it is absurd to expect General Huerta to undertake that all parties will accept peacefully the result of the election." The *New York*

Times agreed: "Mr. Lind . . . could hardly expect to secure an agreement for the suspension of hostilities." Mr. Lind's mission, *El Independiente* of Mexico City asserted, "hurts us, shames us, angers us."[60]

The general, of course, could not have delivered on such a promise, even if he had been disposed to. And he was not so disposed. His minister of foreign affairs, Federico Gamboa, after a five-minute meeting with Lind, delivered a scathing response to the confidential agent: "Mexico cannot for one moment take into consideration the four conditions which His Excellency Mr. Wilson has been pleased to propose." The editorial in the *New York Times* was succinct: "The mission is a failure, and our relations with Mexico are more delicate than ever."[61]

Lind, however, was unbowed, and he reiterated his demands.[62] The Mexican reply was resolute: "If your original proposals were not to be admitted . . . they are now . . . even more inadmissible. . . . Precisely because we comprehend the immense value which is possessed by the principle of sovereignty which the Government of the United States so opportunely invokes in the question of our recognition or non-recognition, precisely for this reason we believe that [we must never] . . . forget our own sovereignty by permitting . . . a foreign government [to tell us what to do in] our public and independent life."[63] Gamboa lectured Lind like a schoolboy, while at the same time informing him that elections had been planned for months and that anyone who had read the Mexican constitution would know that the provisional president could not be a candidate. The *New York Times* pronounced Gamboa's reply to be "lucid and statesmanlike." Secretary of State Bryan put the best possible face on it, sending Lind his "hearty congratulations" and adding, "Huerta's announcement that he will not be a candidate is the one thing necessary to the restoration of peace." But Wilson's wife, saddened that the "Mexican situation" would keep her husband from joining her in New Hampshire, was less enthusiastic. "A plague on the Monroe Doctrine!" she exclaimed.[64]

Fear of Invasion

Wilson dallied (he called it "watchful waiting") while Mexico plunged deeper into chaos. Unable to gain the confidence of international finance and assailed by swelling rebel forces, Huerta struggled to maintain a semblance of control as Mexico splintered and fractured into civil war. Opposition to Huerta crystallized around the rebel leaders who had opposed Díaz and Madero and particularly around Venustiano Carranza, governor of the border state of Coahuila, a man in his fifties with political savvy, a love of history, and a reformist bent. His movement, called the Constitutionalists (a judicious name, given Wilson's devotion to law), would gradually appear to Wilson as a viable alternative to Huerta's dictatorial rule; Wilson would underestimate Carranza's proud and nationalistic resentment of the United States. At this point, however, in mid-1913, President Wilson was unclear and unsure. His utterances on the turbulent and confusing Mexican situation, in private and in public, conveyed his moral discomfort and his indecisiveness, not a policy. "Did you ever know a situation that had more question marks around it?" he asked a group of journalists in late May.[65]

Reading Wilson's, and his administration's, comments on the situation in Mexico, one is struck by the insularity of the policy-making process. Among foreign policy issues, Mexico was of primary concern, but with the exception of the sober voice of John Bassett Moore, no one in the administration seems to have considered the impact of their indecision on foreign governments. In a memorandum to the president in mid-May, Moore's admonition was unique: "The conditions resulting from our non-recognition of the existing government at the City of Mexico are producing serious inconvenience."[66]

The Europeans were left to try to speculate about the meaning of America's "do-nothing policy," as a member of the Reichstag dubbed it. Lind's proposals were so patently unrealistic that they appeared to many Europeans to be a cynical maneuver to pave the way to invasion. In late August, Kardorff reported that the European representatives in Mexico had drawn up a joint resolution condemning any U.S. invasion. Wilhelm was delighted. "Good," he scribbled on the side, with evident relief. "Finally unity against the Yankee."[67]

In fact, Wilson's attitude toward Huerta was hardening. Disappointed by the general's failure to hold early elections in July and influenced by the strongly anti-Huerta tone of Lind's reports, Wilson was beginning to think that something more revolutionary than an election was needed to bring peace to Mexico. He decided to extend the arms embargo to Huerta's forces. Issued by Taft in March 1912, the embargo forbade Americans from exporting arms to any Mexicans; Taft had added an oral provision that arms for the central administration in Mexico City (then the Madero government) should be exempted. Soon after his inauguration, Wilson had requested clarification on the embargo from the State Department. In response, Acting Secretary of State Alvey A. Adee had written a detailed history of the embargo, ending with a request for the president's "guidance . . . particularly with reference to the shipments falling under the fourth classification [the exemption of arms for the central government]." Wilson thanked Adee but provided no guidance. Therefore, arms for Huerta continued to be exempted from the embargo.[68] So when Wilson extended the embargo to Huerta's forces in August 1913, it indicated a tilt toward the Constitutionalists, who controlled northern Mexico along the U.S. border, where enforcement of the embargo was notoriously lax. The extension of the embargo was of greater symbolic than real significance because the Huertistas bought most of their arms from Europe and Japan and, since they controlled Mexico's coasts, they were able to smuggle arms with relative freedom. The Constitutionalists, on the other hand, were landlocked; the United States winked at many arms shipments crossing its border, but the supply was, nevertheless, limited.[69]

On 27 August, Wilson explained his decision about the embargo in the first address on foreign affairs that any president since George Washington had personally delivered to a joint session of Congress. He called for all Americans to leave Mexico, and he concluded by thanking "the great Governments of the world . . . for their generous moral support." (So much for unity against the Yankee.) Although the speech did not mention it and no formal requests were made, the administration let it be known that it hoped that these friendly powers would voluntarily withhold arms and ammunition from the Mexicans. Other than its call for Americans to leave Mexico and its extension of the arms embargo, the speech, which the Mexican *Courier du Mexique* dubbed "a sort of sermon, a homily," dealt in platitudes. The U.S. Congress, press, and public loved it, but the Europeans were skeptical. It "throws no clear light on his future policy," the *Deutsche Tageszeitung* observed, while the London papers declared that the message was "noncommittal, disappointing and in no sense a solution of the problem."[70]

This indicated the emerging communication gap between Washington and the European capitals. Although he refrained from mentioning it in his address, the president was becoming increasingly convinced that foreign financial interests (particularly the British Aguila Oil Company, run by S. Weetman Pearson—Lord Cowdray) were at the root of Mexico's problems.[71] Many Europeans, on the other hand, incredulous that America's policy could be shaped by moral concerns, were increasingly convinced that Wilson was trying to create a situation that would necessitate U.S. intervention and, hence, U.S. control of the Mexican economy. The British were particularly appalled. "It seems scarcely credible that the United States Government should have taken up so hostile an attitude on such insufficient grounds," the British minister in Mexico City declared. "A very large number of people here entertain the conviction," the British chargé there explained, "that the attitude of the United States is, in great part, due to the subtle intrigues of the Standard Oil Company, who play skillfully on President Wilson's rectitude and high moral standard, so that a state of disorder may be continued as long as possible in Mexico, thus retarding the development of the oil industry which threatens to become so serious a rival to their own interests in this hemisphere." From

Washington, Spring-Rice reported a variant on this theme: "According to the language of the Germans here it would seem that the supposed object of American policy in Mexico was to turn us [England] out of the oil fields." The American ambassador in London explained in a letter to the president, "[The British] are stupefied by your concern about anything else [other than order] in Mexico. What matter who rules or how, so long as he keep order? These are the best policemen in the world, these English, in India, in Africa, everywhere; and, about outlying governments, they have policemen's ethics." [72]

The Germans agreed fully. In August, their chargé in Mexico declared in exasperation, "Doesn't Wilson see that his policy against General Huerta is the reason that foreign lives and property are threatened in the north of the country and safety and order have not yet been established?" The generally pro-American *Frankfurter Zeitung* explained, "It is not to the Government at Washington, but to the great private interests, and mainly those of the Standard Oil Company, and its fatal influence on the American policy, that we must lay the account." The influential Berlin financial paper *Boersen Courier* was more bitter: "The sly and undecided policy of the United States has made American diplomacy the laughing-stock of the world. The Government at Washington is aiming in an underhanded way at stripping Mexico of her political independence, but above all at establishing in that country the economic supremacy of the United States. If that Government had desired nothing more than the reestablishment of peace it would have recognized Huerta long ago." Later, the kaiser wrote in the margin of a naval report reporting America's alleged fury that British interests—particularly Pearson oil money—had foiled U.S. plans in Mexico, "Behind Lind is Rockefeller!?? So it's Rockefeller against Pearson!" [73]

As summer turned into fall, the Germans were increasingly concerned that the United States would either intervene or recognize the rebels as cobelligerents, which they believed would increase violence in the countryside and endanger their nationals. European unity, with Germany assiduously avoiding a leadership role, was the only way to square the circle: it was the way to oppose the United States without paying the price. As Wilhelm, Hintze, and several diplomats in the Wilhelmstrasse said time and time again, no single European country could challenge the United States in Mexico, but together, particularly with England at the helm, they could, as the kaiser wrote, ensure that "Wilson bloodied his hand in Mexico." [74] Hintze expressed this position clearly:

> The situation in Europe determines the Mexico policy of the European powers. Many great powers of Europe are currently occupied with problems that are more important and more pressing than those posed by

Mexico. The historical trend of U.S. policy toward Mexico makes it clear that Washington's aim is hegemony. . . . For a single European power to oppose this would be to invite dire consequences and even failure. . . . United . . . the European powers could stop the U.S. advance in Mexico. . . . [In the absence of such unity,] German policy should be neither to help the United States advance, nor to oppose it openly and to protect German citizens and interests. . . . This is the only possible policy for a single European power.[75]

European unity was so attractive, so sensible (wasn't it in England's and France's interest to curb the noxious Monroe Doctrine?), and so much the only possible solution that the kaiser and Hintze clung to it tenaciously. It was the chimera on the horizon.

Of course, it was improbable, given the situation in Europe. The lines between Germany and Austria on the one hand and England, France, and Russia on the other had become starker and more menacing, and the Balkan wars of 1912-13 threatened to engulf all Europe in war. But the notion of European cooperation against the Yankee had a long pedigree. For this generation, it had roots in the undignified scrambling in the capitals of Europe to find a country brave enough to take the lead against the United States in 1898. It resurfaced in Germany's desire to hide in England's shadow in Venezuela and was a persistent refrain in German policy in Mexico. It was taken seriously by the Americans. Lind encouraged the administration to fear that such cooperation was possible.[76]

Predictably, however, although both France and England wanted to avoid U.S. military intervention, neither was willing to take the lead in opposing the United States, and neither was willing to cooperate with the Germans.[77] "Europe has preferred to remain silent at times when, from our perspective in Mexico, it would have been better to have spoken," Hintze wrote in his diary. "Europe cannot do anything contrary to the United States' political wishes." The British minister in Mexico was more blunt: "Europe is an old aunt—joint action by Europe, a piece of nonsense." A French captain on the scene told the captain of the *Bremen*, "We are going to have to stay here [in Tampico] until our neighbor (pointing to the U.S. ships in the harbor) decides the pears have ripened." This comment drew the kaiser's contempt and ire. "That's a nice role for our ships, i.e. for Europe!" he snarled. And on other reports he scrawled contemptuously, "What meekness! La France!" and "Oh, Disraeli, where has your spirit gone?"[78]

As Wilson dallied and the Europeans dreamed of unity, Huerta's control over the Mexican countryside weakened. On 26 August, Lind retired to Veracruz, and U.S. policy foundered. "Mr. Lind . . . lives a prisoner at Veracruz and hearsay is his food," a British admiral wrote. "I fear he is rather like the fleet, having arrived and been here so long, they cannot be removed." [79] Further confounding the situation was the fact that Washington had two official voices in Mexico: Lind was unwavering in his condemnation of Huerta, but Chargé O'Shaughnessy, like Lane Wilson before him, was a stalwart supporter of the general. While the Europeans wanted a prompt resolution to the crisis, the Wilson administration was bombarded by these contrary voices and opted for patience. In so doing, it assumed that it would have the moral support of the Europeans without having to address their concerns. "He [President Wilson] does not believe any diplomatic 'dicker' with European Powers is necessary," the *Herald* explained flatly in early October.[80] All that the Europeans could hope was that the election scheduled for 26 October would finally regularize U.S. relations with Mexico.

October, however, was a month of disappointments. The fall of the key town of Torreón to the Constitutionalists on 1 October undermined not only Huerta's military position but also, because forty German citizens were taken hostage during the battle, foreigners' confidence in his ability to protect them. The Wilhelmstrasse asked the State Department for assistance. On the 10th, Huerta dissolved Congress and arrested 110 deputies he considered disloyal. "Huerta may now be considered an absolute military dictator," the American chargé declared ominously. "If only a *man* would appear in that distracted country," Mrs. Wilson exclaimed. England incurred Wilson's ire by delivering what Mahan called "rather a black eye to the Administration policy": the new British minister to Mexico, Sir Lionel Carden, presented his credentials to the general the day after he had dissolved Congress. The date had been set in advance, but Wilson, already irritated by London's insistence that the elections were a matter of Mexican domestic politics, found Carden's behavior particularly reprehensible because his trusted aide, Colonel Edward House, had reported in July that the British would withdraw their recognition of Huerta if he failed to honor his pledge to "call an election at an early date and abide by its decision." To signal his own extreme displeasure with Huerta's dissolution of Congress, Wilson announced that the United States would refuse to recognize the results of the forthcoming elections.[81]

At that point, Hintze had given the old dream of European unity against the Yankees a novel twist: he had probed the idea of "friendly cooperation" between Europe and the United States—of joint intervention to establish a protectorate over Mexico. This improbable scenario was a desperate attempt to prevent American unilateralism. Hintze, who had maintained close ties with Lind, was worried that the imminent financial collapse of Mexico would lead to a call for foreign (that is, U.S.) financial control. He urged the Wilhelmstrasse to act quickly. Berlin responded—but not by approaching Washington; instead it ordered two cruisers to Mexican waters to rescue German nationals should the need arise. No alarm was expressed in the U.S. diplomatic record or press about these warships. "With the large material interests possessed by the Germans in Mexico," the *Herald* explained, "the sending of . . . warships is not open to objection from the United States." [82]

The minister's idea, however far fetched, was not insane. David Thompson, the former U.S. ambassador to Brazil, agreed with him. In October he asked Bryan, "What humiliation to our country could come from a modification at this time of the Monroe Doctrine, that would permit joint action of our Country and the Powers of Europe . . . to the end of quieting Mexico?" The *Herald* had been pushing for joint action since July. In an editorial on 12 October, it asked "Why should not President Wilson invite the Powers to a conference to devise measures for the pacification, through American instrumentality [that is, the navy], of Mexico?" [83] José Yves Limantour, former Mexican finance minister, had earlier answered this question in the *Herald*'s own pages. "The United States," he explained, "would never entertain the suggestion of such interference, even in collaboration with herself. The Monroe doctrine precluded the possibility of such a thing." Limantour was right, of course: Wilson had neither need of nor interest in a partner. The chair of the Senate Foreign Relations Committee, Augustus Bacon (D-Ga.), explained, "There is no action now contemplated or which is probable where the situation cannot be dealt with solely by the United States. . . . If there should be any difference of views [between the United States and the Europeans about Mexico], the views of the United States should prevail." Bryan was blunt on the point: "If there is anything to be done," he told the British ambassador confidentially, "it will be done by the United States alone." [84]

Wilson was beginning to see, however, as Huerta proved obdurate, that the United States could use the Europeans' help, not as partners but as dutiful servants. To this end, soon after they had expressed their unhappiness with Washington's policy, Wilson turned the tables on the Europeans and asked for their assistance in implementing that very policy. This meant that the president finally had to articulate his government's policy toward Mexico. It was not the awkwardness of the European powers' situation (attempting to safeguard their nationals in Mexico and to fall in step with a policy to which they were not privy) that moved the president. It was the awkwardness of his own situation. "The U.S.G[overnment] seem to be suffering rather from nerves," the British Foreign Office observed. "They do not seem exactly to know what to do and what they mean to do themselves, but they want us to do it with them."[85] Wilson wanted the Europeans' support in isolating Huerta—refusing him arms and loans—and he wanted to persuade them to delay recognizing the victor in the elections to be held on 26 October. So for the first time he planned to explain his Latin American policy in an important speech in Mobile, Alabama, on 27 October and to send a circular note on his Mexican policy to the powers.[86]

The long-awaited election was, predictably, a fiasco. It was preceded by virtually no campaigning and rife with corruption, and voter turnout was, as the preeminent historian of the revolution, Alan Knight, comments, "pathetically low." The results were annulled, and Huerta, to no one's surprise, announced that he would remain president. "Huerta," the *New York Times* commented, "is impossible." While none of the governments that had earlier recognized Huerta formally recognized the "new" government, neither did they break relations with it. They simply let the matter slide, and Huerta did not press them for clarification.[87]

Tension was very high in Mexico. On 30 October, Colonel House wrote in his diary: "The President has in mind to declare war against Mexico. . . . His purpose in this is to keep the powers from interfering and entirely out of the situation. . . . He realizes that his course may possibly bring about a coalition of the European powers against this government, but he seems ready to throw our gauntlet into the arena and declare all hands must be kept off excepting our own." A few days later, Wilson wrote a close friend, "I lie awake at night praying that the most terrible of them [outcomes in Mexico] may be averted. No man can tell what will happen while we deal with a desperate brute like the traitor, Huerta. God save us from the worst!" He drafted (but did not send) a resolution to Congress giving him the power to declare war, and the Europeans expected intervention at any minute. The foreign legations in Mexico City prepared defense plans; Hintze warned that a U.S. blockade was imminent.[88]

Nevertheless, the Wilhelmstrasse decided to accommodate Washington even before receiving the promised circular note.[89] Indeed, when the Spanish government asked the Germans to join in "a joint *démarche*" after the election to persuade the United States to alter its course, the Wilhelmstrasse demurred. "Having agreed to await the United States communication, [the Germans] are not in a position to join in this *démarche*."[90] For Washington, Germany's cooperation was all the more welcome given England's transgressions. "Upon

"The road to the abyss." A Mexican cartoon making fun of Wilson's appeal to the great powers of Europe—Germany, Spain, France, and England—to support his Mexican policy. (*Independiente* [Mexico City]; reprinted in *Literary Digest* [21 February 1914])

Germany and France," the *New York Times* explained, "the Wilson administration places greater reliance [than upon Britain] to follow its lead. Germany has all along shown a disposition to regard this Government as having superior interests in Mexico which foreign nations should respect." The U.S. ambassador in Berlin, James Gerard, expended a great deal of time and energy bolstering the Wilhelmstrasse's support of Wilson's Mexican policy. "My first winter [1913–14]," he wrote in his memoirs, "it was part of my work to secure from Germany promises that she would not recognise this Mexican president [Huerta]."[91]

Wilson's eagerly anticipated speech in Mobile was a disappointment. Foreshadowed by an address at Swarthmore College on 25 October in which the president said, "Nowhere can any government endure which is stained by blood or supported by anything but the consent of the governed," the speech delivered two days later to the Southern Commercial Congress was billed as a full-scale statement of the administration's Latin American policy. "Human rights, national integrity, and opportunity as against material interests—that, ladies and gentlemen, is the issue we now have to face. I want to take this occasion to say that the United States will never again seek one additional foot of territory by conquest. . . . She must regard it as one of the duties of friendship to see that from no quarter are material interests made superior to human liberty and national opportunity." Wilson mentioned no Latin American country by name and spoke in sweeping generalities. The German press was critical; Wilson was suffering from "imperialistic delirium," the *Berliner Neueste Nachrichten* exclaimed. "The speech is a fine one to read," Sir Edward Grey commented, "but its ideas do not seem very practical."[92]

The Europeans awaited the circular note. The evolution of the note is instructive. It began in late October as a verbose, emotional, and illuminating explanation of Wilson's policy, probably drafted by the president himself:

This Government having, in the announcement and maintenance of the Monroe Doctrine, shown its willingness to protect the people of this hemisphere from encroachment at the hands of European powers, having proven by its actions in the [second] Venezuelan contest its willingness to protect a little republic in its rights to have its controversies with great nations settled by arbitration rather than by force, is now prepared to assert with equal emphasis its unwillingness to have an American Republic exploited by the commercial interests of our own or any other country through a government resting upon force. . . . [The United States] will not, therefore, recognize as a legitimate government a government established by force and terrorism.[93]

This draft was leaked to the press: "Wilson to Warn Nations about Mexico," the three-column headline in the *New York Times* blared. Having no time for Wilson's diplomatic nicety of leaving the "commercial interests" unidentified, it added the subheads "Washington Notice That Meddling in Mexico Will Displease Us/Provoked by England." [94] Perhaps anticipating this reaction, or stung by it, the president reduced the draft to an outline and asked for Moore's advice. [95] The counselor's response was, characteristically, dry, brilliant, and deflating. He advised against casting any unsubstantiated blame on foreign interests, and he observed that the Monroe Doctrine was not relevant to the issue at hand. "As the independent States of America are not protectorates of the United States, we do not supervise their diplomatic relations; and it has never therefore been considered necessary for foreign Powers to ask our consent to their recognition of an American government. . . . Nor had the United States said anything to indicate to them that it entertained a different view of their conduct. . . . Of these facts it is pertinent to take note in judging the motives and conduct of other governments." [96] Wilson discussed the draft circular letter with Colonel House. "His idea in brief," House wrote in his diary, "is to insist that Huerta permit the status of affairs to go back where they began when Madero was assassinated, that is the former Congress should be restored and they should be permitted to elect his successor. He was determined not to allow the financiers control. . . . In other words in former years, the Monroe Doctrine was announced to keep Europe from securing political control of any of the states in the Western Hemisphere. The President thinks it is just as reprehensible to permit foreign states to secure financial control of these weak and unfortunate republics." [97]

On 7 November—eight months after he took office—President Wilson finally sent a note to the European powers about his hopes and goals for American policy in Mexico. As the *New York Sun* explained, "The United States Government is not consulting with the other Powers regarding Mexico, but is merely keeping them informed." The note was stripped, edited to obscurity; it had neither Wilson's vehemence nor Moore's crispness. It began, "While the President does not feel that he can yet announce his policy with regard to Mexico in detail," and continued to say merely that the United States would "proceed to employ such means as may be necessary" to force Huerta to resign and that it hoped that the foreign governments would use their influence "to impress upon Huerta the wisdom of retiring." [98]

For the Germans, who dearly wanted to understand America's aims in Mexico, the president's note was frustrating. The *Berliner Tageblatt* was scathing: "Every Mexican knows very well that the policy of the United States in regard to Mexican affairs aims at establishing a protectorate . . . over their Republic." The influential *Kreuzzeitung* predicted that the United States, "as the Palladium of Liberty, will eventually realize the plan of stripping the little States of their freedom," and declared that "the sly and undecided policy of the United States has made America the laughing stock of the world."[99] Nevertheless, the Wilhelmstrasse reassured Washington that it had every desire to continue to follow the U.S. lead in Mexico, and the headline the next day in the *New York Times*, "German Attitude Friendly," reflected this. But the German embassy in Washington also conveyed its exasperation: How could the Germans follow America when they did not know Washington's plans? Who did the Americans think should replace Huerta? From Berlin, Ambassador Gerald reported the German stance succinctly: "The [German] Foreign Office states that Germany has no political interest in the subject but that Mexico must have order and responsible government and wishes to know what candidate for the presidency we have." Given the previous nine months, Wilson's response to the Reich's request for elucidation was disingenuous: "The request . . . is most reasonable, and, of course, we have had it in contemplation to do so." From Washington, Bernstorff cabled the Wilhelmstrasse, "Bryan told me today that here in Washington they do not have a particular successor to Huerta in mind." The kaiser erupted in the margin: "Not the slightest notion!"[100]

In the meantime, Germany's fleeting importance evaporated as the British dispatched Sir William Tyrrell, undersecretary in the Foreign Office, to Washington to smooth over the discord caused by Carden's presentation of his credentials. Although both sides issued vehement denials, it appeared that the U.S. concession on the Panama tolls controversy hammered out by Tyrrell was a quid pro quo for British cooperation in Mexico. The Americans had "put it to Sir Edw[ard] Grey as squarely and as hard as may be prudent," the U.S. ambassador in London explained, "that one way lies a friendly act to us and that the other way lies an unfriendly. . . . This [British] Government will not risk our good will. . . . Our good will is a club they are afraid of." The *New York Times* was sanguine about the future of U.S.-British relations, given that Grey, "one of the most modest and one of the strongest British statesmen of the present day and one who has always held friendliness to the United States to be one of the bases of British foreign policy," was at the helm in the Foreign Office. As expected, Grey put American friendship first: "I do not dispute the inconvenience and untoward results of United States policy, but . . . His Majesty's Government cannot with any prospect of success embark upon an active counterpolicy to that of the United States, or constitute themselves the champions of Mexico. . . . [Such a course would] precipitate the armed intervention by the United States that we desire to avoid." The blow to both Huerta and any future European démarche in Mexico was grave. When the Wilhelmstrasse got wind of the shift in the British stance, any lingering hopes for a united European stance in Mexico evaporated. The United States had firmly secured the advantage. The *Herald* explained the impotence of the foreign powers:

> The impression is growing here that the optimism expressed by President Wilson yesterday [14 November] had its tap root in the assurance that foreign Powers would remain complaisant, or at least acquiescent, to whatever course the United States might elect to follow in Mexico. . . . Color was given to this belief to-day when Mr. Bryan said: — "I think I can say that the foreign Powers will not offer any objection to the United States carrying out its policies in Mexico." "Does that mean," he was asked, "that those nations now indorse [*sic*] our policies?" "Not necessarily so," Mr. Bryan replied, and then he resumed his sphinx-like pose and maintained it to the end of the daily reception.

The *New York Times*'s editorial was more succinct: "Lacking English support, he [Huerta] can hope for none from any other European Power." [101]

The *Berliner Tageblatt*, a left liberal paper that had been consistently critical of U.S. policy, changed its stance, calling for the resignation of Huerta. Even the pan-Germans were forced to face the fact that Britain's stance decisively limited Germany's options in Mexico. The kaiser was left fuming. At the end of November, Bernstorff wrote Berlin, "Unfortunately Europe cannot influence American policy because it does not have the power to counter it." Wilhelm oozed irritation and contempt in the margin: "It would have—and more than enough—if England had been willing to make common cause with the continent." Bernstorff concluded, "Therefore we must be content with being a spectator." In January, Wilhelm scoffed, "The British capitulate completely before the Americans." A few months later, when faced with another example of British collusion with the Americans, he exclaimed: "Unbelievable passivity! How far John Bull has fallen! England has left Europe in the lurch!" [102]

Finally, on 24 November, Wilson delivered on his promise. "As you know," the president wrote Bryan, "the German government is asking very earnestly . . . to be taken into our confidence with regard to our Mexican policy. . . . I am therefore sending you . . . a suggested note." The note, "Our Purposes in Mexico," was sent to fifteen European states, Brazil, and Japan. It finally clarified U.S. policy toward Mexico. "The present policy of the Government of the United States is to isolate General Huerta entirely; to cut him off from foreign sympathy and aid and from domestic credit, whether moral or material, and so to force him out. . . . It hopes and believes that isolation will accomplish this end. . . . If [not,] . . . it will become the duty of the United States to use less peaceful means. . . . It will give other governments notice . . . but no such step seems immediately necessary. . . . It will not permit itself to seek any special or exclusive advantages in Mexico." [103] Nine months into Wilson's term, the Germans finally knew what U.S. policy toward Mexico was, but they still did not, or could not, understand it. Why would the United States seek the destruction of the one man who, in the opinion of almost all the European governments and of all foreigners in Mexico, stood between Mexico and anarchy? This was a policy that would lead only to further instability. And, in fact, the war continued unabated; Huerta grew stronger, his forces recaptured Torreón in mid-December, and the Constitutionalists faltered. "(Entre nous) the Administration was very much alarmed," Admiral Bradley Fiske, a senior member of the General Board, wrote to Rear Admiral Frank Fletcher, commander of the U.S. naval forces in Mexican waters. "You have no idea how important the Administration regards your job, and how worried they are over the whole Mexican situation. Nobody here sees any escape from even worse conditions in the future." [104]

It is a measure of Germany's disenchantment with the idea of European cooperation that even Hintze objected in late November to a proposal of the French and Belgian ministers in Mexico that they send a joint cable to Washington complaining about U.S. policy in Mexico and stating that European troops were needed to protect European citizens. At a meeting that included representatives of Spain, Russia, Britain, Japan, Austria, Norway, and Germany, Hintze spoke against the proposed cable, arguing that the introduction of European troops would only cause the Americans to increase their own presence, give the United States the impression that there was an organized front against it, and hurt the possibility of future U.S.-European cooperation. The Wilhelmstrasse agreed. "I advise reserve in order to avoid open opposition to the collective telegram," Jagow cabled Hintze. A few weeks later, when the minister expressed guarded optimism that the moment might now be opportune for joint American-European cooperation in Mexico, the Wilhelmstrasse disabused him of the notion. "The moment is long gone, if indeed it ever existed," an official wrote in the margin.[105]

Exasperated with England, and with all of Europe, and convinced that a Mexican-American war was on the horizon, the Wilhelmstrasse decided that the only way to prevent U.S. intervention—Washington's ultimate aim—was to help the United States meet its proximate aim, the removal of Huerta. "Please tell Woodrow Wilson," Arthur Zimmermann (then undersecretary of foreign affairs) wrote Bernstorff in November, that we completely understand that the United States cannot recognize Huerta. However, it would be hard for Huerta to look like he was caving in to U.S. pressure. If the negotiations between the United States and Mexico fail, a blockade and recognition of the rebels could follow, which would mean chaos and the endangerment of German lives and property. This would be against our interests—which are limited to the establishment of normalcy in Mexico. Would the United States not welcome our exerting friendly pressure on Huerta and advising him to resign in favor of a candidate acceptable to him and to the United States? [106]

When informed that Wilson had declared his openness to German proposals, the kaiser penned contemptuously, "Of course! He doesn't have the faintest notion of what he wants to do!" From Berlin, the U.S. ambassador reported that during a "long talk with [the] Emperor . . . about Mexico . . . he recognize[d] the justice of your policy and is very friendly to you and our administration." For a short time, Germany succeeded in currying Washington's favor, but not with any pleasure. Wilhelm slammed U.S. policy as "incredible interference in foreign affairs" and predicted that it would end in failure.[107]

By the end of the year it had become clear to virtually all German bankers and businessmen in Mexico that in the absence of American recognition Huerta could not deliver the goods: peace, stability, and the comforts that the privileged class had enjoyed under Díaz. The divorce between Huerta and German business was final (and unpleasant) in early 1914, when the general declared that Mexico would not pay January's interest on its foreign debts. "The failure of Juarez in 1861 to meet foreign obligations led to the invasion of Mexico by the French," the *New York Times* editors reminded their readers. The bankers discussed a joint European response—a note to the Mexican government or even a joint seizure of the customhouses—but, as with comparable government parlays, the démarche never moved beyond discussion. None of these bankers and expatriates relished the idea of U.S. intervention, but they assessed their welfare dispassionately: only the United States could restore order to Mexico, and order was what they needed. American intervention posed less of a threat than continued disorder.[108]

The Wilhelmstrasse looked at the situation differently. It also struggled to find a way—virtually any way—to restore order short of U.S. intervention. It had no desire to help Washington "skim off the cream in Mexico," as Bernstorff said, and it believed that U.S. intervention, though busying the Americans for a while, would unleash a stronger United States with a whetted appetite for empire. "What would happen then to Canada, to Central America and to South America?" asked Hintze.[109]

German officials considered U.S. intervention a very real possibility. Struggling to make sense of Wilson's policy, many Germans feared that Washington was playing a clever and cynical game to destabilize Mexico before invading. "One wonders whether Wilson's policy of postponing a military intervention in the end will not be the cheapest," the captain of the *Bremen* mused. "With the passing of time, Mexico will become ripe for the plucking, and the Mexicans will throw themselves into big brother's arms." Hintze harbored similar suspicions. "The United States' policy is based on thoroughly nationalistic considerations," he confided to his diary. "Its aim is to spare blood and treasure and to subjugate Mexico in the guise of a moral action." He told the wife of the U.S. attaché in Mexico City much the same thing. "In the politest and most veiled of language, [he] intimated to me," she recalled, "that our policy was evidently to weaken the Mexicans by non-recognition, and when they were sufficiently reduced come into Mexico cheaply." John Lind himself lent weight to Hintze's speculations by commenting to the captain of the *Bremen*: "Lots more Mexicans need to kill each other before peace comes to this country. So we're going to let them fight it out, and, eventually, they'll ask us for help." And he wrote to Bryan: "It would be just as well to let them [the Mexicans] use up some more ammunition and exhaust their energies before we appeared on the scene." The German consul in Veracruz reported, "According to his [Lind's] opinion, before anything reasonable could come out of Mexico, all Mexican men had to be killed." [110]

Through the spring of 1914, Hintze hoped that by brokering an agreement between Huerta and the United States he would be able to prevent an American invasion. He also continued to dream of some sort of joint European-American intervention in Mexico. [111] Jagow, on the other hand, had his feet squarely on the ground. In the Reichstag he declared, "Germany's course . . . must be one of neutrality. . . . There was no question of action by Germany alone, if only out of regard for German relations with the United States." Bernstorff, in Washington, understood Wilson's bottom line: "President Wilson wants to hear absolutely nothing about foreigners coming to his aid. All he wants is a free hand, and this is the entire aim of his policy." The English ambassador to Washington agreed. "The President . . . does not propose to ask our advice or to act on it, or to request our assistance." [112]

At a 12 March press conference, when asked whether foreign governments had been informed about the administration's policy toward Mexico, Wilson stated, counterfactually, "We haven't waited for them [foreign nations] to ask us to tell them what our attitude [toward Mexico] was. We, at each important turn of affairs, sent them a note." Senator John Works (R-Calif.) was more blunt: the excruciatingly long delay in the articulation of the policy "made us, as a Government," he declared, "ridiculous." [113]

Treachery on the Ypiranga

On 3 February, frustrated by Huerta's resilience, Wilson had tilted U.S. policy decisively in favor of the Constitutionalists: he had lifted the arms embargo, which, by allowing the Constitutionalists finally to buy all the arms they could afford (something the Huertistas had long been able to do from suppliers in Europe and Japan), signaled his sympathy for the rebel cause. Nevertheless, its immediate impact was counterproductive: it unleashed a wave of nationalist, anti-American sentiment that helped swell Huerta's forces and increase tensions.[114] Later that month, a prominent British citizen, William Benton, was executed by rebel forces in northern Mexico. The British, and Europeans generally, held the United States at least partly responsible and disparaged the inept and feeble attempts of the Wilson administration to bring the perpetrators to justice. European governments sent stern warnings to Washington that if it could not protect the safety of foreigners in Mexico, they would have to take measures themselves. Senator Albert Fall (R-N.Mex.) proclaimed in open Senate debate, "When the German official press says that should a German citizen be murdered in Mexico, Germany would not acquiesce like Great Britain, then I say to you, Senators, there is imminent danger of a conflict with a country with which we should always be at peace." [115]

In early April, the Huertistas and Constitutionalists fought once more for Torreón. Suffering from poor leadership and a lack of ammunition, Huerta's forces once again lost the town to the rebels. The *New York Times* predicted that "the Revolutionary victory [would] have a tremendous moral effect," and, indeed, a string of rebel victories followed; a few days before he returned to Washington, Lind advised from Veracruz that if Huerta could be cut off from supplies arriving on the east coast, his forces might crumble. The air was thick with predictions of U.S. intervention.[116]

On 9 April eight sailors from the USS *Dolphin* were arrested in Tampico. Dissatisfied with Huerta's apology for the incident, Wilson ordered the Atlantic fleet to Mexico's east coast and the Pacific fleet to its west. "The die is cast," the *Herald* intoned. "Once more the United States is called upon to take upon its shoulders the burden of putting in order the house of one of its sister republics. . . . It is a burden we have not sought . . . but civilization demands that the United States exercise primacy upon this hemisphere, and this primacy carries with it responsibility of upholding law and order in the Americas." [117]

The threat was heard, and not only by the Mexicans. Hintze cabled Berlin that he expected the Americans to take aggressive action imminently, and Bernstorff wrote that he thought the United States would take "reprisals, such as . . . the occupation of the customhouses of Tampico and Veracruz." The American ambassador in Berlin called on Foreign Secretary Jagow, who assured him, "The German Government desires the Washington Government to remain in no doubt of its wish that the United States may speedily succeed in restoring order and normal conditions in Mexico." At the same time, the *New York Times* reported, "A semi-official communiqué in the Cologne Gazette indicates unmistakably that the German Government heartily approves American intervention in Mexico. The communiqué says: 'If the intervention of the Americans is destined to restore peace and order there will be nothing objectionable from our point of view. The German nation . . . has no occasion to oppose the action of the United States in any spirit of malicious criticism, which would not only be futile but also injurious to our good relations with America.'" The mainstream German press, however, was caustically critical of U.S. policy. "Germany has no reason to desire an American victory. The American colossus would thereby grow still more gigantic and become more dangerous for us economically than it already is," the *Berlin Post* wrote. "The comedy is about to become a tragedy, involving Mexico's struggle for freedom and independence."[118]

On 20 April, in the midst of the Tampico crisis, General Leonard Wood, chief of staff of the U.S. Army, wrote in his diary, "The custom house at Vera-Cruz must be occupied because a German ship carrying 15,000,000 rounds of ammunition and 260 machine guns is due to arrive tomorrow morning." The *Ypiranga*, a commercial vessel of the Hamburg-American Line (Hapag), was steaming toward Veracruz to deliver arms to Huerta.[119]

The State Department got wind of the *Ypiranga*'s cargo in a cable from the U.S. consul in Veracruz that was received in the early morning of Sunday, 19 April. President Wilson was in West Virginia, and there is no record that he was contacted immediately. When he returned to Washington on Monday morning, he was briefed, and he discussed the situation with his secretaries of state, war, and the navy. (The U.S. public learned of the shipment at the same time, in a page-five article in the *Herald* on Monday morning based on a cable from the paper's correspondent in Mexico entitled "Race with German Vessel Bearing 200 Guns Expected at Vera Cruz.") Although there was nothing either illegal or unusual about the shipment, Wilson and his key advisers agreed that the arms should not be allowed to reach Huerta, in part because they could be used against the Americans who were ready to invade. As the *New York Times* would report, "It would be monstrous negligence to permit machine guns and ammunition to fall into the Dictator's hands." Thus, although most military experts in Washington had favored occupying Tampico, they now shifted their focus to Veracruz and debated whether it would be better to mount a blockade or to occupy the customhouse.[120]

The officials meeting in Washington were well briefed. In response to the Tampico incident, the General Board of the Navy had prepared a report, dated 18 April, analyzing the costs and benefits of occupying Veracruz and Tampico, the two ports key to Mexico's economy. (The customs receipts from Veracruz were Mexico's major source of revenue, and the oil fields of Tampico fueled its trains.) The General Board did not underestimate the difficulty of occupying either: it warned that the seizure of the customhouses "would very probably involve the loss of American lives." A blockade might be less costly, but it would require a declaration of war — that is, an act of Congress.[121]

Later that Monday, 20 April, Wilson addressed a joint session of Congress and asked for its approval to use force in Mexico "in such ways and to such an extent as may be necessary to obtain from General Huerta . . . the fullest recognition of the rights and dignity of the United States." Although he knew about the arms shipment arriving imminently in Veracruz, and although preliminary orders had been sent to the naval commanders in Mexican waters to go to Veracruz, the president did not mention the weapons in his message; he dealt solely with the alleged affront to national honor at Tampico. He did not ask for a declaration of war. "The address was so entirely unlike a trumpet call that it was heard without any enthusiasm," the *New York Times* later editorialized, "and has been frequently criticized as not setting forth a sufficient cause of action." Nevertheless, the House approved the measure overwhelmingly that evening, and the Senate followed suit, albeit more narrowly and after a contentious debate, the next day.[122]

Very early on the morning of 21 April — before the Senate voted — the State Department received confirmation of the arms shipment from its consul and word that the *Ypiranga* was about to pull into Veracruz. Wilson was awakened, and he quickly gave the order: a few hours later the U.S. Navy and Marines hastily occupied the customhouse, cable office, post office, railroad terminal, and harbor of Veracruz. Americans were startled by the suddenness of the operation. "Here in Washington it is taken for granted," the *New York Times* announced, "that to-day's attack on Vera Cruz . . . marks the beginning of a real war." The *Louisville Courier-Journal* was more dramatic: "Yea, verily, we are in for it. Tramp, tramp, tramp, the boys are marching. . . . Southward the star of empire takes its way. . . . Sound the bold anthem, 'On to the Isthmus.' "[123]

Hintze, who was in Mexico City and unaware of the occupation of Veracruz, was relieved that the *Ypiranga* was arriving: he had already decided that he would ask it to carry German refugees from the tense and dangerous port city. When the Americans occupied Veracruz, neither he nor Ambassador Bernstorff was surprised, and neither saw any connection between the ship and the U.S. action. On 20 April, Bernstorff cabled Berlin that the occupation of Veracruz and Tampico was imminent, but he did not mention the *Ypiranga*.[124]

They could not remain in the dark for long. On 21 April, the *New York Times* (printed before the occupation had begun) carried the page-one headline "All Eyes on German Ship: Vessel Reported on Way to Mexico with Big Cargo of Ammunition for Huerta." The report continued: "News that the Hamburg-American liner Ypiranga was due at Vera Cruz to-morrow with 10,000 rifles, a consignment of machine guns, and 15,000,000 rounds of ammunition for Huerta, was said today to have been responsible for the efforts of the Administration to have congress hurry through the joint resolution authorizing President Wilson to use the armed forces of the nation against the dictator." On 22 April, Berlin received an official report that the *Ypiranga* had been the trigger for the American occupation of Veracruz.[125]

As soon as the *Ypiranga* steamed into the harbor at Veracruz, U.S. naval officers boarded it and demanded that it neither dock nor lift anchor without the explicit permission of the U.S. Navy.[126] This was illegal: war had not been declared, and so there could be no formal blockade. The United States had occupied the customhouse specifically to avoid such an incident; occupation provided a way, short of seizing the ship, to seize the cargo (if it was discharged at Veracruz, the U.S. authorities could legally take control of it) or at least to prevent it from being unloaded. As the *New York Times* explained, "The decision to take Vera Cruz without waiting for the authority of Congress . . . was due to delicate international considerations. The President and his advisers realized that unless an actual state of war existed the seizure of the German vessel and her supplies would be illegal and might bring about differences with Germany, which has shown a decidedly friendly feeling toward the United States throughout the Mexican crisis. . . . The easiest way out of the difficulty appeared to be to order the capture of Vera Cruz before the German vessel arrived."[127] Thus, in boarding the *Ypiranga*, the U.S. naval commander, according to the secretary of state, exceeded his orders. On the afternoon of 21 April, the secretary cabled Fletcher, "There has been no declaration of war. . . . Our seizure of custom house . . . does not justify us in controlling movements of a neutral ship in any way. We can only control the disposition of her cargo after it is landed at the custom house. [Under] the circumstances apology and explanations should be made to comander of Ypiranga."[128]

Captain Bonath of the *Ypiranga* cabled the *Dresden*, a German navy cruiser in Veracruz harbor, for advice. Captain Köhler of the *Dresden* informed Bonath, "The *Ypiranga* is called to the service of German Empire to carry refugees. . . . Therefore, do not unload your cargo." [129]

It is difficult to unravel exactly why this order was issued. The most straightforward explanation is that the Germans wanted to avoid losing the cargo to the U.S. authorities at Veracruz. Even the Germans on the scene speculated as to the meaning of the order. "Both Hintze and I," the Hapag agent in Mexico, Carl Heynen, wrote, "have always believed that the prohibition against the unloading of the arms of the *Ypiranga* had originated from . . . the German government in agreement with the U.S. government." Those scholars who see German scheming behind the entire operation regard the order as evidence of the complicity of the German government in the episode: by drafting the ship into government service, Berlin gained control over its actions so that it could be sure that its cargo would ultimately be delivered to Huerta.[130]

Immediately after the occupation of Veracruz, Ambassador Bernstorff called on Bryan and received a briefing on the situation. A day later, the secretary of state visited the ambassador to extend a formal apology to the German government for the illegal interference with the *Ypiranga*. He also indicated that the United States would consider compensating the shippers if the arms were handed over to the Americans in Veracruz. (There is no indication that this suggestion was ever pursued.) Also on the 22d, Rear Admiral Charles J. Badger, the commander in chief of the Atlantic squadron, apologized in person to Captain Bonath and told him that he was free to take his ship wherever he wanted.[131] Washington realized that prohibiting the delivery of the weapons to Huerta legally would require a declaration of war against Mexico, and there was no stomach for this. Furthermore, Wilson wanted to avoid creating an international incident with Germany. Therefore, gentle suasion with the Germans was preferred.

The United States may have been conciliatory because the occupation of Veracruz was not proceeding as painlessly as had been hoped. The Huertistas resisted, resulting in nineteen American deaths, which, the German naval attaché in Washington was quick to point out, was more than had died in the Spanish-American War.[132] Furthermore, even the Constitutionalists roundly denounced the intervention. Captain Köhler reported that it had aroused the people to an "almost fanatical hatred" of the United States. The Mexican authorities handed O'Shaughnessy his passport: his diplomatic mission was "concluded." This not only left U.S. citizens without representation in Mexico but also rendered other foreigners, particularly those living in the interior who had relied on the U.S. representation, defenseless in the face of the Mexican authorities. There were street demonstrations against the occupation throughout South America, and the European press was hostile to the U.S. action. The *Hamburger Nachrichten* condemned Wilson's hypocrisy and declared, "Roosevelt's 'Big Stick' is once more seized and brandished."[133]

However, not a word of protest was heard from Berlin to this clear violation of its sovereign rights. By the time Veracruz was occupied, the Wilhelmstrasse had accepted that, since Wilson was not going to change his attitude toward Huerta, the sooner the United States took action to stabilize the situation the better. "No diplomatic complications with Germany will occur as a result of the Ypiranga incident," the *New York Times* reported confidently. "Germany . . . has shown itself to be a good friend of the United States during the Mexican trouble." During the first week of the occupation, the Germans won points for Hintze's defiance of Huerta and for the *Dresden*'s rescue of 490 American refugees at Tampico. "If any doubt had been created in our minds as to the true position of Germany because of the critical attitude of the Berlin newspapers," the *Herald* editorialized, "it has been blown away. . . . Hoch der Kaiser!"[134]

Flying the German flag, the *Ypiranga* docked at Veracruz, took on refugees, and unloaded all its cargo except the weapons. (This disappointed the U.S. authorities at Veracruz, but there was nothing they could do about it.) Since the ship remained under control of the Reich transporting refugees, and since, as Captain Köhler observed, it "still had materiel on board for the federal government [Huerta], it stayed [in Veracruz] with a flag ship of the German Empire and had a military guard aboard in order to avoid any incident."[135]

On 24 April, Bryan told Bernstorff that the president was most anxious to prevent the *Ypiranga*'s cargo from reaching Huerta. Bernstorff, on querying the Wilhelmstrasse about the ship, was informed that the captain had been told not to unload the arms, which, "presumably," would be returned to Germany. Bernstorff informed Bryan that the arms would be shipped back to Hamburg, and the secretary of state expressed his thanks. Bryan then wrote Daniels, "The German Ambassador thinks there will be no delivery by ship as it now belongs to German Gov't but would cable. I explained that we hoped no delivery would be made. He seemed to have no doubt that they [the arms] would be withheld." For the Wilhelmstrasse, the matter was "settled."[136]

And so it might have been had the *Ypiranga* not steamed down the coast to Puerto México (which the Huertistas controlled) a month after it had precipitated the occupation of Veracruz and unloaded all its cargo of arms right into Huerta's hands.

There are several explanations for the unloading of the weapons. The first, and most widespread, is that the Germans (the Wilhelmstrasse in cahoots with Hapag) had willfully broken their promise to Washington that the weapons would be returned to Hamburg, either through an eruption of anti-Americanism or through stubborn support of Huerta. Barbara Tuchman says of the incident, "Publicly the Germans announced that the munitions would be returned to Hamburg, but while American attention was focused on Veracruz, they privately ordered the *Ypiranga* to slip down the coast . . . [where it] quietly completed delivery of [its] cargo to the Huerta forces." Reinhard Doerries asserts, "[It is] my considered opinion that Berlin had decided to back the caudillo Victoriano Huerta, even in the face of opposition from Woodrow Wilson. . . . President Wilson . . . now assumed correctly that the Germans were not laying all their cards on the table."[137]

This explanation does not make sense. The Wilhelmstrasse consistently put friendly relations with the United States to the fore in its actions in Mexico. It is very unlikely that it would have thrown caution to the winds at this late stage in the Huerta drama. It contradicts the available evidence.

A variant of this explanation is that Hapag, led by Albert Ballin, a strong supporter of Huerta, deliberately misled the Wilhelmstrasse and duped the United States. Again, this seems improbable. By late April, Huerta was isolated, and the arms shipment was not expected to make a significant difference to his chances. Hapag executives had no desire to antagonize the United States, their biggest customer, simply to boost the fortunes of a doomed dictator. As Arthur Zimmermann, the undersecretary of state, and later of telegram fame, cabled Hintze: "Hapag evidently wants to avoid any conflict with the United States."[138]

A more sophisticated explanation is advanced by German historian Thomas Baecker. It is essentially a "whisper down the lane" theory: Hapag told the Wilhelmstrasse that the arms would "presumably" be returned to Hamburg, the message was conveyed to Bernstorff, and to Hintze, and then to the Americans, but somewhere along the transom, the "presumably" was lost. This transformed a comment into a commitment that Hapag had never intended to make. Ballin had meant what he had said: the arms would "presumably" be returned to Europe. On 22 April—when he had made the statement—a Mexican-American war had looked probable, and Ballin had not wanted to incur the wrath of the United States by unloading the arms in the midst of it. However, by mid-May, such a war looked very unlikely, and Martin Schröder & Company of Hamburg, the arms dealers handling the cargo of the *Ypiranga*, demanded that the weapons be delivered. Hapag felt free to offload the weapons, thereby satisfying its customer and freeing the hold for the return cargo. Baecker argues that it was not malevolence but "political blindness" that led to the unloading.[139]

The problem with this theory is that it does not make sense that Hapag would jeopardize its U.S. trade for a relatively small (and prepaid) shipment in Mexico. Furthermore, Baecker's implication that Hapag was unaware that Washington believed that there had been a firm commitment on the part of the shippers to return the arms to Germany does not bear scrutiny. The understanding was even discussed in the Reichstag on 29 April. Jagow said that "the Washington authorities had ordered the Ypiranga to return her cargo. Washington had expressed the wish to keep the cargo on board the Ypiranga in the harbor or to unload it at the Vera Cruz Custom House. . . . The Hamburg-American Company had thereupon ordered the vessel to return home." [140] The *New York Times* and the *Herald* made this understanding clear several times before the ship pulled into Puerto México. On 26 April, the *Times* printed a telegram from Hapag to Captain Bonath: "Hamburg-American Line . . . instruct Captain of Ypiranga leave total arms, ammunition on board and return them to Hamburg." Hapag—in Mexico, Berlin, and New York—must have known that Washington felt it had been given a firm commitment.[141]

Why, then, were the arms offloaded? Certainly part of Baecker's explanation is correct: the situation in Mexico had changed between the stopping of the *Ypiranga* in Veracruz and its arrival in Puerto México a month later. The United States had gained the upper hand; Europe was in line behind U.S. policy; Hintze, who had once been one of Huerta's most ardent backers, was telling the dictator that stepping down would be his last "great patriotic act . . . to save the country from ruin"; the *Ypiranga*'s arms were no longer perceived to be decisive, and they were not likely to be used against invading Americans.[142] Baecker stresses the effect that all this had on Hapag. More relevant is its effect on Washington.

Washington expected the arms to be returned to Germany. It thought as much had been promised and that the matter was "settled." However, it did not press the issue, and it gave mixed signals at two crucial points: the docking of the *Bavaria* at Puerto México and the granting of permission to the *Ypiranga* to leave Veracruz. In early May there were reports of two Hapag ships, the *Kronprinzessin Cecilie* and the *Bavaria*, heading for Puerto México with arms for Huerta aboard. It was also reported that the United States would not prevent them from unloading their cargo.[143] Several days later, the *Kölnische Zeitung* reported that the *Cecilie* had indeed landed its cargo, while the *New York Times* and the *Herald* reported that it had not.[144] The *Bavaria* was expected to dock at Puerto México on 23 May, but it was reported that the State Department had appealed directly to Hapag to stop the shipment and that Hapag had agreed. "Officials are congratulating themselves over the manner in which this coup seems to have been accomplished," the *New York*

Times reported. "The supposition here [in Washington] is that the failure to land the war munitions was a voluntary act on the part of the steamship company. All the information obtainable in Washington indicates that the German Government did not take a hand in the matter."[145] Nevertheless, while the officials at the State Department were congratulating themselves, the *Bavaria* quietly pulled into the harbor at Puerto México on 23 May and proceeded to unload its small shipment of arms for Huerta. The *Herald* covered the incident (somewhat belatedly), but the *Times* did not, and it caused nary a ripple in the diplomatic correspondence.[146] It is reasonable to assume that Hapag weighed the situation—the hold of the *Ypiranga* full of weapons, the calmer situation on the ground in Mexico, the legality of offloading the arms, and the signal sent by the reaction, or nonreaction, to the *Bavaria*—and decided that Washington had blinked, that it would look the other way if the *Ypiranga*'s cargo was quietly unloaded.

Washington did not blink once, but twice. In a complicated series of events, probably injected with human error, the U.S. authorities at Veracruz gave the *Ypiranga* permission to leave despite the fact that they had been informed that it was going to unload its shipment at Puerto México. On 16 May, Hapag in Hamburg cabled Heynen, its agent in Mexico, that it hoped there would be no difficulties with the Americans if the steamer were to proceed to Puerto México, unload its cargo, and pick up a load for the return journey. Heynen consulted with Hintze, with whom he often conferred, and replied that the minister had advised against the *Ypiranga* going to Puerto México; Heynen recommended that the arms be handed over to the American authorities in Veracruz.[147] Hintze feared both the American reaction and a widening of the war. He confided to his diary, however, that he was unsure what to do. "Since I had not been informed of any decision about it, and I could not figure out the U.S. position on it, I asked the Wilhelmstrasse for advice."

On 18 May, the *Ypiranga* was officially—but quietly—released from government service, but Hintze decided (apparently on his own) to continue offering the ship the protection of the flag as long as it remained in Veracruz.[148] On 19 May he was told that the German government had no comment on the unloading of the weapons—Hapag had not approached Berlin, so it had no opinion about the matter.[149] On the same day, Heynen informed the local representative of Schröder & Company that "the *Ypiranga* was at his disposal and that it was his responsibility to make adequate arrangements with the Mexican government to ensure that the unloading of the arms in Puerto México and the loading of the return cargo proceeded without incident even if the Americans insisted that the weapons not be unloaded."[150] Hapag then cabled Heynen: "Please wire confirmation that . . . American authorities in Veracruz have withdrawn opposition before discharging ammunition *Ypiranga* in Puerto México."[151]

On 23 May, Hapag asked for permission from the U.S. port authorities to proceed to Puerto México, indicating, according to Köhler, that it might unload its cargo there. Captain Köhler went on to report that testy negotiations between the port authorities and the representatives of Hapag ensued. "It would have been possible to have resolved the issue to the satisfaction of the Americans. . . . But they were so unhelpful to the representatives of Hapag that the latter saw no reason to come to their aid. . . . The commanding officer at Veracruz later expressed regret that . . . he himself had not dealt with Hapag." In his account, Heynen mentions no acrimony. "The papers were completed openly and freely in the customs house without any question or opposition from the authorities as to the aims of the trip. . . . The Americans never gave the least hint that they would find the unloading of the weapons and ammunition of the *Ypiranga* disagreeable." Captain Bonath asserted, "Before clearance was granted us, I asked him [U.S. captain Herman O. Stickney, collector of the port] specifically: 'What would you do if I were compelled to land these arms at Puerto Mexico?' To this he made no reply."

It is possible that Stickney simply did not hear what was being said to him, so convinced was he that the arms would be returned to Germany. He had no doubt seen the same telegram conveying Hapag's orders to Bonath to "leave total arms, ammunition on board and return them to Hamburg" that had appeared in the *New York Times* on 26 April.[152] Heynen later explained, "The [U.S.] collector of the Port of Veracruz . . . told me that if he had known that the weapons and ammunition were going to be unloaded that he would have refused permission, but that he had never considered this possibility because he had been firmly convinced that the cargo would be returned to Hamburg; he had seen copies of the cables from Hamburg containing these assurances."[153]

Most likely is that Stickney heard exactly what was said but knew that he could not legally object and that Washington was no longer particularly interested in the *Ypiranga*'s cargo. In any case, on 25 May, Captain Bonath received permission from the port authorities, and the *Ypiranga* steamed to Puerto México, arriving shortly after noon on 27 May—four days, that is, after the *Bavaria*. The U.S. press reported the ship's movements without alarm. The *New York Times* speculated, "Many believe that the Ypiranga's departure is for the purpose of taking him [Huerta, leaving for exile] aboard at Puerto Mexico. The ship still has in her cargo the arms . . . but it is known to a certainty that they will not be landed at Puerto Mexico." In full view of U.S.

warships, the *Ypiranga* docked at Puerto México, and the crew immediately began to unload its cargo. The weapons were unloaded "without problem."[154]

"Washington's Hands Tied," announced the *New York Times*. "To seize German boats would be piracy, to seize Puerto Mexico would be war. . . . Long ago the State Department declared that if the agreement with the ship owners failed to prevent the importation of arms for Gen. Huerta, no aggressive measures could be taken to prevent it."[155] This was particularly true because Washington had submitted its dispute with Mexico over the Tampico incident to the mediation of the ABC powers (Argentina, Brazil, and Chile) and any aggressive action would jeopardize these promising efforts.

The official reaction in Washington was therefore very reserved, lending credence to the argument that the administration had indeed blinked. "There is reason to believe . . . that the Administration is not seriously concerned over the incident," the *New York Times* observed in its first report on the episode. "The President has been quoted circumstantially within the last few days as indicating that the approach of the Ypiranga simply supplied the 'psychological moment' for the sharp stroke that he considered necessary to bring the Mexican controversy to a head. The landing of the arms, it is thought, comes too late to bolster the tottering regime of Gen. Huerta."[156]

Public opinion, however, was not so placid. Nineteen American servicemen had died to stop Huerta from getting these arms. As Karl Boy-Ed, the German naval attaché in Washington, reported, "Not only those in government, but also the general public in the United States is very critical of the behavior of Hapag. . . . Letters [to] . . . the majority of newspapers . . . include bitter comments that the actions of the *Ypiranga* at Puerto México meant that the sacrifice of the nineteen [Americans] who died in Veracruz was in vain." Furthermore, it was embarrassing. "Europeans and Mexicans in Vera Cruz are quietly laughing," the *Herald* reported, "at the way the Americans were outwitted." And it was sinister: perhaps Huerta had agreed to mediation only to render Washington impotent to protest the landing of this huge arms shipment.[157]

The official response hardened. "The State and Navy Departments undoubtedly feel that they have been roughly dealt with by the shipping agents of the Hamburg-American line." Years later, Secretary of the Navy Daniels remembered, "It was to the [U.S.] Navy like a blow on the head."[158]

U.S. customs authorities fined Hapag nine hundred thousand pesos for the *Ypiranga*'s discharging its cargo at a port other than that to which it was addressed. Heynen called the fine "petty revenge," and Captain Köhler commented, "This incident is indicative of the arrogant presumption on the part of the United States that whatever goes against its interests is an offence against everything that is 'Right.' " Boy-Ed, on the other hand, noted the cost of the incident for Germany in a letter to Tirpitz, "There is no doubt as to the legality of the delivery of the weapons . . . [but] whether it was in Germany's interest is very much to be doubted." [159]

The Wilhelmstrasse's response to the fine was muted. "No German Protest Yet" was the headline in the *New York Times* on 3 June. Nor was a protest forthcoming. "This is not a matter between the Washington and Berlin Governments," Heynen explained, "for there was no understanding that we should not land the *Ypiranga*'s cargo elsewhere, the American Admiral commanding at Vera Cruz having said on 22 April that the ship was free to go where it pleased. We made all arrangements for landing at Puerto Mexico and the German Government had nothing to do with the matter." [160]

Heynen was right: the Wilhelmstrasse considered the arms shipment on the *Ypiranga* to be Hapag's responsibility; it was a business deal, not a political matter. It had been willing to be the intermediary between Hapag and the U.S. government, but after it had relayed the message the Americans wanted to hear, it took no official position on the matter.[161] It did not understand U.S. policy in Mexico. As with Wilson's twists and turns in the decision to withhold recognition from Huerta, so with the administration's reversals and threats concerning the *Ypiranga*: the Germans were left groping for a coherent, credible explanation of Washington's policy. Bernstorff, who believed that the Americans had given the *Ypiranga* a green light to unload its cargo anywhere, speculated that Washington was laying the groundwork to seize more customhouses. Otherwise, he argued, it simply made no sense. Hintze hazarded the explanation that the Americans must have wanted (their rhetoric notwithstanding) Huerta to be strengthened as a counterweight to Carranza. "This explains the U.S. embargo on weapons and ammunition as well as the permission to unload the *Ypiranga*," he concluded.[162]

Furthermore, the arms on the *Ypiranga* were not German, and there is no evidence that Berlin was even aware of their existence before the storm burst. Michael Meyer has exhaustively traced the circuitous path of the arms of the *Ypiranga*—from New York to Odessa to Hamburg to Le Havre before crossing the Atlantic. Yes, New York. "Her cargo," Jagow announced, "was principally of American origin." This shipment included arms from the Colt Automatic Arms Company in Hartford, Connecticut; from the French firms Cartoucheries Françaises and Saint Chamond; and from the British firm Vickers and Armstrong. Both the French and Swiss governments appear to have assisted the shippers to amass the arms, but not the German.[163]

The Wilhelmstrasse would have been informed about the arms shipment before the *Ypiranga* sailed but for the obstinacy of the Hamburg senate. When the cargo arrived in Hamburg—14,750 cases of ammunition and weapons worth more than $1 million—the American consul feared that it was headed for Huerta. (U.S. consuls were on the lookout for large arms shipments that could have been destined for Huerta.) His anxiety, however, was never relayed to Berlin. The Hamburg senate, irritated with U.S. policy in Mexico, stonewalled the consul and dismissed the police report that stated, "Weapons have been sent by this circuitous route destined for Mexico in order to obscure the destination and make it difficult for the Americans to trace the cargo." The actions of the ship, the Hamburg senate bristled, were perfectly legal.[164]

The cargo ended up in a German bottom because Hapag provided the most regular and reliable steamer service from Europe to Mexico. (It is tempting to speculate that the choice of a German bottom was doubly pleasing as it would transfer the heat—if there was any—to the hapless Germans, but there is no evidence to prove this.)[165] The weapons were paid for in Mexican bonds to a Swiss bank. The hand of the German government was nowhere to be found.

Nevertheless, much of the U.S. press of the day and historians since refer to the trigger for the U.S. occupation of Veracruz as the arrival of a shipment of "German arms" and cite the incident as another example of the perfidy of the Germans. In fact, the opposite conclusion seems more true. Reconsider the bald facts of the story. A German company shipped a cargo of arms to Huerta. The action was thoroughly legal. At Veracruz, U.S. officers illegally boarded the ship and ordered it not to leave. Several weeks later, U.S. officers gave the ship permission to leave, having been told that the captain's intention was to (legally) offload the cargo at Puerto México. When a storm erupted in the U.S. press, Washington expressed its dismay at the German action, and the ship was fined almost half a million dollars.

Major international incidents have been spawned from less, but throughout it all the German government stoically endeavored to maintain good relations with Washington. It protested neither the violation of sovereignty implicit in the boarding of the *Ypiranga* nor the fine. At no point did it challenge the highly questionable right of the Americans to stop a ship from delivering its cargo when no formal blockade or state of war had been declared. Rather, it consistently kept a low profile and let Hapag deal with the matter. Its actions were true to the assertion that it did not perceive it to be a political matter and, more important, consistent with its policy in Mexico to avoid offending Washington.

Nor did the State Department treat it as a political matter. It tried to deal directly with the shipping company, and its desire to safeguard its relationship with Germany conditioned many of its actions during the affair, particularly the hasty occupation of Veracruz itself. It was careful not to blame the German government for what happened. This led Heynen to surmise after the arms were unloaded, "I believe that the incident will have no consequences and will be consigned to a pigeon hole in Washington." [166] If it had been simply an intergovernmental matter, Heynen would have been right.

However, the State Department could not control the spin, and the incident was etched onto the lengthening list of examples of German treachery and aggression in the hemisphere. Hintze understood that this would be the inevitable outcome. "Our enemies," he wrote, "will not fail to exploit it in Washington as evidence of duplicity and deviousness." [167]

Reflections

The *Ypiranga* resonates in the echo chamber created by the Zimmermann telegram. It resonates in hindsight. It gives depth to the image of a German threat to the hemisphere. It is, however, a red herring.

"The entire handling of the affair by the Foreign Office and the German Admiralty," Reinhard Doerries asserts,

> shows clearly that Berlin . . . had opted for Huerta and, despite America's expressed interest and obvious distress, could not be swayed from its position. The Foreign Office, which was in contact with the Hamburg-American Line, revealed that consideration for the political views of the United States, at least in Mexico, was not necessarily a determining factor for German actions. Thus it happened that, even before the outbreak of the World War, Count Bernstorff . . . was maneuvered into a very unpleasant, if not to say somewhat discreditable position vis-à-vis the American government. . . . When war broke out in Europe, Berlin was already fully engaged in Mexico. In contrast to the United States, Germany had supported . . . Huerta and underlined its policy by supplying the dictator with arms.[168]

But this is not what the story of the *Ypiranga* shows. What it shows is that when war broke out, Germany changed its traditional policy in Mexico. What it actually shows is that before the war Berlin acted with remarkable consideration for the political views of the United States.

How could such divergent interpretations emerge? In some ways the problem is comparable to that in Brazil, where the pan-Germans said one thing (lurid sound bites) and the Wilhelmstrasse did another (cautious inactivity). In Mexico, however, it was not the garrulous pan-Germans but Minister Hintze, the German community, and the kaiser who spouted the quotable, anti-American rhetoric. (The important difference between the two situations is that the jingoistic talk about Brazil was much more public and gave rise to a debate in the U.S. press.)

Let us deal first with Hintze. He, like the British and American representatives in Mexico City, was still behaving like the freewheeling, virtually autonomous diplomats of yore, like the British, German, and American triumvirate who hammered out the Samoa settlement in the 1880s — diplomats who did what they thought best and wrote home to inform their bosses afterward. The telegraph changed that, and with new communications technology, control flowed to the center. In the early years of this century, diplomats increasingly could — which slipped into should — consult with their superiors before making decisions. But the habit was still to think for oneself. Therefore, Hintze's letters to Berlin convey a certain sense of authority that is as quotable as it is deceptive. When push came to shove, he was overridden by the Wilhelmstrasse time and time again.

Similar conclusions apply to the statements of German businessmen with interests in Mexico. Like the navy captains who reported their dreams for the flowering of *Deutschtum* in Brazil, German businessmen in Mexico allowed themselves to dream and to speculate, initially about schemes to bolster up Huerta and eventually about the necessary evil of U.S. intervention. The Wilhelmstrasse received their comments in stony silence. The businessmen and the Foreign Office were running on separate tracks; their aims frequently overlapped, but they were not identical. Both the Wilhelmstrasse and the businessmen wanted stability in Mexico in order to protect German interests there, but the Wilhelmstrasse also had to deal with the balance of power. In its view, German interests would not be protected simply by the iron hand of a neo-Díaz (whether imposed by the United States or not); stability was not just a function of Mexican domestic politics, it was also the by-product of the maintenance of the balance of power in the region — a balance of power, that is, in which Germany avoided conflict with the United States but maintained a role in Mexico, albeit limited, and a voice, albeit muted.

The kaiser, in his running commentary on Mexican affairs along the margins of reports forwarded to him, conveyed his frustration with England, with France, and with the United States. His marginalia reveal the emotional side of German policy, the turbulence beneath the surface. It is reasonable to speculate that his opinions on Mexico were shared by others in government, and it is reasonable to suppose that they affected policy. It is very difficult, however, to find proof of either assertion. Take, for example, Wilhelm's clearly expressed support for a joint European action to challenge U.S. hegemony in Mexico. The quotations are there: he wanted to see that "Wilson bloodied his hand in Mexico," and he rejoiced when a joint démarche was in the offing, "Good. Finally unity against the Yankee." [169] But where is the policy? Hintze tried to begin a joint action, and Wilhelm scribbled approval, and it can all seem ominous, but, as in Brazil, where's the fire?

There were Germans—even the kaiser himself—voicing dreams of German grandeur in Mexico, dreams of the destruction of the Monroe Doctrine, dreams of a more just geography. These dreams are not insignificant, but they are not policy. German policy toward Mexico—what Germany actually did— was remarkably consistent and restrained. In Mexico, Germany tried to promote stability to protect its citizens and investments and to remain a player in an increasingly complex game. As the wind changed, it changed tack in order to sail steadily toward these goals.

Germany both resented its fate—being bested by the Americans in Mexico —and bowed to it. It would be wrong, however, to characterize German policy—stretched between these two tendencies—as inconsistent, twisting and turning. Diplomacy frequently strains to straddle a divide, to have it both ways. This is not the same as inconsistency: German policy was *consistently* pulled between its desire to denounce the Monroe Doctrine and its need to placate the Americans. But in Mexico, where the German stake was marginal and the American stake, both economic and strategic, significant, the desire to placate prevailed until Germany and the United States were almost at war. The Wilhelmstrasse was realistic: no gain in influence in Mexico would be worth risking the displeasure of the United States. Hintze summed up the Reich's predicament: "Those who can't bite shouldn't bark." [170]

Throughout the year and a half of Huerta's rule, Berlin struggled to find a way to halt or slow the spread of American hegemony without damaging Germany's relationship with the United States. As the U.S. military attaché in Berlin wrote, "The German papers have given a good deal of space to the Mexican revolutions. . . . It is asked, 'why should we alienate the Americans, who are sensitive with respect to anything that looks like an infringement of the Monroe Doctrine, at this time and drive them into the English camp?' The Germans don't care about the Monroe Doctrine, but they want friends." Whatever its desires, the Reich's actions in Mexico were consistently deferential to Washington. The *Ypiranga* was no exception: the delivery of arms to Huerta was a legal business transaction of Hapag that had been approved by the U.S. authorities; it was not an insolent ploy of the German government. The U.S. government and press repeatedly acknowledged and lauded German support for the United States in Mexico. "The German government has occupied a most dignified position in the matter," President Wilson said at a press conference in March 1914. "It hasn't gone around with a chip on its shoulder." [171]

Berlin was attempting to defend a very weak position: it had relatively few nationals in Mexico, relatively minor business interests, and its insecurity in Europe dictated that it was not free to pursue adventure in the Western Hemisphere. It did not even have sufficient cruisers available to protect its nationals in the country. In February 1913 — while revolution was raging — Jagow stated in the Reichstag that Berlin had asked for Washington's assistance in protecting its citizens in Mexico because it had no ships close by. "Only His Majesty's ship *Bremen* is at present on the East America station . . . and she must undergo extensive repairs. . . . It is therefore not possible to send her to Veracruz at the moment." Throughout the early years of the revolution the United States looked after the safety of German citizens, particularly in the interior. Even during the *Ypiranga* affair, Berlin asked for special assistance, as the *Nürnberg* (which was usually off the west coast of Mexico) was going to Panama for repairs.[172]

Moreover, Mexico bordered the United States; by 1913 Americans had established their preeminence in the sprawling country. The international struggle in Mexico was between an England in strategic retreat and a United States on the march; while it suited London to hand the naval burden to Washington, it was not willing to forgo the financial stakes without a struggle. Berlin is hardly in the game. It is striking that in both the U.S. and British records on Mexico during the Huerta period, Germany plays an utterly marginal role.

The story of Germany's accommodation to the twists and turns of Wilson's policy in Mexico helps deflate the idea of a German threat to the hemisphere, and it also provides a case study in the problems of communication between the two countries, problems that bred the mistrust underlying the perception of threat. Even after November 1913, when Wilson finally articulated his policy toward Mexico, the Germans did not understand it. This makes their willingness to support it all the more remarkable.

Why did they find it incomprehensible? In a sense, it comes down to the old realist/idealist debate. Baldly, the Germans found Wilson's declarations of his idealistic aims unbelievable. When the U.S. ambassador in London told his German counterpart that the United States had no interest in Mexican territory, "He looked at me — a mere glimpse of 1/100th of a second — and I saw this flit across his mind: 'You are either a consummate liar or an irresponsible idiot.'" Here were people speaking two mutually unintelligible languages. The words can be translated, but the meanings slip away. Why?[173]

Wilson's motives in Mexico will probably always be debated; they are a rich and deep field for historical archaeology. Scholars have tended, naturally, to focus on Wilson's words and their correlation with (or lack thereof) his actions. However, especially when looking at his speeches from a non-

American perspective, it also seems important to remember to whom he was speaking. Clearly he was not addressing the Europeans. Nor was he addressing the Mexicans. In 1913, he simply did not know enough about Mexico to be talking about reality there. Hintze saw this clearly: countering Carden's comment that "Woodrow Wilson is a model of duplicity," Hintze said, "My impression is that Wilson is pursuing a consistent policy that is based, apparently, on a failure to understand the Mexican people." [174]

The point is deceptively simple: in his pronouncements on Mexico, Wilson was talking about what Americans believe. He was saying that Americans believe in democracy and justice. For Americans, this is a powerful message. It resonates.

And what did this message, meant for Americans, mean to foreigners? Foreigners took Wilson's policy statements literally and were confused by them. "[Lind is] at pains to explain how difficult he found it to convince the Mexicans the USG[overnment] could be actuated by higher motives than those of mere commercialism," the British minister in Mexico wrote the Foreign Office. Undersecretary Mallet minuted: "A great deal of explanation seems to be required." In June 1914—eighteen months into Wilson's Mexico policy— the kaiser was still baffled by it. When he met Colonel House in Berlin, he "broke in . . . to say what a great man Diaz was and why we did not send for him and put him in charge." [175]

For many Germans, since Huerta was the key to stability, and since the United States had no replacement for Huerta in mind, Wilson's goal in removing Huerta must have been to weaken Mexico prior to an American invasion. According to this theory, Wilson was either a cynical, duplicitous realist with "very sinister designs towards Mexico" or a dupe, an unwitting tool of big business. "The [German] secretary of state [Jagow] is convinced that [the] American refusal to recognize is entirely due to the influence of the American ambassador in Mexico, whose personal policy is, he says, to annex at least northern provinces," the British ambassador in Berlin cabled home.[176] The Socialist *Vorwärts* commented, "If the United States gains its end, the result will be that Mexico will become more than ever the domain of American trusts—the delectable result of the policy of a democratic President who has always boasted so loudly of his opposition to capitalism." Kardorff agreed: "Does he [Wilson] not see that he, the declared enemy of the big syndicates, is serving quite well the interests of the trusts in Mexico?" The Mexican minister in Berlin demurred. "He did not himself believe so much in an American desire to annex as in their wish to see a Government set up in Mexico who would be completely subservient to them. He thought that their present unfriendly attitude was very largely due to the fact of Lord Cowdray having secured the oil concession, and was entirely engineered by financial interests." [177] Or perhaps, some speculated, Wilson had simply developed an obsessive hatred for Huerta. Or perhaps he was just a naive, incompetent American with a "theatrical desire of seeing a free suffrage exercised by . . . all the . . . bandits throughout the country." [178] In any case, he was not what he said he was: a man seeking justice in Mexico.

The notion that Wilson was using an important issue in foreign affairs to express inchoate ideals to a domestic audience was foreign to most Europeans. They did not have that luxury, living cheek by jowl with powerful neighbors and not blessed with a vast land full of natural resources. Nor did they have the need. While it might be of central significance for an American president to express ideals, to preach a vision, what is central to European foreign policy is what is central to realpolitik, the theory of politics that was forged in Europe. That is, power: control over land and resources and people. But for an unchallenged island nation with abundant resources, power is a different commodity; power to rally, power to unite, power to create a sense of nationhood vie with raw power in importance. "There are many things that come before business and there are some things that come before order," the U.S. ambassador in London wrote to Wilson. [179]

Wilson was stirring the American people; he was stating American ideals; he was articulating what Americans believe. This is what religious talk does. And the impasse between Wilson and the Europeans about his goals in Mexico is reminiscent of the impasse that can result when people of two different religions talk about their faiths. There is a slipperiness in comparing one's own beliefs with the actions—rather than the beliefs—of others.

It is tempting to compare our intentions in foreign policy with the actions of other countries. Intentions can seem more important than actions, which frequently (through external evil, personal failure, bad luck, "irony") fall far short of intentions. This emphasis on intentions is alien to the dominant mode of political thought among Europeans. It stumps them. To fit it into the realpolitik, power-centric model, this kind of moralistic policy must be seen as cynical, or inept, or naive.

It is, in fact, not quite any of the above. It is, simply, different. It is not the opposite of realpolitik; it is a variant of it, a variant that developed in luxury, where foreign policy was rarely a matter of life or death, or even war or peace. And it is a variant that developed where the need for security vied with the need for the creation of nationalism. (This is not what Link calls Wilson's "higher realism"; it is more like "coddled realism.") [180]

What might have been reckless idealism for the Europeans—the refusal to recognize an established government on moral grounds—was not reckless on

"The new gown." In this German cartoon, Wilson drapes Mexico in the American flag. (*Lustige Blätter* [7 January 1914])

Wilson's part. It had a very low cost for the United States and benefits beyond the articulation of American ideals. In a report to the Foreign Office about his mission to Washington in November 1913, Tyrrell zeroed in on the realpolitik behind Wilson's policy:

> I was sent for to the White House where the President gave me his views on Mexico. . . . With the opening of the Panama Canal it is becoming increas-

ingly important that the Governments of the Central American Republics should improve, as they will become more and more a field for European and American enterprise: bad government may lead to friction and such incidents as the Venezuela affair under Castro. . . . With this object in view, the President made up his mind to teach these countries a lesson by insisting on the removal of Huerta. . . . Huerta exceeded . . . the limit of what is permissible. . . . The President did not seem to realise that his policy will lead to a "de facto" American protectorate over Central American republics; but there are others here who do, and who intend to achieve that object.[181]

In taking a stand against the British, and winning, the United States solidified its hegemony throughout the region. It signaled loudly and clearly that it had the power and the will to act unilaterally in the hemisphere.

For the Mexicans, of course, the costs were higher. Wilson, and all the foreigners put together, did not determine the course of the Mexican Revolution. He affected it, but the story had its own internal, Mexican dynamic. Alan Knight argues that Wilson had a more sensitive grasp of the revolution than did the European leaders and that as president of the United States his actions would inevitably affect Mexico—Wilson could not avoid interfering, if not by commission, then by omission.[182] There is certainly truth in this, and a useful corrective to the cheap shots frequently hurled at Wilson. But Knight sidesteps the fundamental arrogance of Wilson's stance. Wilson presumed that he had the moral right—even duty—to decide what was best for Mexico, to pass judgment on the legitimacy of its revolution, and to tinker with the outcome. As the wife of the American chargé in Mexico said, "We can but express the pious hope that, with the help of God, no foreign nation will ever have a chance to serve us to the same extent."[183]

5

Image and Reality

The Utility
of Misperception

The last words of John Knowles's novel *A Separate Peace* are a haunting reflection on the enemy. "All of them," he writes about his characters, "constructed at infinite cost to themselves these Maginot Lines against this enemy they thought they saw across the frontier, this enemy who never attacked that way—if he ever attacked at all; if he was indeed the enemy." [1] By 1900, many Americans saw an enemy across the frontier, and the enemy was Germany. The U.S. Navy had decided that the next war would be fought in the Caribbean and that it would be against Germany.

The uncertainty of it all, of perception and of reality. To determine who is and who is not an enemy, one must predict the future; one must guess what could happen, what might happen. It is an art. And passing judgment on these guesses, even with the benefit of hindsight, is almost as difficult as making the original determination, particularly if the purported enemy never attacked at all. Was it the prudent and prescient countermeasures that stopped the threat from materializing? Or does the passing of the threat—not with a bang but a whimper—show instead that the precautions were unnecessary, provocative, counterproductive?

This has been a study of threat perception. It illuminates how the image of the enemy was constructed, what validity this image had, and what its significance was. It has investigated two related questions: what did Germany do in Latin America and what did the United States think it did? The gap between German actions and U.S. perceptions has been the study's keynote. This gap matters because this was the era of protective imperialism. From the victory over Spain in 1898 through the purchase of the Danish West Indies in 1917, the

United States unfurled its umbrella over the Caribbean and Central America. If it was protecting these small, weak countries from German aggression, the United States was not necessarily behaving like a traditional imperial power in its acquisition of empire; it could have been, instead, benevolently enforcing the Monroe Doctrine. If, on the other hand, there was no German threat, U.S. imperialism is laid bare, and ordinary.

This study of Berlin's behavior in Latin America shows that the Reich was, in fact, at all times hesitant to act aggressively and eager to avoid a clash with the United States. What did Germany actually do to establish hegemony in the region? The simple answer is nothing. There was no German threat. True, one branch of the Imperial Navy drew up war plans aimed at destroying the Monroe Doctrine, but the plans were toothless: the German army refused to respond to the navy's call—and the kaiser was silent—and so the navy was left with a rousing overture to a war, which would have been followed by disastrous silence. True, Germany blockaded Venezuelan ports, but it cleared the operation carefully with the United States well beforehand, and it followed England's lead. True, many Germans moved to southern Brazil, and some dreamed of establishing a full-fledged colony there, but their government's help was lackluster, failing even to promote the construction of a railroad that would link an important German settlement to the port. True, the Wilhelmstrasse sent the Zimmermann telegram in the thick of war, but before the war broke out, its policy in Mexico had been accommodating to the United States despite the irritations caused by Wilson's dallying. Even more striking, with the exception of its occasional promotion of the arms trade, Berlin made no serious attempt to establish informal empire in Latin America. Look, for example, at Brazil: despite the opportunity, despite the pan-German rhetoric, despite the Germans living in Brazil, the Reich failed to negotiate favorable trade treaties, initiate helpful stock market reforms, promote capital investment, or save the Hansa colony.

Nevertheless, many Americans—including Dewey, the General Board of the Navy, Mahan, the editors of the *New York Herald*—looked in their teacups in 1900 and saw a clear and present German danger. They fed on each other: the pro-naval U.S. press reflected the navy's concerns, and the navy picked up concerns expressed in the press, both U.S. and British. Thus there was an intricate fugue of various voices—the pan-Germans, the U.S. pro-naval press, U.S. Navy officers, German navy officers, the British press—who sang about the German threat. The cumulative impact was more powerful than any solo voice. To use Jack Snyder's image explaining empires that overexpand, these separate groups "logrolled" and in so doing created an image that had both durability and momentum.[2] Against a backdrop of trade tensions and the burgeoning German fleet, these voices formed an image of German ambitions in Latin America.

It is important to avoid overstatement: the idea of a German threat to Latin America was not uppermost in the minds of most of those who did embrace it. It was not a hotly debated issue. Furthermore, it is impossible to gauge the sincerity of those who did argue that there was a German threat; they could have been motivated more by the lure of economic or political gain than by concern for U.S. security. Emphasizing a threat helped bolster support for a larger navy. For the British, it was a way to widen the gap between the United States and Germany.

Moreover, it was not the only image of Germany. One of the most striking aspects of this study has been the chasm between the State Department's and executive's image of Germany on the one hand and that of the navy and pro-naval press on the other. Teddy Roosevelt spanned this divide. An avid expansionist and friend of Lodge and Mahan, Roosevelt beat the drum of the German threat—until he became vice president. Then he precipitously dropped his dire predictions and professed his desire to cooperate with Berlin. While the navy was drawing up war plans in the early years of the twentieth century, the secretary of state asked U.S. representatives in Brazil, where the German threat was considered most serious, whether they themselves had seen signs of danger. The ministers and consuls replied with remarkable unanimity that although there were many Germans in Brazil's three southern states, there was no German threat. The Germans in Brazil, they stressed, were loyal to their new country, not to the kaiser. Nor did the White House, whether occupied by Roosevelt of by Taft, express any anxiety about a German threat to Brazil. In Mexico, President Wilson and the State Department went out of their way to stress how cooperative Berlin had been during the Huerta period; Wilson blamed English intrigue for his troubles, not German.

Thus there were two American images of Germany, the "official" one that the diplomats tended to espouse, and the "unofficial" one that much of the navy and popular press promoted. These two images were not in competition; they were on separate tracks. Their differences were ones of interpretation rather than fact.

Both agreed that Berlin had a reason to challenge the Monroe Doctrine. There was a compelling logic to the idea of German expansion in the Western Hemisphere. The spirit of the day in the politics of the great powers was expand or perish. Germany was considered both overpopulated and in need of overseas markets. Africa and Asia were already carved up by European powers with whom Germany did not want to clash. Latin America was the logical destination for German expansion.

Both agreed that at the turn of the century the German navy had the where-withal to threaten the U.S. Navy in the Caribbean, a region of increasing interest to the United States because of the desire for an isthmian canal and the closing of the continental frontier. Anxiety about German strength was the flip side of anxiety about American weakness. By both American and German reckoning, Germany would have won a naval war waged in the region. And even if it was far fetched to imagine that Germany might provoke such a war, it is the business of strategists to imagine the worst. As Mahan wrote in 1909, "It made no difference to us what object she [Germany] had in view; . . . her navy was the big fact, that called on us to sit up and take notice." For the U.S. Navy the important point was that Germany had the capability to threaten the Monroe Doctrine.[3]

For the State Department and White House, however, the equation was more complex and the threat less dire because capability concerned more than hardware. It also involved opportunity. While aware that the U.S. Navy would have been hard pressed to enforce the Monroe Doctrine in the Caribbean, to say nothing of south Brazil, the State Department—unlike the General Board, which recommended in 1901 that the doctrine be limited to north of the Amazon—was comforted by the fact that the doctrine was protected by the rivalries that preoccupied the European powers.

Where the navy and the State Department divided most sharply was in their interpretation of Germany's intentions. Gauging intentions is soothsaying; it is a deeply subjective act. Every action, every utterance of the putative enemy becomes a sign to be interpreted, a variation in the tea leaves to be read. Hunches about what these actions and words signify are colored, even determined, by a complicated mind-set made up of prejudices, experiences, information, fears.

For much of the American public and navy, the analysis of German intentions was simple: the ultranationalists articulated them clearly—Berlin wanted to conquer the world. What the pan-Germans said made sense out of a complicated morass of information. The public and the navy had no need for the oft tortuous analysis of the relationship between pan-Germans and Berlin that has dogged historians to this day. Like any military's determination of the threat it faces, the U.S. Navy's assessment was based on the extrapolation of a worst-case scenario from the evidence—the assumption that smoke means fire. That Berlin actually did very little to expand its influence in Latin America carried less weight than the alarmist rhetoric of the pan-Germans and their critics. Words spoke louder than deeds.

For the State Department, however, deeds mattered, and the assurances of the officials in the Wilhelmstrasse carried more weight than the fantasies of the pan-Germans and the popular press. Thus the State Department could look on the German need to expand and on German naval strength and not be alarmed because it did not believe that the Reich had either the political freedom or the intention of embroiling itself in a war with the United States.

These two images coexisted at the turn of the century, leading separate lives. There was very little contact between the Navy and State departments. Naval reports were routinely forwarded to the State Department, but the courtesy was not often reciprocated. The detailed minutes of the meetings of the General Board reveal how separate war planning was from diplomacy and even current events: the views of the State Department were never sought, and even crises with a clear naval dimension, such as the blockade of Venezuela and the Russo-Japanese War, were barely mentioned. The immutability of the navy's image of Germany as a marauder in the hemisphere—the repetitiveness of its war scenarios, the persistence of the nightmares dreamed up in Newport—is explained, in part, by the simple fact that the navy developed its plans in a political vacuum. The State Department, on the other hand, was aware of the navy's fears, of the articles about the German threat in the press, and of the international politics of the day. It occasionally checked with its representatives in Latin America about the Germans in their midst. It did little to correct the image because it seemed insignificant; it did not inhibit or impinge upon diplomacy. Reality was determined by diplomat-to-diplomat exchanges, not by the popular press.

What is interesting is that the State Department, by considering the navy's image of Germany irrelevant, condemned its own version of reality to irrelevance. It did not broadcast its image. Despite the occasional reports in the *New York Times* parroting the State Department's viewpoint, its image of Germany did not "stick." The navy's did.

Of course, Wilhelm bears a great deal of responsibility. His actions were cautious, but he underestimated—badly—the power of language, of ambiguity, and of fear. Looming behind the caution of the Germans in Latin America was the ominous growth of the fleet, and behind that of German industrial power, which made pan-German rhetoric credible. Wilhelm chose not to curb the pan-Germans for domestic political reasons (and because of his visceral sympathy with their point of view), and he paid a price abroad. He did, in fact, bow to the Monroe Doctrine, but he could not bring himself to do it with grace, and his audible grumblings carried more weight than all his caution.

This fits a pattern: German dreams and German actions were out of sync in Latin America, and the former, not the latter, was the stuff that compelling images are made of. This was true of Berlin's policy toward Venezuela during the Anglo-German blockade, toward Brazil, and toward Mexico before the outbreak of war in Europe. It is reasonable to surmise, although it can never be more than that, that if history had been radically different, if Germany had been confident of its position in Europe, it might have sought empire in Latin America. This dream, passionately asserted by the pan-Germans, and not convincingly denied by the government, seemed more real than the blandness of official policy.

The Wilhelmstrasse strove to control the damage: to contain the kaiser without antagonizing him, to appease the imperialists without alienating the Agrarians, to avoid offending the United States while at the same time hoping to increase Germany's prestige abroad. This was a government that wanted too much in Latin America and did not want any of it badly enough. It wanted the fruits of expansion, but it was unwilling to risk antagonizing the United States.

Why was Wilhelm's policy in Latin America so flaccid? Perhaps the Reich made the same fundamental error in Latin America that it did in Europe: perhaps it believed that time was on its side. The Tirpitz plan was based on the bizarre premise that the world would stand still while Germany built its world-class fleet, that battleships could dance on eggs. At the turn of the century, those in Berlin who thought about Latin America may have hoped to forestall a decisive confrontation until the 1920s and then, fleet in hand and Europe subdued, to sally forth. But Germany could no more stop time in the Americas than it could in Europe. The United States, like England across the water, did not play the fiddle while Tirpitz built the fleet. Or perhaps some in Berlin feared that a more vigorous policy in Latin America—as in Europe—would propel the world toward war. The evidence, however, points to a simpler explanation: that Berlin was not interested in Latin America, despite the clamorings of the jingoes.

The Germans seemed to have been dealt a good hand (their navy could beat the U.S. Navy; many Germans had settled in Latin America; Germany had well-established trade ties to the region), but they could not play it. The Monroe Doctrine might have been an arrogant conceit, but once Britain began to withdraw its fleet from the region, Monroe Doctrine or no Monroe Doctrine, it was America's to take. This was not because of American military power— Germany could defeat the U.S. fleet in its own backyard. Nor was it due to U.S. proximity to the region—the speed with which the German navy could mobilize negated that potential advantage. It was due to brute geography—to the United States' lack of strong neighbors.

Wilhelm and his courtiers refused to make the hard choices that clear policy requires. They were cautious but refused to be humble; they yielded to the Monroe Doctrine but refused to recognize it. They were cautious, but in a prickly, begrudging way. Thus they failed to reap any of the benefits of caution: trust and friendship. They ended up with the worst of both worlds. They got nothing but distrust.

This was because the image of Germany as a marauder in the hemisphere gradually overwhelmed the more sedate view of the State Department and entered the public discourse. It became reality. By 1913, when Wilson came into office, it should have been clear to all that whatever capacity Berlin may have had to challenge the Monroe Doctrine in 1900 had evaporated by the end of the decade. This was due neither to a deterioration of the German navy nor to a strengthening of the U.S. Navy, but to Germany's increasing isolation on the Continent. What was clear to the prescient after the second Venezuela crisis should have been clear to all after the 1905 Morocco crisis. Fearing encirclement, Berlin was unable to undertake any adventure in the Americas. As its isolation on the Continent deepened, it shed any optimism about Latin America. By 1905, the German navy had shelved its war plans about a showdown in the Caribbean, and the flamboyance and energy of pan-German rhetoric about Latin America had waned. Berlin, however, did not signal this shift clearly, and the U.S. Navy remained suspicious of every German cruiser trolling the waters of the Western Hemisphere. Wilson and the State Department, on the other hand, were still sober in their assessment of Germany's behavior. By 1915, however, when Wilson's imperial surge began in earnest, he appropriated the popular image of Germany. In Mexico, he had not needed it: there he was standing tall for democracy; he was teaching the Mexicans to elect good men. But when his marines occupied Haiti in 1915 and the Dominican Republic a year later, and when he bought the Danish West Indies in 1917, the idea of a German threat was useful. He could unfurl the American umbrella and announce with authority — despite the collapse of the German navy and the total preoccupation of the German army with the war in Europe — that he was protecting the weak and vulnerable from the German bully.

This helps to explain why the image of a German marauder in the hemisphere has had such remarkable staying power, despite the fact that it is not supported by an investigation of Berlin's actions and is gutted by the obvious constriction of German freedom of maneuver. It is still a common refrain in the scholarly literature. Why? Why has it been so tempting to believe that Wilhelm was plotting?

The answer must be speculative. Determining the enemy is like playing cards. Even when, after the fact, the historian can reveal the Reich's cards, it is impossible to determine all its possible strategies with certainty. Even with hindsight, there are too many variables. Thus, for example, Ragnild Fiebig-von Hase can look in the German archives and proclaim that there was a

German threat to Latin America because only the cards can be revealed with certainty, not how they would have been played.

But the question must be one of probability, of emphasis. The onus is on the historian, as it was on the executive and the State Department at the time, to discern the possible from the probable, the likely from the unlikely. The question is parallel to the critical legal distinctions needed to argue a case of self-defense: the defendant must be able to persuade the jury that his or her perception of an imminent threat was reasonable. There are, in this regard, two significant facts about German policy toward Latin America at the time. First, Berlin was very cautious in all its actions toward the region. Second, even if for the sake of argument one assumes that it would have liked to have seen the realization of every dream of the pan-Germans, an increasingly unlikely set of events would have had to have occurred for these dreams to have been put into motion: England would have had to have supported Germany, and Europe would have had to have been at peace. Therefore, while it is understandable that many Americans saw Germany as a competitor in the hemisphere, and while in the card game of threat assessment it was reasonable to speculate on the possibility of a German threat, the likelihood of such a threat became increasingly remote after 1900. What is interesting is the almost total failure to take either fact—both of which were accessible at the time (the General Board's interest in the plan against Germany lapsed in 1903)—into account in the popular and naval assessment of the German role during the period of protective imperialism.

In part this is due to inertia: once established, images are hard to shed. Throughout the era, Germany did nothing dramatic to counter the negative image of its Latin American policy in the United States. (The contrast with London's frank appeasement of the United States in the hemisphere is striking.) It would have taken something more dramatic than prudence to dislodge the prevailing perception. The key question for the navy was not Germany's intentions, or the changing nature of these intentions, but its capabilities. Therefore, Germany would have had to have sent a very strong signal to have penetrated the world of naval planning. Indeed, it is probable that as long as Germany was expanding its fleet, no signal would have been strong enough to have changed the American navy's image of Germany.[4]

As for the verdict of historians about the German threat, the residue of history has made the idea of an aggressive, expansionist Germany in the Western Hemisphere easy to believe. How can we read the kaiser's marginalia, or the bombast of the pan-Germans, today, in light of Hitler, and not shudder? But hindsight, when clouded by the two world wars, is not always twenty-twenty.

These explanations of the persistence of the idea of a German threat to the hemisphere—the difficulty of all threat assessment, inertia, hindsight—may be inadequate to explain the phenomenon. It is startling: it is considered plausible that the French and Germans were hatching plots to take over Brazil in 1914, Haiti in 1915, and the Danish West Indies in 1917; historians to this day refer to a German threat without a serious analysis of it; and yet, this study of the key examples of a German challenge—the war plans, the Venezuela crisis, colonization in southern Brazil, intrigue in Mexico—shows that in every instance Berlin deferred to the Monroe Doctrine, that the threat was tenuous in 1900 and nonexistent in 1914. And yet, it was credible, in 1914 and to the present day. Something more may be needed to explain the allure of the image.

The image of Germany as a threat to the hemisphere fills a need. The need is not just for an enemy in the simple sense that the U.S. Navy required—an adversary around which to structure force planning and rally the Congress and the American people. The resonance and persistence of the image are explained by something deeper.

At the turn of the century, the government-to-government exchanges between Washington and Berlin about the latter's actions in Latin America were not, in general, overblown. But the press in the United States, Germany, England, and Latin America entered the picture, and parts of it played up the image, interest groups fed into it, and the image took hold. The fundamental point is that the United States wanted—and presumed it had the right to— more than it could seize or defend. It wanted to replace the British in Latin America; it wanted to put muscle behind the Monroe Doctrine. The U.S. Navy, however, was not yet strong enough to fulfill these desires. Impotence is the seedbed of paranoia.

What was at the turn of the century a reasonable, if pessimistic, image of German policy toward Latin America had hardened by 1913 into an article of faith. The result is that scholars can write with perfect ease and good conscience that Germany posed a threat to the hemisphere despite the fact that the evidence of German actions presents, as the State Department recognized at the time, a very different picture.

This is, in part, because the need to see Germany as a threat to the region is great. Berlin's actions were beside the point because this was not really a discussion about Berlin. It was not really about the German threat. It was about American expansionism, and it was about American exceptionalism. The image of Germany as a marauder derives in part from Americans' presumption that they deserve absolute security, the security geography blessed them with and ruthlessness secured. Americans seem to accept this security as their right because they are the last best hope of humankind, the bastion of freedom.

"Uncle Sam: 'It is hard to bring 'em all under one hat!' " (*Beiblatt zum Kladderadatsch* [Berlin], 1 December 1901)

They have developed zero tolerance for any challenger, particularly in this hemisphere. A challenge is an affront, blasphemy, a stab at freedom's core.

Perhaps nations become accustomed to levels of threat, and in 1900 the United States was accustomed to a very low level indeed. After the decision of the British to seek American friendship, the Germans took their place as designated enemy number one. Or perhaps there is a constant ratio of power to sense of threat, and with the dramatic expansion of U.S. power after the Spanish-American war, there was a corresponding expansion of Americans' sense of exposure.

But it is more. If the United States invades a small island, as Wilson invaded Haiti in 1915, because the costs are low and the benefits, while not great, are nevertheless worth the low cost—that is, if the United States behaves like a typical imperial power—how do Americans square this behavior with their conviction that they are exceptional?

The idea of a German threat does more than explain (poorly) American imperialism; it justifies it. It squares the circle: the United States acts like a great power but can maintain its self-image as exceptional. Its imperialism might superficially resemble the European variety, but it is seen as fundamentally different: whereas the Europeans acted aggressively for their own good, the Americans reacted protectively for the good of others. This is the essence of the Monroe Doctrine, that the United States pledges itself to protect freedom in the hemisphere; the establishment of hegemony is merely a burdensome side effect and not what it seems. There is an assumption in much U.S. political thought that the default position for U.S. foreign policy is passive, that the United States is pulled reluctantly into action by the evil world and that this somehow proves its humanitarian intentions. To maintain this perception an enemy is essential. Thus, in explaining U.S. imperialism at the turn of the century, the idea of a German threat is the missing piece of the jigsaw puzzle. It fits so well that it must be true. Without a threat, there could be no "protection," and without protection there was just imperialism. The horror of this was not due to the pejorative meaning that imperialism developed as the twentieth century wore on but rather to the ordinariness of it all. Having established its continental boundaries, the United States at the dawn of the new century was entering the world of other great powers. This was, and remains, extremely threatening to the basic self-perception of Americans. If the United States is ordinary, if it behaves in ordinary ways, then what is it? The essence of U.S. nationalism is the conviction that the United States is a revolutionary experiment, a new world, a city on the hill. In this perspective, a cold, sobering light falls on American behavior in the hemisphere, where, unlike in Europe, the United States had a free hand and could have been what it declares it is: different and better. Instead, the United States behaved like an old world power and convinced itself that it had not.

The Europeans and the Latins saw the ordinariness of U.S. policy very clearly. The Germans bore no illusions about U.S. ambitions. "It is generally assumed that the object of our government," the U.S. chargé in Berlin wrote in 1901, "is to . . . remodel the phrase 'America for the Americans' so as to make it 'America for the North Americans.'"[5] Not only the Germans but also many Latins realized very early that the United States was vying for hegemony in their region and that their self-interest lay either in courting the colossus of the north, as the Brazilian government chose to do, or in playing the powers off against each other as best they could, as Haiti and the small, weak states closer to the threat of U.S. domination tried to do.[6]

Suspicion of U.S. goals in the region had deep roots. In 1873, a European commentator on U.S. immigrants to Brazil noted that the Brazilians harbored "a not unnatural prejudice against the keen, hard, adventurers of the North, much such as an oyster might have against admitting a nail as bedfellow . . . that nation of filibusters, those grey-eyed fanatics of a destiny of Empire."[7] And an American observer noted in 1902, "Since the war with Spain, Brazilians have been saying that the Anglo-Saxon blood has broken out in the trait for land-grabbing . . . and that the Philippines, Porto Rico, and Cuba, the last left on the limb to ripen, are the first fruits to be gathered by the new policy.

The 'humane war' aspect, which so aroused enthusiasm in our own country, has been regarded here [in Brazil] with more than skepticism. Texas and its history are fresher in the minds of Brazilians than in those of many Americans."[8] And after the Venezuela crisis, an editor in Rio wrote, "[The Monroe Doctrine is] a pure eccentricity. . . . [It] has no value whatever. At best it is simply another document for the benefit of those who would determine the characteristic psychology of the North American."[9] The contrast between the U.S. perspective on the one hand and that of the Germans and Latins on the other is pervasive and significant. It continues, in varied forms, to the present day, and it has been a persistent rift in the scholarly explanations of American imperialism.

There have been several waves of explanations of U.S. expansionism at the turn of the century that have stressed different motives: security, humanitarianism, domestic politics, economic gain. All point to triggers for interventionism but shy away from the discussion of the underlying disposition. From the earliest days, Americans presumed that they would exercise hegemony over the entire hemisphere, over Cuba when the pendulous pear ripened, and over the rest of the "sister republics" as they threw off the yoke of Old World oppression and joined the empire for liberty. The Monroe Doctrine was the articulation of this presumption, which seemed as self-evident as it did inevitable.

Throughout the nineteenth century, the presumption of hegemony played itself out on the continent, and by the turn of the century it was spilling overseas. This was the organic continuation of manifest destiny. By 1895, with the first Venezuela crisis, it was time for the United States to grab the baton the withdrawing British offered and claim hegemony over its rightful sphere to the south.

Yes, there were spurs to the plucking—spurs that explain why this island was occupied now and that one was spared. Yes, business interests (bananas, railroads, bankers), security interests, and humanitarian interests entered the equation. They were catalysts and switches on the tracks, but they were not decisive. The story is so simple it is anticlimactic: by 1898 the United States, not Latin America, had "ripened." It was ready to pluck the fruit that was growing in what it had always presumed to be its orchard.

This is, quite simply, the behavior of an imperial power. There is nothing extraordinary about it. It is as old as international relations. And while it may be obvious to non-Americans, it is hard for Americans to accept; it is easier to slip into explanations that allow us to preserve our sense of exceptionalism. But there is no escape, no exit through business or security or goodwill. It is simple imperialism: we presumed it was ours, we had the power to take it, and the cost was extraordinarily low. The basic American mind-set had always been to exercise hegemony, hegemony so predestined that it was barely felt as hegemony: it was simply the natural way of things.

While the U.S. Navy was declaring its alarm about the German threat, it was in fact establishing its hegemony over Latin America. What looked like a vacuum of power was simply a pause while the United States built the naval strength and developed the trade and diplomatic ties to claim its sphere. German dreams, expressed by the kaiser and the pan-Germans and given substance by the fleet, allowed Americans to act like an ordinary power and to feel exceptional.

Notes

Abbreviations

AA	Auswärtiges Amt (German Foreign Office)
AA-PA	Auswärtiges Amt-Politisches Archiv, Bonn
BA-MA	Bundesarchiv-Militärarchiv, Freiburg
Bz	Brazil Files, in AA-PA
CDN	*Chicago Daily News*
Con	*Atlanta Constitution*
DC	*Daily Chronicle*
DM	*Daily Mail*
DN	*London Daily News*
DZA	Deutsches Zentralarchiv, Potsdam
ed.	editorial
ES	*Washington Evening Star*
FO	Foreign Office (London)
FR	U.S. Department of State, *Papers Relating to the Foreign Relations of the United States*
GBL	General Board, Letters, RG 80, NA
GBM	General Board, Minutes of Proceedings, RG 80, NA
GBS	General Board, Subject File, RG 80, NA
GBW	General Board War Portfolios, RG 80, NA
Ge	Germany Files, in AA-PA
GP	*Grosse Politik der Europaischen Kabinette*, edited by Johannes Lepsius et al.
Her	*New York Herald*
LC	Library of Congress, Washington, D.C.
LD	*Literary Digest*
LTR	*The Letters of Theodore Roosevelt*, edited by E. Morison
M	Microfilm, reel number
MG	*Manchester Guardian*
MP	*Morning Post*
Mx	Mexico Files, in AA-PA
NA	National Archives, Washington, D.C.
Nat	*Nation*
NWCA	Naval War College Archives, Newport, R.I.
NYT	*New York Times*
Ob	*Observer*

ONI   U.S. Office of Naval Intelligence
Pic   *New Orleans Daily Picayune*
PMG   *Pall Mall Gazette*
PRO   Public Records Office, Kew
r   roll
RG   Record Group
SFC   *San Francisco Chronicle*
Sp   *Spectator*
SR   *Saturday Review*
Sun   *New York Sun*
T   *Times* (London)
TR   Theodore Roosevelt
UNOpP   U.S. Naval Operations Plans
Vz   Venezuela Files, in AA-PA
WG   *Westminster Gazette*
Wor   *New York World*
WSJ   *Wall Street Journal*
WW   Woodrow Wilson
WWP   *The Papers of Woodrow Wilson*, edited by Arthur Link

Introduction

1. Edward M. House Diary, 25 Nov. 1914, Edward M. House Papers, Sterling Library, Yale University, New Haven, Conn. (hereafter cited as "House Diary, Yale"). See also 22 Jan. 1913, 21 June 1914, and 15 Oct. 1915.

2. Bryan to WW, 27 Mar. 1915, *WWP*, 33:456; WW to Bryan, 31 Mar. 1915, ibid., 458.

3. Lansing, "Drama," 4. See House Diary, Yale, 24 July 1915, 11 Oct. 1915.

4. Fiske, "Naval Power," 735.

5. Bismarck, in *Hamburger Nachrichten*, 9 Feb. 1896.

6. Cain and Hopkins, *British Imperialism*; Crapol, "From Anglophobia," 13–19; Smith, *Illusions of Conflict*, 3–24.

7. Vagts, *Deutschland*. Two earlier books touched on the issue but suffered from a paucity of sources and a pronounced postwar bias. See Keim, *Forty Years*; Schieber, *Transformation*.

8. Bemis, *Latin American Policy* and "Wilson and Latin America." For an extreme statement of this viewpoint, see Colby, "American Interests." Langer's "preclusive imperialism" is also based on the presumption of a threat (see Langer, "Farewell to Empire").

9. See esp. Williams, *Tragedy*, *Contours*, and *Empire*.

10. See, for example, Bailey, *Diplomatic History*, 466–68, 499–506, 553–54; Callcott, *Western Hemisphere*, 56–58, 136–38; Collin, *Theodore Roosevelt's Caribbean*, 69–75; Healy, *Drive to Hegemony*, 72–76; Langley, *Banana Wars*, 20–21. Schoonover, who is currently writing a book on German relations with Central America, places U.S. expansionism in its international context and sees a German challenge to the spread

of U.S. hegemony in Central America in the late nineteenth century. See Schoonover, *United States*, esp. 73–74.

11. For a succinct summary of the debate, see Hull, *Entourage*, 1–8. See also Moeller, "Kaiserreich Recast?"

12. For Fischer on Latin America, see *Griff nach der Weltmacht*, 22; it is not mentioned in *Krieg der Illusionen*.

13. See Hell, "Der Griff nach Südbrasilien"; Baecker, *Mexikopolitik*; Brunn, *Deutschland*; Katz, *Secret War*; Herwig and Trask, "Naval Operations Plans"; Herwig, *Politics of Frustration*; Herwig, *Vision*; Fiebig-von Hase, *Lateinamerika* and "Die Rolle."

Chapter 1

1. For an overview of U.S.-German relations at the turn of the century, see Pommerin, *Der Kaiser*; Kaikkonen, *Deutschland*; Jonas, *United States*, 35–94; Vagts, "Hopes"; Vagts, *Deutschland*; Fiebig-von Hase, *Lateinamerika*.

2. For quote, see White, *Autobiography*, 2:139–40.

3. Ibid., 144.

4. Berghahn, *Modern Germany*, 253–60, tables 1–10. See Ashley, *Modern Tariff History*, 124, 199, 232–33; Crouse, "Decline," 27–28.

5. On MFN, see John Sherman (secretary of state) to White, 31 Jan. 1898, M77:71, NA; Kanitz, and Bülow's response, in *Stenographische Berichte 1898/1900*, 10th leg., 1st sess., 30th sitting (11 Feb. 1899), 1:789–90; *NYT*, 12 Feb. 1899; White to Hay, 13 Feb. 1899, *FR 1899*, 297–99; White to Hay, 27 Mar. 1899, M44:87, NA; Chargé George Fisk to Hay, 16 May 1899, and encl. Memo from Richthofen (undated), M44:88, NA; Fisk to Hay, 17 May 1899, and enclosures, M44:88, NA. On fears of closed zones, see White to Hay, 7 Jan. 1898, M44:84, NA; White to Sherman, 3 Feb. 1898, M44:84, NA; White to Hay, 10 Aug. 1898, M44:85, NA; White to Hay, 13 Feb. 1899, M44:87, NA; White to Hay, 26 Sept. 1899, M44:89, NA. See also Fisk, "German-American"; Sartorius, *Schriften*, 47–55; Stone, "International Aspect," 386–87; Stone, "New German Customs Tariff," 392–406; Stone, "Most Favored"; Isaacs, *International Trade*, 343.

6. Crouse, "Decline," 33; Pflanze, *Bismarck*, 2:282–85; Craig, *Germany*, 88.

7. Germany supplied 16 percent of America's sugar. The primary intent of the U.S. sugar duty was to raise revenue ($55 million annually, making it the single most important source of revenue), not to protect the small domestic sugar industry, which provided only 10 percent of U.S. sugar. Taussig, *Tariff History*, 275.

8. Everett to Evarts, 15 Feb. 1879, *FR 1879*, 361. See Pflanze, *Bismarck*, 3:4–11, 43–45, 62–69, 179–82; Stolberg-Wernigerode, *Germany*, 135–73; Craig, *Germany*, 85–100; Jonas, *United States*, 35–41; Webb, "Agricultural Protection."

9. Snyder, *Roots*, 93. See Crouse, "Decline," 58–204; Wendlandt, "German View"; Snyder, "Dispute"; Gignilliat, "Pigs"; Hoy and Nugent, "Public Health."

10. Stone, "International Aspect," 388, 390. They also followed Germany's lead in lifting the ban.

11. See Pendleton to Bayard, 1 Dec. 1887, *FR 1887*, 584; Pendleton to Bayard, 30 Jan. 1888, *FR 1888*, 609.

12. *NYT*, 23 Dec. 1882; Vance (D-N.C.), quoted in Gignilliat, "Pigs," 10. See Cleveland, "Message to Congress," 3 Dec. 1888, *FR 1889*, xiii; response to Cleveland in *National Zeitung*, 28 Mar. 1888, encl. in Pendleton to Bayard, 2 Apr. 1888, *FR 1888*, 629–30.

13. Chailley, in *LD* (8 Nov. 1890): 5; *The Statutes at Large of the United States of America*, vol. 26/27, *Public Acts and Resolutions of Congress*, Dec. 1889–Mar. 1891, 51st Cong., 1st sess., ch. 1244, 1890, p. 612; *Chicago Tribune*, in *LD* (12 Sept. 1891): 20. See Senate Report no. 345, 48th Cong., 1st sess., 1884, p. 2.

14. *Kölnische Zeitung*, quoted in *NYT*, 12 Feb. 1899.

15. On the impact of the Saratoga Agreement, see Sherman to Reichenau, 22 Sept. 1897, *FR 1898*, 178–79. Berlin occasionally seemed to agree that the Saratoga Agreement had lapsed, but it more often argued the contrary. On German protest to the new tariff, see White to Sherman, 12 Feb. 1898, M44:84, NA; White, *Autobiography*, 2:134; *LD* (15 Sept. 1894): 22.

16. See Jackson to Bülow, 27 Oct. 1897, encl. in Jackson to Sherman, 28 Oct. 1897, *FR 1897*, 179–80; Sherman to White, 31 Jan. 1898, M77:71, NA; Crouse, "Decline," 288–89.

17. See White to Sherman, 5 Feb. 1898, M44:84, NA; Jackson to Hay, 27 Dec. 1898, M44:86, NA; *NYT*, 26 Feb. 1899; Crouse, "Decline," 104–204.

18. For an overview, see *The New York Times Index*, 1891–98. On a tariff war, see "A German 'Tariff War,'" *NYT*, ed., 1 June 1900; *Berliner Tageblatt*, 4, 6 Dec. 1895; *Freisinnige Zeitung* (Berlin), 5 Dec. 1895; *Kreuzzeitung* (Berlin), 8 Dec. 1895; Runyon to Olney, 9 Dec. 1895, M44:77, NA; *Kreuzzeitung*, 20 July 1897, encl. in White to Sherman, 29 July 1897, M44:82, NA; *Norddeutsche Allgemeine Zeitung*, 5 Aug. 1897, encl. in White to Sherman, 12 Aug. 1897, M44:82, NA.

19. See esp. Marschall's vigorous arguments against retaliation, 3 May 1897, *Stenographische Berichte 1895/1897*, 9th leg., 4th sess., 8:5706–9; 5718–19; 5724.

20. *LD* (1 Aug. 1891): 23.

21. Taussig, *Tariff History*, 282.

22. Fisk, "German-American," 326. See White to Sherman, 28 Dec. 1897, M44:83, NA; Sherman to White, 31 Jan. 1898, M77:71, NA; White to Sherman, 11 Feb. 1898, M44:84, NA; White to Hay, 27 Mar. 1899, M44:87, NA; White to Hay, 21 Apr. 1899, M44:88, NA; Fisk to Hay, 18 May 1899, enclosing Memo from Reichstag, ibid.; White, *Autobiography*, 2:131–33. Until 5 February 1910, when Germany finally extended its conventional tariff to all U.S. exports, 4 percent of U.S. exports had higher tariffs. See Roosevelt, 1907 Message to Congress, *FR 1907*, lxvi.

23. Kanitz quoted in Runyon to Gresham, 18 Dec. 1894, M44:75, NA.

24. Cleveland, "Third Annual Message, December 2, 1895, to the Congress of the United States," in *Messages and Papers of the Presidents*, 12:6061–62. For statistics on U.S. beef exports to Germany, see Crouse, "Decline," 182 n. 50. The United States considered the fear of Texas fever to be patently ludicrous. (See Jackson to Richthofen, 18 July 1899, encl. in Jackson to Hay, 18 July 1899, *FR 1899*, 496.) For a detailed discussion and statistical charts of the impact of the ban on U.S. exporters, see Crouse, "Decline," 488–90; 522–23 nn. 293–95.

25. *LD* (19 Feb. 1898): 216.

26. See esp. debate in the Reichstag, 3 May 1897, *Stenographische Berichte 1895/1897*, 9th leg., 4th sess., 8:5701–28.

27. *NYT*, ed., 4 Mar. 1900; White to Hay, 10 Mar. 1900, *FR 1900*, 501. For a good discussion of the meat ban, see Crouse, "Decline," 205–82; 402–524. For U.S. reaction to the ban, see White to Hay, 13 May 1899, M44:88, NA; *FR 1900*, 485–513.

28. See Jackson to Hay, 16 Nov. 1899, M44:89, NA; encl. in Jackson to Hay, 18 Apr. 1901, M44:93, NA; Crouse, "Decline," 29, 52–53 n. 78; Lammersdorf, "Kaiser."

29. For statistics, see Crouse, "Decline," 380–82 n. 100; *NYT*, 22 May 1900; Fiebig-von Hase, "Wirtschaftsbeziehungen," 333–34, tables 1 and 2; Fiebig-von Hase, "United States," 37–44. By 1904, German exports to the United States were valued at $106,909,600, while U.S. exports to Germany were valued at $216,841,800 (Mason to Hay, 15 Mar. 1905, *FR 1905*, 457). In 1904, Germany received 24 percent of all U.S. products destined for Europe. It remained a distant second to England but well ahead of its nearest competitor, France. Stone, "International Aspect," 387.

30. See esp. Hoy and Nugent, "Public Health."

31. Holborn, *History*, 379–80; LaFeber, *New Empire*, 17–18.

32. White to Hay, 13 May 1899, M44:88, NA.

33. Schierbrand, "Our Tariff Differences," 205.

34. *LD* (8 Jan. 1898): 55.

35. Sartorius, *Schriften*, 68–84 (quotes, 75). For the Agrarian point of view, see *Berliner Neueste Nachrichten*, 27 Aug. 1897, encl. in White to Sherman, 27 Aug. 1897, M44:82, NA; Kardorff, *Stenographische Berichte 1898/1900*, 10th leg., 1st sess., 22d sitting (31 Jan. 1899), 1:547; Kanitz, ibid., 30th sitting (11 Feb. 1899), 1:789–90; Jackson to Hay, 31 May 1899, M44:88, NA. See also Crouse, "Decline," 345–52.

36. Quoted in White to Sherman, 12 Feb. 1898, M44:84, NA. See Sherman to White, 14 Dec. 1897, M77:71, NA; White to Hay, 26 Sept. 1899, M44:89, NA.

37. Sherman to White, 14 Dec. 1897, M77:71, NA; White to Hay, 26 Sept. 1899, M44:89, NA.

38. *Staats-Zeitung*, quoted in *LD* (2 May 1890): 22; *Berliner Tageblatt*, 22 Sept. 1899.

39. *NYT*, ed., 1 June 1900.

40. Holleben to Hohenlohe, 1 Jan. 1898, USA1:10, AA-PA.

41. White to Day, 12 Aug. 1898, M44:85, NA.

42. *NYT*, 28 Nov. 1897.

43. White to Day, 18 June 1898, M44:85, NA.

44. For the kaiser, see Röhl, *Kaiser and His Court* and *Wilhelm II*; Röhl and Sombart, *Kaiser Wilhelm II*; Kohut, *Wilhelm II*; Cecil, *Wilhelm II*, vol. 1, *Prince and Emperor*, and vol. 2, *Emperor and Exile*; Balfour, *Kaiser*; Hull, *Entourage*.

45. Meriwether, "Navy," 856; Herwig, *Officer Corps*, 17. On Weltpolitik, see Kehr, *Der Primat* and *Schlachtflottenbau*; Berghahn, *Der Tirpitz-Plan* and *Rüstung und Machtpolitik*; Cecil, *Wilhelm II*, vol. 1, *Prince and Emperor*, 291–339; Eley, "*Sammlungspolitik*"; Hillgruber, "Zwischen Hegemonie"; Kennedy, "Kaiser." Winzen argues that Weltpolitik failed by 1900 and that thereafter Tirpitz and Bülow (without the kaiser's knowledge) directed German policy toward war against England. To signal this shift, he prefers to call the later policy Weltmachtpolitik. See Winzen, *Bülows Weltmachtkonzept*.

46. The "Oedipal" hatred of England stemmed from the fact that Wilhelm's maternal grandmother was Queen Victoria. His mother, Victoria's eldest daughter, said, "William's one idea is to have a navy which shall be larger and stronger than the British Navy." Langer, *Diplomacy*, 428.

47. On Tirpitz, see Kaulisch, *Tirpitz*; Kennedy, "Fischer and Tirpitz." On the German naval bureaucracy, see Lambi, *Navy*, and Sondhaus, *Preparing for Weltpolitik*, 190–226.

48. White, *Autobiography*, 2:140; Bülow, *Denkwürdigkeiten*, 1:412. On Bülow, see Winzen, *Bülows Weltmachtkonzept*; Fesser, *Bülow*; Hull, *Entourage*, 230–31; Lerman, *Chancellor as Courtier*; Cecil, *Emperor*, 2:68–73.

49. Tirpitz, in Eckardstein, *Lebenserinnerungen*, 2:40.

50. Article by Hartmann, encl. in Adee to Long, 11 Aug. 1900, RG 45, VN:German Navy, box 680, NA.

51. Tirpitz, "Memo No. 9: General Lessons Drawn from the Fall Fleet Maneuvers," 16 June 1894, Tirpitz Papers, N253:34, BA-MA.

52. Baecker, "Mahan über Deutschland," 14. On the influence of Mahan in Germany, see Mahan to Ellen Mahan, 30 Nov. 1893, in Seager and Maguire, *Mahan*, 2:185–87; Mahan to Ellen Mahan, 8 and 10 Aug. 1894, in Seager and Maguire, *Mahan*, 2:310–13; White, *Autobiography*, 2:224. On Mahan, see Seager, *Alfred Thayer Mahan*; Sprout, "Mahan"; Livezey, *Sea Power*; Graham, *Supremacy*.

53. Bülow to Wilhelm II, 7 Apr. 1898, *GP*, 15:20–21. On Germany and the Spanish-American war, see *GP*, 15:3–105; Count E. Reventlow, "Diederichs and Dewey at Manila Bay," *Deutsche Tageszeitung*, 17 and 18 Feb. 1914; Diederichs, "Darstellung"; "Diederichs gegen Dewey," *Berliner Tageblatt*, 28 Feb. 1914; Dewey, *Autobiography*, 220–31; Gottschall, "Germany," 22–40; Clifford, "Admiral Dewey"; Offner, *Unwanted War*, 29–30, 59–60, 89–90, 159–85; Kaikkonen, *Deutschland*, 77–115, 134–73; Shippee, "Germany"; Fiebig-von Hase, *Lateinamerika*, 428–46; Vagts, *Deutschland*, 1128–1410; Einstein, "British Diplomacy"; Rippy, "European Powers"; Bailey, "Dewey"; Spector, *Admiral*, 72–82.

54. White to Day, 30 July 1898, M44:85, NA; Spring-Rice to Hay, 7 May 1898, John Hay Papers, box 14, LC; Bülow to Hatzfeldt, 8 May 1898, quoted in Gottschall, "Germany," 103. See Spring-Rice to Hay, 30 Apr. 1898; 14 May 1898; 16 July 1898; 23 July 1898, Hay Papers, box 14. See also White to Day, 18 June 1898, M44:85, NA; Richthofen, "Memo," 10 July 1898, *GP*, 15:54–59; White to Day, 13 July 1898, M44:85, NA; Day to White, 15 Aug. 1898, M77:71, NA; Jackson to Hay, 28 Nov. 1898, M44:86, NA; White to Hay, 12 Jan. 1899, M44:87, NA. On Germany's interest in the West Indies during the Spanish-American War, see Fauenzi, "Memo," 6 Apr. 1898, BA-MA; Knorr to Wilhelm II, 13 July 1898, RM2:1834, BA-MA; "Memo of a Conversation between Bülow and Heeringen," 4 Apr. 1899, RM3:39, BA-MA. On Tirpitz's desires, see Notiz 110, Tirpitz Papers, N253:153. See also *Alldeutsche Blätter*, 8 May 1898.

55. Heinrich to Bülow, 11 April 1898, *GP*, 15:33–39; Bülow to Wilhelm II, 14 May 1898, quoted in Gottschall, "Germany," 44.

56. Bülow to Krüger, 18 May 1898, and Bülow to Wilhelm II, 14 May 1898, quoted in Gottschall, "Germany," 50 n. 47, 45.

57. Knorr to Diederichs, 2 June 1898, RM38:43, BA-MA.

58. Sargent, "Admiral Dewey and the Manila Campaign," 10 Nov. 1904, pp. 24–25, George Dewey Papers, box 75, LC.

59. Langer, *Diplomacy*, 519; Diederichs to Knorr, 9 Aug. 1898, RM38:44, BA-MA.

60. White to Day, 18 June 1898, M44:85, NA.

61. Diederichs, "Darstellung," 277, 259, 278; Williams to Wildman, 22 June 1898, quoted in Gottshall, "Germany," 70.

62. Sargent, "Admiral Dewey and the Manila Campaign," 10 Nov. 1904, p. 36, Dewey Papers, box 76.

63. Braisted, *Navy*, 35–39.

64. Marginalia on Bülow to Wilhelm II, 15 Jan. 1899, quoted in Gottschall, "Germany," 137; Spring-Rice to Hay, 16 July 1898, Hay Papers, box 14; *American Monthly Review of Reviews* 20, no. 1 (July 1899): 18. See Knox, "1898 Efforts toward Caroline Islands," Feb. 1944, RG 45, subject file VI, box 665, NA; Brown, "Caroline Islands"; Gottschall, "Germany," 127–38.

65. White, speech at Leipsig, *LD* (6 Aug. 1898): 171. See White, *Autobiography*, 2:168.

66. Chamberlain, quoted in Offner, *Unwanted War*, 199–200.

67. *NYT*, 12 Feb. 1899.

68. Quoted in *NYT*, 13 Feb. 1899. For a sample of U.S. opinion, see "Topics in Brief," *LD* (6 Aug. 1898): 38.

69. "Z," "Noticeable Tendency of Improved Relations between England and Germany, Involving Possibly the Monroe Doctrine," no. 62, 15 Apr. 1913, C-9-d, box 453, RG 38, NA; Tirpitz quoted in Herwig, *Politics of Frustration*, 26.

70. McCalla, "Lessons of the Spanish American War," 1899, NWCA. See Pratt, "An Outline of the Policy of the Navy, and Its General Strategy in Relation to the Defense of the Canal," 1 June 1916, GBS, box 146.

71. TR to Kimball, 9 Jan. 1900, in *LTR*, 2:1130–31.

72. Quoted in Morison and Commager, *Growth*, 2:416.

73. Representative McAdoo (D-N.J.), quoted in Spector, *Professors of War*, 54. Spector provides a lively account of the early years of the college. See also Adm. Austin Knight and Lt. William Puleston, "History of the Naval War College," 1916, NCWA; LaFeber, *New Empire*, 121–27.

74. Mahan to Roosevelt, 1 May 1897, in Seager and Maguire, *Mahan*, 2:505–6; Mahan to Thursfield, 1 Dec. 1897 and 25 Jan. 1898, ibid., 529, 536–37.

75. Mahan, "Report to Naval War Board," 1898, quoted in Dewey to Morton, 1 Feb. 1905, GB 406, GBL. The report was unsigned, but Dewey assumed that its author was Mahan.

76. Quoted in Kennedy, *Antagonism*, 203.

77. Berghahn, *Der Tirpitz-Plan*. On the seizure of Kiaochow, see Ganz, "German Navy." For alarm in the United States, see *NYT* 27, 28 Nov. 1897; 8, 16, 18 Dec. 1897; 7, 25 Jan. 1898. See also White to Sherman, 28 Nov. 1897, RG 45, subject file VP, box 685, NA.

78. *Outlook* (London) quoted in *LD* (29 Apr. 1905): 636.

79. "Z," "Noticeable Tendency of Improved Relations between England and Germany, Involving Possibly the Monroe Doctrine," no. 62, 15 Apr. 1913, C-9-d, box 453,

RG 38, NA. On the first Venezuela crisis, see Lodge, "England"; LaFeber, *New Empire*, 242-83; Schoultz, *Beneath*, 107-24.

80. Mahan, "The United States Looking Outward," in *LD* (6 Dec. 1890): 3. On Samoa, see subject file VI: "International Relations and Politics," box 668, RG 45, NA; Ryden, *Samoa*, 207-574; Kennedy, *Samoan Tangle*; Kennedy, "Tridominium"; Vagts, *Deutschland*, 636-937; Pommerin, *Der Kaiser*, 49-62; Ide, "Samoa."

81. Quoted in Vagts, *Deutschland*, 1794 and 1076.

82. Dewey to Long, 12 Nov. 1901, GB 187, GBL; "Germany and the United States," *Harper's Weekly* (2 June 1900): 500. On suspicions of German activity in the Danish West Indies (which became the U.S. Virgin Islands in 1917), see the following documents from GBM: 21 May 1901; 25 June 1901; 27 Feb. 1902. See also Dewey to Long, 12 Nov. 1901, GB 187, GBL; "Memorandum on St. Thomas and St. John," 14 Nov. 1901, envelope 6, box 27 SL, RG 8, NWCA; Dewey to Long, 18 Nov. 1901, GB 187, GBL; Tower to Hay, 14 Jan. 1903, M44:97, NA; "Report of the Second Committee," 20 Dec. 1904, GBM; *Hamburger Nachrichten*, 18 Oct. 1905; O'Brien to Root, 23 Oct. 1905, *FR 1905*, 550-51; Lorillard to Root, 24 Nov. 1905, ibid., 551-52; Egan to Root, 23 Aug. 1911, *FR 1911*, 573-75. See also Tansill, *Purchase*, 373-453; Nørregaard, *Vore Gamle Tropekolonier*, 4:74-80; Adams, "Strategy," 260-65. For Margarita and Martinique, see 23 Apr. 1901, GBM; Dewey to Long, 24 Apr. 1901, GB 155, GBL; *Her*, 1, 3, 4, 7, 12 May 1901; Taylor to Sigsbee, 8 Aug. 1901, GB 163, GBL; "Haiti Santo Domingo Plan," box 3:5-d, GBW; "Joint Army and Navy War Plan," no. 32, UNOpP, box 48, RG 8, NWCA; Hood, "Reconnaissance of Margarita Region, Venezuela," envelope 8, box 28 SL, NWCA; "Preliminary Examination of Margarita Island with War Plans," 1901, box 27 SL, NWCA; *NYT*, 17 Aug. 1902, 2:23; "Does Germany Aim to Control the Caribbean?," *Harper's Weekly* (22 Nov. 1902): 1765. For Haiti, the reports are voluminous, but see esp. "Joint Army and Navy War Plans, Problem no. 2," UNOpP, box 48, NWCA. For southern Brazil, see below, chapter 3. For a war plan assuming a German attack on St. Thomas, Haiti, and Margarita, see "Solution of Problem of 1901: Strategy," envelope C-1, RG 12, NWCA.

83. On the Lüders incident, see the "Lüders" file in RG 45, subject file VP, box 685, NA; Gaillard, *La République*, 217-50; Fiebig-von Hase, *Lateinamerika*, 405-6. Originally fined forty-eight dollars and given a one-month sentence, Lüders unwisely requested a second trial, which resulted in a five-hundred-dollar fine and a one-year sentence.

84. Powell to Sherman, 21 Oct. 1897, RG 45, subject file VP, box 685, NA. See Powell to Sherman, 22 Oct. 1897, ibid.; "Pardon Decree of T. A. S. Sam," encl. in Powell to Sherman, 26 Oct. 1897, ibid. For the Haitian government's official proclamation, see *Le Moniteur* (Port au Prince), 8 Dec. 1897.

85. Bismarck, in *Hamburger Nachrichten*, 2 Dec. 1897; Powell to Sherman, 12 Nov. 1897, RG 45, subject file VP, box 685, NA; *Impartiel*, 21 Oct. 1897, encl. in Powell to Sherman, 21 Oct. 1897, ibid.; White, *Autobiography*, 2:149-50; *Her*, 11 Dec. 1897; *Wor*, 8 Dec. 1897.

86. See esp. Day to Powell, 12 Nov. 1897, RG 45, subject file VP, box 685, NA; Sherman to Powell, 19 Nov. 1897, ibid.

87. *Le Temps*, 10 Dec. 1897.

88. *Wor*, 30 Nov. 1897; *Her*, 12 Dec. 1897. The *Herald*'s coverage was more ex-

tensive and alarmist than the *New York Times*. It carried twenty-five articles on the topic between 12 Nov. and 23 Dec. 1897. The most important articles in *NYT* are 21, 28 Nov. 1897. The *World* carried fifteen articles about the incident from 20 November to 10 December. For Washington's instructions, see esp. Sherman to Powell, 19 Nov. 1897, RG 45, subject file VP, box 685, NA.

89. Bigelow, "German Press," 20–21.

90. Crowninshield to Long, 28 Feb. 1898, GB 414-3, box 42, GBS. See Jackson to Hay, 10 Nov. 1899, M44:89, NA.

91. *NYT*, ed., 13 Dec. 1899. See *NYT*, 24 Dec. 1899.

92. Driggs, quoted in Dorwart, *Naval Intelligence*, 58. For a survey of British press reaction to the First Fleet Bill, see *LD* (30 Apr. 1898): 532–33. The silence of the U.S. press is striking. (An exception is Bigelow, "German Press," 21.)

93. Meriwether, "Navy," 862.

94. Sperry to wife, 6 Aug. 1901, Charles Sperry Papers, LC.

95. *Neueste Nachrichten* (Berlin), quoted in *Her*, 11 May 1900; *Buffalo Courier*, quoted in *Her*, 29 May 1900; *Her*, 2 May 1900. For press comment, see *Her*, 28 Apr. 1900; *Boston Evening Transcript*, 28 Apr. 1900 (which deems the speech "claptrap"); *Her*, 29 Apr. 1900 (with the headline "Root's Warning Is for Germany"); *Boston Evening Transcript*, 1 May 1900; *Con*, 1 May 1900; *NYT*, 6 May 1900. For a good summary of editorial opinion, see *Her*, 2 May 1900, and *LD* (12 May 1900): 566–67 and (19 May 1900): 598. See also *National Zeitung*, quoted in *NYT*, 6 May 1900; *Vossische Zeitung*, quoted in *Her*, 1 May 1900.

96. *Her*, 12 May 1900; Lodge, *Congressional Record*, 56th Cong., 1st sess., 11 May 1900, 33:5403.

97. *Times* (Philadelphia) quoted in *Her*, 14 May 1900; *Denver Republican* quoted in *Her*, 19 May 1900.

98. Daniel, *Congressional Record*, 56th Cong., 1st sess., 14 May 1900, 33:5487; Holleben to Hohenlohe, 18 May 1900, AA30307, DZA; *Sp*, quoted in *NYT*, 6 May 1900; *National Review* (June 1900): 612.

99. TR to Mahan, 3 May 1897, in Turk, *Ambiguous Relationship*, 115. See TR to McCalla, 3 Aug. 1897, in *LTR*, 1:636; Sprout and Sprout, *Rise*, 253; Lodge, *Selections*, 1:494.

100. TR to Lodge, 27 Mar. 1901, in Lodge, *Selections*, 1:484–86.

101. Lodge to TR, 30 Mar. 1901, in Lodge, *Selections*, 1:487–88.

102. *Her*, 28 July 1899; *NYT*, 30 July 1899; 1, 6 Aug. 1899.

103. For comparisons of the two navies, see *Congressional Record*, 56th Cong., 1st sess., 11 May 1900, 33:5402; Richard Guenther, U.S. consul general in Berlin, "The Total Strength of the German Navy," 1 Apr. 1900, encl. in Adee to Long, 11 Aug. 1900, RG 45, VN: "German Navy," box 680, NA; ONI, "Memo comparing the American and the German Navies," 26 Mar. 1902, GBM; "Solution of the Problem of 1903," envelope C-1, RG 12, NWCA; "Germany War Plan," box 10, no. 1: 5-Y, GBW; "War with Germany" (1897, no. 266), UNOpP 1896 to 1900, subfile 1, UNOpM–UNOpP box 47, RG 8, NWCA; Rogers, "Tactical Study of the Black Fleet. 'E' of Report of Tactical Committee 1903," envelope 6, RG 12, NWCA; Bernadou, "Tactical Study of the Black Fleet. 'F' of the Report of the Tactical Committee 1903," NWCA; "Joint Army and Navy War Plans. Problem no. 2: Table Showing the Comparative Strength of the

Naval Forces of Germany and the United States," UNOpP box 48, RG 8, NWCA; Evans to Long, 27 Mar. 1902, GB 420-2, GBL; Pitman Pulsifer, "Information (in tabular form) Relating to Vessels, the Personnel of and Appropriations for the Navy, and the Comparative Strength of the Great Naval Powers," 58th Cong., 3d sess., 25 Jan. 1905, S. Doc. 117; *NYT*, 27 Aug 1905; Dewey to Bonaparte, 20 June 1906, GB 438, GBL; ONI, "Naval Expenditures of the Powers, 1900–1907," 9 Apr. 1908, C-11-a, box 662: "Naval Expenditures," RG 38, NA; Meriwether, "Navy"; Cooling, *Gray Steel*, 49, 136; Fiebig-von Hase, *Lateinamerika*, 500–506, 819–25; Sprout and Sprout, *Rise*, 252–55; Spector, "Roosevelt"; Lambi, *Navy*, 142, 146.

104. See Cooling, *Grey Steel*, 157.

105. Fiebig-von Hase, *Lateinamerika*, 819–24. See Evans to Moody, 27 Mar. 1902, GB 420-2, GBL; Wilson, "New German Navy."

106. *NYT*, ed., 20 Feb. 1905. See Mahan to Low, 15 Feb. 1900, in Seager and Maguire, *Mahan*, 2:682–84; A. Maurice Low, "American Affairs," *National Review* (June 1902): 625; Taylor, "Fleet."

107. Wiley to Commander, U.S. Asiatic Fleet, 1 Sept. 1904, E-6-a, box 771: "Efficiency and Discipline of German Navy," RG 38, NA. For a representative sample, see the following documents from just one year (1901) of weekly meetings, all in GBM: 20 Mar.—ONI report about "the rapid increase of the German navy"; 23 Apr.—ONI report about the German Nautical Society; 26 Apr.—ONI report about German Navy League; 21 May—ONI report about German naval preparedness and building program; 23 May—ONI reports on German Navy League and German naval developments; 21 Aug.—ONI report about German activity in the Dominican Republic; 24 Aug.—ONI report about German gunnery practice; 30 Oct.—ONI report "showing the growth of German naval and commercial power and giving a building programme for the United States that would be equivalent to the German programme until 1906"; 31 Oct.—naval attaché in Berlin report about speed of the German fleet; 19 Dec.—ONI reports about German naval tactics, Germans at Shanghai; naval attaché report about the Navy League. See also the very thorough ONI reports: "Z," "Recruiting and Discharges, Organization and Training, and Promotions in the Enlisted Force of the German Navy," 1903, E-6-a, box 770, RG 38, NA; Ferber, "Organization and Administration of the German Navy," 1908, ibid.; "Z," "Training of Seamen and Apprentices in the German Navy," 1902, E-6-b, ibid.; and Dorwart, *Naval Intelligence*, 75.

108. ONI, "Report to the General Board," 23 May 1901, GBM.

109. Wilson, "New German Navy," 536.

110. See, for example, the scathing criticism of the U.S. Navy in Mantey's *Winterarbeit*, RM5:5964, pp. 68–93, BA-MA.

111. On Tirpitz, see Kennedy, "Fischer and Tirpitz."

112. House Diary, Yale, 2 Dec. 1913 and 1 June 1914; TR to Mahan, 12 May 1890, Alfred Thayer Mahan Papers, LC; TR to Sternburg, 17 Jan. 1898, *LTR*, 1:764.

113. Roosevelt, in *Her*, 11 Mar. 1900.

114. Mahan to Roosevelt, 12 Mar. 1901, in Turk, *Ambiguous Relationship*, 128.

115. See Spector, *Admiral*, 107–17.

116. TR to Lodge, 9 Apr. 1900, in Lodge, *Selections*, 1:455. A year later, Roosevelt wrote, "I think that Dewey now cares very little for the navy people, or for the real interest of the navy." TR to Lodge, 20 Aug. 1901, ibid., 497.

117. Dewey to Brownson, 26 Oct. 1906, Dewey Papers, box 75. After the 1902–3 Venezuela crisis, the General Board decided that forty-eight ships (one for each state) would be needed to combat the German "menace" (31 Jan. 1903, GBM:1:237; Dewey to Moody, 9 Feb. 1903, GB420-2, GBL). The war college called for a force that would give "crushing superiority" over the Germans, that is, one and a half times larger than the German fleet; this meant forty-eight ships (Chambers, "Memo," [ca. 1904], GB420-2, GBL). See Schilling, "Admirals," 39.

118. Fiebig–von Hase, *Lateinamerika*. See U.S. Congress, Senate, 65th Cong., 3d sess., S. Doc. 418, *Navy Yearbook*, 802–4.

119. Edelsheim, *Operationen über See*; *NYT*, ed., 19 Nov. 1901.

120. Holleben to Bülow, 14 Dec. 1901, AA-PA; Sigsbee to Moody, 21 Jan. 1903, GBS.

121. See Rebeur-Paschwitz to Tirpitz, 7 Mar. 1901, RM3:6658, BA-MA.

122. *NYT*, 27 Apr. 1971. See *NYT*, 24 Apr. 1971.

123. See Herwig and Trask, "Naval Operations Plans"; Fiebig–von Hase, *Latein-amerika*; Forstmeier, "Deutsche Invasionspläne."

124. Mantey, "*Winterarbeit* of 1898," RM5:5964, pp. 68–93, BA-MA. For the early plan, see Karcher to Goltz, 13 Mar. 1889, RM5:5960, BA-MA.

125. Quoted in Vagts, "Hopes," 2:60.

126. For four variations on the plan, see Bendemann, "Draft of a Memo," 2 Feb. 1899, RM5:5960, BA-MA; Admiralstab, "Memo," Mar. 1899, ibid.; Mantey, "*Winter-arbeit* of 1899: 'The War Fleet of a Great European Power Moves against the United States,'" Mar. 1899, RM5:5964, BA-MA; Thomsen's comments on Mantey, "*Winter-arbeit* of 1899," [n.d.], ibid.

127. Tirpitz to Diederichs, 3 Dec. 1899, RM3:6657, BA-MA.

128. Diederichs, "Memo for the Budget Committee of the Reichstag," 12 Jan. 1900, RM5:5960, BA-MA.

129. Kaiser's comment on Rebeur-Paschwitz to Tirpitz, 20 Jan. 1900, RM5:5960, BA-MA; Diederichs to Schlieffen, 1 May 1900, ibid. Grenville and Young state that in December 1899, Wilhelm II "personally instructed . . . Diederichs and . . . Schlieffen . . . to prepare a war plan against the United States," but they cite no document, and none giving such an order can be found. Grenville and Young, *Politics*, 305.

130. Diederichs to Schlieffen, 28 Nov. 1900, RM5:5960, BA-MA.

131. Diederichs, notes on *Immediatvortrag*, 9 Dec. 1900, RM5:880, BA-MA. See Schlieffen to Diederichs, 1 Dec. 1900, ibid.

132. Diederichs's marginalia on Schlieffen to Diederichs, 14 Dec. 1901, RM5:5960, BA-MA.

133. Büchsel, "Memo," 21 Mar. 1903, Tirpitz Papers, vol. 8.

134. Büchsel to Captain of *Vineta*, 25 Apr. 1903, RM5:5960, BA-MA.

135. Fourteen special studies were drawn up about the problems of supply. See, for example, "Memo: Preliminary Works for Operations Plan III through 1 Oct. 1904," RM5:5961, BA-MA.

136. Büchsel, "Memo," 9 May 1906, RM5:5962, BA-MA. See Hebbinghaus, "Memo," 10 Sept. 1906, RM5:885, BA-MA.

137. Comments of Thomsen on Mantey, "*Winterarbeit* of 1899," [n.d.], RM5:5964, BA-MA. This phrase is quoted in Herwig and Trask, "Naval Operations Plans," 12; Herwig, *Politics of Frustration*, 48; Lambi, *Navy*, 131.

138. Lambi, *Navy*.

139. Bendemann, "Memo," 19 Sept. 1899, RM5:5960, BA-MA; Diederichs, "Memo," 1 Feb. 1900, ibid. See Herwig and Trask, "Naval Operations Plans," 15.

140. Diederichs to Schlieffen, 25 Jan. 1901, RM5:5960, BA-MA; Schlieffen to Diederichs, 13 Mar. 1901, ibid.

141. Herwig and Trask, "Naval Operations Plans," 19-20.

142. Büchsel, "Memo," 21 Mar. 1903, Tirpitz Papers, vol. 8. See Diederichs, "Memo for the Budget Committee of the Reichstag," 12 Jan. 1900, RM5:5960, BA-MA.

143. See Luce, "A Short Study in Naval Strategy," lecture delivered 27 Aug. 1910 at Naval War College, NWCA.

144. See Bourne and Boyd, "Captain Mahan's 'War.'"

145. See "War with Germany," 1897, no. 266, UNOpP 1896 to 1900, subfile 1, UNOpM–UNOpP box 47, RG 8, NWCA; Dorwart, *Naval Intelligence*, 49, 58.

146. Cited in Fiske, *Midshipman*, 479.

147. See "The Naval War College and Its Work," *Harper's Weekly* (7 Feb. 1895): 149-50. See Taylor, "Study of War"; McHugh, *Fundamentals*.

148. Dewey to Morton, 1 Feb. 1905, GB 406, GBL. See Dewey to Long, 10 Dec. 1900, GB 87, GBL; Dewey to Long, GB 187, 12 Nov. 1901, GBS, box 148.

149. Daniels, *Wilson Era*, 322. On the creation of the General Board, see Costello, "Planning for War"; Wainwright, "General Board." On Taylor, see Spector, *Admiral*, 125.

150. Dewey to Crowninshield, 11 Apr. 1900, GB 401, with Taylor memo attached, GBL.

151. 21 May 1900, GB 20, GBM. See 23 May 1900, GB 22, GBM with encl. "Appendix A," which states "place, date and enemy—viz. the *West Indies in 1905* against *Germany*" (italics in original).

152. GBM (1900-1901) in which the Haiti/Santo Domingo Plan is discussed: 22 Nov. 1900; 23 Nov. 1900; 24 Nov. 1900; 20 Mar. 1901; 21 Mar. 1901; 23 Apr. 1901; 25 Apr. 1901; 22 May 1901; 23 May 1901; 25 June 1901; 26 June 1901; 21 Aug. 1901; 22 Aug. 1901; 24 Aug. 1901; 19 Dec. 1901; 20 Dec. 1901. By 1912, the east coast variant had been almost completely eliminated. See Germany War Plan, 5-7, portfolio 1, box 10, GBW.

153. Mahan to Taylor, 7 Dec. 1903, GB 420-1, GBS, box 58. See Moody to General Board, 20 Nov. 1903, and GB report, 5 Dec. 1903, ibid.

154. "Report of the 2nd Committee," 20 Dec. 1904, GBM; 22 Nov. 1904, GBM. See 12 Feb. 1906, GBM.

155. 24 Jan. 1906, GBM; Costello, "Planning for War," 107; "Report of the 2nd Committee," 20 Dec. 1904, GBM. See Dewey to Commander of Caribbean Squadron, 6 May 1904, GB 425-1, GBL.

156. Fiske, *Midshipman*, 477; Dewey to President of Naval War College, 19 June 1912, GBL.

157. War Portfolio No. 1 includes: (box 1) 1-a,b,c,d: "General Considerations and Data," approved 19 Oct. 1910, dated Feb. 1915, updated Jan. 1919; "Nicaragua," approved 22 June 1910; (box 2) "Bahia and 4-5: Kingston, Jamaica," approved May 1908 and 23 June 1908, dated Feb. 1913; (box 3) 5-d: Hi-Sd, July 1915 and 5-6: Fort [sic] de France Harbor; (box 4) "Mexico," May 1913; (box 8) "Naval War Plan for

Mexico," approved 15 Apr. 1912, dated 1 May 1912 and "Strategic Plan—Margarita District"; (box 9) 5-i: "Culebra, P. R.: Advanced Base Plan," Apr. 1916; (box 10) 5-y: Germany War Plan, cover page dated July 1915; (box 11) Sigsbee, "Germany vs. the US—West Indies," 21 May 1900; Central America Plan, June 1910.

158. 24 Jan. 1905, GBM.

159. The plan was sent for comment to the Army War College in December 1900 (Long to Root, 13 Dec. 1900, GBL). See Dewey to Long, 23 Apr. 1901, GB no. 87, GBL; acting secretary of navy to Root, 24 Apr. 1901, GB 88, ibid. The Joint Navy-Army Board was not established until 1903. The General Board was still actively amending the Hi-Sd plan in 1905 and 1906. See "Review by the General Board of the Army War College Papers on the Hi-Sd Plan," 29 Mar. 1905(?—handwritten), portfolio no. 1, box 3, GBW; "Report of the Second Committee," 23 Nov. 1905, GBM; "Report of the Second Committee," 24 Jan. 1906, ibid.

160. 22 Sept. 1903, GBM.

161. Sigsbee, "Report to the General Board: Germany versus the United States—West Indies," 21 May 1900, box 11, register 374, GBW. See 21 May 1900, GB 20, GBM.

162. Other occupation plans, developed in much less detail and rarely, if ever, discussed in the General Board meetings, concerned Nicaragua, Central America, the French in Saigon, the English territories in Canada and the West Indies, and the Russians in Vladivostock. Costello, "Planning for War," 107.

163. Germany War Plan, 5-Y, portfolio 1, box 10, GBW.

164. Vagts, "Hopes," 67; Challener, *Admirals*, 405; Herwig, *Politics of Frustration*, 105; Lambi, *Navy*, 131; Baecker, "Blau gegen Schwarz," 354. See Schilling, "Admirals," 16; Fiebig-von Hase, *Lateinamerika*, 788–89.

165. "General Considerations and Data," 19 Oct. 1913, War Portfolio 1, box 1, GBW.

166. "Political Situation—Causes for War—Finances of War," [1910-11], Portfolio 1:5-Y Germany War Plan, box 10, GBW (italics in original).

167. Dewey to Bonaparte, 28 Sept. 1906, GB 436, GBL.

168. Taylor, in Costello, "Planning for War," 282.

169. Dewey to Long, 21 Aug. 1901, GB 28, GBL.

170. See *NYT*, ed., 6 Oct. 1900.

171. Vagts, *Deutschland*.

172. See Dewey to Moody, 3 Dec. 1903, GB 420-1, GBL; Dewey to Bonaparte, 2 Oct. 1906, GB 404, GBL. See TR to Knox, 8 Feb. 1909, *LTR*, 6:1513; Braisted, *Navy*, 115-24, 148-53, 169-73, 232-39; Maurer, "Concentration"; Livermore, "American Navy as a Factor," 873.

173. Dewey to Moody, 27 May 1904, GB 414-1, GBL. See Dewey to Morton, 1 Feb. 1905, GB 406, GBL, which reviews the General Board's policy on bases; Challener, *Admirals*, 36-39; Fiebig-von Hase, *Lateinamerika*, 447-71.

174. Portfolio 1, box 10, GBW: Germany War Plan, Forward.

Chapter 2

1. Hebbinghaus, "Memo," 10 Sept. 1906, RM5:885, BA-MA.

2. Bowen to Hay, 28 Nov. 1902, M79:T56, NA. Germany, England, France, Italy, Belgium, Holland, Sweden, Spain, Mexico, and the United States had claims against Venezuela. The estimated amounts of these claims vary. U.S. claims were about $4.2 million; German claims were about $2.5 million; British claims were about $25 million (based on 1902 exchange rate of 19.3 bolivars = £5 = $1). See, for example, U.S. Senate documents, 58th Cong., 3d sess., no. 119, serial 4769; *NYT*, 11 June 1902; Buchanan to Lansdowne, 11 Nov. 1902, FO 420:206, PRO; Bax-Ironside to Lansdowne, 23 Dec. 1903, FO 420:224, PRO; Mühlberg to Metternich, 17 July 1902, Vz1:21, AA-PA; Bülow, "Memo on German Claims in Venezuela," presented to the Reichstag on 8 Dec. 1902, *Stenographische Berichte 1900/1903*, 10th leg., 2d sess., sup. 7, doc. 786, pp. 4957–59.

3. See, for example, Fiebig-von Hase, *Lateinamerika*, 846–1044; Herwig, *Politics of Frustration*, 76–80; Healy, *Drive to Hegemony*, 100–106; Collin, *Theodore Roosevelt's Caribbean*, 95–123.

4. On the German community in Venezuela (about one thousand strong), see Vagts, *Deutschland*, 1525–1635; Herwig, *Vision*, 17–79, 87–92; Fiebig-von Hase, *Lateinamerika*, 44–88, 120–40. On the pan-Germans, see below.

5. On the diversion of ships, see Fiebig-von Hase, *Lateinamerika*, 410, 850. On the use of foreign disturbances to rally support for the fleet bills, see Kennedy, "Tirpitz, England," esp. 33–34.

6. See Bülow to Wilhelm II, 30 Dec. 1901, Vz1:18, AA-PA; Bülow to Wilhelm II, 1 Sept. 1902, *GP*, 17:244–46; Bülow to Wilhelm II, 3 Nov. 1902, *GP*, 17:246–49. See Hebbinghaus, Memo, 24 Aug. 1901, RM5:5966, BA-MA; Bülow, "Memo on German Claims in Venezuela," 4957–59; Bülow's speech in the Reichstag, 19 Mar. 1903, *Stenographische Berichte*, 287th sitting, 10:8719.

7. For strain in their relationship, see Mühlberg to Metternich, 17 July 1902, Vz1:21, AA-PA; Holstein to Bülow, 4 Aug. 1901, in Rich and Fisher, *Holstein Papers*, 4:234–35. On Bülow and the kaiser, see esp. Lerman, *Chancellor as Courtier*, 29–40, 86–102.

8. See Hebbinghaus, "Memo," 24 Aug. 1901, RM5:5966, BA-MA, with comments by Diederichs. See Holleben to Richthofen, 21 Sept. 1901, D138, AA-PA.

9. See Bülow to Wilhelm II, 30 Dec. 1901, Vz1:18, AA-PA; diary, 11 Jan. 1902, in Rich and Fisher, *Holstein Papers*, 4:245–46.

10. Captain of *Vineta* to Admiralstab, 6 Oct. 1900, RM5:5954, BA-MA. For U.S. suspicions, see Loomis to Hay, 28 July 1900, M44:r96, NA; *Sun*, ed., 29 Jan. 1900; White to Hay, 5 June 1901, M44:93, NA. For British suspicions, see *T*, 18 Dec. 1902; Lord Tweedmouth, 2 Mar. 1903, *Parliamentary Debates*, 118:1049.

11. See Diederichs to Wilhelm II, 23 Dec. 1901, Vz1:18, AA-PA; Kriege, "Wilhelmstrasse Memo," 7 Jan. 1902, Vz1:19, AA-PA; Diederichs to Richthofen, 8 Jan. 1902, ibid.; Herwig and Helguera, *Alemania y el bloqueo*, 22–23; Fiebig-von Hase, *Lateinamerika*, 458.

12. Diary, 11 Jan. 1902, Rich and Fisher, *Holstein Papers*, 4:245–46.

13. See the kaiser's marginalia on Bülow to Wilhelm II, 20 Jan. 1902, *GP*, 17:241–43.

14. Bülow to Prince Heinrich, 30 Jan. 1902, *GP*, 17:243 n.*; *Revue Bleue*, 4 Jan. 1902, 492; Jackson to Hay, 19 Mar. 1902, M44:r95, NA. See White to Hay, 5 Mar. 1902, and Jackson to Hay, 12 Mar. 1902, ibid. On the possible source of the rumors of British intrigue, see Offner, *Unwanted War*, 184–85.

15. *SR*, 22 Feb. 1902; *Le Temps* (Paris) quoted in *LD* (25 Apr. 1903): 626. See Trommler, "Inventing the Enemy."

16. Castro, in *La República* (Caracas), in *LD* (4 Jan. 1902): 24, and in Commander of *Vineta* (Stiege), "Military-Political Report, 27 December 1901–3 February 1902," 3 Feb. 1902, encl. in Schröder to Richthofen, 5 Mar. 1902, Vz1:20, AA-PA; Haggard to Villiers, 23 Feb. 1902, FO 80:443, PRO. On plans for the operation, see Diederichs to Wilhelm II, 23 Dec. 1901, Vz1:18, AA-PA.

17. Admiralstab to Richthofen, 31 Jan. 1902, Vz1:19, AA-PA.

18. Haggard to Lansdowne, 4 Apr. 1902 and 12 May 1902, with minute of 17 May 1902, FO 80:443, PRO.

19. Sondhaus, *Preparing for Weltpolitik*, 207.

20. *Stenographische Berichte*, 112th sitting (8 Jan. 1902), 3209. For Bülow's Anglophobia, see diary, 7 Nov. 1902, Rich and Fisher, *Holstein Papers*, 4:270; Winzen, *Weltmachtkonzept*, 353–94. On the Anglo-German alliance talks, see Kennedy, *Antagonism*, 223–66; Kennedy, "German World Policy"; Langer, *Diplomacy*, 485–536, 711–46. On the Granite speech, see diary, 11 Jan. 1902, Rich and Fisher, *Holstein Papers*, 4:244.

21. Kiderlen-Wächter, quoted in Taylor, *Course of German History*, 147.

22. Kneer, *Great Britain*, 11; Herwig, *Vision*, 223.

23. De Lemos to Lansdowne, 27 Aug. 1902, FO 80:444, PRO; memorandum on British claims, encl. in White to Hay, 24 Dec. 1902, M30:r193, NA. The Foreign Office was greatly preoccupied with the perambulations of the British-registered *Ban Righ*, a ship that Castro accused, with justice, of aiding the rebels. (See any volume of Foreign Office correspondence for this period. The documentation is voluminous.) For a list of the seventeen notes that Haggard sent Castro, see Haggard to Lansdowne, 30 June 1902, FO 420:206, PRO.

24. Eckardstein to AA, 2 Jan. 1902, with Richthofen's and Bülow's comments, Vz1:19, AA-PA; Lansdowne to Colonial Office (draft), 16 Jan. 1902, FO 80:443, PRO. See Lascelles to Richthofen, 30 Jan. 1902, with Richthofen's comments, Vz1:19, AA-PA; Lansdowne to Villiers, 8 Feb. 1902, FO 80:443, PRO.

25. See Lansdowne, 2 Mar. 1903, *Parliamentary Debates*, 1060–61; Lansdowne to Lascelles, 22 Apr. 1902, FO 800:r111, PRO.

26. For the two diplomats working together, see their joint response to Castro's blockade of the Orinoco: Haggard to Lansdowne, 27 Aug. 1902, FO 80:444, PRO; Haggard to Lansdowne, 1 Sept. 1902, ibid.; Haggard to Lansdowne, 3 Oct. 1902, FO 80:445, PRO.

27. Minutes of Hurst, Davidson, and Lansdowne on Haggard to Lansdowne, 30 June 1902, FO 80:443, PRO. See Villiers to Lansdowne, 19 July 1902, with Lansdowne's minute, ibid. Every document passing through the Foreign Office was folded in three, the outside fold covered in the scrawl of increasingly senior officials in the Foreign Office, with minutes about the dispatch, the general trend of policy, recommendations, comments on previous minutes, and draft replies that sometimes sprawled over onto loose sheets of paper.

28. See Colonial Office to Foreign Office, 19 Feb. 1902, FO 80:443, PRO; Bülow to Wilhelm II, 1 Sept. 1902, *GP*, 17:244-46.

29. Mühlberg to Metternich, 17 July 1902, Vz1:21, AA-PA. On 12 July, Richthofen, Bülow, Sack, and Büchsel had met and recommended joint action in the fall. See "Remarks on the Meeting of 12 July 1902," Vz1:21, AA-PA.

30. Lansdowne to Villiers, filed with Larcom, Memo, 20 July 1902, FO 80:443, PRO. See Lansdowne to Buchanan, 23 July 1902, FO 420:206, PRO; Metternich to Bülow, 24 July 1902, Vz1:21, AA-PA; Metternich to Bülow, 7 Aug. 1902, ibid.

31. See Lansdowne's minute on Haggard to Lansdowne, tel. 40, 5 Aug. 1902, FO 80:444, PRO; Lansdowne to Admiralty (draft), 8 Aug. 1902, ibid.; Admiralty to Lansdowne, 14 Aug. 1902, ibid.; Lansdowne to Lascelles, 19 Aug. 1902, with Thomas's minute, 22 Aug. 1902, FO 420:206, PRO.

32. Lansdowne's memo on cabinet meeting, 21 Oct. 1902, and Villiers to Lansdowne (memo), 8 Nov. 1902, FO 80:445, PRO.

33. Lansdowne's minute on Villiers to Lansdowne, 8 Nov. 1902, FO 80:445, PRO; Lansdowne to Villiers, telegram from Sandringham, 10 Nov. 1902, ibid.; Villiers's minute on Lansdowne to Haggard, 11 Nov. 1902, ibid.; Lansdowne to Herbert, tel. 49, 11 Nov. 1902, ibid. It is curious that Lansdowne, in trying to anticipate issues that might arise in Sandringham, failed to mention Venezuela. See Lansdowne to Sanderson, 8 Nov. 1902, add 49727, Balfour Papers, British Museum, London.

34. "Iron-clad" from *NYT*, 26 Jan. 1903.

35. Lansdowne to Buchanan, 11 Nov. 1902, FO 80:445, PRO. See Lansdowne's minute on Villiers, "Points Raised by Count Metternich," 13 Nov. 1902, ibid.

36. *DN*, ed., 13 Dec. 1902; *DM*, ed., 16 Dec. 1902.

37. Lansdowne to Haggard, 11 Nov. 1902, FO 80:445, PRO; Bülow to Wilhelm II, 13 Nov. 1902, *GP*, 17:118. See Metternich to Wilhelmstrasse, 11 Nov. 1902, *GP*, 17:250-52.

38. *DM*, 16 Dec. 1902; Hamilton, quoted in Monger, *End of Isolation*, 105-6. Lansdowne was preoccupied with the education bill, just as Bülow was absorbed with the tariff debate. Lansdowne was also dealing with Salisbury's illness and the Boer War. At that moment, Ambassador White was packing in Berlin to begin his retirement, and Ambassador Herbert had arrived in Washington only in October.

39. *National Review* and *Sp*, quoted in *LD* (15 Nov. 1902): 645-46.

40. See, for example, Morris, "Pregnant Days"; Fiebig–von Hase, *Lateinamerika*, 880-900; Marks, *Velvet on Iron*, 37-54; Parsons, "German-American Crisis"; Beale, *Roosevelt*, 403-32; Livermore, "Venezuelan Crisis."

41. Roosevelt, "Message of the President," 3 Dec. 1901, *FR 1901*, xxxvi-xxxvii. This message gave rise to much adverse comment in the German press. See White to Hay, 10 Dec. 1901, no. 1804, M44:94, NA.

42. TR to McCalla, 3 Aug. 1897, *LTR* 1:636.

43. TR to Kimball, 17 Dec. 1897, *LTR*, 1:743.

44. TR to Moore, 5 Feb. 1898, *LTR*, 1:768-69.

45. TR to Moore, 9 Feb. 1898, *LTR*, 1:771.

46. TR to Strachey, 27 Jan. 1900, *LTR*, 2:1145.

47. TR to Meyer, 12 April 1901, *LTR*, 3:552.

48. TR to Lodge, 19 June 1901, *LTR*, 3:98. See TR to Spring-Rice, 3 July 1901, *LTR*, 3:109.

49. TR to Sternburg, 11 Oct. 1901, *LTR*, 3:172; TR to Sternburg, 12 July 1901, *LTR*, 3:116. On Roosevelt's desire to work with Germany, see also TR to Sternburg, 6 Mar. 1902, *LTR*, 3:239.

50. See esp. Paget to Lansdowne, 18 Sept. 1901, FO 15:344, PRO; Hunter to Hay, 26 Feb. 1902, M219:r65, NA, with enclosed European and Guatemalan notes; Villiers, "Memo for Lansdowne," 28 Mar. 1902, FO 15:352, PRO; Lascelles to Lansdowne, 6 Apr. 1902, ibid.; Paget to Lansdowne, 17 Apr. 1902, ibid. For a very good account, see Kneer, *Great Britain*, 1–31.

51. Hay to Hunter, 22 Mar. 1902, M77:r34, NA; Hay to Hunter, 10 Apr. 1902, ibid. See Adee to Bowen, 10 Aug. 1901, M77:r175, NA; Hunter to Hay, 22 Mar. 1902, M219:r65, NA; Bailey to Hay, 24 July 1902, ibid. The *New York Times* did not mention the incident. The Foreign Office initiated discussions about joint pressure in March 1901; the elaborate scheme evolved over the course of one year, and its every twist and turn is preserved in voluminous documentation. The United States is not mentioned once, not even in a minute. See esp. vols. FO 15:344 and FO 15:352, PRO.

52. Commander of *Falke* (Lieutenant Commander Musculus) to Admiralstab, 26 June 1902, in Hebbinghaus to Richthofen, 21 July 1902, Vz1:21, AA-PA; Haggard to Lansdowne, 27 June 1902, FO 80:443, PRO.

53. *Le Temps*, 29 June 1902. See Commander of *Gazelle* (Count von Oriola) to Admiralstab, 30 June 1902, encl. in Hebbinghaus to Richthofen, 21 July 1902, Vz1:21, AA-PA; *Le Figaro*, 28 and 29 June 1902; *L'Intransigeant*, 29 June 1902; *Le Temps*, 30 June 1902.

54. Bertie to Admiralty, 6 Aug. 1902, ADM 1:7618, PRO; Bowen to Hay, 10 Aug. 1902, and Adee's minute, M79:T56, NA. See Adee to Bowen, 21 Aug. 1902, M77:r175, NA; Hay to Bowen, 11 July 1902, ibid.; Hill to Bowen, 25 July 1902, ibid. The *New York Times* briefly reported the incident with no comment (27 and 29 June 1902).

55. Powell to Hay, 6 Sept. 1902, *FR 1902*, 645.

56. Powell to Hay, 13 Sept. 1902, subject file VI, box 665: "Political Situation in Haiti," RG 45, NA.

57. Vagts, *Deutschland*, 1497; Jackson to Hay, 10 Sept. 1902, M44:r96, NA; Moore to Adee, 15 Sept. 1902, Hay Papers; Adee to Moody, 9 Sept. 1902, subject file VP, box 685, RG 45, NA; *NYT*, 11 Sept. 1902. The kaiser's comment was leaked to the U.S. and British press. See *NYT*, 26 Jan. 1903; *Her*, 22 Jan. 1903 and 13 Dec. 1905; *MG*, 26 Jan. 1903. For the reaction in the German press, see *Frankfurter Zeitung und Handelsblatt*, 8 Sept. 1902; *Hamburger Nachrichten*, 8 Sept. 1902; *Tägliche Rundschau*, 7 Sept. 1902. See also Schröder to Richthofen, 31 Oct. 1902, with encl. Military Political Reports of Captain Eckermann of the *Panther*, Haiti 1:12, AA-PA. On the boarding of the German steamer, *Markomannia*, see Firmin to Killick, 1 Sept. 1902, subject file VI, box 665: "Political Situation in Haiti," RG 45, NA; Killick to Firmin, 2 Sept. 1902, ibid.; Powell to Hay, 3 Sept. 1902, *FR 1902*, 644; Powell to Hay, 6 Sept. 1902, *FR 1902*, 645–49; Powell to Hay, 7 Sept. 1902, *FR 1902*, 649–50. For the *Crête à Pierrot*, see Rogers to Moody, 5 July 1902, subject file VI, box 665: "Political Situation in Haiti," RG 45, NA. For the Haitian background, see Plummer, *Haiti*, 95–105.

58. Wharton's minute on Thomas to Kerr, 22 Dec. 1902, ADM 1:7696, PRO. See Haggard to Lansdowne, 1 Oct. 1901, FO 420:206; Haggard to Lansdowne, 26 Oct. 1901, ibid.; Haggard to Lansdowne, 13 June 1902, ibid.; Haggard to Lansdowne, 3 Oct. 1902, ibid.; Admiralty to Foreign Office, 27 Dec. 1902, FO 80:468, PRO; Haggard to Lansdowne, 13 Jan. 1903 (incorrectly dated 1902), ibid.; Haggard to Lansdowne, tel. 23, 18 Feb. 1903, ibid. On the British claim to Patos, see esp. vols. FO 80:468, PRO, and ADM 1:7696, PRO. The *New York Times* and the *Herald* reported the dispute in a most cursory fashion. See *NYT*, 21, 23 Sept. and 24 Nov. 1902; *Her*, 21, 22 Sept. 1902.

59. Villiers's minute on Lucas to Villiers, 24 Jan. 1902, FO 80:468. See Hertslet, "US and Patos Island," 24 Jan. 1902, ibid. In 1943 Britain ceded Patos to Venezuela. Rodríguez Campos, *Venezuela, 1902*, 230.

60. Bowen to Hay, 4 Oct. 1902, M79:T56, NA.

61. Russell to Hay, 30 June 1901, and Hay to Russell, 17 July 1901, *FR 1901*, 550–51.

62. Holleben to Hay, 13 Dec. 1901, enclosing Imperial German Embassy, "Pro-memoria," 11 Dec. 1901, and Hay to Holleben, 16 Dec. 1901, enclosing Department of State, "Memorandum," 16 Dec. 1902, *FR 1901*, 192–95. See TR to Sternburg, 12 July 1901, *LTR*, 3:115–17. After the German memorandum was made public, the *New York Times* commented editorially on the German government's "perfect consideration and politeness" (29 Aug. 1902).

63. Vernassa, *Emigrazione*, 56. This is the authoritative source on the Italian role.

64. Lansdowne, "Proposed Coercion of Venezuela," memo no. 144, 17 Oct. 1902, CAB 37:r18, vol. 63, PRO; Hay to Herbert, 11 Nov. 1902, U.S. Senate documents, 58th Cong., 3d sess., no. 119, 782–83.

65. Metternich to AA, 15 Dec. 1902, *GP*, 17:263; Lansdowne, 2 Mar. 1903, *Parliamentary Debates*, 118:1066–67. See Villiers to Lansdowne, 11 Oct. 1902, FO 80:445, PRO; Lansdowne to Buchanan, 26 Nov. 1902, FO 420:206, PRO.

66. Villiers, Memo for Lansdowne, 18 Oct. 1902, FO 80:445, PRO; Lansdowne, "Proposed Coercion of Venezuela," memo no. 144, 17 Oct. 1902, CAB 37:r18, vol. 63, PRO. See Lansdowne to Herbert, 11 Nov. 1902, FO 420:206, PRO.

67. Lansdowne, minute on Admiralty to Foreign Office, 14 Aug. 1902, FO 80:444, PRO. See Sanderson, Memo, 16 Aug. 1902, with Lansdowne's minute, FO 80:444, PRO; Lansdowne to Lascelles, 19 Aug. 1902, FO 420:206, PRO; Metternich to Bülow, 17 Aug. 1902, Vz1:21, AA-PA; Mühlberg to Metternich, undated, ibid.

68. See Campbell, *Anglo-American Understanding*, 274; Grenville, "Great Britain."

69. Selborne's minute on Villiers to Admiralty, 22 Oct. 1902, ADM 1:7620, PRO; Haggard to Lansdowne, 29 Nov. 1902, with Villiers's minute, FO 80:446, PRO. This same fear probably explains the Foreign Office's dilatoriness in informing Haggard of the impending action. "I think Haggard should have notice of what is coming," Villiers wrote on 27 November. "He will want a little time to pack up, etc." (Villiers to Lansdowne, 27 Nov. 1902, FO 80:446, PRO). Bowen was not informed of the blockade until after Haggard and Pilgrim-Baltazzi had left Caracas. Bowen to Hay, 13 Dec. 1902, M79:T56, NA.

70. See Grenville, "Great Britain"; Lammersdorf, "Advantages of Cooperation," 88–89.

71. Jackson to Hay, 5 Oct. 1901, M44:r94, NA. See White to Day, 13 May 1898, M44:85, NA.

72. Quadt to Bülow, 23 Aug. 1902, *GP*, 17:111. See Vagts, *Deutschland*, 1554; Holleben to AA, 30 Nov. 1901, Vz1:18, AA-PA; Holleben to Richthofen, 21 Sept. 1901, D138:21, AA-PA.

73. Wilhelm II, marginalia no. 2 on Bülow to Wilhelm II, 20 Jan. 1902, *GP*, 17:241–43.

74. See Bülow to Wilhelm II, 1 Sept. 1902, *GP*, 17:244–46; Bülow to Wilhelm II, 3 Nov. 1902, ibid., 246–49.

75. Rodd to Lansdowne, 6 Dec. 1902, FO 800:132, PRO; Haggard to Lansdowne, 12 Sept. 1902, FO 80:444, PRO.

76. Buchanan to Lansdowne, tel. 44, 2 Dec. 1902, with minutes of Villiers, Larcom, and Lansdowne, FO 80:447, PRO. See Bülow to Wilhelm II, 20 Jan. 1902, *GP*, 17:242; Thomas to Kerr, 6 Dec. 1902, ADM 1:7620, PRO; Vernassa, *Emigrazione*, 71–85.

77. Lansdowne to Rodd, 20 Dec. 1902, FO 800:132, PRO. See Lansdowne to Rodd, 4 Dec. 1902 (draft), FO 80:447, PRO; Prinetti to Panza, 4 Dec. 1902, in Vernassa, *Emigrazione*, 138; Lansdowne to Rodd, 5 Dec. 1902, FO 80:447, PRO; unsigned Foreign Office memo reporting conversation with the Italian ambassador, no date but filed after 5 Dec. 1902, ibid.; Vernassa, *Emigrazione*, 85–89.

78. Bülow to Wilhelm II, 12 Dec. 1902, *GP*, 17:258–59; *Il Mattino*, 15 Dec. 1902, in Vernassa, *Emigrazione*, 100. For Germany's reservations about Italian participation, see Metternich to Lansdowne, 10 Dec. 1902, FO 80:447, PRO; Lansdowne to Buchanan, 7 Dec. 1902 (draft), ibid.

79. Douglas to Admiralty, 27 Sept. 1902, ADM 1:7620, PRO.

80. Lansdowne's memo on cabinet meeting, 21 Oct. 1902, FO 80:445, PRO; Bülow to Wilhelm II, 3 Nov. 1902, with Wilhelm's marginalia, *GP*, 17:246–49.

81. Villiers to Thomas, 25 Nov. 1902, ADM 1:7620, PRO. See Villiers to Lansdowne, 24 Nov. 1902, with Lansdowne's minute, FO 80:446, PRO; Haggard to Lansdowne, 7 Dec. 1902, FO 420:206, PRO.

82. Bülow to Wilhelm II, 12 Dec. 1902, *GP*, 17:258. The correspondence on this issue is extensive. See esp. Bülow to Wilhelm II, 20 Jan. 1902, *GP*, 17:241–43; Metternich to Lansdowne, 21 Nov. 1902, FO 80:446, PRO; Richthofen to Metternich, 5 Dec. 1902, *GP*, 17:257; Davidson, "Memo," 8 Dec. 1902, FO 80:448, PRO; Metternich to AA, 9 Dec. 1902, *GP*, 17:257–58; Bülow to Wilhelm II, 12 Dec. 1902, ibid., 258–60; Villiers's minute to Lansdowne, 13 Dec. 1902, FO 80:448, PRO. For Bülow's recommendations, see esp. Kriege, "Memo," 7 Jan. 1902, and Diederichs to Richthofen, 8 Jan. 1902, Vz1:19, AA-PA. On Germany's yielding to the British demand, see Scheder to de Jong van Beek, 29 Dec. 1902, RM38:131, BA-MA. The dispute went to arbitration before war was declared.

83. Lansdowne's minute on Haggard to Lansdowne, 20 Nov. 1902, FO 80:446, PRO.

84. Phillips, 15 Dec. 1902, *Parliamentary Debates*, 116: col. 1257; Rodríguez Campos, *Venezuela*, 1902, 227; *T*, ed., 11 Dec. 1902. See Douglas to Admiralty, 11 Dec. 1902, ADM 1:7620, PRO; Ship's log, *Retribution*, 10 Dec. 1902, ADM 53:25490, PRO.

85. Montgomerie to Admiralty, 16 Dec. 1902, ADM 1:7620, PRO. See Douglas to

Admiralty, 15 Dec. 1902, ibid. and Ship's log, *Charybdis*, 13 and 14 Dec. 1902, ADM 53:18468, PRO. The captain of the *Marietta* asserted that the Venezuelans did apologize on time but that the British did not consider the apology adequate (Diehl to Moody, 16 Dec. 1902, subject file VI, box 671: "Venezuela Situation," RG 45, NA). For the ultimatum and the reply, see *Venezuelan Herald*, encl. in Diehl to Moody, 4 Jan. 1903, subject file VI, box 671: "Venezuela Situation," RG 45, NA.

86. Castro, quoted in *El Pregonero*, 15 Dec. 1902; Venezuelan Ministry of Foreign Affairs, "Protest to the Bombardment of Puerto Cabello," 15 Dec. 1902, encl. in Bowen to Hay, 27 Dec. 1902, M79:T56, NA; Volkmar to Hill, 16 Dec. 1902, T229:r12, NA. For Montgomerie's views, see Montgomerie to Scheder (*Vineta*), 16 Dec. 1902, encl. in Montgomerie to Douglas, 20 Dec. 1902, ADM 1:7696, PRO. See also ship's log, *Charybdis*, 13, 14 Dec. 1902, ADM 53:18468, PRO; Montgomerie to Scheder, 16 Dec. 1902, RM38:131, BA-MA; "Blockade of Venezuela, Vol. 3," RM38:132, BA-MA. For a vivid description of the sinking of the boats, see report of commanding Venezuelan General, *El Pregonero*, 15 Dec. 1902; Haggard to Lansdowne, 14 Dec. 1902, FO 80:448, PRO. The Admiralty did not share Montgomerie's assessment. "Commodore's action . . . most unexpected and uncalled for" (Douglas to Admiralty, 17 Dec. 1902, FO 80:448). The bombardment caused questions to be raised in the British Parliament (see *Parliamentary Debates* 116 [Commons, 15 Dec. 1902]: 1212–13, 1246–87). The U.S. commander on the scene reported that the prison was evacuated and that the only casualties were a broken leg and a broken ankle, "presumably . . . through jumping off the . . . fort." Diehl to Moody, 16 Dec. 1902, subject file VI, box 671: "Venezuela Situation," RG 45, NA.

87. Montgomerie to Admiralty, 16 Dec. 1902, ADM 1:7620, PRO; Wilhelm's marginalia on Bülow to Wilhelm II, 12 Dec. 1902, *GP*, 17:260. On the separation of the blockades, see "Remarks on the Joint Blockade of the Coast of Venezuela," 25 Sept. 1902, Vz1:22, AA-PA; Lansdowne to Buchanan, 29 Nov. 1902, FO 80:446, PRO; Davidson, Memo, 9 Dec. 1902, with Lansdowne's minute, FO 80:448, PRO; Lansdowne on Villiers, Memo, 21 Dec. 1902, FO 80:449, PRO; Bülow to Quadt, 20 Jan. 1903, *GP*, 17:272–73.

88. Villiers's minute on Douglas to Admiralty, tel. 114, 13 Dec. 1902, FO 80:448, PRO; Lansdowne's minute on Montgomerie to Admiralty, 16 Dec. 1902, ibid.; Lansdowne's minute on Douglas to Admiralty, tel. 119, 17 Dec. 1902, ibid.; Villiers's minute on Douglas to Admiralty, tel. 114, 13 Dec. 1902, ibid. For notification of the request, see Bowen to Hay, 9 Dec. 1902, *FR 1902*, 790; Hay to Tower, 12 Dec. 1902, ibid., 420; Hay to White, 12 Dec. 1902, ibid., 453; White to Hay, 13 Dec. 1902, M30:r193, NA; White to Lansdowne, 13 Dec. 1902, FO 80:448, PRO. For a copy of the official notice, see FO 80:449, PRO. For the delays, see Douglas to Admiralty, 2 Dec. 1902, ADM 1:7620, PRO; Montgomerie to Douglas, 18 Dec. 1902, RM38:131, BA-MA. For the German blockade, see Plumacher to Scheder, 24 Dec. 1902, RM38:137, BA-MA; Brewer to Scheder, 23 Dec. 1902, ibid.; Scheder, "Military Political Report: 27 Dec. 1902–5 Jan. 1903," Curaçao, 5 Jan. 1903, encl. in Schröder to Richthofen, 4 Feb. 1903, Vz1:23, AA-PA; Douglas to Admiralty, 22 Dec. 1902, FO 80:449, PRO; and Bowen to Hay, 22 Dec. 1902, M79:T56, NA. For acceptance of arbitration, see Tower to Hay, 18, 19 Dec. 1902, M44:r96, NA; White to Hay, 18 Dec. 1902, M30:r193, NA.

89. For Roosevelt's claim see TR to Thayer, 21, 23, 27 Aug. 1916, *LTR*, 8:1101–8.

For less dramatic claims, which reach a crescendo in 1916, see TR to Reid, 27 June 1906, ibid., 5:319; TR to White, 14 Aug. 1906, ibid., 358–59; TR to Reid, 4 Dec. 1908, ibid., 6:1410. For the believers, see Morris, "Pregnant Days," 2–13; Fiebig-von Hase, *Lateinamerika*, 880–900; Marks, *Velvet on Iron*, 37–54; Parsons, "German-American Crisis," 436–52; Beale, *Roosevelt*, 403–32; Livermore, "Roosevelt," 452–71; Ricard, *Théodore Roosevelt*, 279–94. For the mildly skeptical, see Holbo, "Perilous Obscurity"; Spector, "Roosevelt," 257–63; Esthus, *International Rivalries*, 40–41; Gould, *Presidency*, 75–79; Brands, *T.R.*, 463–71. For the incredulous, see Pringle, *Theodore Roosevelt*, 198–203; Vagts, *Deutschland*, 1555–57, 1567–68, 1593–94, 1622; Perkins, *Monroe Doctrine*, 215–27; Herwig, *Vision*, 205–7. The General Board worked on a plan "covering a situation in Venezuela" in April 1902 (23 April 1902, GBM). In June, the German government's offical notification of its intentions was passed to the board, but the Venezuela plan was not completed until October 1903. See 17 June 1902, and 27 Oct. 1903, GBM.

90. Douglas to Admiralty, 1 Jan. 1903, ADM 1:7696, PRO. For the admiralty ledgers, see ADM 12:1371–76, PRO. See Marks, *Velvet on Iron*, 37–54. For a restatement of Marks's thesis, see Morris, "Pregnant Days," 2–13. For a twist, arguing that the ultimatum was delivered in February, see Ricard, *Théodore Roosevelt*, 279–94. For a defense of Ricard, see Tilchin, *British Empire*, 32–34.

91. See Metternich to Bülow, 1, 16, 17, 20, 22, 23, 27 Dec. 1902; 23, 24, 30 Jan. and 3, 4, 9, 17, 22 Feb. 1903, Vz1:21–22, AA-PA.

92. Lascelles to Sanderson, 27 Dec. 1902, FO 800:111, PRO. See Lascelles to Lord Francis Knollys (private secretary to Edward VII), 9 Jan. 1903, ibid.; Lascelles to Lansdowne, 30 Jan. 1903, ibid.; Lascelles to Lansdowne, 6 Feb. 1903, ibid.; Cecil, *Emperor*, 2:76–77.

93. This analysis of the British press is based on a close reading of the *Times*, the *Morning Post*, the *Daily Chronicle*, the *Pall Mall Gazette*, the *Daily Mail*, the *Spectator* (a weekly), the *Westminster Gazette*, the *London Daily News*, the *Manchester Guardian*, the *Observer* (a weekly), and the *Saturday Review* (a weekly). The *Times* was technically independent but leaned toward the Conservatives. The *Morning Post*, *Spectator*, *Daily Mail*, and *Pall Mall Gazette* were allied with the Conservatives. The *Manchester Guardian*, *Westminster Gazette*, *Daily Chronicle*, *Daily News*, and *Observer* were allied with the opposition Liberals. In the London *Review of Reviews*, William Stead ranked the papers as follows: the *Times* and *Westminster Gazette* were first rank—read by members of both parties; in the second rank, in descending order of importance were the *Daily News*, *Morning Post*, *Daily Chronicle*, *Pall Mall Gazette*; and in the third rank was the *Daily Mail* (*Review of Reviews* 30 [Dec. 1904]: 604–5). In this section (through n. 123), all dates are 1902 unless otherwise noted.

94. *DM*, ed., 9 Dec.; *T*, ed., 27 Nov.; *DN*, ed., 11 Dec. See *DM*, ed., 12 Dec. For the lack of alarm, see *T*, 25 (ed.), 29 Nov., 5, 10, 11 (ed.) Dec.; *MP*, 22 (ed.), 25 Nov.; *DM*, 27 Nov. (ed.), 9 Dec.; *MG*, 5 (ed.), 9 Dec.; *Ob*, 7 Dec.; *WG*, 8 Dec.; *PMG*, 27 Nov. (ed.), 9, 10 Dec.; *DC*, 25, 27, 28 (ed.) Nov., 4 (ed.), 11 (ed.) Dec.; *SR*, 29 Nov. 1902, 662; *Sp*, 29 Nov. 1902, 817. (The *Saturday Review* was unique in its sympathetic view of the Venezuelans. See 13 Dec. 1902, 728–29.)

95. *NYT*, ed., 9 Sept. See *SR*, 1901–03.

96. *PMG*, ed., 27 Nov. See *T*, 3 and 9 Dec. (eds.), 10 Dec.; *DC*, ed., 28 Nov.; *DM*,

3 Dec.; *PMG*, 3 Dec.; *Sp*, 6 Dec. 1902, 881; *DN*, ed., citing the *Crête-à-Pierrot* incident as an indicator of Washington's hands-off policy, 12 Dec.; *PMG*, 13 Dec.

97. *DN*, ed., 1 Dec. See *DN*, 4 Dec. By 11 December, the *Daily News* had broadened its concerns to the lives of Britons in Venezuela and the Balfour government's predilection to be the world policeman. On the 12th it condemned secret diplomacy, and on the 13th it stressed the priority of domestic issues. On the *Daily News*, see Koss, *Press*, 365.

98. Koss, *Press*, 378; *MP*, 9 Dec. 1902. The *Morning Post* was more virulently anti-German than the other papers (see, for example, 28 Nov. and 4 Dec., ed.). Only the iconoclastic *Saturday Review* was never critical of the alliance: "There is no reason in scientific politics why we should be in antagonism to Germany; least of all in South America." *SR*, 20 Dec. 1902, 761.

99. See *DM*, ed., 12 Dec.; *MG*, 12 Dec.; *WG*, ed., 12 Dec. For a concise illustration of the shift, see the editorials in *DC*, 11–13 Dec. The *Pall Mall Gazette*, stiffened by its contempt for all things Venezuelan, held out until 15 December and then hardened its opposition to the venture on 16 December (eds., 15 and 16 Dec.). The *Saturday Review* still expected no complications on 13 December (p. 728). Interestingly, it was closest to the *Times* (and the Foreign Office, on which it heaped scorn) in its confidence that England had a clear right and need to enforce claims in South America and that the United States had no right to interfere. See esp. *SR*, 20 Dec. 1902, 760.

100. *MG*, ed., 12 Dec. For the assumption that the allies would seize the custom-houses, see *MP*, ed., 7 Dec.; *DM*, ed., 9 Dec. For criticism of seizing the ships, see *WG*, ed., 16 Dec.; *DC*, ed., 11 Dec.; *DN*, eds., 11, 12, and 17 Dec.

101. *WG*, ed., 12 Dec. See *MG*, 12 Dec.; *DC*, ed., 12 Dec.; *DM*, ed., 12 Dec.

102. *MP*, ed., 11 Dec. The *Daily News*, as usual, was ahead of the pack. On 11 December, it mused, "Unless we have a free hand, Pres. Castro may be able to defy our blockades and ultimatums. Are the Government quite certain that we have a free hand?" (ed.). See *DN*, ed., 12 Dec., and *WG*, ed., 13 Dec.

103. Lee, *Popular Press*, 160; *WG*, ed., 15 Dec.; *WG*, ed., 16 Dec.; *MG*, ed., 16 Dec.; *MP*, ed., 17 Dec. See *DN*, ed., 16 Dec.

104. This analysis of the U.S. press is based on a close reading of the *New York Times*, the *New York Sun*, the *Wall Street Journal*, the *New York World*, the *New York Herald*, the *Chicago Daily News* (CDN), the *Atlanta Constitution* (Con), the New Orleans *Daily Picayune*, the Washington *Evening Star*, the *San Francisco Chronicle*, and the *Nation*, a weekly. The *Herald* had particularly extensive coverage of Venezuela, but its objectivity was suspect: its correspondent was Bowen's private secretary (see Haggard to Lansdowne, 24 Nov. 1902, FO 80:446, PRO). For the U.S. press, see also Angermann, "Ein Wendepunkt."

105. See *NYT*, eds., 5, 10, and 11 Dec.; *Sun*, eds., 7 and 12 Dec.; *Her*, 4, 6, and 11 Dec.; *CDN*, eds., 10 and 11 Dec.; *Con*, eds., 4 and 9 Dec.; *ES*, ed., 10 Dec.; *Nat* (4 Dec. 1902): 434; (11 Dec. 1902): 457–58. The *Wall Street Journal* did not mention the incident until December 15. The *Picayune* and the *World* were more alarmed from the beginning but still saw no threat to the Monroe Doctrine. See *Pic*, eds., 2 and 9 Dec.; *Wor*, ed., 11 Dec. The *San Francisco Chronicle* was critical of the collection of private debts by warships from the beginning. See *SFC*, eds., 10, 11, and 12 Dec. For a very rare column expressing early anxieties, see *NYT*, 17 Aug. 1902, 2:23.

106. Mahan to Maxse, 22 Dec. 1902, in Seager and Maguire, *Mahan*, 3:50. For the

possible threat to the Monroe Doctrine, see *Wor*, 16 Dec.; *Pic*, 12 Dec.; *NYT*, ed. and p. 1, 16 Dec.; *Con*, eds., 13 and 17 Dec.; *CDN*, eds., 12 and 13 Dec.; *Her*, eds., 15 and 16 Dec.; *ES*, ed., 11 Dec. The *Sun* emphasized that the administration perceived no threat to the Monroe Doctrine (ed. and p. 1, 16 Dec.; ed., 17 Dec.)

107. During the first week of December 1902, the naval war games were well covered by several papers (see *NYT*, 3, 5, and 6 Dec.; *Her*, 2, 5, 7, 10, and 11 Dec.; *Wor*, 10 Dec.; *Sun*, 5, 7, and 9 Dec.; *ES*, 5, 9, and 11 Dec.). Only a few papers explicitly linked Dewey's presence to the events in Venezuela before 11 December. (See *Wor*, 4 Dec.; *Pic*, ed., 5 Dec.) However, after the 11th, the linkage was widespread (see *SFC*, 14 and 17 Dec.; *Sun*, 16 and 17 Dec.; *Wor*, 17 Dec.; *Her*, ed., 11 Dec.; *CDN*, ed., 12 Dec.; *Con*, ed., 13 Dec., 17 Dec.; *Pic*, eds., 12 and 15 Dec.; *ES*, 13 and 16 Dec.). Prior to the acceptance of arbitration, the *New York Times* and the *Wall Street Journal* never linked the two stories, and the *Nation* never mentioned the fleet. Only the *World* and *Evening Star* were specific—the fleet would escort U.S. ships to Venezuela if Germany insisted on imposing a peace blockade (the press did not know that Berlin had bowed to London's wish for a war blockade), which the United States would not recognize. *ES*, 15 Dec.; *Wor*, 17 Dec.

108. *WG*, 5 Dec., citing the *Times*'s report that the fleet would not interfere with England or Germany. *MP*, 17 Dec.: "The Navy Department is preparing orders for the disposition of Admiral Dewey's fleet during Christmas week. The plans avoid concentration at any point. This decision is simply in accordance with the original programme, decided on before the maneouvres began."

109. *MG*, 13 Dec. See *MG*, 5 Dec. (a Reuters telegram that simply mentions the U.S. Navy, not Dewey's fleet in particular); *DN*, 12 and 17 Dec.; *DM*, 12 and 14 Dec.

110. *T*, 6 Dec. The *Times* reported the plans for the winter maneuvers on November 10 and the presence of the fleet on December 5.

111. See *Parliamentary Debates* 116:237–38, 653–55, 914–15, 1105–9, 1212–13, 1224, 1245–87 (the debate), 1289–90, 1335, 1487–92, 1612.

112. In his study of Roosevelt's use of the press to signal American naval preparedness in the Caribbean, Paul Holbo concludes that the president's public diplomacy was ambiguous and therefore subject to differing interpretations abroad. As for the British press's handling of the U.S. fleet maneuvers, he notes that the *Manchester Guardian* did not mention them (in fact it did, twice, but only obliquely; see above, n. 99), that the *Times* mentioned them in the first week of December and then let the subject drop, and that the *Daily News* became alarmed as soon as it heard about them. But both the *Times* and the *Daily News* are anomalous in that they mention the U.S. fleet at all, and Holbo's interpretation of the *News* is inaccurate: its concern about the American reaction was not linked to the fleet. The article that Holbo cites in support of this notion was penned by a chatty columnist (reminiscent of Alistair Cooke's "Letter from America"), whose opinions were distinct in tone and content from the paper's reportorial and editorial line. ("And anyhow," the occasional columnist wrote, "there are the United States ships of war . . . waiting about.") Holbo's study indicates the perils of relying on a small sample, even one that should have been, on the face of it, representative. Had he looked at more British newspapers, he would have seen that in England, Roosevelt's signal—if such it was—was worse than ambiguous: it was all but inaudible. Furthermore, scholars who have relied on Holbo's work have tended to ignore his nuanced and modest conclusions and have taken from his article the bald notion that

the press, worldwide, was concerned with the U.S. fleet maneuvers. (Holbo, "Perilous Obscurity," 428–48. For the article in *Daily News* cited by Holbo, see "American Notes: What Befell at La Guayra," *DN*, 11 Dec. For other scholars' use of Holbo, see Collin, *Theodore Roosevelt's Caribbean*, 106; Fiebig–von Hase, *Lateinamerika*, 849.)

113. If there was any concern about war, it referred to the possibility that war might break out between the powers and Venezuela, with no mention of the participation of the United States. See *DN*, eds., 13 and 15 Dec.; *MG*, eds., 9 and 12 Dec.; *MP*, ed., 18 Dec.; *DM*, ed., 15 Dec.

114. The extent of the ignorance can be seen in the *Daily Mail*: "It would be wise on our part to make clear what we believe to be the fact—that there is no co-operation between England and Germany" (ed., 13 Dec.).

115. *DN*, 15 Dec.; *PMG*, ed., 15 Dec.; *DC*, ed., 16 Dec.

116. *DC*, 15 Dec. For the press's irritation with the lack of information, see *DN*, eds., 9, 11, 12, and 13 Dec., 15 Dec.; *T*, eds., 13, 15 Dec.; *WG*, eds., 12, 15 Dec.; *MP*, eds., 9, 15 Dec.; *DC*, ed., 12 Dec.; *SR* (13 Dec. 1902): 726.

117. Reid, "Last Month"; Campbell-Bannerman, 15 Dec. 1902, *Parliamentary Debates* 116: col. 1270.

118. Reid, "Last Month"; *St. James Gazette*, quoted in *DM*, 17 Dec.; *MG*, ed., 16 Dec.

119. *DN*, ed., 16 Dec.

120. *DN*, ed., 12 Dec.; *WG*, ed., 13 Dec. See, for example, *SR* (29 Nov. 1902): 662; *DN*, eds., 1, 16 Dec.; *Ob*, ed., 7 Dec.; *MP*, 9 Dec., 15 Dec. (ed.); *DM*, eds., 9, 12 Dec.; *WG*, eds., 12, 15, 16 Dec.; *DC*, ed., 13 Dec.; *PMG*, ed., 16 Dec.

121. Brooks, "Venezuelan Imbroglio"; Metternich to Bülow, 4 Feb. 1903, Vz1:23, AA-PA.

122. *T*, 17 Dec., quoting *Her*, ed., 15 Dec; *T*, 15 Dec. The *Times* insisted throughout the episode that there was no alarm in the United States and that there was no crisis (see 10, 12 [ed.], 13, and 16 Dec.). However, the *Times*'s New York correspondent frequently reported a slightly more agitated mood in the United States than did the Washington correspondent; the leader writers reflected the latter's reports more often than the former's (see, for example, the two reports and editorial of December 12). After the acceptance of arbitration, in an abrupt change in the paper's stance, the *Times* published a poem by Rudyard Kipling that was searing in its sarcastic treatment of the government. See "The Rowers," *T*, 22 Dec.

123. *DC*, ed., 12 Dec.; *MP*, ed., 13 Dec.; *DN*, ed., 13 Dec.; *DM*, ed., 16 Dec. See *DN*, 15 and 16 (ed.) Dec. The *Westminster Guardian* asserted only that England was unable to accept arbitration without Germany's agreement (*WG*, ed., 16 Dec.). The weekly *Saturday Review*, published on 13 and 20 December, missed the debate but welcomed arbitration on 20 December (*SR* [20 Dec. 1902]: 760–61). The *Spectator* was opposed to arbitration (*Sp*, "News of the Week" [13 Dec. 1902]: 925).

124. For questions and debate on Venezuela before the Christmas recess, see n. 111 above. For the fierce attack in Parliament on the government's lack of consultation with the United States, see esp. *Parliamentary Debates* (Lord Cranborne, 19 Feb. 1903) 118:281 and (Lansdowne, 3 Mar. 1903) 118:1066.

125. Metternich to AA, 14 and 15 Dec. 1902; Bülow to Metternich, 17 Dec. 1902, *GP*,

17:262, 266–67. "Inevitable bow" from Metternich to Bülow, 1 Feb. 1903, Vz1:23, AA-PA.

126. Metternich to Bülow, 4 Feb. 1903, with Bülow's marginalia no. 4, *GP*, 17:288–89. The Conservatives' loss of a significant by-election in one of their strongholds was attributed, in part, to the public's displeasure with the government's cooperation with Germany in Venezuela. See *Sp*, quoted in *LD* (7 Feb. 1903): 196 and (11 Apr. 1903): 543.

127. Holleben to AA, 16 Dec. 1902, with Bülow's marginalia no. 1, *GP*, 17:264.

128. White to Hay, 17, 18 Dec. 1902, M30:r193, NA; White, memo for Lansdowne, 17 Dec. 1902, FO 80:442, PRO. The delivery of this note caused a diplomatic flap in London. Its timing was awkward. As White explained to Hay, "The decision to accept arbitration was arriged [*sic*] at by Cabinet at Tuesday's council [16 December], and . . . [the] German Ambassador's instructions to assent thereto came yesterday [17 December] before my conversation with his Lordship [Lansdowne], but he could not communicate decision till after today's Cabinet council [18 December]. . . . His Majesty's Government are the better pleased to find that they had of their own accord adopted a course which would find favor with the Government of the United States" (White to Hay, 18 Dec. 1902, M30:r193, NA). In order to be sure that there was no misunderstanding on this point, Lansdowne requested that the diplomatic record be gently adjusted. White had cabled Hay: "Told him [Lansdowne] you had instructed me to represent desirability of arbitration, which I did urgently." The last phrase was omitted from the printed record at Lansdowne's request. See White to Hay, 17 Dec. 1902, M30:r193, NA; White to Hay, 18 Dec. 1902, ibid.; White, Memo for Lansdowne, 17 Dec. 1902, FO 80:442, PRO.

129. TR to Thayer, 21 Aug. 1916, *LTR*, 7:1102–3.

130. Haggard to Lansdowne, 21 Sept. 1901, FO 80:427, PRO; Haggard to Lansdowne, 15 Sept. 1901, FO 80:435, PRO. See Pilgrim-Baltazzi to Bülow, 27 Sept. 1901, Vz1:18, AA-PA; *NYT*, 16 Dec. 1901; Commander of *Vineta* (de Fonseca-Volleim) to Admiralstab, 14 Nov. 1901, and Commander of *Stein* (Bacher) to Admiralstab, 1 Dec. 1901, encl. in Admiralstab to Richthofen, 9 Jan. 1902, Vz1:18, AA-PA; Commander of *Moltke* (Frantz) to Admiralstab, 23 Dec. 1901, encl. in Admiralstab to Richthofen, 29 Jan. 1902, Vz1:19, AA-PA.

131. Wilhelm's marginalia on Bülow to Wilhelm II, 20 Jan. 1902, *GP*, 17:241–43.

132. Bülow to Wilhelm II, 3 Nov. 1902, *GP*, 17:248. The response in Latin America to the Anglo-German blockade was muted: only Peru and Argentina voiced support for Venezuela; the other governments were "evasive, neutral or even frankly hostile" (Rodríguez Campos, *Venezuela, 1902*, 302–3).

133. Metternich to Bülow, 9 Nov. 1902, *GP*, 17:115 n. 1.

134. Wilhelm II to Bülow, 12 Nov. 1902, *GP*, 17:116; Bülow to Wilhelm II, 13 Nov. 1902, *GP*, 17:118; Mühlberg to Metternich, 17 July 1902, Vz1:21, AA-PA.

135. Wilhelm's marginalia on Bülow to Wilhelm II, 3 Nov. 1902, *GP*, 17:246–49.

136. White, *Autobiography*, 2:247.

137. Bülow to Wilhelm II, 23 Jan. 1902, with Wilhelm's marginalia, *GP*, 17:275–76.

138. Vagts, *Deutschland*, 1497.

139. Metternich to AA, 28 Jan. 1903, with Wilhelm's marginalia no. 1, *GP*, 17:281–82; Bülow to Metternich, 4 Feb. 1903, *GP*, 17:286; Tirpitz, *Erinnerungen*, 137.

140. *Her*, 14 Feb. 1903; Bülow, speech in the Reichstag, 19 Mar. 1903, *Stenographische Berichte*, 287th sitting, 10:8719.

141. TR to Theodore Roosevelt Jr., 9 Feb. 1903, *LTR*, 3:422.

142. *Washington Times*, 15 Feb. 1903. The discrepancy in settlement awards was due to the fact that Germany's first-rank claims ($325,000) far surpassed Britain's. Also, England was eager to settle the affair before Parliament reconvened on 17 February. The details were hammered out at the Hague, where the negotiations dragged on until February 1904. By August 1907, Venezuela had, to the surprise of most people, paid its debt in full. The best account of the claims negotiations is Guthrie, "Intervention," 193-315. See also Sullivan, "Despotism," 342-49.

143. See *Her*, 18 Dec. 1902; *NYT*, 23 Dec. 1902. Castro had ridiculed the blockade before the attack on Fort San Carlos, saying that Venezuela could break it at will as long as the allies did not control the lagoon (see *NYT*, 26 Jan. 1903). See also ONI, "The Bombing of Fort San Carlos," [n.d.], subject file VI: "International Relations and Politics," box 671, RG 45, NA; Dorwart, *Naval Intelligence*, 76.

144. See Russell to Hay, 23, 28 Jan. 1903, M79:r56, NA. For a recent restatement of this view, see Rodríguez Campos, *Venezuela, 1902*, 225.

145. Scheder, "Military Political Report: 14-24 January, 1903," 24 Jan. 1903, encl. in Admiralstab to Richthofen, 18 Feb. 1903, Vz1:24, AA-PA; Captain of *Ariadne* to Admiralty, 30 Jan. 1903, ADM 1:7696, PRO. See Douglas to Admiralty, encl. in Admiralty to Foreign Office, 23 Jan. 1903, FO 420:212, PRO. The British themselves had "caused considerable panic ashore" when they had fired blanks at the mainland on 25 January. Johnson to Eustace, 25 Jan. 1903, ADM 1:7696, PRO; see also Eustace to Senior Naval Officer, 27 Jan. 1903, ibid.

146. *NYT*, 30 Jan. 1903; Plumacher, "Memorandum and Impression on the Events at Maracaibo from 1st of January until 15th of February 1903," encl. in Plumacher to Hill, 18 Feb. 1903, T62:r19, NA. The American press reported the incident as a German defeat. *Sun*, 21 Jan. 1903; *Her*, 19 and 21 Jan. 1903; *SFC*, 19 Jan. 1903; *Con*, 19 Jan. 1903; *Pic*, 19 and 20 (ed.) Jan. 1903.

147. Scheder, "Military Political Report: 14-24 Jan. 1903."

148. Richthofen to Quadt, 24 Jan. 1903, Vz1:23, AA-PA.

149. *Nat* (29 Jan. 1903): 81; *Harper's Weekly* (27 Jan. 1903): 181; *NYT*, ed., 23 Jan. 1903; 29 Jan. 1903, GBM.

150. For comment on Dewey, see *Con*, 23 Jan. 1903; *SFC*, 24, 26 Jan. 1903; *Sun*, 24 Jan. 1903; *Her*, 24 Jan. 1903. On the March war scare, see *NYT*, 7, 20, 22, 28 Mar. 1903; *LD* (11 Apr. 1903): 523-24; *LD* (25 Apr. 1903): 624-26.

151. *Detroit Journal*, quoted in *LD* (14 Feb. 1903): 217.

152. *Her*, 31 Jan. 1903; Quadt to AA, 23 Jan. 1903, *GP*, 17:274.

153. TR to Hale, 17 Dec. 1901, *LTR*, 3:209.

154. For Wilson in Mexico in 1913, see below, chapter 4.

155. Bülow, 19 Mar. 1903, *Stenographische Berichte*, 287th sitting, 10:8719.

156. TR to Root, 7 June 1904, *LTR*, 4:821-22. That February, the Hague had completed its arbitration of the Venezuela matter by favoring the claims of the blockading powers.

157. For an excellent discussion of the corollary, see Schoultz, *Beneath*, 180-85.

158. TR to Cleveland, 26 Dec. 1902, *LTR*, 3:398. See TR to Root, 2 June 1904, *LTR*, 4:811.

Chapter 3

1. Tonnelat, *L'expansion*, 91; Williams, "Naval War Plan for the Attack of Rio De Janeiro, Brazil," 1 Feb. 1908, U-1-c, box 1330, RG 38, NA. For a comprehensive and interesting contemporary account of the German colonies in southern Brazil, see Behnke, "Military-Political Report," 24 Sept. 1904, encl. in Büchsel to AA, [illegible] Nov. 1904, Bz1:35, r:16525, AA-PA; see also Seeger to Hay, 23 May 1902, RG 59, r70:v68, NA. For background on the Germans in Brazil, see Müller, *Die Deutsche*; Ballod, "Die Bedeutung"; Backhaus, *Welche*; Becker, *Deutsche Siedler*; Sudhaus, *Deutschland*; Benicke, "Rio Grande do Sul"; Roche, *La colonisation*; Hell, "Der Griff nach Südbrasilien"; Hell, "Das 'südbrasilianische Neudeutschland' "; Brunn, *Deutschland*; Luebke, *Germans in Brazil*; Fiebig-von Hase, *Lateinamerika*, 193–247. For population estimates based on varying definitions of "German," see Jannasch, quoted in *Deutsche Zeitung*, 5 Dec. 1902, and "The Germans in Brazil," *Deutsche Zeitung*, 1 Aug. 1903, encl. in Barnes, "Report on Southern Brazil, June 2 to September 16, 1903" [hereafter "Report"], RG 38, box 1330, file U-1-c, NA; "Solution of the Problem of 1903," RG 12, envelope C-1, p. 2, NWCA; Schierbrand, "Germany's Expansion Policy," *NYT*, 22 Mar. 1903; Benicke, "Rio Grande do Sul," pt. 3: 40; Tonnelat, *L'expansion*, 142; De Barros Basto, *Síntese*, 45; Luebke, *New World*, 93–95, 98, 111; Blancpain, *Migrations*, 25–31. On the pan-Germans, see esp. Chickering, *We Men*. On pan-German dreams in Brazil, see Baum, "Designs"; Bonsal, "Greater Germany"; Wagner, "Germany and Pan-Germany"; de Magalhães, "Germany"; Chéradame, *Pan German Plot*, 193–98.

2. Portfolio 1, box 1, GBW: "General Considerations and Data," 1-d: "Plans for the United States Fleet," 19 Oct. 1910. See GBM and GBL, 1900–1914. For the Naval War College reports on Germany's west African ports, see Walker, "Notes on Hayti and Puerto Rico," box 11, GBW.

3. Lodge, quoted in *Her*, 12 May 1900.

4. Assu, *Brazilian Colonization*, 4 (emphasis in original).

5. Stolberg-Wernigerode, *Germany*, 187–95, (191, quoted). See Brunn, *Deutschland*; Pflanze, *Bismarck*, 3:113–42.

6. See, for example, marginalia on Krauel to Hohenlohe, 6 Oct. 1995, Bz1:33, r:16523, AA-PA, and on Bülow, memo, 15 Feb. 1905, AA38403, DZA.

7. Brunn, *Deutschland*, 47. For the naval revolt, see documents in RG 45, file VI: "International Relations and Politics," box 663, NA. The U.S. minister never mentioned Germany in his reports to the State Department during the revolt and mutiny (see M121:r60–61, RG 59, NA). See Fiebig-von Hase, *Lateinamerika*, 193–230; Smith, *Illusions of Conflict*, 169–84; Smith, "Britain"; Love, *Rio Grande do Sul*, 57–72; Graham, *Great Britain*, 307–10; LaFeber, *New Empire*, 210–18; LaFeber, "Depression Diplomacy"; Calhoun, "American Policy."

8. Krauel to AA, 15 Sept. 1896, AA30335, DZA. See Krauel to AA, 10, 11, 12, and 29 June and 1 July 1895, Bz1:33, r:16523, AA-PA.

9. Kapff-Cannstatt, "New Immigration Law."

10. Kaerger to Hohenlohe, 13 Jan. 1896, AA30410, DZA.

11. Chickering, *We Men*, 81; Langer, *Diplomacy*, 417. See Kruck, *Geschichte*.

12. Walter Kundt, quoted in Rocca, "German Colonization in .Brazil," *Bollettino dell' Emigrazione* 12 (1906), AA30288, DZA. See Jordan, "Aspects." For an interesting article about the indigenous peoples of southern Brazil, see Sellin, "Indians in the Hansa Colony," *Export* 23, no. 34 (22 Aug. 1901): 472-74.

13. Sargent to Frelinghuysen, 12 Mar. 1883, *FR 1883*, 350; quoted in *NYT*, 15 June 1902.

14. Gleich, *Germany and Latin America*, 7, table 1. See Hell, "Der Griff nach Südbrasilien," 64; Luebke, *New World*, 12, 93; Holborn, *History*, 367-68.

15. Karl von Koseritz, "Ratschläge für Auswanderer nach Südbrasilien," 1864, quoted in Sudhaus, *Deutschland*, 168.

16. Backhaus, *Welche*, 3. See Jackson to Hay, 25 Oct. 1901, *FR 1901*, 191.

17. Jannasch, quoted in *Deutsche Zeitung*, 5 Dec. 1902, encl. in Barnes, "Report," RG 38, box 1330, file U-1-c, NA; Heinze to Reichenau, 17 July 1907, encl. in Reichenau to Bülow, 4 Aug. 1907, AA30290, DZA; Goetsch to Kries, 24 Jan. 1905 (report prepared by emigration expert to brief Bülow for Immediatvortrag), AA38403, DZA.

18. See Brunn, *Deutschland*, 138; Jackson to Hay, 28 Nov. 1899, M44:89, NA.

19. See "The Lifting of the Heydt'sche Reskript," *Export* 18, no. 33 (13 Aug. 1896): 453-54; Brunn, *Deutschland*, 127-44. The lifting of the *Heydt'sche Reskript* was viewed with alarm by many across the Atlantic but turned out to be inconsequential. Emigration to Brazil failed to increase. The number of Germans leaving their homeland was tied to economic conditions, not to official or unofficial promotional efforts. And the overwhelming majority of those who did leave continued to head straight for the United States, despite their government's desire that they go to Brazil. See the careful report on immigration trends in Brazil: Griscom to Root, 28 Aug. 1906, Case 1112: Immigration, M862:141, RG 59, NA. See also how Sternburg uses the declining emigration statistics to buttress his argument that the German threat is a "phantom" (Sternburg, "Phantom Peril," 641-50; for a related letter, see Sternburg to Bülow, 30 Sept. 1906, AA 30287, DZA). For another careful report on immigration trends, see Stemrich to Reichenau, 23 Mar. 1908, AA 30290, DZA. For further statistics, see Ballod, "Die Bedeutung," 631-55, and Tonnelat, *L'expansion*, chart p. 142. For an article bemoaning the slow pace of emigration to Brazil, see *Deutsche Kolonialzeitung*, 1 May 1901.

20. Marginalia on Krauel to Hohenlohe, 6 Oct. 1895, Bz1:33, r:16523, AA-PA.

21. "The Significance of German Expansion," *Review of Reviews* 32 (Jan. 1905): 116.

22. Anonymous, quoted in Baum, "Designs," 588; Wintzer quoted in "Vigilans sed Aequus," *German Ambitions*, 45.

23. German Colonial Congress, resolution of 11 Oct. 1902, quoted in Shalack, Sellin, and Mörsch, "Prospectus," Dec. 1902, encl. in Sellin to Aichberger, 3 Feb. 1903, AA30831, DZA. A similar resolution was passed in 1905. Resolution of the German Colonial Congress, section 6, 15 Dec. 1905, AA30328, DZA.

24. Herman Leyser, quoted in Bonsal, "Greater Germany," 64.

25. *Sp*, 18 Oct. 1902, 554.

26. Schmoller, quoted in Rocca, "German Colonization in Brazil," *Bollettino dell'*

Emigrazione 12 (1906), AA30288, DZA; Kapff-Cannstatt, "New Immigration Law." Not everyone agreed with these hopes. Koser, for example, scrawled on the margin of a newspaper about the possibility of secession, "Impossible! It could never survive against American and Argentine objections and competition" (marginalia on *Kölnische Zeitung*, 8 Apr. 1898, AA 30337, DZA).

27. *Kreuz Zeitung*, enclosed in Jackson to Hay, 28 Nov. 1899, M44:89, NA; *Deutsche Post* quoted in "German Expansion," *Outlook* 98 (1901): 1501.

28. "Ey" [Captain Samuel G. Shartle, U.S. military attaché in Berlin], "The German Navy League," 10 June 1914, 286, RG 165, NA. For the historiographical trends in the interpretation of the influence of the Pan-German League on the Reich, see Chickering, *We Men*, 2–8, and Coetzee, *German Army League*, 6–11. See also Eley, "Thoughts"; Blackbourn, "Politics."

29. Wagner, "Germany and Pan-Germany," 174; *Times*, quoted in Chickering, *We Men*, 2; Usher, *Pan-Germanism*, 1–2.

30. Archibald Hurd quoted in Usher, *Pan-Germanism*, 1 n. 1.

31. Strachey, introduction to "Vigilans sed Aequus," *German Ambitions*, v–vi.

32. Wagner, "Germany and Pan-Germany," 186. See AA to Krauel, 20 Apr. 1895, Bz1:26, AA-PA; Krauel to Hohenlohe, 29 May 1895, Bz1:27, r:16517, AA-PA; Dodge to Hay, 3 Oct. 1903, M44:98, NA.

33. On the argument about the relationship between *Sammlungspolitik* and imperialism, see especially the classic study by Kehr, *Schlachtflottenbau*, which focuses on the Navy League but applies to the Pan-German League as well.

34. Kaiser's marginalia on Bülow, "Memo," 15 Feb. 1905, AA38403, DZA.

35. Wagner, "Germany and Pan-Germany," 180, 175.

36. Chickering, *We Men*, 302.

37. *Her*, 3 May 1901.

38. *Diario Oficial* (Rio), 6 Dec. 1903, quoted in Thompson to Hay, 10 Dec. 1903, RG 59, r71:v69, NA.

39. Chamberlain, "Germany in Southern Brazil," 1022; the *German Democrat*, 4 June 1903, encl. in German consul in Chicago to Bülow, 18 Sept. 1903, Bz11:3, r:16579, AA-PA.

40. *Die Grenzboten* (Leipzig) 57 (1898): 720. Established in 1841, the progovernment *Die Grenzboten* was for a long time the most important German political magazine. See Leupolt, *Die Aussenpolitik*.

41. *Die Grenzboten* 60 (1901): 845–46.

42. Ibid., 62 (1903): 94.

43. Ibid., 376.

44. Krauel to Hohenlohe, 29 May 1895, Bz1:27, r:16517, AA-PA; marginalia on "German Foreigners in Southern Brazil," *Deutsche Zeitung* (Pôrto Alegre), 1 Jan. 1897, AA30305, DZA; Thompson to Hay, 9 May 1903, RG 59, r70:v68, NA, enclosing an article from the *Jornal do Comercio* (Rio); Sellin, "Germany's Interests."

45. "Z," "Anti-American Feeling in Germany," 7 Feb. 1911, c-6-b, 415, RG 38, NA.

46. "Germany and the Monroe Doctrine," *Sp*, 6 Jan. 1900, 37–38. See *NYT*, ed., 18 Jan. 1900, and *Her*, 7 and, esp., 28 Jan. 1900. The pattern was repeated five months later: see *NYT*, 6 May 1900, for an article about the Germans in Brazil based on the *Spectator*. See also *Sp*, 26 Mar. 1902, 87, which states: "We have repeatedly pointed out

that this policy [Weltpolitik] must in the nature of things include a wish for territory in South America." For the magazine's continuing alarums against German designs in Brazil, see also 30 Aug. 1902, 280; 18 Oct. 1902, 554; 13 Dec. 1902, 928; 21 Feb. 1903, 280; 28 Feb. 1903, 318; 25 Apr. 1903, 646. The loop went from the U.S. press to the German press as well: see the *National Zeitung*, 18 July 1903, for an article about a report in the *New York Tribune* about German ambitions in Brazil and see the *Tägliche Rundschau*, 23 July 1903, for a similar article based on the *Herald* and the *Newport Tribune*.

47. *SR*, 27 Apr. 1901; *Her*, 6 May 1901; *NYT*, 29 Apr. 1901. See *NYT*, 26 Feb. 1902, repeating an alarmist *Times* story about German policy toward Brazil.

48. HKG to AA, 23 Apr. 1903, Bz11:2, r:16578, AA-PA. The *Saturday Review* story was reprinted in Rio's *El Paiz* (see *Her*, 9 May 1901). The *Herald*'s story mentioned above, for example, was reprinted in Brazil. See *Gaceta da Notícias* (the organ of the Brazilian Foreign Ministry), 16 Apr. 1902. For an article in the mainstream German press attacking the more reckless statements of the pan-Germans about Brazil, see *Kölnische Zeitung*, 6 June 1899. See also Tonnelat, *L'expansion*, 142, for pan-German press articles fueling a series in 1904 on the German threat in the Pôrto Alegre daily *Correio do Povo*. For frequent attacks on the *Herald* by Germans in southern Brazil, and for numerous examples of the German Brazilian press reprinting inflammatory articles from U.S., British, and German papers, see Barnes, "Report," RG 38, box 1330, file U-1-c, NA; Chamberlain, "Letter from Brazil."

49. "The Lifting of the Heydt'sche Reskript," *Export* 18, no. 33 (13 Aug. 1896): 453–54.

50. Under Brazilian law, everyone born in Brazil was considered a Brazilian citizen, and it was easy for immigrants to become citizens. The *Herald* reported that only about 1-2 percent retained their German citizenship (*Her*, 11 May 1901). See "On the Subject of Naturalization," *Deutsche Zeitung*, 23 June 1903, encl. in Barnes, "Report," RG 38, box 1330, file U-1-c, NA. For population estimates, see n. 1 above. An interesting document on this question is C. Fabri (Hanseatic Colonization Society) to Hohenlohe, 14 Dec. 1898, AA30827, DZA, in which the society bemoans the fact that their concession stipulated that they could only bring German nationals to the Hansa colony. They feared that this could fuel the suspicions of those Brazilian nativists who believed that Germany intended to take over southern Brazil. The society asserted that it fully intended to maintain the German character of the Hansa, but it asked to be allowed to admit all German speakers, even those who were not German citizens. It promised, however, to exclude all Slavs and Jews.

51. See Luebke, *Germans in Brazil*, 28; Luebke, *New World*, 28–32, 103, 114–16.

52. Assu, *Brazilian Colonization*, 37. For an overview of German colonization in Blumenau, see "Yearly Report of the Imperial German Consulate at Blumenau for 1900," consul to AA, [n.d.], AA53935, DZA; Benicke, "Rio Grande Do Sul"; Becker, *Deutsche Siedler*; Centro de Estudos Sociais, *Colóquio*; Funke, *Deutsche Siedlung*; Fouquet, *Der deutsche Einwanderer*. For a good description of the harshness of life in the rural parts of German southern Brazil, see Tonnelat, *L'expansion*, 91ff. See also the strong distinction drawn between life for Germans in the northern tropical regions of Brazil, "where they were degraded and treated like coolies," and in the south, "where they have been able to transform themselves into small peasants" ("The Lifting of the Heydt'sche Reskript," *Export* 43, no. 33 [13 Aug. 1896]: 454).

53. Behnke, "Military-Political Report," 24 Sept. 1904, encl. in Büchsel to AA, [illegible] Nov. 1904, Bz1:35, r:16525, AA-PA. The German population of Curitiba was five thousand; of Joinville, fourteen thousand.

54. Barnes, "Report," RG 38, box 1330, file U-1-c, NA.

55. Behnke, "Military-Political Report," 24 Sept. 1904, encl. in Büchsel to AA, [illegible] Nov. 1904, Bz1:35, r:16525, AA-PA.

56. *Nat* (16 Dec. 1897): 471.

57. Shaw, "German Colonists in South America," *American Monthly Review of Reviews* 25 (Jan. 1902): 9.

58. German consul in Florianópolis to AA, 31 Mar. 1911, Bz1:41, r:16531, AA-PA.

59. "The Significance of German Expansion," *Review of Reviews* 32 (1905): 116. For a sociological discussion of the assimilation of Germans in Brazil, see Willems, *A aculturação* and *Assimilação*. See also Luebke, *New World*, 93–109.

60. MacKintosh, "German Aims," 21.

61. For the Germans, see, for example, Reichardt, "Promemoria," 28 Nov. 1885, AA30252, DZA; Koser to AA, 1 Mar. 1899, AA30337, DZA; Treutler to AA, 1 Mar. 1906, Bz11:6, r:16582, AA-PA; Walter to Treutler, 25 Nov. 1906, encl. in Treutler to Bülow, 10 Dec. 1906, AA30346, DZA. For the Americans, see Bryan to Hay, 25 June 1900, RG 59, r67:v65, NA; Bryan to Hay, 2 Apr. 1901, RG 59, r68:v66, NA; Dawson to Hay, 1 Nov. 1901, RG 59, r69:v67, NA; Thompson to Hay, 9 May 1903, RG 59, r70:v68, NA; Thompson to Hay, 10 Dec. 1903, RG 59, r71:v69, NA.

62. Reichardt, "Promemoria," 28 Nov. 1885, AA30252, DZA.

63. Treutler to AA, 1 Mar. 1906, Bz11:6, r:16582, AA-PA (emphasis in original). See Treutler to Bülow, 9 Jan. 1906, ibid. Sternburg echoed Treutler's reports in "Phantom Peril."

64. Bryan to Hay, 25 June 1900, RG 59, r67:v65, NA; *NYT*, ed., 5 July 1901. See *Washington Post*, 8 May 1901. For Lodge's speech, see above, chapter 1, n. 96.

65. "Solution of the Problem of 1903," RG 12, envelope C-1, p. 2, NWCA.

66. See, for example, Bonsal, "Greater Germany," 58–59; *Das Echo*, 14 May 1903, 1470; Treutler to Bülow, 12 May 1906, AA30345, DZA.

67. *Kölnische Zeitung*, 8 Apr. 1898.

68. Thompson to Hay, 9 May 1903, RG 59, r70:v68, NA. On the desire of the upper class to "whiten" the population, see Luebke, *New World*, 10, 94, 114.

69. Bryan to White, [n.d.] 1901, RG 84, Diplomatic Posts—Brazil, vol. 139, NA.

70. Thompson to Hay, 9 May 1903, RG 59, r70:v68, NA.

71. *Deutsche Zeitung* (Pôrto Alegre), 12 June 1903, encl. in Barnes, "Report," RG 38, box 1330, file U-1-c, NA.

72. Schröder, "A Study," 31 Dec. 1895, RM5/v5918, BA-MA; Steinberg, "German Plan," 155.

73. Captain of *Geier*, 15 Feb. 1898, RM5/5918, BA-MA; Jacobsen, "Wargames on Board the Cruiser *Geier* during January and February 1899," [n.d.] 1899, ibid.

74. Chadwick, "Coal," 1901, NWCA; Loomis, "The Influence of an Isthmian Canal upon Central and South America," 1901, NWCA.

75. Portfolio 1, box 1, GBW: "General Considerations and Data," 1-d: "Plans for the United States Fleet," [19 Oct. 1910]. (For date of Black Plan, see chapter 1.) For very cursory plans for the defense of Brazilian ports, see no. 5-q, Major W. N. McKelvy,

"Naval War Plan for Bahia Bay, Brazil," 23 June 1908, and no. 5-p, Major Dion Williams, "Naval War Plan for the Attack of Rio de Janeiro, Brazil," 25 May 1908, portfolio 1, box 1, GBW.

76. 24 Apr. 1901, GBM; Dewey to Long, GB 171, 25 June 1901, GBL. See GBM: 26 Apr. 1901; 21 May 1901; 22 May 1901; 23 May 1901; 25 June 1901; and 20 Aug. 1901. See Mahan to Fitzhugh, 9 Mar. 1912, in Seager and Maguire, *Mahan*, 3:446.

77. Wintzer, quoted in "Vigilans sed Aequus," *German Ambitions*, 44. The idea was also voiced in the mainstream press. See *Grenzboten* 62 (1903): 181–85.

78. Münsterberg, *Americans*, 216, 217. See discussion of Münsterberg in de Magalhães, "Germany," 69, and in Shartle to Chief of War College Division, General Staff, 19 July 1912, RG 165, file 6370, box 1901/2, NA.

79. "Solution of the Problem of 1903," RG 12, envelope C-1, p. 2, NWCA; "Solution," p. 1, Germany War Plan, 5-Y, portfolio 1, box 10, GBW; "Political Situation—Causes for War—Finances of War," ibid.; Barnes, "Report," RG 38, box 1330, file U-1-c, NA.

80. Barnes, "Report," RG 38, box 1330, file U-1-c, NA.

81. "Solution of the Problem of 1903," RG 12, envelope C-1, p. 1, NWCA.

82. GBM, 21 June 1904.

83. "Solution of the Problem of 1903," RG 12, envelope C-1, p. 1, NWCA. See GBM, 27 Feb. 1903 and 30 Dec. 1903.

84. In the *New York Times*, for example, not one article on the Germans in Brazil appeared in 1899. Then, in the first six months of 1900—while the Second Fleet Bill was being debated and passed (in March)—there was a spate of articles. See ed., 18 Jan. 1900; 21 Jan. 1900; 20 Apr. 1900; 6 May 1900; 15 May 1900; 19 May 1900.

85. "Solution of the Problem of 1903," RG 12, envelope C-1, p. 32, NWCA.

86. "Political Situation—Causes for War—Finances of War," [1910–11], portfolio 1:5-Y, Germany War Plan, box 10, GBW.

87. Hebbinghaus, "Memo," 10 Sept. 1906, RM5:885, BA-MA.

88. Wilhelm II to TR, *LTR*, 5:544 n. 1; TR to William II, 8 Jan. 1907, *LTR*, 542. See TR to Reid, 10 Jan. 1907, *LTR*, 543–44.

89. TR to Mahan, 12 Jan. 1907, *LTR*, 5:551.

90. See TR's letters in August, September, and November 1905 to Aldrich, Sternburg, Shaw, and Allison, *LTR* 4:1329, 5:15, 26–27, 31–33, 41, 89. See Schierbrand, "Tariff Differences"; Marvin, "America in Foreign Trade"; Stone, "How the Germans"; "Germany as Our Future Rival in This Hemisphere," *LD* (21 Apr. 1906): 619; Crapol, "From Anglophobia," 166–90.

91. TR to Spring-Rice, 13 May 1905, *LTR*, 4:1178.

92. TR to Root, 8 Aug. 1908, *LTR*, 6:1164.

93. TR to Lee, 17 Oct. 1908, *LTR*, 6:1292. See TR to White, 17 Oct. 1908, *LTR*, 6:1292; TR to Lee, 23 Nov. 1908, *LTR*, 6:1378–79; TR to Reid, 4 Dec. 1908, *LTR*, 6:1410–11; TR to Reid, 6 Jan. 1908, *LTR*, 6:1465–67.

94. TR to Reid, 4 Dec. 1908, *LTR*, 6:1411.

95. TR to Knox, 8 Feb. 1909, *LTR*, 6:1511.

96. Posadowsky in "Minutes of a Session of the Ministry of State," 8 June 1898, AA30825, DZA. See "The society has acquired a territory of 650,000 hectares. . . . Each emigrant needs about 25 hectares, so there is enough land for 20,000 families

[a family consisting of 2.5 people]. Of the remaining 150,000 hectares, one third will be for communal use—streets, municipal buildings—and the rest for the use of the Hansa society" ([Management HKG], "Prospectus," [undated], AA30824, DZA). See also Hill to Vereker, 23 Aug. 1897, RG 84, Consular Posts–Rio Grande do Sul, vol. 13, NA; Vereker to Hill, 28 Sept. 1897, RG 84, Consular Posts–Rio Grande do Sul, vol. 17, NA; Shalack to Hohenlohe, 24 June 1898, AA30825, DZA; Wile, "German Colonisation," 131–32.

97. *NYT*, 9 Dec. 1896. See *NYT*, ed., 12 Sept. 1896.

98. "Minutes of a Session of the Ministry of State," 8 June 1898, AA30825, DZA. See Posadowsky to Bülow, 2 Oct. 1898, AA30826, DZA; Wiegand to Bülow, 9 Sept. 1898, ibid. For reaction in the German Brazilian press, see *Deutsche Zeitung* (Pôrto Alegre), 17 Aug. 1898. For the German press, see *National Zeitung*, 16 Aug. 1898; *Berliner Neueste Nachrichten*, 17 Aug. 1898.

99. Maps of the colony vary in the generosity of their definition of the HKG's grant. Compare, for example, the map encl. in HKG to Bülow, 25 July 1902, AA30831, DZA, with that in Sellin to Aichberger, 30 Apr. 1903, AA30832, DZA. These discrepancies might be due to the fact that the original HKG colony later absorbed the older colonies of Blumenau and Dona Francisca. For a professional evaluation of the land bought by the society, see Sellin to Reichardt, 13 Dec. 1897, AA30824, DZA. For population statistics, see Solingen to AA, 6 Feb. 1902, "Annual Report, 1901," AA53935, DZA; German consul in Blumenau to AA, 21 Jan. 1903, "Annual Report, 1902," ibid.; Schmidt to Bülow, 4 Dec. 1904, AA30836, DZA.

100. Wagner, *Pan-Germanic Doctrine*, 276; *Illinois Staats Zeitung*, quoted in "The Germans in Brazil," *Deutsche Zeitung*, 1 Aug. 1903, encl. in Barnes, "Report," RG 38, box 1330, file U-1-c, NA. On gerrymandering, see Luebke, "Prelude to Conflict," 4.

101. Koser to German consul in Pôrto Alegre, 11 Nov. 1902, AA30341, DZA. For complaints about the screening process, see Wangenheim to HKG in Hammonia, 29 Dec. 1904, AA30328, DZA; Asseburg, "Annual Report 1902," AA30832, DZA. For complaints against the Hamburg-America Line, which refused to dock at the undeveloped ports in southern Brazil to discharge the emigrants, see Asseburg to d'Oliveira, 16 Sept. 1901, AA30830, DZA. For an indication of difficulties faced by the colonists, see "The Hansa Colony in Southern Brazil," *Berliner Tageblatt*, 28 July 1899; Her, 9 May 1901; *Kölnische Zeitung*, 10 Mar. 1902 and 19 Apr. 1902; *Rheinisch-Westfälische Zeitung*, 13 Mar. 1902 and 21 May 1902; "A Warning," *Südamerikanische Rundschau*, 1 Apr. 1902; *Frankfurter Zeitung*, 15 May 1902; *Münchner Post*, 26 Nov. 1902. Nevertheless, rosy propaganda about the life in southern Brazil continued to appear. See Central Bureau for Emigration, "Rio Grande do Sul," (Berlin, 1903), AA30342, DZA, and "About Colonization in South Brazil and the Hansa Colony," *Export* 25, no. 13 (26 Mar. 1903): 164–65. *Export* frequently reported on conditions in Brazil, especially Rio Grande do Sul. See, for example, 32 (5 Aug. 1897); 33 (12 Aug. 1897); 34 (19 Aug. 1897).

102. Wiegand to Bülow, 9 Sept. 1898, AA30826, DZA.

103. "Deutschtum in Southern Brazil," *Kölnische Zeitung*, 7 May 1899. For an official document that discusses similar dreams, see Haniel (chargé d'affaires) to Bülow, 27 Nov. 1904, AA30328, DZA. For early discussions of the railway, see [Management HKG], "Prospectus," [undated], AA30824, DZA; Jencke to Reichardt, 11 and 18 May

1897, AA30336, DZA. For an early professional assessment of the railway with a map, see Koppel to AA, 28 Mar. 1900, AA30824, DZA. The correspondence on the importance of the railway is voluminous. For a selection of early letters, see Sellin to Aichberger, 27 July 1901, AA30830, DZA; Solingen to AA, "Annual Report, 1901," 6 Feb. 1902, AA53935, DZA; Sellin to Aichberger, 31 Oct. 1902, AA30326, DZA; Consulate of Santa Catarina, "Commercial Report, 1902," AA30327, DZA; Shalack, Sellin, and Mörsch, "Prospectus," Dec. 1902, encl. in Sellin to Aichberger, 3 Feb. 1903, AA30831, DZA. See also *National Zeitung*, 14 July 1902.

104. Meuriot, "Un nouvel essai."

105. Shalack, Sellin, and Mörsch, "Prospectus," Dec. 1902, encl. in Sellin to Aichberger, 3 Feb. 1903, AA30831, DZA; Sellin and Mörsch to Bülow, 3 Feb. 1903, encl. in ibid.; Weigand to Mühlberg, 20 Dec. 1904, AA30328, DZA. For early efforts to raise the capital, see "Minutes of Meeting at Hotel du Nord, Köln," 15 Aug. 1899, AA30323, DZA. For a description of the colony directed to banks, see Sellin to [open], "Hanseatic Colonization Society GmbH," [undated], AA30831, DZA.

106. [Unidentified newspaper quoting 1903 Annual Report of HKG], 11 June 1904, AA30285, DZA.

107. Behnke, "Military-Political Report," 24 Sept. 1904, encl. in Büchsel to AA, [illegible] Nov. 1904, Bz1:35, r:16525, AA-PA; German consul in Santa Catarina to AA, "Commercial Report," 28 Jan. 1904, AA30327, DZA.

108. Sellin to Cahensly, 16 May 1903, AA30832, DZA. See HKG to Weigand, 11 May 1903, ibid.; Goetsch to Kries, 24 Jan. 1905, AA38403, DZA, which is the briefing paper prepared for Bülow by the emigration expert for an Immediatvortrag. For a petition from the HKG to the kaiser (11 Oct. 1900) about the importance of the railway, see Sellin to *Export* 48 (19 Nov. 1900).

109. Wagner, "Germany and Pan-Germany," 184–5; "Germany's Dispute with Brazil," *LD* (8 Feb. 1902): 193; "Brazil's Firmness toward Germany," ibid., 616.

110. Robert Gernhard, "The Meaning of Southern Brazil for Germany," *Tägliche Rundschau*, 24 Oct. 1901; Jannasch, quoted in *Deutsche Zeitung*, 5 Dec. 1902, encl. in Barnes, "Report," RG 38, box 1330, file U-1-c, NA. See Bryan to Hay, 25 Sept. 1900, RG 59, r67:v65, NA. On the unprofitability of railways in Brazil, see Chamberlain, "Letter from Brazil," 824; Forbes, "Commercial Relations," 242–43.

111. Behnke, "Military-Political Report," 24 Sept. 1904, encl. in Büchsel to AA, [illegible] Nov. 1904, Bz1:35, r:16525, AA-PA. See Laves, "Governmental Influence"; Feis, *Europe*, 174.

112. Reichenau to Bülow, 4 Aug. 1907, AA30290, DZA, and enclosures from German consuls in Florianópolis, Petropolis, Rio Grande do Sul, São Paulo, and Curitiba. See Stemrich to Reichenau, 23 Mar. 1908, ibid.

113. Koerner (for Bülow) to Reichenau, 31 Dec. 1907, AA30290, DZA.

114. "Why Germany Should Have a Great Navy," *Review of Reviews* 31 (1905): 626; Wangenheim to Bülow, 28 Feb. 1905, AA30328, DZA.

115. *Der Urwaldsbote* (Blumenau), 11 Mar. 1900, AA30324, DZA; Griscom to Root, 2 Jan. 1907, RG 59, r380:case 4202, NA; Reichenau to Bülow, 4 Aug. 1907, AA30290, DZA. For early U.S. interest in financing the railway, see Dawson to Bryan, 16 May 1902, encl. in Bryan to Hay, 23 May 1902, RG 59, r68:v66, NA.

116. See Goes and Bergmann [for Board of Directors of Santa Catarina Joint Stock

Company], "Financial Report of First Year of Business, 2 Feb. 1907–31 Sept. 1907," 26 May 1908, AA30329, DZA; Goetsch to Sellin, 12 Jan. 1907, AA30840, DZA; Mühlberg to Waldthausen, 29 Jan. 1907, AA30328, DZA; Bethmann to Wilhelm II, 31 Dec. 1911, Bz1:41, AA-PA.

117. *Der Urwaldsbote*, ed., 5 May 1906, AA30838, DZA. On this article, see HKG, "Communiqué," 6 June 1906, AA30839, DZA. On the continuing calls for a railway, see German consul in Santa Catarina to AA, "Commercial Report," 28 Jan. 1904, AA30327, DZA; "The Construction of the Railroad in Santa Catarina," *Export* 28, no. 7 (16 Feb. 1905): 97–98; Wiegand to Mühlberg, 10 Mar. 1905, AA30836, DZA; Sellin to AA, 30 Mar. 1905, AA30836, DZA; *Kölnische Zeitung*, 12 Aug. 1905; Treutler to Bülow, 8 Dec. 1905, AA30838, DZA; Lehmann to AA, 5 Jan. 1906, AA30327, DZA; Treutler to Bülow, 8 Oct. 1906, AA30840, DZA; Asseburg, "Supplemental Consular Report From Itajaí, 1900–1906," AA53966, DZA; *Frankfurter Zeitung*, 8 July 1907.

118. Sellin to Charlock, 14 Aug. 1906, encl. in Sellin to Bülow, 17 Aug. 1906, AA30840, DZA. See Charlock to HKG, 16 Aug. 1906, encl. in Sellin to Bülow, 24 Oct. 1906, ibid.; Charlock to Bülow, 1 Oct. 1906, and enclosures, ibid.

119. Sellin, "Germany's Interests."

120. Marginalia on Bethmann to Wilhelm II, 31 Dec. 1911, Bz1:41, r:16531, AA-PA. By 1913, the railway had reported a 412,000 mark loss (see "Annual Report of the Board of the Santa Catarina Railway Company AG for the First Year of Operation, 2 Feb.–31 Dec. 1907," AA30329, DZA, and encl. map). For emigration statistics to the Hansa, see "Commercial Report of German Consulate, Rio Grande do Sul, 1903," AA30344, DZA, and Schmidt to Bülow, 10 Dec. 1904, AA30328, DZA. For a lengthy analysis of the problems with the colony, see Wagenheim to Bülow, 22 Nov. 1905, AA30838, DZA. For a description of the colony in 1911, see Michahelles to Bethmann, 6 May 1911, Bz1:41, r:16531, AA-PA. See also "Southern Brazil and the German Colony," *Deutsche Kolonialzeitung*, 14 Mar. 1908. In late 1906, a fifteen-page questionnaire was sent to German immigrants throughout Brazil. The detailed responses, which are included in several volumes in the Potsdam archives, give a vivid picture of life in Brazil at that time. See, for example, AA30328, AA30329, AA30347, DZA.

121. Tonnelat, *L'expansion*, 129; Behnke, "Military-Political Report," 24 Sept. 1904, encl. in Büchsel to AA, [illegible] Nov. 1904, Bz1:35, r:16525, AA-PA. The percentage of German children attending the German schools was low. For example, in Florianópolis, a community of ten thousand Germans, the German school had a student body of fifty. See Aldinger to Central Bureau for Emigration, 1 Oct. 1907, AA30289, DZA; Baum, "Designs," 593.

122. Chamberlain, "Letter from Brazil," 821–31.

123. See Hell, "Der Griff nach Südbrasilien." See the "Coriolan articles" encl. in Haniel to Bülow, 4 May 1903, Bz11:2, AA-PA. For the churches, see Jackson to Hay, 19 Mar. 1902, M44:95, NA; Luebke, *New World*, 97. The Germans in Brazil were almost equally divided between Protestants and Roman Catholics. For the press fund, see Forbes, "Commercial Relations," 70 n. 108; Brunn, *Deutschland*, 176–78. For the cable, see Brunn, *Deutschland*, 180–81. For the citizenship laws, see White to Day, 30 June 1898, M44:85, NA; Schmidt to Bülow, "Consular Report for the Years 1902–1904," 10 Dec. 1904, AA53939, DZA; Tonnelat, *L'expansion*, 144; Brunn, *Deutschland*, 167–200.

124. "German Brazilians," *Koloniale Zeitschrift*, 7 Jan. 1904 (reprint of an article from *Deutsche Zeitung* [Pôrto Alegre]), AA30342, DZA. See the article by a German consul, D. Koser, *Deutsche Zeitung*, 11 June 1903, encl. in Barnes, "Report," RG 38, box 1330, file U-1-c, NA. For official correspondence about the creation of consulates, see Colonial League to Hohenlohe, 30 Dec. 1896, AA30305, DZA; Jannasch to Bülow, 29 Mar. 1902, AA30326, DZA; Aichberger to Jannasch, 21 Apr. 1902, ibid.; Treutler to Bülow, 22 Sept. 1905, AA30837, DZA. For reports from German consuls in Brazil in the late nineteenth century, see AA52628-52669, DZA. For an article about the usefulness of consuls in Brazil, see "The Importance of Professional Consuls in Desterro Brazil," *Export* 24, no. 13 (27 Mar. 1902): 171-72.

125. Treutler to Bülow, 29 Sept. 1903, AA30343, DZA; Aichberger, "Memo," 18 Jan. 1904, ibid.

126. Treutler to AA, 1 Mar. 1906, Bz11:6, r:16582, AA-PA.

127. Thompson to Hay, 13 Nov. 1903, RG 80, r71:v69, NA. In 1890, Germany's imports from the ABC countries (Argentina, Brazil, Chile) were 274.3 million marks, while its exports were 109.3 million marks; in 1913, the figures were, respectively, 942.3 million and 563.6 million (Forbes, "Commercial Relations," 118). See Asseburg, "Supplemental Consular Report From Itajaí, 1900-1906," AA53966, DZA. For Brazilian trade patterns during this period, see Graham, *Great Britain*, 298-315.

128. Dodge to Root, 10 Oct. 1905, M44:104, NA.

129. Forbes, "Commercial Relations," 112, quoted; see 85-106, 113, 141, 168. In 1890, Germany's trade with Brazil was worth almost twice its trade with Argentina (190.1 million marks versus 101.3 million). By 1899, Argentina absorbed more German exports than did Brazil; by 1913, German imports from Argentina were worth twice as much as those from Brazil. See the report encl. in Dettmann to AA, 27 Nov. 1911, AA4883, DZA.

130. Thompson to Hay, 13 Nov. 1903, RG 59, r71:v69, NA.

131. Capt. Paul Malone, "The Military Geography of the Atlantic Seaboard, considered with reference to an invading force," Army Staff College, 1909-10, MID correspondence, RG 165, NA; Cordier, "The German Military Mission to Bolivia," [rec'd. 15 Oct. 1912], file 6370, box 1901/02, RG 165, NA. See Forbes, "Commercial Relations," 207; de Magalhães, "Germany," 76-77. For similar French comments about the German traders' proficiency in Latin America, see Blancpain, *Migrations*, 259. Only Britain carried more Brazilian shipping, and its share of the trade was falling, particularly in southern Brazil (Graham, *Great Britain*, 301-2). The only U.S. company linking New York and Brazil, the United States and Brazil Mail Steamship Company, went out of business in 1892 (Callcott, *Western Hemisphere*, 56). See also *NYT*, 2 May 1901.

132. *Neueste Nachrichten*, encl. in Jackson to Hay, 6 July 1899, M44:89, NA; quoted in Tonnelat, *L'expansion*, 149. See Small, "German 'Threat,'" 255 (table 1); Graham, *Great Britain*, 305; Burns, *Unwritten Alliance*, 63.

133. Rosenberg, *Spreading the American Dream*, 48-59; LaFeber, *New Empire*, 210. See LaFeber, "Depression Diplomacy"; Pletcher, "Reciprocity"; Smith, *Unequal Giants*, 14-19; Smith, *Illusions of Conflict*, 163-69. See Dawson to Dawes, 11 Dec. 1899, RG 84, Diplomatic Posts–Brazil, vol. 136, NA; Holleben to Hohenlohe, 15 Dec. 1899, AA30307, DZA.

134. Dünhoff to Caprivi, 17 Feb. 1891, Bz1:14, r:16504, AA-PA; TR to Sternburg, 11 Oct. 1901, *LTR*, 3:172. See Sellin, "Germany's Interests"; Seebohm, "Military Political Report," 8 Aug. 1913, RM2/v1759, BA-MA. The treaty was terminated in 1894, but it had achieved its purpose: it gave the Americans an economic and a political wedge into Brazil. See Hutchinson, "Results," 300–303; Burns, *Unwritten Alliance*, 63.

135. Forbes, "Commercial Relations," 158.

136. Herwig, *Vision*, 110–40. For German military influence in Latin America, see Nunn, *Yesterday's Soldiers*, 56–61, and Livermore, "Battleship Diplomacy." See also Ruggles, "German Military Influence in South America," 2 Mar. 1911, encl. in Broughtan to secretary, General Staff, 20 May 1911, W.C.D. #6370-4, RG 165, box 1901/2, NA.

137. Coleman, "German Influence and Activities in Brazil," 9 June 1912, RG 165, box 1901/2, NA. For U.S. concern about military links being established between Germany and Brazil, see *NYT*, 20 Apr. 1900; Bryan to Hay, 18 Mar. 1902, RG 59, r68:v66, NA; Thompson to Hay, 13 Oct. 1903, r70:v68, NA.

138. See Treutler to Bülow, 30 Dec. 1901, Bz3:4, r:16541, AA-PA; Treutler to Bülow, 14 Mar. 1902, ibid.

139. Coleman, "German Influence and Activities in Brazil," 9 June 1912, RG 165, box 1901/2, NA. See Reissman to Bülow, 11 and 24 May 1908, Bz3:8, r:16545, AA-PA; AA to Reissman, 20 and 21 June 1908, ibid.; "Ey" [Captain Samuel G. Shartle, U.S. military attaché in Berlin], "Monthly Military Notes for January 1912," 8 Feb. 1912, box 135, RG 165, NA.

140. Kaiser's marginalia, quoted in Brunn, *Deutschland*, 61, and in Herwig, *Vision*, 115; Treutler to Bülow, 16 June 1906, AA29056/1, DZA.

141. Coleman to the Chief of General Staff, War College Division, 12 Sept. 1912, file 6370, box 1901/2, RG 165, NA. See German minister in Rio to AA, 18 Nov. 1911, Bz1:42, r:16532, AA-PA. On the German mission to Brazil, see AA29056/1, DZA, and Ge127:1, r:1766, AA-PA. For German officers for the Brazilian navy, see the correspondence with Tirpitz in AA29056/1, DZA. Berlin sent military instructors to many Latin American countries in this period. See AA29056 (Bolivia), AA29068 (Honduras), AA29072 (Nicaragua), AA29073–74 (Paraguay), AA29076 (Peru), AA29078 (Santo Domingo), AA29079 (El Salvador), AA29084 (Uruguay), and AA29085 (Venezuela), DZA. For a detailed report from a U.S. military intelligence officer, see Cordier, "The German Military Mission to Bolivia," [rec'd. 15 Oct. 1912], file 6370, box 1901/2, RG 165, NA.

142. Arco-Valley to AA, 6 July 1909, Ge127:1, r:1766, AA-PA. See Biel to AA, 4 Sept. 1909, ibid.; AA to Arco-Valley, 11 Sept. 1909, ibid. See also Thompson to Hay, 1 Apr. 1905, RG 59, r73:v71, NA; Coleman to the Chief of General Staff, War College Division, 12 Sept. 1912, file 6370, box 1901/2, RG 165, NA.

143. See Small, "German 'Threat,'" 253–54.

144. Behnke, "Military-Political Report," 24 Sept. 1904, encl. in Büchsel to AA, [illegible] Nov. 1904, Bz1:35, r:16525, AA-PA.

145. Commander of *Von der Tann* to Wilhelm II, 4 Apr. 1911, RM5/v5539, BA-MA. See Memo for Secretary of Navy, 27 Feb. 1911, case 11709, General Correspondence, ONI, RG 38, NA.

146. Bryan to Hay, 25 June 1900, RG 59, r67:v65, NA.

147. Treutler to AA, 11 Sept. 1906, Bz11:6, r:16582, AA-PA; Sternburg to AA, 4 Apr. 1906, ibid.

148. Kaiser's marginalia on Waldthausen to Bülow, 24 Nov. 1904, Argentina 1:24, AA-PA.

149. Burns, *Unwritten Alliance*, 16.

150. See Gilderhus, *Visions*, esp. ix–xi.

151. Richardson to Root, 1 Dec. 1905, RG 59, r74:v72, NA; clipping enclosed in Richardson to Root, 27 Dec. 1905, RG 84, Diplomatic Posts–Brazil, vol. 146, NA. The first conference had been held in Washington in 1889–90; the second, in Mexico City, in 1901.

152. Burns, *Unwritten Alliance*; Smith, *Unequal Giants*, 35–76. José Maria da Silva Paranhos Jr. was named Baron of Rio-Branco in 1884.

153. Thompson to Hay, 15 Jan. 1905, RG 80, r73:v71, NA; Nabuco, *Life*, 307. See Da Costa, *Nabuco*, 226–40.

154. Knight, *Americans*, 27.

155. *LD* (2 May 1903): 657; Tower to Hay, 11 Nov. 1903, M44:r99, NA. See Tower to Hay, 21 Jan. 1903, M44:97, NA.

156. German consul in Rio to AA, 10 Dec. 1905, Bz1:36, r:16526, AA-PA. See Saurma to Admiralstab, 28 Aug. 1905, RM5/v5542, BA-MA; German consul in Bahia to AA, 5 Sept. 1905, Bz1:36, r:16526, AA-PA; German consul in Rio to AA, 24 Sept. 1905, ibid.; Saurma to German consul at Rio, 31 Oct. 1905, encl. in German consul at Rio to AA, 10 Dec. 1905, ibid.; Treutler to AA, 8 and 9 Dec. 1905, Bz11:4, r:16580, AA-PA; Saurma to Admiralstab, 10 Dec. 1905 encl. in Büchsel to AA, 10 Dec. 1905, ibid.

157. Treutler to Bülow, 19 Dec. 1905, Bz11:4, r:16580, AA-PA, and Richardson to Root, 26 Dec. 1905, RG 59, r74:v72, NA. See Treutler to AA, 8 and 11 Dec. 1905, Bz11:4, r:16580, AA-PA; Saurma to Admiralstab, 13 Dec. 1905, encl. in Büchsel to Richthofen, 14 Dec. 1905, ibid.; the semiofficial account in *Norddeutsche Allgemeine Zeitung*, 17 Dec. 1905.

158. Rio-Branco to Treutler, 15 Dec. 1905, encl. in Treutler to Bülow, 19 Dec. 1905, Bz11:5, r:16581, AA-PA. See Treutler to AA, 10 and 11 Dec. 1905, ibid.; *Jornal do Comercio*, 7 Dec. 1905; Sellin, "Germany's Interests." For a thorough American account of both sides, see Richardson to Root, 12 Dec. 1905, RG 59, r74:v72, NA; Richardson to Root, 26 Dec. 1905, ibid.; Richardson to Root, and enclosures, 15 Jan. 1906, RG 84, Diplomatic Posts–Brazil, vol. 146, NA.

159. Büchsel to Richthofen, 14 Dec. 1905, Bz11:4, r:16580, AA-PA.

160. Rio-Branco to Nabuco, 11 Dec. 1905, Rio-Branco to Moore, 22 Nov. 1907, and Rio-Branco to Nabuco, quoted in Burns, *Unwritten Alliance*, 103–4. See Nabuco, *Life*, 305–16. *The Unwritten Alliance* is the definitive account of U.S.-Brazilian relations in the early years of this century. Smith asserts that Rio-Branco was concerned about the German immigrants, but his source is a book published in Rio in 1916, that is, during the war. Smith, *Unequal Giants*, 49, 226.

161. *Washington Post*, 11 Dec. 1905. The *New York Times* printed a brief report on 12 December 1905, but did not give the incident any play until after Nabuco's interview (see *NYT*, 17 Dec. 1905). The *Herald* reported the incident briefly on 8 December

1905, with a brief follow-up on 9 December 1905; following Nabuco's interview, it printed a long article with drawings of the Panther on 10 December 1905 and others on 12-14, 16-21, 27 December 1905. See also Burns, *Unwritten Alliance*, 104-5. Nabuco went to the State Department on 9 December (Richardson to Root, 19 Dec. 1905, RG 59, r74:v72, NA). On Nabuco's generally friendly attitude toward the Germans, see Sternburg to AA, 19 Dec. 1905, Bz11:5, r:16581, AA-PA.

162. Sternburg to AA, 10 Dec. 1905, Bz11:4, r:16580, AA-PA; Sternburg to AA, 19 Dec. 1905, Bz11:5, r:16581, AA-PA. See Joffily, *O Caso Panther*, 29; Burns, *Unwritten Alliance*, 104-6.

163. Rio-Branco to Treutler, 15 Dec. 1905, Bz11:5, r:16581, AA-PA.

164. See *Estado de São Paulo*, 12 Dec. 1905, and Sellin's rejoinder, ibid., 12 Jan. 1906. See Treutler to AA, 11 Dec. 1905, Bz11:5, r:16581, AA-PA.

165. Dodge to Root, 19 Dec. 1905, M44:104, NA. See AA to Treutler, "Orders," 14 Dec. 1905, Bz11:4, r:16580, AA-PA; Immediatbericht Bülows, 16 Dec. 1905, with kaiser's marginalia, ibid.; Büchsel to Richthofen, 17 Dec. 1905, ibid.; AA to Treutler, 17 Dec. 1905, ibid.

166. *Her*, 21 Dec. 1905; Treutler to Bülow, tel. 29, 31 Dec. 1905, Bz11:5, r:16581, AA-PA. See Treutler to AA, 21, 23, 24, 27 (no. 27 and 28) Dec. 1905, 1, 5 Jan. 1906, Bz11:4, r:16580, ibid.

167. AA to Treutler, 10 Jan. 1906, Bz11:5, r:16581, AA-PA. See Treutler to AA, 25, 30, and 31 Dec. 1905, Bz11:4, r:16580, AA-PA; Costa Motta, "Memo," 29 Dec. 1905, ibid.; AA to Treutler, 31 Dec. 1905, ibid.; Treutler to AA, 1 and 3 Jan. 1905, Bz11:5, r:16581, AA-PA; AA to Treutler, 1 and 4 Jan. 1906, ibid.

168. AA to Treutler, 10 Jan. 1906, Bz11:5, r:16581, AA-PA. See Treutler to Bülow, 5 and 6 Jan. 1906, ibid.; Rio-Branco to Treutler, 6 Jan. 1906 encl. in Treutler to AA, 9 Jan. 1906, ibid.; AA to Treutler, 7 and 8 Jan. 1906, ibid.; Treutler to AA, 7 (no. 4 and 5), 8 Jan. 1906, ibid. For the U.S. point of view and a complete account of the exchange, see Richardson to Root, 26 Dec. 1905, RG 59, r74:v72, NA; Richardson to Root, 15 Jan. 1906, ibid.

169. See Steinhoph's testimony, 7 May 1906, encl. in Treutler to Bülow, 29 May 1906, Bz11:6, r:16582, AA-PA.

170. Tonnelat, *L'expansion*, 145-47.

171. Sellin, "Germany's Interests." In a State Department summary of U.S.-German relations written in 1917, the Panther incident is labeled "a high handed German proceeding" (Putney, "Germany's Foreign Policies from 1897 to 1914, with particular reference to her attitude toward the United States," 29 Aug. 1917, M355:r1, 711.6213½, NA).

172. Sternburg to AA, 4 Apr. 1906, Bz11:6, r:16582, AA-PA. See Sternburg to AA, 19 Dec. 1905 and 12 Jan. 1906, Bz11:5, r:16581, AA-PA.

173. Sternburg to AA, 19 Dec. 1905, Bz11:5, r:16581, AA-PA.

174. Thompson to Hay, 9 May 1903, RG 59, r70:v68, NA.

175. Büchsel, "Memo," 9 May 1906, RM5/v5962, BA-MA.

176. *Speeches Incident to the Visit*, 12. A year later, the British minister in Rio declared that the U.S. ambassador was "the only representative here who has any influence" (Haggard to Grey, 7 Apr. 1907, FO 371/201, PRO).

177. See, for example, Callcott, *Western Hemisphere*, 56–58, 136–38; Collin, *Theodore Roosevelt's Caribbean*, 69–75; Healy, *Drive to Hegemony*, 72–76; Langley, *Banana Wars*, 20–21.

Chapter 4

1. Meyer, "Conspiracy," 76.
2. Katz, *Secret War*, 62.
3. Munro, *Intervention*, 270; Doerries, *Imperial Challenge*, 33; Lansing to E. Smith, draft, 3 Mar. 1917, Robert Lansing Papers, LC. See "Method of Determining a Course of Action," 17 Nov. 1919, ibid. Lloyd Gardner asserts, "Indeed, it was fear of German-Mexican connections that both stimulated and restrained Anglo-American diplomacy in response to the revolution" (Gardner, "Wilson," 4).
4. Kiderlen-Wächter to Hintze, 15 Aug. 1911, Mx1/30, AA-PA.
5. Lane Wilson, quoted in "A Report by William Bayard Hale," 18 June 1913, *WWP*, 27:540. As with the German population statistics in Brazil, those in Mexico are approximate. Katz cites a figure of 2,500 Germans in 1910, while *Leslie's Weekly* cited 5,000 for the same year; Baecker counts 4,000 in 1913; the *Vossische Zeitung* put the number at 5,000–6,000 in 1914 (Katz, *Secret War*, 50; *Leslie's Weekly*, 14 Aug. 1913; *LD* [10 Jan. 1914]: 56; Baecker, *Mexikopolitik*, 94). Estimates of the American population ranged from 20,000 to an implausible high of 75,000. Platt puts the figure at 19,568 in 1910; Clark says 33,000–41,000 in 1912; Lane Wilson spoke of some 30,000 Americans "still left in Mexico" in 1913, while Link cites 40,000 in 1913 (Platt, *Latin America*, 130; "The Mexican Situation," 1 Oct. 1912, Philander C. Knox Papers, container 19, p. 3107, LC; H. L. Wilson to Bryan, 9 July 1913, *WWP*, 28:37; Link, *Wilson: The New Freedom*, 349).
6. The ABC countries were Germany's first three largest trading partners in Latin America, and Mexico lagged well behind them (El Colegio de México, *Estadisticas*, 524, 546). For slightly different statistics, see *NYT*, 16, 17 May 1914; *LD* (23 May 1914): 1243; and Darius, *Die Entwicklung*, 43. See also Baron Geiser, in *Vossische Zeitung*, quoted in *LD* (10 Jan. 1914): 56. On Hapag (Hamburg-Amerikanische-Paketfahrt-Aktien-Gesellschaft), see Cecil, *Albert Ballin*, 14–26. For Hapag and Mexico, see Eversbusch, "Die deutsche Mexiko-Schiffahrt," 42–50; Katz, "Hamburger Schiffahrt."
7. Katz uncovered one instance of German private enterprise investigating the potential of Mexican oil (Katz, *Secret War*, 203–5). What is significant, however, is that this interest was not shared by either the government or the navy.
8. Doerries, *Imperial Challenge*, 36. See Wangenheim to Bülow, 22 Dec. 1906, Mx1/19, AA-PA; Wangenheim to Bülow, 4 Mar. 1907, ibid.; Wangenheim to Bülow, 26 Feb. 1907, encl. in Tschirschky, "Confidential Memo," 18 Mar. 1907, ibid. See also Mx1:20, AA-PA; Nunn, *Yesterday's Soldiers*; Smith, *Revolutionary Nationalism*, 10; Schiff, "German Military Penetration."
9. Katz, *Secret War*, 51.
10. See esp. Kiderlen-Wächter to Hintze, 15 Aug. 1911, Mx1:30, AA-PA.
11. See Katz, *Secret War*, 54–55. For background, see Conant, "The Banking System of Mexico," 61st Cong., 2d sess., 10 Oct. 1910, S. Doc. 493.

12. See Kemnitz, "Mexiko," 19 Nov. 1913, Mx1:39, AA-PA; Jagow to Reichstag, 29 Apr. 1914, Mx1:45, AA-PA; Rippy, "German Investments"; Smith, *Revolutionary Nationalism*, 6; Feis, *Europe*, 74, 193. With the proviso that the figures are estimates based on inadequate records, total German capital abroad in 1914 was 22 billion gold marks, 3.8 billion of which were in Latin America, including 500 million in Mexico.

13. O'Shaughnessy, *Intimate Pages*, 249–50; Köhler, "Political Military Report," 20 June 1914, RM5:5826, BA-MA. Lane Wilson frequently relied on Hintze (Wilson, *Episodes*, 183). Hintze was also close to the British minister, Sir Lionel Carden (see Spring-Rice to Tyrrell, 3 Feb. 1914, and Spring-Rice to Tyrrell, 17 Feb. 1914, FO 800:84, PRO). See also Katz, *Secret War*, 75–76.

14. Wilson, *Episodes*, 189. See "First Centennial of the Republic of Mexico," 61st Cong., 2d sess., 16 June 1910, H. Rept. 1611.

15. The literature on the Mexican Revolution is vast. Knight, *Mexican Revolution*, is the new standard. For a comprehensive list, the reader is referred to the excellent bibliography by John Womack in Bethell, *Cambridge History*, 5:835–45.

16. Katz, *Secret War*, 74.

17. "A Report by William Bayard Hale," 18 June 1913, RG 59, 812.00:7798 ½, NA; Wood, quoted in Bryce to Grey, 6 Jan. 1913, FO 414:235, PRO; Hintze to Bethmann, 7 Dec. 1911, Mx1:28, AA-PA, with kaiser's marginalia.

18. O'Shaughnessy, *Intimate Pages*, 191–92. Wilson's special envoy William Bayard Hale called him "an ape-like man, of almost pure Indian blood" (Hale, "Memorandum on Affairs in Mexico," 9 July 1913, WWP, 28:43). Wilson described him as "a diverting brute!" (WW to Hulbert, 24 Aug. 1913, WWP, 28:153). The British minister commented, "While . . . his morals are base, he is a strict disciplinarian. . . . He is nearly blind. He is a drunkard" ("Memorandum by Mr. Hohler," encl. in Stronge to Grey, 21 Feb. 1913, FO 414:235, PRO).

19. "A Report by William Bayard Hale," 18 June 1913, RG 59, 812.00:7798½, NA. For a particularly dramatic account, see "Memorandum by Mr. Stronge," encl. in Stronge to Grey, 21 Feb. 1913, FO 414:235, PRO. See also Stronge to Grey, 24 Feb. 1913, and enclosures, ibid.; Hohler to Grey, 30 Sept. 1913, ibid.

20. See Buchenau, *Shadow*, 56–62; Smith, *Revolutionary Nationalism*, 8–12; Krauze, *Mexico*, 6.

21. Hintze Diary, 22 May 1914, Mx1:50, AA-PA. See Stronge to Grey, 30 Dec. 1912, FO 414:235, PRO. See Blaisdell, "Henry Lane Wilson"; Blasier, "United States and Madero."

22. Knox to H. L. Wilson, 28 Feb. 1913, *FR 1913*, 748. This exchange was leaked to the press (see *Her*, 28 July and 24 Nov. 1913). During Wilson's first week in office, Huntington Wilson advised the president to extend recognition to Huerta (Wilson, *Episodes*, 249).

23. Bryce to Grey, 28 Feb. 1913, FO 414:235, PRO. Taft's delay in recognition was not due to doubts about Huerta's legitimacy (see Wilson, *Episodes*, 296–97; Link, *Wilson: The New Freedom*, 348 n. 4). For an opposing view, see Gardner, "Wilson," 10, 42 n. 22.

24. Bryce to Grey, 18 Feb. 1913, FO 371:1671, PRO; "The Mexican Situation," 14 May 1913, encl. in Moore to WW, 15 May 1913, WWP, 27:437–38. See *Her*, 20 Feb. 1913; Bryce to Grey, 24 Feb. 1913, FO 371:1670, PRO; "Legality, etc., of the Provi-

sional Government," in H. L. Wilson to Bryan, 12 Mar. 1913, *FR 1913*, 772–73. For U.S. press reaction, see *LD* (8 Mar. 1913): 497. For the reception, see H. L. Wilson to Knox, 21 Feb. 1913, *FR 1913*, 726–27; Stronge to Grey, 23 Feb. 1913, FO 414:235, PRO.

25. "Out of 35 [ministers] in the [foreign] service, 22 have been replaced by appointees whose diplomatic and other abilities have been sedulously concealed from the public" (*Nat* [18 Dec. 1913]: 582).

26. Bryce to Grey, 24 Mar. 1913, FO 414:235, PRO; Bryce to Grey, 31 Mar. 1913, ibid.; Spring-Rice to Grey, 19 Aug. 1913, FO 800:83, PRO.

27. Wilson, quoted in Thompson to Bull, 22 May 1913, *WWP*, 27:465; *WWP*, 27:158 n. 1.

28. "A Statement on Relations with Latin America," 12 Mar. 1913, *WWP*, 27:172; Press Conference, 11 Apr. 1913, *WWP*, 27:289; *Wor*, 12 Apr. 1913. See entry dated 11 Mar. 1913, in Daniels, *Cabinet*, 6–7; Bernstorff to AA, 13 Mar. 1913, Mx1:33, AA-PA; "From the Diary of Josephus Daniels" (hereafter cited as "Daniels Diary"), 18 Apr. 1913, *WWP*, 27:331; "From the Diary of Colonel House" (hereafter cited as "House Diary"), 2 May 1913, *WWP*, 27:383. Wilson's 12 April statement followed a lengthy discussion in the cabinet (see entry dated 11 Apr. 1913, in Daniels, *Cabinet*, 42–43).

29. Calvert, *Mexican Revolution*, 172; *NYT*, 12 Apr. 1913. For agitation by U.S. business in Mexico, see Speyer to Moore, 1 May 1913, RG 59, 812.00:7473, NA; House to WW, 6 May 1913, *WWP*, 27:404–5 (enclosing Ludlow to House, 29 Apr. 1913; Speyer to House, 5 May 1913; and Kruttschnitt to House, 6 May 1913); McAdoo to WW, 7 May 1913, RG 59, 812.00:7545, NA; Speyer to Moore, 19 May 1913, RG 59, 812.00:7546, NA. See also Bryan and Bryan, *Memoirs*, 357–58.

30. Kardorff to Bethmann, 2 Apr. 1913, Mx1:34, AA-PA. See Kardorff to Bethmann, 26 Mar. 1913, ibid.; House Diary, 27 Mar. 1913, *WWP*, 27:253 n. 2; Stronge to Grey, 17 May 1913, FO 414:235, PRO; "The Mexican Situation, Veracruz," 22 July 1913, Josephus Daniels Papers, LC, Navy: Mexico, reel 47.

31. See Bernstoff to AA, 25 Feb. 1913, Mx1:33, AA-PA; Kardorff to Bethmann, 26 Mar. 1913, Mx1:34, AA-PA; Kemnitz, "Memorandum about America," 27 Mar. 1913, ibid. The Wilhelmstrasse had been similarly hesitant about recognizing de la Barra (the interim president after Díaz) and Madero.

32. On friction with the Europeans over U.S. recognition of China, see *Her*, 22 Mar., 10 May 1913; Stronge to Grey, 14 May 1913, FO 414:235, PRO; Stronge to Grey, 13 June 1913, ibid.

33. See Grey to Stronge, 22 Feb. 1913, FO 414:235, PRO; Grey to Stronge, 3 Mar. 1913, ibid.; Grey to Stronge, 12 Mar. 1913, ibid.; Bryce to Bryan, 31 Mar. 1913, *FR 1913*, 784–85; *Her*, 17 Apr. 1913; *NYT*, 4 May 1913; minute on Spring-Rice to Grey, 16 May 1913, FO 371:1673, PRO; Moore to WW, 28 Oct. 1913, *WWP*, 28:460; Grey on Laughlin to Paget, 3 Nov. 1913, FO 371:55582, PRO. For an excellent discussion of the British decision, see Calvert, *Mexican Revolution*, 150–66.

34. Grey on Stronge to Grey, 28 Feb. 1913, FO 371:1671, PRO; Grey to Spring-Rice, 8 Nov. 1913, FO 414:235, PRO; Bryce to Grey, 1 Apr. 1913, FO 371:1672, PRO; Press Conference, 18 Apr. 1913, *WWP*, 27:325. British recognition did not give rise to adverse comment in the U.S. press. Spring-Rice, however, referring to the reaction in official circles, commented, "Our recognition of President [Huerta] seems to have created an unfavorable impression" (Spring-Rice to Grey, 16 May 1913, FO 371:1673,

PRO). In August, a debate flared in the U.S. press when the Foreign Office stated that it had recognized Huerta after Lane Wilson had delivered the speech of congratulations to him. "Great Britain had expected the United States also to recognize the Huerta Government because Ambassador Wilson had read the speech" (*NYT*, 14 Aug. 1913; see also *Her*, 14 Aug. 1913). In November, when U.S. criticism of Britain's action was harsh, Grey wrote, "The earliest mention after President Wilson's inauguration of what attitude the U.S. might adopt towards the Mexican situation, that I can trace, is in a conversation between Mr. Bryce and Mr. Bryan on 1 April 1913. Mr. Bryce mentioned to Mr. Bryan H.M.G.'s recognition of Huerta . . . and asked him what the intentions of the U.S.G. were. Mr. Bryan said that he has quite understood . . . that . . . recognition . . . must be accorded in the way it had been done, but as regards the action of the U.S.G. he was not able to give any definite indication. He thought they would at any rate wait some while longer before recognizing Huerta's Govt. H.M.G.'s recognition of Huerta therefore took place before Pres[iden]t Wilson had declared any policy" (Grey on Laughlin to Paget, 3 Nov. 1913, FO 371:55582, PRO; see Spring-Rice to Grey, 19 May 1913, FO 414:235, PRO; Grey to Spring-Rice, 21 May 1913, FO 414:235, PRO; Grey to Spring-Rice, 28 Oct. 1913, FO 800:83, PRO; Spring-Rice to Grey, 29 Oct. 1913, FO 414:235, PRO).

35. The *Universal* (Mexico City) quoted in *LD* (17 May 1913): 1117. Spain extended recognition on 1 April, France and Austria-Hungary on 12 May, Belgium on 20 May. By October, nine Latin American nations—but not the ABC powers—had recognized the de facto president. None of these actions occasioned critical comment in the U.S. press. See de Bunsen to Grey, 2 Apr. 1913, FO 371:1672, PRO; H. L. Wilson to Bryan, 12 Apr. 1913, *FR 1913*, 790; Stronge to Grey, 13 May 1913, FO 371:1673, PRO; Moore to WW, 28 Oct. 1913, *WWP*, 28:460; Hitch, "Chronology of Important Events in Mexico from the Overthrow of Porfirio Diaz down to the Present Time (July 1, 1914)," RG 59, 812.00:24267, NA; "A Suggestion by William Bayard Hale," ca. 15 Oct. 1913, *WWP*, 28:412.

36. On the German decision to recognize Huerta, see Hintze to Bethmann, 28 Feb. 1913, Mx1:34, AA-PA; Hintze, "Background to the February Revolution in Mexico," 28 Feb. 1913, ibid.; Kardorff to Bethmann, 2 Apr. 1913, with kaiser's marginalia of 9 Apr., ibid.; Kardorff to AA, 14 May 1913, ibid.; Spring-Rice to Grey, 19 May 1913, FO 414:235, PRO; Spring-Rice to Grey, 20 May 1913, FO 371:1673, PRO.

37. Moore to WW, 28 Oct. 1913, *WWP*, 28:460.

38. H. L. Wilson, quoted in *NYT*, 14 Aug. 1913. See *NYT*, 25 Oct. 1913.

39. *Her*, 17 May 1913; Daniels, *Wilson Era*, 182; Press Conference, 26 May 1913, *WWP*, 27:471.

40. *Her*, 17 Mar. 1913. See Bryan to WW, 26 May 1913, *WWP*, 27:477–79; Seebohm, "Political Military Report," 11 June 1913, RM5:5822, BA-MA; Stronge to Grey, 23 July 1913, FO 371:1674, PRO.

41. *NYT*, 6 June 1913; Baecker, *Mexikopolitik*, 287 n. 113; *NYT*, ed., 6 June 1913. See Stronge to Grey, 21 May 1913, FO 371:1673, PRO; H. L. Wilson to Bryan, 2 June 1913, *FR 1913*, 806; *Her*, 2 June, 20 July 1913; *NYT*, 21 June, 27 July 1913; Turlington, *Mexico*, 249–50; Baecker, *Mexikopolitik*, 76–80; Knight, *Mexican Revolution*, 133.

42. WW to H. L. Wilson, 14 June 1913, *WWP*, 27:518; Press Conference, 17 July 1913, *WWP*, 28:37. On Wilson's call for elections, see Wilson, *Episodes*, 300–305.

For Lane Wilson's most adamant request for information, see H. L. Wilson to Bryan, 9 June 1913, *FR 1913*, 807. For requests from foreign dignitaries in Mexico, see H. L. Wilson to Bryan, 8 Mar. 1913, *FR 1913*, 760; *NYT*, 17 May 1913.

43. See H. L. Wilson to Bryan, 9 June 1913, RG 59, 812.00:7743, NA; H. L. Wilson's statement to the U.S. Senate Committee on Foreign Relations, *NYT*, 31 July 1913. See also *Her*, 26, 27 July 1913. While the *Herald* supported the administration's policy, the *NYT* urged the ambassador's approach throughout July. See *NYT*, eds., 17, 28 July, 5 Aug. 1913.

44. Daniels, *Wilson Era*, 180–81; Wilson, *Episodes*, 308; Spring-Rice to Grey, 15 Aug. 1913, FO 414:235, PRO. See "A Report by William Bayard Hale," 18 June 1913, RG 59, 812.00:7798 ½, NA. For an editorial sympathetic to the ambassador's plight, see *NYT*, 16 Aug. 1913. See also *Her*, 27 July 1913. In 1908, Hale had found himself at the center of a firestorm involving the kaiser. Thinking of Hale as a minister (which he had been) and not as a *New York Times* correspondent (which he was), Wilhelm granted him an audience and proceeded to spout virulently anti-English, bellicose threats. Fearing the interview too explosive, the *New York Times* did not print it, but President Roosevelt learned of its contents and was alarmed by the kaiser's indiscretion and truculence. See Johnson, *Remembered Yesterdays*, 229–37; TR to Hammond, 8 Aug. 1908, and TR to Root, 8 Aug. 1908, *LTR*, 6:1163–64; TR to White, 17 Oct. 1908, and TR to Lee, 17 Oct. 1908, *LTR*, 6:1292–94; TR to Reid, 6 Jan. 1909, *LTR*, 6:1465–67.

45. Stronge to Grey, 12 May 1913, FO 414:235, PRO. See Stronge to Grey, 28 June 1913, ibid. The presentation of credentials of a new ambassador would have signaled de facto recognition of Huerta. For Lane Wilson's threat, couched in diplomatic terms, see H. L. Wilson to Bryan, 9 July 1913, *FR 1913*, 808–9; H. L. Wilson to Bryan, 11 July 1913, *FR 1913*, 810.

46. For the tension between the ambassador and the administration, see the exchange: H. L. Wilson to Bryan, 9 June 1913, RG 59, 812.00:7743, NA; Bryan to H. L. Wilson, 15 June 1913, ibid. See also the vitriolic account of the period, stressing the untenable position in which the president's policy placed him, in Wilson, *Episodes*, 299–322.

47. National Railways of Mexico, Minutes: "Meeting in Paris on 18 July 1913," encl. in Bank für Handel und Industrie to Jagow, 21 July 1913, Mx1:35, AA-PA.

48. "Draft Telegram," encl. in Stronge to Grey, 5 July 1913, FO 414:235, PRO. See Stronge to Grey, 4 July 1913, FO 371:1673, PRO; Kardorff to Bethmann (nos. 69 and 70), 5 July 1913, Mx1:37, AA-PA; AA to Lichnowsky, 7 July 1913, ibid.; Stronge to Grey, 23 July 1913, FO 414:235, PRO.

49. Granville to Grey, 8 July 1913, FO 371:1673, PRO (emphasis in original). See Lichnowsky to Bethmann, 10 July 1913, Mx1:35, AA-PA.

50. Spring-Rice to Grey, 11 July 1913, FO 371:1674, PRO; Granville to Grey, 25 July 1913, FO 414:235, PRO. See Grey to Granville and Bertie, 11 July 1913, FO 371:1673, PRO; Grey to Spring-Rice, 11 July 1913, FO 414:235, PRO; Spring-Rice to Grey, 14 July 1913, FO 371:1674, PRO.

51. *NYT*, ed., 19 July 1913; *NYT*, 29 July 1913; Grey on Spring-Rice to Grey, 18 July 1913, FO 371:1674, PRO. See *Her*, 15, 18 July 1913; *Nat* (24 July 1913): 71.

52. *Her*, ed., 16 July 1913; *NYT*, ed., 19 July 1913.

53. Press Conference, 17 July 1913, *WWP*, 28:38.

54. Link, *Wilson: The New Freedom*, 358; *Her*, ed., 8 Aug. 1913; Hohler to Grey, 6 Apr. 1914, FO 414:239, PRO; Lind to Bryan, 19 Sept. 1913, *WWP*, 28:293–94 (emphasis in original). On Lind, see Stephenson, *Lind*; Hill, *Emissaries*, 63–187. For a German viewpoint, see Köhler, "Political Military Report," 11 Apr. 1914, RM5:5825, BA-MA.

55. "A Circular Note to the Powers," 8 Aug. 1913, RG 59, 812.00:8284A, NA. See Bryan to Bernstorff, 8 Aug. 1913, Mx1:36, AA-PA; Grey to Stronge, 11 Aug. 1913, FO 414:235, PRO; Grey to Spring-Rice, 13 Aug. 1913, ibid.; Grew to Jagow, 13 Aug. 1913, Mx1:36, AA-PA; Stronge to Grey, 15 Aug. 1913, FO 371:1675, PRO; Spring-Rice to Grey, 17 Aug. 1913, ibid. The White House felt that the circular note was necessary to persuade Huerta to receive Lind, who would not be presenting official credentials as an ambassador. See *Her*, 6 Aug. 1913; Garza Aldape to O'Shaughnessy, 6 Aug. 1913, encl. in O'Shaughnessy to Bryan, 7 Aug. 1913, *FR 1913*, 819.

56. Grey to Spring-Rice, 8 Nov. 1913, FO 414:235, PRO; Spring-Rice to Grey, 19 Aug. 1913, FO 800:83, PRO.

57. Grew to Jagow, 13 Aug. 1913, Mx1:36, AA-PA, with kaiser's marginalia. See Jagow to Kardorff, 10 Aug. 1913, ibid.; Jagow to Kardorff, 12 Aug. 1913, ibid.; Kardorff to AA, 16 Aug. 1913, ibid.; Kardorff to Bethmann, 19 Aug. 1913, Mx1:37, AA-PA. For Spain and Russia, see Scholle to Bryan, 29 Aug. 1913, *FR 1913*, 829; C. S. Wilson to Bryan, 30 Aug. 1913, ibid.

58. Spring-Rice to Grey, 19 Aug. 1913, FO 800:83, PRO. For a review of the U.S. press, see *Her*, 14 Aug. 1913. See also *Her*, 13, 15, 17, 29 Aug. 1913; *NYT*, 14 Aug. 1913.

59. Instructions to John Lind, 4 Aug. 1913, *WWP*, 28:110.

60. *Le Temps*, in *NYT*, 29 Aug. 1913; Leslie on Stronge to Grey, 10 July 1913, FO 371:1674, PRO; Knatchbull-Hugessen on Stronge to Grey, 17 Aug. 1913, FO 371:1675, PRO; *NYT*, ed., 8 Aug. 1913; *El Independiente*, quoted in *LD* (16 Aug. 1913): 235.

61. Gamboa to Lind, 16 Aug. 1913, *WWP*, 28:168–75; *NYT*, ed., 23 Aug. 1913. Gamboa's note—seven thousand words long—was not deciphered until 21 August.

62. Lind to Bryan (nos. 1 and 2), 27 Aug. 1913, *WWP*, 28:232–33.

63. Mexican Foreign Office to Lind, 26 Aug. 1913, encl. in O'Shaughnessy to Bryan, 27 Aug. 1913, *WWP*, 28:236.

64. *NYT*, ed., 28 Aug. 1913; Bryan to Lind, 27 Aug. 1913, *WWP*, 28:239; Ellen Axson Wilson to WW, 19 Aug. 1913, *WWP*, 28:195.

65. "Address of the President to Congress," 2 Dec. 1913, *FR 1913*, x; Press Conference, 26 May 1913, *WWP*, 27:471.

66. Moore, "The Mexican Situation," 14 May 1913, encl. in Moore to WW, 15 May 1913, *WWP*, 27:437. See Moore to WW, 28 Oct. 1913, *WWP*, 28:458–63.

67. Richthofen, quoted in *Zeitung am Mittag*, in *Her*, 27 Aug. 1913; marginalia on Kardorff to Bethmann, 26 Aug. 1913, Mx1:36, AA-PA.

68. Adee to WW, 24 Mar. 1913, *FR 1913*, 872–75. See WW to Adee, 25 Mar. 1913, *FR 1913*, 875–76; "Note: Violations of Neutrality," *FR 1913*, 867–72; "A Memorandum by John Bassett Moore," 22 Aug. 1913, *WWP*, 28:214–15.

69. See *Her*, 24, 25 July, 26 Aug. 1913; *NYT*, 29 July 1913; Breckinridge to WW, 10 Sept. 1913, *WWP*, 28:280.

70. "An Address on Mexican Affairs to a Joint Session of Congress," 27 Aug. 1913, *WWP*, 28:230-31; *Her*, 28 Aug. 1913; *LD* (27 Sept. 1913): 516; *Deutsche Tageszeitung*, quoted in *NYT*, 29 Aug. 1913; *T*, quoted in *Her*, 29 Aug. 1913. See *NYT*, 26 Aug. 1913.

71. For early hints, see, for example, Daniels Diary, 18 Apr. 1913, *WWP*, 27:331; House Diary, 2 May 1913, *WWP*, 27:383; Daniels, *Wilson Era*, 181. For the most impassioned statement, see "A Draft of a Circular Note to the Powers," 24 Oct. 1913, *WWP*, 28:431-32. For Lind, see Lind to Bryan, 25 Oct. 1913, *WWP*, 28:444-47. For Bryan, see Bryan to WW, 28 Oct. 1913, *WWP*, 28:455-57. Wilson's analysis of Mexican affairs paralleled his critique of the role of trusts and big business in domestic politics. Both the U.S. and British documents are rife with reports of the Wilson administration's suspicion that British policy was manipulated by the oil companies. See, for example, "A Draft of a telegram to Walter Hines Page," 11 Oct. 1913, *WWP*, 28:388; O'Shaughnessy to Bryan, 20 Oct. 1913, *WWP*, 28:420-21; Page to Bryan, 21 Oct. 1913, *WWP*, 28:421; Lind to Bryan, 23 Oct. 1913, *WWP*, 28:429; Lind to Bryan, 25 Oct. 1913, *WWP*, 28:444-45; Grey to Spring-Rice, 28 Oct. 1913, FO 800:83, PRO; Spring-Rice to Grey, 29 Oct. 1913, FO 414:235, PRO; House Diary, 30 Oct. 1913, *WWP*, 28:476; Spring-Rice to Grey, 13 Nov. 1913, FO 414:235, PRO. See also *NYT*, eds., 30 June, 10, 22 Nov. 1913. Suspicion of Cowdray's influence also peppers the reports in the *Herald* (see, for example, 17 July, 1, 19 Oct., 15, 16, 18 Nov. 1913).

72. "Memorandum by Sir L. Carden," encl. in Carden to Grey, 12 Sept. 1913, FO 414:235, PRO; Hohler to Grey, 24 Sept. 1913, ibid.; Spring-Rice to Tyrrell, 17 Feb. 1914, FO 800:84, PRO; Page to WW, 2 Nov. 1913, *WWP*, 28:484-85.

73. Kardorff to AA, n. 47, 10 Aug. 1913, Mx1:36, AA-PA; *LD* (15 Nov. 1913): 936; *LD* (22 Nov. 1913): 998; marginalia on Seebohm, "Political Military Report," 28 Nov. 1913, RM5:5823, BA-MA.

74. Marginalia on Kardorff to Bethmann, 10 Aug. 1913, Mx1:36, AA-PA.

75. Hintze to Bethmann, 26 Sept. 1913, Mx1:38, AA-PA.

76. See Lind to Bryan, 28 Jan. 1914, *WWP*, 29:190. See also Herrick to Bryan, 25 Oct. 1913, *FR 1913*, 850.

77. See Kühlmann to Bethmann, 29 Oct. 1913, Mx1:39, AA-PA; German Embassy in Paris to Bethmann, 2 Nov. 1913, ibid.; Schön to Bethmann, 6 Nov. 1913, ibid.; Bernstorff to AA, no. 140, (undated, rec'd 10 or 11) Nov. 1913, ibid.; Kühlmann to Bethmann, 11 Nov. 1913, ibid.; Bernstorff to AA (nos. 144 and 146), 14 Nov. 1913, ibid.; Kühlmann to Bethmann, 18 Nov. 1913, ibid. See also Link, *Wilson: The New Freedom*, 369-77; Hendrick, *Page*, 1:209-15.

78. Hintze Diary, 11 and 16 May 1914, Mx1:50, AA-PA; Carden, quoted in Hintze to Bethmann, 11 Nov. 1913, Mx1:40, AA-PA; marginalia on Seebohm, "Political Military Report," 28 Nov. 1913, RM5:5823, BA-MA; marginalia on Schön to Bethmann, 5 Mar. 1914, Mx1:44, AA-PA; marginalia on Bernstorff to Bethmann, 25 Nov. 1913, Mx1:40, AA-PA.

79. Craddock to Admiralty, 19 Feb. 1914, encl. in Admiralty to Foreign Office, 12 Mar. 1914, FO 414:239, PRO. See *NYT*, ed., 17 Oct. 1913; Köhler, "Political Military Report," 11 Apr. 1914, RM5:5825, BA-MA.

80. *Her*, 10 Oct. 1913.

81. O'Shaughnessy to Bryan, 11 Oct. 1913, *FR 1913*, 837; Ellen Wilson to WW, 13 Oct. 1913, *WWP*, 28:400; Mahan to Clark, 23 Oct. 1913, in Seager and Maguire,

Mahan, 3:512; House Diary, Yale, 3 July 1913. See Bryan to O'Shaughnessy, 13 Oct. 1913, *WWP*, 28:399. On Carden's presentation of his credentials, see *NYT*, 17, 29 Oct. 1913; Page to Bryan, 27 Oct. 1913, *FR 1913*, 851.

82. *Her*, 20 Oct. 1913. See Hintze to Bethmann, 19 Oct. 1913, M x1:38, AA-PA; Haniel to AA, 23 Oct. 1913, ibid.

83. Thompson to Bryan, rec'd 29 Oct. 1913, 710.11/159, M1276:1; *Her*, ed., 12 Oct. 1913. See *Her*: 18 July, 31 Aug., 1, 2 Sept., 9, 19, 20, 21 Oct. 1913. See also *Nat* (24 July 1913): 71.

84. *Her*, 20 July 1913; *Her*, 18 Oct. 1913; Spring-Rice to Grey, 28 Oct. 1913, FO 414:235, PRO.

85. Paget on Spring-Rice to Grey, 23 Oct. 1913, FO 371:1677, PRO. See Goschen to Zimmermann, 14 Nov. 1913, M x1:39, AA-PA.

86. On the development of the request to the powers, see "A Suggestion by William Bayard Hale," ca. 15 Oct. 1913, *WWP*, 28:411–12; Bryan to WW, 22 Oct. 1913, *WWP*, 28:422; "A Draft of a Circular Note to the Powers," *WWP*, 28:431–33; Press Conference, 3 Nov. 1913, *WWP*, 28:485–87; Goschen to Zimmermann, 14 Nov. 1913, M x1:39, AA-PA. For the U.S. request to delay recognition, see Bryan to Certain Diplomatic Officers of the United States (sent to Austria, France, Germany, Britain, Italy, Japan, Russia, and Spain), 24 Oct. 1913, *FR 1913*, 849. To the press, Wilson denied asking for the assistance of the foreign powers, saying instead that their "voluntary concurrent action . . . will be appreciated" (*NYT*, 14 Nov. 1913). See also "What the United States is seeking is an acquiescence in its policy by the Powers, such an approval to carry with it a discouragement of financial aid to the Huerta regime" (*Her*, 12 Nov. 1913).

87. Knight, *Mexican Revolution*, 76; *NYT*, ed., 31 Oct. 1913.

88. House Diary, 30 Oct. 1913, *WWP*, 28:477–78; WW to Hulbert, 2 Nov. 1913, *WWP*, 28:484. See "A Draft of an Address to Congress," ca. 31 Oct. 1913, *WWP*, 28:479–81; "Naval War Plan for Mexico" and "Memorandum Relative to Naval Cooperation in War with Mexico," box 8, GBW; *Her*, 19 Nov. 1913; Bernstorff to AA, (rec'd. 21) Nov. 1913, M x1:39, AA-PA; *NYT*, 24 Nov. 1913; Seebohm, "Political Military Report," 28 Nov. 1913, RM5:5823, BA-MA.

89. See Gerard to Bryan, 26 Oct. 1913, *FR 1913*, 851; *NYT*, 29 Oct., 2 Nov. 1913; *Her*, 2 Nov. 1913.

90. Goschen to Grey, 27 Oct. 1913, FO 414:235, PRO. The British also rebuffed the Spanish. See Grey to Rennie, 29 Oct. 1913, FO 414:235, PRO; *NYT*, 9 Nov. 1913.

91. *NYT*, 29 Oct. 1913; Gerard, *Four Years*, 47. On Germany, see Laughlin to Bryan, 11 July 1913, *FR 1913*, 811; *Her*, 16 Oct. 1913; Bryan to WW, 22 Oct. 1913, *WWP*, 28:422–23; *NYT*, 27 Oct. 1913; Gerard to Bryan, 27 Nov. 1913, *FR 1913*, 863.

92. "A Talk at Swarthmore College," 25 Oct. 1913, *WWP*, 28:441; "An Address on Latin American Policy at Mobile, Alabama," 27 Oct. 1913, *WWP*, 28:451; *Neueste Nachrichten*, quoted in *Her*, 2 Nov. 1913, I-1:4; Grey on Spring-Rice to Grey, 30 Oct. 1913, FO 371:55582, PRO. On the Swarthmore speech, see "The President's Ideal," *Nat* (30 Oct. 1913): 402. For an excellent analysis of the Mobile speech, see Calvert, *Mexican Revolution*, 248–53.

93. "A Draft of a Circular Note to the Powers," 24 Oct. 1913, *WWP*, 28:431–33.

94. *NYT*, 25 Oct. 1913.

95. "An Outline of a Circular Note to the Powers," ca. 24 Oct. 1913, *WWP*, 28:434.

96. Moore to WW, 28 Oct. 1913, *WWP*, 28:458–63, quotations, 458, 460. Enclosed in this letter is Moore's draft circular letter, *WWP*, 28:464.

97. House Diary, 30 Oct. 1913, *WWP*, 28:476.

98. *LD* (8 Nov. 1913): 857; "A Note to the Powers [England, Germany, France, Italy, Japan, Norway, Argentina, Brazil, Chile, Belgium]," 7 Nov. 1913, *FR 1913*, 856. See Press Conference, 30 Oct. 1913, *WWP*, 28:471–74; "Draft of a Circular Note to the Powers," 7, 8, 10, Nov. 1913, *WWP*, 28:502–4.

99. *LD* (22 Nov. 1913): 998.

100. *NYT*, 14 Nov. 1913; Gerard to Bryan, 8 Nov. 1913, *FR 1913*, 858; WW to Moore, 21 Nov. 1913, *WWP*, 28:571; Bernstorff to AA, 21 Nov. 1913, M*x1*:39, AA-PA. See Goschen to Grey, 12 Nov. 1913, FO 371:55582, PRO; Goschen to Zimmermann, 14 Nov. 1913, M*x1*:39, AA-PA; *Nat* (13 Nov. 1913): 447; Lersner to Moore, 19 Nov. 1913, *WWP*, 28:567 n. 2.

101. Page to WW, 25 Oct. 1913, *WWP*, 28:443; *NYT*, ed., 17 Nov. 1913; Grey to Carden, 17 Oct. 1913, FO 371:1676, PRO; *Her*, 15 Nov. 1913; *NYT*, ed., 12 Nov. 1913. See Grey to Spring-Rice, 2 Apr. 1914, FO 800:84, PRO; Calvert, *Mexican Revolution*, 254–55, 269–71; Link, *Wilson: The New Freedom*, 375–77; Hendrick, *Page* 1:200–214; Scholes and Scholes, "Wilson, Grey."

102. Bernstorff to Bethmann, 25 Nov. 1913, M*x1*:40, AA-PA, with kaiser's marginalia; kaiser on Hintze to AA, no. 4, [undated, rec'd. 11] Jan. 1914, M*x1*:42, AA-PA; kaiser on Lichnowsky to Bethmann, 1 Mar. 1914, M*x1*:44, AA-PA. See *Berliner Tageblatt*, 18 Nov. 1913; Dehn, "England and the Monroe Doctrine," *Alldeutsche Blätter*, 27 Dec. 1913, 450.

103. WW to Bryan, 23 Nov. 1913, and encl., "International Note: 'Our Purposes in Mexico,'" *WWP*, 28:585.

104. Fiske to Fletcher, 27 Nov. 1913, "C" 196(4), RG 45, NA.

105. Jagow to Hintze, 2 Dec. 1913, M*x1*:40, AA-PA; Kenmitz on Hintze to Bethmann, 9 Dec. 1913, M*x1*:41, AA-PA. See Hintze to Bethmann, 27 Nov. 1913, ibid.; Hintze to AA, 2 Dec. 1913, M*x1*:40, AA-PA.

106. Zimmermann to Bernstorff, 10 Nov. 1913, M*x1*:39, AA-PA.

107. Kaiser (in English) on Bernstorff to AA, no. 138, (rec'd. 7) Nov. 1913, M*x1*:39, AA-PA; Gerard to Bryan, 2 Jan. 1914, RG 59, NA; kaiser on Hintze to Bethmann, 4 Nov. 1913, M*x1*:40, AA-PA.

108. *NYT*, ed., 14 Jan. 1914. See Hintze to Bethmann, 9 Dec. 1913, M*x14*:1, AA-PA; Schwabach to Zimmermann, 15 Jan. 1914, ibid.; Bleichröder, Deutsche Bank, Dresdner Bank et al. to AA, 16 Jan. 1914, ibid.; Goschen to Grey, 30 Jan. 1914, FO 414:239, PRO; Lichnowsky to Bethmann, 28 Jan. 1914, M*x14*:1, AA-PA; Carden to Grey, 8 Feb. 1914, FO 414:239, PRO; Bleichröder to AA, 7 May 1914, M*x14*:2, AA-PA; Schwabach to AA, 11 May 1914, ibid. Katz's argument that German bankers' interest ebbed and flowed with their interest in Mexican oil seems tenuous at best (Katz, *Secret War*, 204–5). The fear that the Mexican financial failure could precipitate European intervention was discussed extensively in the *New York Times* (see *NYT*, 4, 17, 21, 25 Jan. 1914).

109. Bernstorff to Bethmann, 25 Nov. 1913, M*x1*:40, AA-PA; Hintze to Bethmann, 27 Nov. 1913, M*x1*:41, AA-PA.

110. Seebohm, "Political Military Report," 28 Nov. 1913, RM5:5823, BA-MA;

Hintze Diary, 10 and 11 May 1914, Mx1:50, AA-PA; O'Shaughnessy, *Intimate Pages*, 234; Seebohm, "Political Military Report," 4 Dec. 1913, RM5:5823, BA-MA; Lind to Bryan, 19 Sept. 1913, *WWP*, 28:299; German naval attaché to Admiralstab, "US Military Intervention in Mexico," 21 May 1914, RM5:5825, BA-MA.

111. See Jagow to Bernstorff, 15 May 1914, Mx1:46, AA-PA.

112. Jagow, *Stenographische Berichte*, 13th leg., 1st sess., 244th sitting (29 April 1914); Bernstorff to Bethmann, 23 Feb. 1914, Mx1:44, AA-PA; Spring-Rice to Grey, 17 Feb. 1914, FO 800:84, PRO.

113. Press Conference, 12 Mar. 1914, *WWP*, 50:408; Works, *Congressional Record*, 63d Cong., 2d sess., 6 Mar. 1914, 4405.

114. See *NYT*, 27 Jan. 1914; Bryan to all diplomatic missions, (circular telegram), 31 Jan. 1914, *FR 1914*, 446–47, enclosing Proclamation Lifting Embargo; "A Press Release," 3 Feb. 1914, *WWP*, 29:216–17; *NYT*, 4 Feb. 1914; Daniels, *Life*, 179–80; Knight, *Mexican Revolution*, 138–40.

115. *LD* (21 Mar. 1914): 602. For a dramatic rendition of the Benton affair, see Eisenhower, *Intervention!*, 69–78. See also *FR 1914*, 842–54; Page to WW, 24 Feb. 1914, *WWP*, 29:285–86; Page to WW, 28 Feb. 1914, *WWP*, 29:300–301.

116. *NYT*, ed., 5 Apr. 1914. See Lind to Bryan, 1 Apr. 1914, 812. 11371, NA.

117. *Her*, ed., 20 Apr. 1913. On the Tampico incident, see esp. case c-10-a, box 471, RG 38, NA; Quirk, *Affair of Honor*, 1–34; Knight, *Mexican Revolution*, 150–62.

118. Bernstorff to AA, 20 Apr. 1914, Mx1:45, AA-PA; *NYT*, 20, 21 Apr. 1914. See Hintze to AA, 16 Apr. 1914, Mx1:45, AA-PA; Hintze to AA, 19 Apr. 1914, ibid.

119. Wood Diary, 20 Apr. 1914, Leonard Wood Papers, LC. For the story of the *Ypiranga*, see Meyer, "Arms"; Katz, *Secret War*, 232–40; Baecker, *Mexikopolitik*.

120. *Her*, 20 Apr. 1914; *NYT*, ed., 22 Apr. 1914. See Canada to State Department, 18 Apr. 1914, *WWP*, 29:464; Bryan to O'Shaughnessy, 19 Apr. 1914, *WWP*, 29:464–65. The occupation of Veracruz is well covered in the literature. See especially Quirk, *Affair of Honor*.

121. General Board to Daniels, 18 Apr. 1914, GB no. 427, GBL.

122. "An Address to Congress on the Mexican Crisis," 20 Apr. 1914, *WWP*, 29:474; *NYT*, ed., 23 Apr. 1914. See "Enforcing Certain Demands Made upon Victoriano Huerta, of Mexico," 63d Cong., 2d sess., 20 Apr. 1914, H. Rept. 560; "Enforcement of Certain Demands against Victoriano Huerta," 63d Cong., 2d sess., 21 Apr. 1914, S. Rept. 437. Congressional action on the resolution was not required before Wilson took action (see Bryan to O'Shaughnessy, 21 Apr. 1914, *FR 1914*, 478).

123. *NYT*, 22 Apr. 1914; *LD* (2 May 1914): 1032. See Canada to Bryan, 20 Apr. 1914, encl. in Bryan to WW, 21 Apr. 1914, *WWP*, 29:477; Canada to Bryan, 21 Apr. 1914, *FR 1914*, 479. Daniels to Fletcher, 21 Apr. 1914, Daniels Papers, Navy: Mexico, reel 47; Fletcher, "Seizure and Occupation of Vera Cruz, April 21st–April 30th, 1914," ibid. For German accounts of the occupation, see Köhler, "Political Military Report," 28 Apr. 1914, RM5:5825, BA-MA; Köhler, "Political Military Report," 10 May 1914, ibid.

124. See Bernstorff to AA, 20 Apr. 1914, Mx1:45, AA-PA. See also Bernstorff to AA (nos. 47–50), 20 Apr. 1914, ibid.; Hohler to Grey, 18 Apr. 1914, FO 414:239, PRO; Hintze to AA, 19 Apr. 1914, Mx1:45, AA-PA; Telegram to German residents in Mexico, 24 Apr. 1914, RM5:5825, BA-MA. Until 1 May, Hintze, relying completely on rumors swirling around Mexico City, was confused about the *Ypiranga* and about

events in Tampico and Veracruz (see, for instance, Hintze to Bethmann, 16–24 Apr. 1914, Mx1:48, AA-PA).

The use of a Hapag ship for rescuing refugees was not unusual. On 13 February 1914, Zimmermann stated in the Reichstag that the German government had sent two navy ships to Mexico and that it had asked for the cooperation of Hapag. The *Ypiranga* had been mentioned in connection with rescuing refugees several months earlier in Tampico, when revolution had gripped that city (see AA to Admiralstab, 5 Feb. 1914, RM5:5824, BA-MA; Hapag to AA, 7 Feb. 1914, encl. in AA to Admiralstab, 8 Feb. 1914, ibid.; Zimmermann, *Stenographische Berichte*, 13th leg., 1st sess., 213th sitting [13 Feb. 1914]: 7278). Tuchman alleges that Hintze had offered the Mexicans the arms aboard the *Ypiranga* in exchange for a pledge to cut off oil to the English in time of war (Tuchman, *Zimmermann Telegram*, 47). Not only does she offer no evidence, but the available evidence about Hintze's motivations and actions contradicts her.

125. *NYT*, 21 Apr. 1914. The next day, the paper sported an eight-column banner headline that included the statement "Landing Ordered by Wilson to Stop Import of Arms" (*NYT*, 22 Apr. 1914). On informing Berlin, see Boy-Ed to Tirpitz, "US Military Intervention in Mexico," 22 Apr. 1914, RM5:5825, BA-MA; Köhler, "Political Military Report," 28 Apr. 1914, RM5:5825, BA-MA (for the suspicion that the *Ypiranga* had triggered the occupation); Köhler, "Political Military Report," 10 May 1914, RM5:5825, BA-MA (for the confirmation, via accounts in the U.S. press). See also Hughes to Maas, undated, encl. in Köhler, "Political Military Report," 24 May 1914, RM2:1780, fiche 4, BA-MA. The British were formally informed of the connection on 23 April (Spring-Rice to Grey, 23 Apr. 1914, FO 414:239, PRO).

126. See Canada to Bryan, 21 Apr. 1914, *WWP*, 29:480; Heynen to Hapag, Hamburg, 4 June 1914, Mx1:49, AA-PA. See also O'Shaughnessy, *Wife*, 288.

127. *NYT*, 22 Apr. 1914.

128. Daniels to Fletcher, 21 Apr. 1914, Daniels Papers, Navy: Mexico, reel 47. See Bryan to WW, 21 Apr. 1914, *WWP*, 29:476–77 n. 1; Bryan to Canada, 21 Apr. 1914, *FR 1914*, 477; Fletcher to Daniels, 22 Apr. 1914, Daniels Papers, Navy: Mexico, reel 47. See also Daniels, *Wilson Era*, 201. Köhler believed that the U.S. captain had simply not known how to prevent the landing of the cargo (which had been his orders) in the absence of an official declaration of war (see Köhler, "Political Military Report," 28 Apr. 1914, RM5:5825, BA-MA).

129. Köhler, "Political Military Report," 28 Apr. 1914, RM5:5825, BA-MA. See Kemnitz to Bernstorff, 25 Apr. 1914, Mx1:45, AA-PA; Baecker, *Mexikopolitik*, 337.

130. Heynen to Hapag, 4 June 1914, Mx1:50, AA-PA.

131. Bernstorff to AA, 21 Apr. 1914, Mx1:45, AA-PA; Bryan, "Memorandum," 21 Apr. 1914, RG 59, 812.00:17170, NA; *NYT*, 22, 23 Apr. 1914; *Her*, 22 Apr. 1914; Baecker, *Mexikopolitik*, 337 n. 379 (Baecker had access to Hapag archives). Hapag suggested that the captain of the *Ypiranga* should demand 6,000 pounds compensation if the ship couldn't take on its return cargo because of the undeliverable arms (Heynen to Hapag, 4 June 1914, Mx1:50, AA-PA; Hintze Diary, 23 May 1914, ibid.).

132. Boy-Ed to Tirpitz, 30 Apr. 1914, RM5:5826, BA-MA. Two hundred Mexicans were killed in the operation (Knight, *Mexican Revolution*, 153).

133. Köhler, "Political Military Report," 28 Apr. 1914, RM5:5825, BA-MA; López Portillo y Rojas to O'Shaughnessy, 22 Apr. 1914, encl. in O'Shaughnessy to Bryan,

25 Apr. 1914, *FR 1914*, 490; *Hamburger Nachrichten*, in *LD* (23 May 1914): 1243. See *NYT*, 23 Apr. 1914; *Her*, 27 Apr. 1914.

134. *NYT*, 23 Apr. 1914; *Her*, ed., 27 Apr. 1914. See *Her*, 26, 27 Apr. 1914; Mayo to Daniels, "Report of Events at Tampico from April 17th, 1914 to April 30, 1914," 30 Apr. 1914, Daniels Papers, Navy: Mexico, reel 47; RMA to Jagow, 5 June 1914, RM5:5825, BA-MA, enclosing letters of thanks from Americans to Köhler. Daniels later claimed that Bernstorff had presented a formal protest to the State Department, and Tuchman makes much of this. There is, however, no documentary evidence of it, and Berlin denied it (Daniels, *Wilson Era*, 200; Tuchman, *Zimmermann Telegram*, 51–52; AA to Hintze, 25 Apr. 1914, Mx1:45, AA-PA).

135. Köhler, "Political Military Report," 24 May 1914, RM5:5825, BA-MA. Köhler reported that about one hundred refugees availed of the offer (Köhler, "Political Military Report," 10 May 1914, RM5:5825, BA-MA).

136. Bernstorff to AA, 24 Apr. 1914, Mx1:45, AA-PA; Bryan to Daniels, n.d. (filed with April 1914 memos), Daniels Papers, Special Correspondence, reel 43; marginalia on Hintze to AA, 23 Apr. 1914, Mx1:45, AA-PA. See Hans-Adolf von Bülow to Bethmann, 23 Apr. 1914, ibid.; Kemnitz to Bernstorff, 25 Apr. 1914, ibid.; Bernstorff to AA, 26 Apr. 1914, ibid.; Bryan to Bernstorff, 29 Apr. 1914, encl. in Bernstorff to Bethmann, 1 May 1914, Mx1:46, AA-PA; Bernstorff to AA, 30 Apr. 1914, ibid.; Daniels, *Wilson Era*, 200. For the British perception that a commitment had been made, see Goschen to Grey, 30 Apr. 1914, FO 414:239, PRO; Spring-Rice to Grey, 13 May 1914, FO 800:84, PRO.

137. Tuchman, *Zimmermann Telegram*, 52; Doerries, *Imperial Challenge*, 37. See Katz, *Secret War*, 237–38; Teitelbaum, *Wilson*, 245; Quirk, *Affair of Honor*, 151.

138. AA to Hintze, 19 May 1914, Mx1:47, AA-PA. See Hintze Diary, 23 May 1914, Mx1:50, AA-PA. See also Cecil, *Albert Ballin*. Doerries stresses Ballin's sympathy with Huerta (Doerries, *Imperial Challenge*, 36). Hapag headquarters in New York asserted that it had not ordered the *Ypiranga* to unload its cargo and that if such an order had been given, it must have been "due to independent action on the part of our agents" (*NYT*, 31 May 1914).

139. Baecker, *Mexikopolitik*, 183.

140. Jagow, *Stenographische Berichte*, 13th leg., 1st sess., 244th sitting (29 April 1914).

141. *NYT*, 26 Apr. 1914. See *NYT*, 27 Apr. 1914; *Her*, 22 Apr. 1914.

142. Hintze Diary, 30 Apr. 1914, Mx1:50, AA-PA. See Hintze Diary, 1 and 8 May, 9 June 1914, ibid.

143. See *NYT*, 9 May 1914; *Her*, 9 May 1914.

144. *Kölnische Zeitung*, 10 May 1914; *NYT*, 10 May 1914; *Her*, 10 May 1914. On 11 May the *Herald* reported that the *Kronprinzessin Cecilie* had in fact landed its cargo; on the 26th, when reporting the unloading of the *Bavaria*'s arms, it retracted the story about the *Cecilie* (*Her*, 11, 26 May 1914).

145. *NYT*, 10 May 1914; *NYT*, 11 May 1914.

146. See *Her*, 26, 28 May 1914.

147. Heynen to Hapag, 4 June 1914, Mx1:50, AA-PA. See Hintze Diary, 23 May 1914, ibid.; Daniels, *Wilson Era*, 210.

148. Hintze Diary, 17 May 1914, Mx1:50, AA-PA. See Hintze to Bethmann, 3 June

1914, Mx1:49, AA-PA; Köhler, "Political Military Report," 20 June 1914, RM5:5826, BA-MA. The *Ypiranga* stopped flying the flag on 25 May when it left Veracruz.

149. AA to Hintze, 19 May 1914, Mx1:47, AA-PA. Later, after the arms were landed, the German legation in Mexico City said it knew nothing of the ship's movements (*NYT*, 28 May 1914).

150. Heynen to Hapag, 4 June 1914, Mx1:50, AA-PA.

151. Baecker, *Mexikopolitik*, 340 n. 413. See Hapag to Zimmermann, 4 June 1914, Mx1:48, AA-PA, and enclosure: "Halboard Newyork"; *NYT*, 29 May 1914. Heynen did not send the desired confirmation until 30 May 1914.

152. Köhler, "Political Military Report," 20 June 1914, RM5:5826, BA-MA; Heynen to Hapag, 4 June 1914, Mx1:50, AA-PA; Bonath, in *NYT*, 31 May 1914; *NYT*, 26 Apr. 1914. See Hintze Diary, 23 May 1914, Mx1:50, AA-PA.

153. Heynen to Hapag, 4 June 1914, Mx1:50, AA-PA.

154. *NYT*, 27 May 1914; Heynen to Hapag, 4 June 1914, Mx1:50, AA-PA. See Rear Admiral Sir C. Craddock to Admiralty, 28 May 1914, encl. in Admiralty to Foreign Office, 29 May 1914, FO 414:239, PRO.

155. *NYT*, 28 May 1914. See *Her*, 28, 29 May 1914.

156. *NYT*, 28 May 1914.

157. Boy-Ed to Tirpitz, 11 June 1914, RM5:5826, BA-MA; *Her*, 28 May 1914. See *Her*, 30 May 1914.

158. *NYT*, 29 May 1914; Daniels, *Wilson Era*, 200.

159. Heynen to Hapag, 4 June 1914, Mx1:50, AA-PA; Köhler, "Political Military Report," 20 June 1914, RM5:5826, BA-MA; Boy-Ed to Tirpitz, 11 June 1914, ibid. See *NYT*, 31 May, 1 June 1914; Carden to Grey, 12 June 1914, FO 414:240, PRO.

160. *NYT*, 3 June 1914; *NYT*, 31 May 1914.

161. See AA to Hintze, 19 May 1914, Mx1:47, AA-PA; Bülow to Bethmann, 25 May 1914, ibid.; Hintze Diary, 24 May 1914, Mx1:50, AA-PA.

162. Hintze Diary, 23 May 1914, Mx1:50, AA-PA. See Bernstorff to Bethmann, 25 Apr. 1914, Mx1:46, AA-PA; Hintze to Bethmann, 17 May 1914, Mx1:47, AA-PA.

163. *NYT*, 30 Apr. 1914. See Meyer, "Arms," 547; Goschen to Grey, 30 Apr. 1914, FO 414:239, PRO; *NYT*, 29 May 1914; Quirk, *Affair of Honor*, 98; Baecker, *Mexikopolitik*, 176–79 (which stresses the French role). The *Herald* reported that the arms were of French origin (*Her*, 22 Apr. 1914).

164. Meyer, "Arms," 549. The head of the U.S. Atlantic fleet agreed that the action was perfectly legal. See Badger to Daniels, 28 Apr. 1914, encl. in Daniels to Bryan, RG 59, 812.00:11768, NA.

165. For a defense of this theory, see Katz, *Secret War*, 234–35.

166. Heynen to Hapag, 4 June 1914, Mx1:50, AA-PA.

167. Hintze to Bethmann, 3 June 1914, Mx1:49, AA-PA.

168. Doerries, *Imperial Challenge*, 37 and 165.

169. Kaiser on Kardorff to Bethmann, 10 Aug. 1913, Mx1:36, AA-PA; kaiser on Kardorff to Bethmann, 26 Aug. 1913, ibid.

170. Hintze Diary, 10 May 1914, Mx1:50, AA-PA.

171. Shartle, "Monthly Report for March 1912," 8 Apr. 1912, RG 165, box 135, NA; Press Conference, 9 Mar. 1914, *WWP*, 50:406.

172. See Lersner to Bryan, 27 May 1914, *FR 1914*, 887–88; Lansing to Bernstorff,

2 June 1914, ibid., 889. For U.S. protection of Germans in Mexico, see correspondence in *FR 1913*, 915; *FR 1914*, 884–95.

173. Page to Wilson, 22 Feb. 1914, quoted in Grieb, *Huerta*, 128. For the debate about Wilson's realism and idealism, see, for example, Clements, who asserts that Wilson's policy in Mexico "met a standard rare in human affairs" ("Mexican Policy," 136), and Grieb, who argues that Wilson was acting out of misguided moralism (*Huerta*), and Smith, who argues that Wilson was following the mandates of big business and economic imperialism (*Revolutionary Nationalism*).

174. Hintze Diary, May 4, 1914, Mxi:50, AA-PA. For comments on Wilson's ignorance, see Braniff, "Distinguished Mexican Tells of Situation Here," *NYT*, 20 July, 29 Aug. 1913.

175. Stronge to Grey, 21 Aug. 1913, FO 371:1675, PRO; House Diary, Yale, 1 June 1914.

176. Spicer on Spring-Rice to Grey, 2 Dec. 1913, FO 371:1678, PRO; Granville to Grey, 8 July 1913, FO 371:1673, PRO. On speculation about the annexation of the northern provinces and the "Madero lobby," see Stronge to Grey, 16 June 1913, FO 371:1673, PRO, and minutes; Hale to WW, ca. 25 June 1913, *WWP*, 28:8; Spring-Rice to Grey, 16 July 1913, FO 371:1674, PRO; Spicer on Spring-Rice to Grey, 19 July 1913, ibid.; *NYT*, ed., 3 Mar. 1913; *Nat* (14 Aug. 1913): 223.

177. *NYT*, 21 Apr. 1914; Kardorff to Bethmann, 21 Aug. 1913, Mxi:37, AA-PA; Granville to Grey, 25 July 1913, FO 414:235, PRO. See *NYT*, ed., 5 Dec. 1913. For rebuttal, see Grey to Spring-Rice, 28 Oct. 1913, FO 800:83, PRO; Wood on Bryce to Grey, 16 Jan. 1913, FO 414:235, PRO.

178. Hohler to Grey, 24 Sept. 1913, FO 414:235, PRO.

179. Page to WW, 28 Feb. 1914, *WWP*, 29:300.

180. Link, "Higher Realism."

181. Tyrrell, through Spring-Rice, to Grey, 14 Nov. 1913, FO 371:55582, PRO. Many people, at the time and subsequently, have pointed to the ways in which Wilson's policy served the U.S. national interest. See, for example, entry of 11 Mar. 1913, Daniels, *Cabinet*, 6–7; "Press Statement on Latin America," 12 Mar. 1913, *WWP*, 27:172; Nordholt, *Woodrow Wilson*, 119; Heckscher, *Woodrow Wilson*, 298.

182. See Knight, *Mexican Revolution*, 68–77, 138–40, 150–57.

183. O'Shaughnessy, *Intimate Pages*, 307.

Chapter 5

1. Knowles, *Separate Peace*, 196.

2. Snyder, *Myths of Empire*, esp. 17–19.

3. Mahan to Clark, 23 July 1909, in Seager and Maguire, *Mahan*, 3:307.

4. On the inertia of images, see Jervis, *Perception*.

5. Jackson to Hay, 5 Oct. 1901, M44:r94, NA.

6. On Brazil, see Burns, *Unwritten Alliance*; on Haiti, see Plummer, *Haiti*.

7. Assu, *Brazilian Colonization*.

8. Chamberlain, "Letter from Brazil," 821–31.

9. *Correio da Manha* (Rio), 30 Mar. 1903, encl. in Thompson to Hay, 16 Apr. 1903, RG 59, r70:v68, NA.

Bibliography

Manuscripts

Germany

Bonn

Auswärtiges Amt, Politische Abteilung
  Files of the Foreign Office:
    Argentina 1: General Affairs of Argentina
    Brazil 1: General Affairs of Brazil
    Brazil 3: Brazilian Military and Naval Affairs
    Brazil 11: Relations with Germany
    Germany 127: Political Affairs
    Germany 138: The Imperial Navy
    Haiti 1: General Affairs of Haiti
    Mexico 1: General Affairs of Mexico
    Mexico 14: Mexican Finances
    USA 1: General Affairs of USA
    Venezuela 1: General Affairs of Venezuela

Freiburg

Bundesarchiv-Militärarchiv
  RM 2: The Kaiser's Naval Cabinet
  RM 3: The Reichsmarineamt
  RM 5: The Admiralstab
  RM 38: Ships Logs
  N 253: Tirpitz Papers

Potsdam

Deutsches Zentralarchiv
  AA II: Files of the Foreign Office
    Emigration outside Europe
    Commercial Relations with South and Central America
    Consular Reports (Blumenau, Joinville, Itajahy)

Great Britain

Kew
Public Records Office
  Files of the Admiralty
    ADM 1 Admiralty and Secretariat Papers
    ADM 12 Military Affairs
    ADM 53 Ships Logs
    ADM 116 Secretary's Casebooks
  Files of the Cabinet
    CAB 37 Cabinet Memoranda
  Files of the Foreign Office
    FO 15 Guatemala
    FO 35 Haiti
    FO 80 Venezuela
    FO 371 Political
    FO 414 Mexico
    FO 420 Confidential Print
    FO 800 Papers
      Sir Edward Grey
      Lansdowne
      Frank Lascelles
      Cecil Spring-Rice
      Francis Villiers

London
British Museum
  Balfour Papers

United States

New Haven, Connecticut
Sterling Library, Yale University
  Edward M. House Papers

Newport, Rhode Island
Naval War College
  RG 8 Intelligence and Technological Archives
  RG 12 Student Problems and Solutions

Washington, D.C.
Library of Congress
  Josephus Daniels Papers
  George Dewey Papers
  John Hay Papers
  Philander C. Knox Papers
  Robert Lansing Papers
  Elihu Root Papers
  Charles Sperry Papers

Alfred Thayer Mahan Papers
Henry White Papers
Leonard Wood Papers
National Archives
RG 38 Records of the Office of the Chief of Naval Operations
RG 45 Naval Records Collection of the Office of Naval Records and Library
RG 59 General Records of the Department of State
RG 80 General Records of the Department of the Navy
RG 84 Records of Foreign Service Posts of the Department of State
RG 165 Records of the War Department General And Special Staffs
RG 225 Records of the Joint Army-Navy Board

Published Sources

Adams, William. "Strategy, Diplomacy, and Isthmian Canal Security, 1880–1917."
Ph.D. diss., Florida State University, 1974.
Anderson, Pauline. *The Background of Anti-English Feeling in Germany, 1890-1902.*
New York: Octagon, 1969.
Angermann, Erich. "Ein Wendepunkt in der Geschichte der Monroe-Doktrin und
der deutsch-amerikanischen Beziehungen: Die Venezuelakrise von 1902/03 im
Spiegel der amerikanischen Tagespresse." In *Jahrbuch Für Amerikastudien,* edited
by Walther Fischer, 3:22-58. Heidelberg: Carl Winter Universitätsverlag, 1958.
Ashley, Percy. *Modern Tariff History: Germany—United States—France.* 3d ed. New
York: E. P. Dutton and Co., 1926.
Assu, Jacaré. *Brazilian Colonization from an European Point of View.* London:
E. Stanford, 1873.
Backhaus, [no first name]. *Welche Aussichten bieten sich den Deutschen in Südamerika?*
Berlin, 1910.
Baecker, Thomas. *Die deutsche Mexikopolitik, 1913/1914.* Berlin: Colloquim, 1971.
———. "Blau gegen Schwarz. Der amerikanische Kriegsplan von 1913 für einen
deutsch-amerikanischen Krieg." *Marine-Rundschau* 69 (1972): 347-60.
———. "Los intereses militares del imperio alemán en México: 1913-1914." *Historia
Mexicana* 20, no. 3 (Jan.-Mar. 1972): 347-62.
———. "The Arms of the *Ypiranga*: The German Side." *Americas* 30 (1973): 1-17.
———. "Mahan über Deutschland." *Marine-Rundschau* 73 (Jan.-Feb. 1976): 10-19,
86-102.
Bailey, Thomas. "Dewey and the Germans at Manila Bay." *Hispanic American
Historical Review* 45 (Oct. 1939): 59-81.
———. *A Diplomatic History of the American People.* 10th ed. Englewood Cliffs, N.J.:
Prentice-Hall, 1980.
Balfour, Michael. *The Kaiser and His Times.* New York: Norton, 1964.
Ballod, Karl. "Die Bedeutung von Südbrasilien für die deutsche Kolonisation."
Jahrbuch für Gesetzgebung 23 (1899): 631-55.
Baum, Loretta. "German Political Designs with Reference to Brazil." *Hispanic
American Historical Review* 2 (Nov. 1919): 586-99.

Beale, Howard. *Theodore Roosevelt and the Rise of America to World Power.* Baltimore: Johns Hopkins Press, 1956.

Becker, Rudolf. *Deutsche Siedler in Rio Grande do Sul: Eine Geschichte der deutschen Einwanderung.* Ijuhy, Brazil: Loew, 1938.

Bemis, Samuel Flagg. *The Latin American Policy of the United States.* New York: Harcourt, Brace, 1943.

———. "Woodrow Wilson and Latin America." In Buehrig, *Wilson's Foreign Policy*, 105–40.

Benicke, Wolf. "Rio Grande do Sul 'Südbrasilien': Werden und Wesen eines südamerikanischen Kolonisationsraumes." Ph.D. diss., Munich, 1950.

Berghahn, Volker R. *Der Tirpitz-Plan: Genesis und Verfall einer innenpolitischen Krisenstrategie unter Wilhelm II.* Düsseldorf: Droste, 1971.

———. *Rüstung und Machtpolitik: Zur Anatomie des "Kalten Krieges" vor 1914.* Düsseldorf: Droste, 1973.

———. *Modern Germany: Society, Economy, and Politics in the Twentieth Century.* New York: Cambridge University Press, 1982.

Bethell, Leslie, ed. *The Cambridge History of Latin America.* Vols. 4–5. Cambridge: Cambridge University Press, 1986.

Bigelow, Poultney. "The German Press and the United States." *North American Review* 164 (Jan. 1897): 12–23.

Blackbourn, David. "The Politics of Demagogy in Imperial Germany." *Past and Present* 113 (Nov. 1986): 152–84.

Blaisdell, Lowell. "Henry Lane Wilson and the Overthrow of Madero." *Southwestern Social Science Quarterly* 43, no. 2 (Sept. 1962): 126–35.

Blancpain, Jean-Pierre. *Migrations et mémoire germaniques en Amérique Latine.* Strasbourg: Presses Universitaires de Strasbourg, 1994.

Blasier, Cole. "The United States and Madero." *Journal of Latin American Studies* 4, no. 2 (Nov. 1972): 207–310.

Bonsal, Stephen. "Greater Germany in South America." *North American Review* 176 (Jan. 1903): 58–67.

Bourne, Kenneth, and Carl Boyd. "Captain Mahan's 'War' with Great Britain." *Proceedings of the United States Naval Institute* 94, no. 7 (July 1968): 71–78.

Braisted, William. *The United States Navy in the Pacific, 1897-1909.* Austin: University of Texas Press, 1958.

Brands, H. W. *T.R.: The Last Romantic.* New York: BasicBooks, 1997.

Brooks, Sydney. "The Venezuelan Imbroglio." *Fortnightly Review* (Feb. 1903): 247–57.

Brown, Richard. "The German Acquisition of the Caroline Islands, 1898–99." In Moses and Kennedy, *Germany in the Pacific and Far East*, 137–55.

Brunn, Gerhard. *Deutschland und Brasilien (1889-1914).* Cologne: Böhlau, 1971.

Bryan, William Jennings, and Mary Baird Bryan. *The Memoirs of William Jennings Bryan.* Philadelphia: John C. Winston Co., 1925.

Buchenau, Jürgen. *In the Shadow of the Giant: The Making of Mexico's Central America Policy, 1876-1930.* Tuscaloosa: University of Alabama Press, 1996.

Buehrig, Edward, ed. *Wilson's Foreign Policy in Perspective.* Bloomington: Indiana University Press, 1957.

Bülow, Bernhard von. *Denkwürdigkeiten*. Berlin: Ullstein, 1930.

Burns, E. Bradford. *The Unwritten Alliance: Rio-Branco and Brazilian-American Relations*. New York: Columbia University Press, 1968.

Cain, P. J., and A. G. Hopkins. *British Imperialism: Innovation and Expansion, 1688-1914*. London: Longman, 1993.

Calhoun, Charles. "American Policy toward the Brazilian Naval Revolt of 1893-94: A Reexamination." *Diplomatic History* 4 (Winter 1980): 39-56.

Callcott, Wilfrid. *The Western Hemisphere*. Austin: University of Texas Press, 1968.

Calvert, Peter. *The Mexican Revolution, 1910-1914: The Diplomacy of Anglo-American Conflict*. Cambridge: Cambridge University Press, 1968.

Campbell, Charles. *Anglo-American Understanding, 1898-1903*. Westport, Conn.: Greenwood, 1980.

Canis, Konrad. *Von Bismarck zur Weltpolitik: Deutsche Aussenpolitik 1890 bis 1902*. Berlin: Akademie Verlag, 1997.

Cecil, Lamar. *Albert Ballin: Business and Politics in Imperial Germany, 1888-1918*. Princeton: Princeton University Press, 1967.

———. *Wilhelm II*. Vol. 1, *Prince and Emperor, 1859-1900*. Chapel Hill: University of North Carolina Press, 1989.

———. *Wilhelm II*. Vol. 2, *Emperor and Exile, 1900-1941*. Chapel Hill: University of North Carolina Press, 1996.

Centro de Estudos Sociais da Faculdade de Filosofia da Universidade Federal do Rio Grande do Sul. *I Colóquio de estudos teuto-brasileiros*. Pôrto Alegre, Brazil: Universidade Federal do Rio Grande do Sul, 1963.

Challener, Richard. *Admirals, Generals, and American Foreign Policy, 1898-1914*. Princeton: Princeton University Press, 1973.

Chamberlain, George. "Letter from Brazil." *Atlantic Monthly* (Dec. 1902): 821-31.

———. "Germany in Southern Brazil." *Independent* 56 (5 May 1904): 1016-22.

Cheny, Robert. *A Righteous Cause: The Life of William Jennings Bryan*. Boston: Little, Brown, 1987.

Chéradame, André. *The Pan German Plot Unmasked*. Translated by Lady Frazer. London: John Murray, 1916.

Chickering, Roger. "Patriotic Societies and German Foreign Policy, 1890-1914." *International History Review* 1, no. 4 (Oct. 1979): 470-89.

———. *We Men Who Feel Most German: A Cultural Study of the Pan-German League, 1886-1914*. Boston: Allen and Unwin, 1984.

Clements, Kendrick A. "Woodrow Wilson's Mexican Policy, 1913-15." *Diplomatic History* 4 (Spring 1980): 113-36.

———. *William Jennings Bryan: Missionary Isolationist*. Knoxville: University of Tennessee Press, 1982.

———. *The Presidency of Woodrow Wilson*. Lawrence: University Press of Kansas, 1992.

Clifford, John. "Admiral Dewey and the Germans, 1903: A New Perspective." *Mid-America* 49 (July 1967): 214-20.

Coetzee, Marilyn. *The German Army League: Popular Nationalism in Wilhelmine Germany*. New York: Oxford University Press, 1990.

Colby, Elbridge. "American Interests in the West Indies." *Proceedings of the United States Naval Institute* 57, no. 4 (Apr. 1931): 468–72.

El Colegio de México. *Estadisticas Económicas del Porfiriato, Comercio Exterior de México.* Mexico City: El Colegio de México, 1960.

Coletta, Paolo, ed. *American Secretaries of the Navy.* Vol. 1, *1775-1913.* Annapolis: Naval Institute Press, 1980.

Collin, Richard. *Theodore Roosevelt: Culture, Diplomacy, and Expansion: A New View of American Imperialism.* Baton Rouge: Louisiana State University Press, 1985.

———. *Theodore Roosevelt's Caribbean: The Panama Canal, the Monroe Doctrine, and the Latin American Context.* Baton Rouge: Louisiana State University Press, 1990.

Connell-Smith, Gordon. *The United States and Latin America.* New York: John Wiley and Sons, 1974.

Cooling, Benjamin. *Gray Steel and Blue Water Navy: The Formative Years of America's Military-Industrial Complex, 1881-1917.* Hamden, Conn.: Archon Books, 1979.

Costello, Daniel. "Planning for War: A History of the General Board of the Navy, 1900-1914." Ph.D. diss., Fletcher School of Law and Diplomacy, 1968.

Craig, Gordon A. *Germany, 1866-1945.* New York: Oxford University Press, 1978.

Crapol, Edward. "From Anglophobia to Fragile Rapprochement: Anglo-American Relations in the Early Twentieth Century." In Schröder, *Confrontation and Cooperation,* 13–32.

Crouse, Janet Kay Wellhousen. "The Decline of German-American Friendship: Beef, Pork, and Politics 1890-1906." Ph.D. diss., University of Delaware, 1980.

Da Costa, João Frank. *Joaquim Nabuco e a política exterior do Brasil.* Rio: Gráfica Récord Editôra, 1968.

Daniels, Josephus. *The Life of Woodrow Wilson.* Chicago: Will H. Johnston, 1924.

———. *The Cabinet Diaries of Josephus Daniels, 1913-1921.* Edited by David Cronon. Lincoln: University of Nebraska Press, 1963.

———. *The Wilson Era: Years of Peace—1910-1917.* Westport, Conn.: Greenwood, 1974.

Darius, Rudolf. *Die Entwicklung der deutsch-mexikanischen Handelsbeziehungen von 1870-1914.* Cologne: Kalk, 1927.

Davis, George. *A Navy Second to None: The Development of Modern American Naval Policy.* New York: Harcourt, Brace, 1940.

De Barros Basto, Fernando Lázaro. *Síntese da História da Imigração no Brasil.* Rio de Janeiro, 1970.

De Magalhães, Edgardo. "Germany and South America: A Brazilian View." *Nineteenth Century and After* 81 (Jan. 1917): 67–80.

Dewey, George. *Autobiography of George Dewey.* 1913. Annapolis: Naval Institute Press, 1987.

Diederichs, Otto von. "Darstellung der Vorgänge vor Manila von Mai bis August 1898." *Marine-Rundschau* 25 (Mar. 1914): 253–79.

Doerries, Reinhard. *Imperial Challenge: Ambassador Count Bernstorff and German-American Relations, 1908-1917.* Chapel Hill: University of North Carolina Press, 1989.

———. "Empire and Republic: German-American Relations before 1917." In Trommler and McVeigh, *America and the Germans,* 2:3–17.

Dorwart, Jeffery. *The Office of Naval Intelligence: The Birth of America's First Intelligence Agency, 1865-1918*. Annapolis: Naval Institute Press, 1979.

Dreher, William. "A Letter from Germany." *Atlantic Monthly* (Mar. 1903): 388-98; (Mar. 1904): 389-99.

Dülffler, Jost; Martin Kröger, and Rolf-Harald Wippich, eds. *Vermiedene Kriege: Deeskalation von Konflikten der Großmächte zwischen Krimkrieg und Erstem Weltkrieg, 1865-1914*. Munich: Oldenbourg, 1997.

Eckardstein, Hermann von. *Lebenserinnerungen und politische Denkwürdigkeiten*. 3 vols. Leipzig, 1919-21.

Edelsheim, Franz. *Operationen über See*. Berlin, 1901. Translated into English as *Germany's Naval Campaign against Great Britain and the United States (Operationen über See)*. Translated by Alexander Gray. London: Hodder and Stoughton, 1915.

Edsel, Carlos. *Cipriano Castro y Teodoro Roosevelt*. Distrito Sucre, Miranda: Comisión Centenario del Nacimiento de don Rómulo Gallegos, 1986.

Einstein, Lewis. "British Diplomacy in the Spanish-American War." *Massachusetts Historical Society Proceedings* 76 (1964): 30-54.

Eisenhower, John. *Intervention!: The United States and the Mexican Revolution, 1913-1917*. New York: Norton, 1993.

Eley, Geoff. "*Sammlungspolitik*: Social Imperialism and the Navy Law of 1898." *Militärgeschichtliche Mitteilungen* 15 (1974): 29-63.

———. *Reshaping the German Right: Radical Nationalism and Political Change after Bismarck*. New Haven: Yale University Press, 1980.

———. "Some Thoughts on the Nationalist Pressure Groups in Imperial Germany." In Kennedy and Nicholls, *Nationalist and Racialist Movements*, 40-67.

Esthus, Raymond. *Theodore Roosevelt and International Rivalries*. Claremont, Calif.: Regina Books, 1970.

Eversbusch, Wolfgang. "Die deutsche Mexiko-Schiffahrt." Ph.D. diss., Universität Berlin, 1941.

Feis, Herbert. *Europe, the World's Banker, 1870-1914: An Account of European Foreign Investment and the Connection of World Finance with Diplomacy before the War*. New Haven: Yale University Press, 1931.

Fesser, Gerd. *Reichskanzler Bernhard Fürst von Bülow*. Berlin: Deutscher Verlag der Wissenschaften, 1992.

Fiebig-von Hase, Ragnhild. *Lateinamerika als Konfliktherd der deutsch-amerikanischen Beziehungen 1890-1903*. 2 vols. Göttingen: Vandenhoeck and Ruprecht, 1986.

———. "Die deutsch-amerikanischen Wirtschaftsbeziehungen, 1890-1914." *Amerikastudien* 33 (1988): 329-57.

———. "Die Rolle Kaiser Wilhelm II. in den deutsch-amerikanischen Beziehungen, 1890-1914." In Röhl, *Der Ort*, 223-57.

———. "The United States and Germany in the World Arena, 1900-1917." In Schröder, *Confrontation and Cooperation*, 33-68.

———. "Großmachtkonflikte in der Westlichen Hemisphäre: Das Beispiel der Venezuelakrise vom Winter 1902/03." In Dülffler, *Vermiedene Kriege*, 527-78.

Fiebig-von Hase, Ragnhild, and Ursula Lehmkuhl, eds. *Enemy Images in American History*. Providence, R.I.: Berg, 1997.

Fischer, Fritz. *Griff nach der Weltmacht: Die Kriegszielpolitik des kaiserlichen Deutschland 1914/18.* Düsseldorf: Droste, 1961.

———. *Krieg der Illusionen: Die deutsche Politik von 1911 bis 1914.* Düsseldorf: Droste, 1969.

Fisk, George. "German-American Diplomatic and Commercial Relations, Historically Considered." *American Monthly Review of Reviews* 25 (Mar. 1902): 323-28.

———. "German American 'Most Favored Nation' Relations." *Journal of Political Economy* 2, no. 2 (Mar. 1903): 220-36.

Fiske, Bradley. "Naval Power." *Proceedings of the United States Naval Institute* 37, no. 3 (Sept. 1911): 683-736.

———. *From Midshipman to Rear-Admiral.* New York: Century Co., 1919.

Forbes, Ian. "German Commercial Relations with South America, 1890-1914." Ph.D. diss., University of Adelaide, 1975.

Forstmeier, Friedrich. "Deutsche Invasionspläne gegen die USA um 1900." *Marine-Rundschau* 68 (June 1971): 344-51.

Fouquet, Carlos. *Der deutsche Einwanderer und seine Nachkommen in Brasilien, 1808-1824-1974.* São Paulo: Instituto Hans Staden, 1974.

Friedberg, Aaron. *The Weary Titan: Britain and the Experience of Relative Decline, 1895-1905.* Princeton: Princeton University Press, 1988.

Funke, Alfred. *Deutsche Siedlung über See: Ein Abriss ihrer Geschichte und ihrer Gedeihen in Rio Grande do Sul.* Halle, 1902.

Gaillard, Roger. *La République exterminatrice, deuxième partie: L'Etat vassal (1896-1902).* Port-au-Prince: Roger Gaillard, 1988.

Ganz, A. Harding. "The German Navy in the Far East and Pacific: The seizure of Kiautschou and after." In Moses and Kennedy, *Germany in the Pacific and Far East,* 115-36.

Gardner, Lloyd. "Woodrow Wilson and the Mexican Revolution." In Link, *Revolutionary World,* 3-48.

———. *Safe for Democracy: The Anglo-American Response to Revolution, 1913-1923.* New York: Oxford University Press, 1987.

Gerard, James. *My Four Years in Germany.* New York: Grosset and Dunlap, 1917.

———. *Face to Face with Kaiserism.* New York: George H. Doran, 1918.

German Reichstag. *Stenographische Berichte über die Verhandlungen des Reichstages.* Berlin, 1890-1914.

Gignilliat, John. "Pigs, Politics, and Protection: The European Boycott of American Pork, 1879-1891." *Agricultural History* 35 (Jan. 1961): 3-12.

Gilderhus, Mark T. *Pan American Visions: Woodrow Wilson in the Western Hemisphere, 1913-1921.* Tucson: University of Arizona Press, 1986.

Gleich, Albrecht von. *Germany and Latin America.* Santa Monica, Calif.: Rand, 1968.

Gottschall, Terrell Dean. "Germany and the Spanish-American War: A Case Study of Navalism and Imperialism, 1898." Ph.D. diss., Washington State University, 1981.

Gould, Lewis. *The Presidency of Theodore Roosevelt.* Lawrence: University Press of Kansas, 1991.

Graham, G. *The Politics of Naval Supremacy.* Cambridge: Cambridge University Press, 1965.

Graham, Richard. *Great Britain and the Onset of Modernization in Brazil, 1850-1914.* Cambridge: Cambridge University Press, 1968.

Grenville, J. A. S. "Great Britain and the Isthmian Canal, 1898-1901." *American Historical Review* 60 (Oct. 1955): 48-69.

———. "Diplomacy and War Plans in the United States, 1890-1917." *Transactions of the Royal Historical Society*, 5th ser., no. 11 (1961): 1-21.

Grenville, J. A. S., and G. B. Young. *Politics, Strategy, and American Diplomacy: Studies in American Foreign Policy, 1873-1917.* New Haven: Yale University Press, 1966.

Grieb, Kenneth J. *The United States and Huerta.* Lincoln: University of Nebraska Press, 1969.

Guthrie, Wayne. "The Anglo-German Intervention in Venezuela, 1902-3." Ph.D. diss., University of California, San Diego, 1983.

Healy, David. *Drive to Hegemony: The United States in the Caribbean, 1898-1917.* Madison: University of Wisconsin Press, 1988.

Heckscher, August. *Woodrow Wilson: A Biography.* New York: Scribner's, 1991.

Hell, Jürgen. "Der Griff nach Südbrasilien: Die Politik des Deutschen Reiches zur Verwandlung der drei brasilianischen Südstaaten in ein überseeisches Neudeutschland (1890 bis 1914)." Ph.D. diss., Universität Rostock, 1966.

———. "Das 'südbrasilianische Neudeutschland': Der annexationistische Grundzug der wilhelminischen und nazistischen Brasilienpolitik (1895 bis 1938)." In *Der deutsche Faschismus in Lateinamerika, 1933-1943*, 103-10. Berlin: Humboldt-Universität zu Berlin, 1966.

Hendrick, Burton. *The Life and Letters of Walter H. Page.* New York: Doubleday, Page and Co., 1924.

Herwig, Holger. *The German Naval Officer Corps: A Social and Political History, 1890-1918.* Oxford: Clarendon Press, 1973.

———. *The Politics of Frustration: The United States in German Naval Planning, 1889-1941.* Boston: Little, Brown, 1976.

———. *Germany's Vision of Empire in Venezuela, 1871-1914.* Princeton: Princeton University Press, 1986.

Herwig, Holger, and J. León Helguera. *Alemania y el bloqueo internacional de Venezuela, 1902/03.* Caracas: Ministerio de Relaciones Exteriores/Editorial Arte, 1977.

Herwig, Holger, and David Trask. "Naval Operations Plans between Germany and the United States of America, 1898-1913: A Study of Strategic Planning in the Age of Imperialism." *Militärgeschichtliche Mitteilungen* 2 (1970): 5-32.

Hildebrand, Klaus. *Das vergangene Reich. Deutsche Aussenpolitik von Bismarck bis Hitler, 1871-1945.* Stuttgart: Deutsche Verlags-Anstalt, 1995.

Hill, Larry. *Emissaries to a Revolution: Woodrow Wilson's Executive Agents in Mexico.* Baton Rouge: Louisiana State University Press, 1973.

Hillgruber, Andreas. "Zwischen Hegemonie und Weltpolitik." In Stürmer, *Das kaiserliche Deutschland*, 187-204.

Holbo, Paul. "Perilous Obscurity: Public Diplomacy and the Press in the Venezuelan Crisis, 1902-1903." *Historian* 32 (May 1970): 428-48.

Holborn, Hajo. *A History of Modern Germany, 1840-1945*. Princeton: Princeton University Press, 1969.

Hoy, Suellen, and Walter Nugent. "Public Health or Protectionism? The German-American Pork War, 1880-1891." *Bulletin of the History of Medicine* 63 (1989): 198-224.

Hubatsch, Walther. *Der Admiralstab und die obersten Marinebehörden in Deutschland, 1848-1945*. Frankfurt: Verlag für Wehrwesen Berard und Graefe, 1958.

Hull, Isabel. *The Entourage of Kaiser Wilhelm II, 1888-1918*. New York: Cambridge University Press, 1982.

Hutchinson, Lincoln. "Results of Reciprocity with Brazil." *Political Science Quarterly* 18, no. 2 (1903): 282-312.

Ide, Henry. "Our Interest in Samoa." *North American Review* 165 (Aug. 1897): 167.

Isaacs, Asher. *International Trade: Tariff and Commercial Policies*. Chicago: Richard D. Irwin, 1948.

Jervis, Robert. *Perception and Misperception in International Politics*. Princeton: Princeton University Press, 1976.

Joffily, José. *O Caso Panther*. Rio de Janeiro: Paz e Terra, 1988.

Johnson, Robert Underwood. *Remembered Yesterdays*. Boston: Little, Brown, 1923.

Jonas, Manfred. *The United States and Germany: A Diplomatic History*. Ithaca, N.Y.: Cornell University Press, 1984.

Jordan, Gerald, ed. *Naval Warfare in the Twentieth Century, 1900-1945*. New York: Crane Russak, 1977.

Jordan, Terry. "Aspects of German Colonization in Southern Brazil." *Southwestern Social Science Quarterly* 42, no. 4 (Mar. 1962): 346-53.

Junior, Junius. "A Letter to Uncle Sam." *Atlantic Monthly* (Feb. 1912): 172-79.

Kaikkonen, Olli. *Deutschland und die Expansionspolitik der USA in den 90er Jahren des 19. Jahrhunderts*. Jyväskyla, Finland: Jyväskylan Yliopisto, 1980.

Kapff-Cannstatt, E. "The New Immigration Law and the Political Situation in South Brazil." *Export* 17, no. 50 (12 Dec. 1895): 697.

Katz, Friedrich. "Hamburger Schiffahrt nach Mexiko, 1870-1914." *Hanseatische Geschichtsblätter*, special ed., 83 (1965): 139-50.

―――. *The Secret War in Mexico: Europe, the United States, and the Mexican Revolution*. Chicago: University of Chicago Press, 1981.

―――. "Mexico: Restored Republic and Porfiriato." In Bethell, *Cambridge History of Latin America*, 5:3-78.

Kaufman, Burton. "United States Trade and Latin America: The Wilson Years." *Journal of American History* 58 (1971-72): 342-63.

Kaulisch, Baldur. *Alfred von Tirpitz und die imperialistische Flottenrüstung: Eine politische Biographie*. Berlin: Militärverlag der Deutschen Demokratischen Republik, 1982.

Kehr, Eckart. *Schlachtflottenbau und Parteipolitik 1894-1901: Versuch eines Querschnitts durch die innenpolitischen, sozialen und ideologischen Voraussetzungen des deutschen Imperialismus*. Berlin: E. Ebering, 1930.

―――. *Der Primat der Innenpolitik*. Berlin: de Gruyter, 1965.

Keim, Jeanette. *Forty Years of German-American Relations*. Philadelphia: William J. Dornan, 1919.

Kennedy, Paul. "Tirpitz, England, and the Second Navy Law of 1900: A Strategical Critique." *Militärgeschichtliche Mitteilungen* 11 (1970): 33–57.

———. "German World Policy and the Alliance Negotiations with England, 1897–1900." *Journal of Modern History* 495 (Dec. 1973): 606–25.

———. *The Samoan Tangle: A Study in Anglo-German Relations, 1878–1900.* New York: Barnes and Noble, 1974.

———. "Germany and the Samoan Tridominium, 1889–98: A Study in Frustrated Imperialism." In Moses and Kennedy, *Germany in the Pacific and Far East*, 89–114.

———. "Fischer and Tirpitz: Political Admirals in the Age of Imperialism." In Jordan, *Naval Warfare*, 45–59.

———. *The Rise of Anglo-German Antagonism, 1860–1914.* London: Allen and Unwin, 1980.

———. "The Kaiser and German *Weltpolitik*." In Röhl and Sombart, *Kaiser Wilhelm II*, 143–68.

———, ed. *The War Plans of the Great Powers, 1880–1914.* Boston: Unwin Hyman, 1979.

Kennedy, Paul, and Anthony Nicholls, eds. *Nationalist and Racialist Movements in Britain and Germany before 1914.* London: Macmillan, 1981.

Kneer, Warren. *Great Britain and the Caribbean, 1901–1913: A Study in Anglo-American Relations.* East Lansing: Michigan State University Press, 1975.

Knight, Alan. *The Mexican Revolution.* 2 vols. Cambridge: Cambridge University Press, 1986.

Knight, Melvin. *The Americans in Santo Domingo.* New York: Vanguard Press, 1928.

Knowles, John. *A Separate Peace.* New York: Bantam, 1959.

Kohut, Thomas. *Wilhelm II and the Germans: A Study in Leadership.* New York: Oxford University Press, 1991.

Koss, Stephen. *The Rise and Fall of the Political Press in Britain.* London: Fontana, 1981.

Krauze, Enrique. *Mexico: Biography of Power: A History of Modern Mexico, 1810–1996.* Translated by Hank Heifetz. New York: HarperCollins, 1997.

Kruck, Alfred. *Geschichte des Alldeutschen Verbandes, 1890–1939.* Wiesbaden: Franz Steiner, 1954.

LaFeber, Walter. "United States Depression Diplomacy and the Brazilian Revolution, 1893–1894." *Hispanic American Historical Review* 40 (Feb. 1960): 107–18.

———. *The New Empire: An Interpretation of American Expansion, 1860–1898.* Ithaca, N.Y.: Cornell University Press, 1963.

———. "The 'Lion in the Path': The U.S. Emergence as a World Power." *Political Science Quarterly* 101, no. 5 (1986): 705–18.

Lambi, Ivo. *The Navy and German Power Politics, 1862–1914.* Boston: Allen and Unwin, 1984.

Lammersdorf, Raimund. "The Advantages of Cooperation." In Schröder, *Confrontation and Cooperation*, 87–92.

———. "Amerika und der Kaiser." *Amerikastudien* 31 (1986): 295–302.

———. *Anfänge einer Weltmacht: Theodore Roosevelt und die transatlantischen Beziehungen der USA, 1901–1909.* Berlin: Akademie Verlag, 1994.

Langer, William. "A Farewell to Empire." *Foreign Affairs* 41 (Oct. 1922): 115–30.

———. *The Diplomacy of Imperialism, 1890–1902*. 1935. New York: Knopf, 1950.

Langley, Lester. *The Banana Wars*. Chicago: Dorsey Press, 1988.

Lansing, Robert. "Drama of the Virgin Islands Purchase." *New York Times Magazine*, 19 July 1931, 4–5.

Laves, Walter. "German Governmental Influence on Foreign Investments, 1871–1915." *Political Science Quarterly* 43 (1928): 498–519.

Lee, A. J. *The Origins of the Popular Press*. London: Croom Helm, 1976.

Lepsius, Johannes, et al., eds. *Die grosse Politik der europäischen Kabinette, 1871–1914*. Vol. 15. Berlin: Deutsche Verlagsgesellschaft für Politik und Geschichte, 1924.

Lerman, Katharine. *The Chancellor as Courtier: Bernhard von Bülow and the Governance of Germany, 1900–1909*. Cambridge: Cambridge University Press, 1990.

Leupolt, Erich. *Die Aussenpolitik in den bedeutendsten politischen Zeitschriften Deutschlands, 1890–1909*. Leipzig: Reinicke, 1933.

Link, Arthur. *Wilson: The New Freedom*. Princeton: Princeton University Press, 1956.

———. "The Higher Realism of Woodrow Wilson." *Journal of Presbyterian History* 41 (Mar. 1963): 1–13.

———, ed. *The Papers of Woodrow Wilson*. 69 vols. Princeton: Princeton University Press, 1966–94.

———, ed. *Woodrow Wilson and a Revolutionary World*. Chapel Hill: University of North Carolina Press, 1982.

Livermore, Seward. "Battleship Diplomacy in South America: 1905–1925." *Journal of Modern History* 16 (Mar. 1944): 31–48.

———. "Theodore Roosevelt, the American Navy, and the Venezuelan Crisis of 1902–1903." *American Historical Review* 51 (Apr. 1946): 452–71.

———. "The American Navy as a Factor in World Politics, 1903–1913." *American Historical Review* 63 (July 1958): 863–79.

Livezey, William. *Mahan on Sea Power*. Norman: University of Oklahoma Press, 1947.

Lodge, Henry Cabot. "England, Venezuela, and the Monroe Doctrine." *North American Review* 160 (June 1895): 651–58.

———, ed. *Selections from the Correspondence of Theodore Roosevelt and Henry Cabot Lodge, 1884–1918*. 2 vols. New York: Scribner's, 1925.

Love, Joseph. *Rio Grande do Sul and Brazilian Regionalism, 1882–1930*. Stanford: Stanford University Press, 1971.

Luebke, Frederick. "A Prelude to Conflict: The German Ethnic Group in Brazil, 1890–1917." *Ethnic and Racial Studies* 6, no. 1 (Jan. 1983): 1–17.

———. *Germans in Brazil: A Comparative History of Cultural Conflict during World War I*. Baton Rouge: University of Louisiana Press, 1987.

———. *Germans in the New World*. Urbana: University of Illinois Press, 1990.

McHugh, Francis. *Fundamentals of War Gaming*. 3d ed. Newport, R.I.: Naval War College Press, 1966.

MacKintosh, C. N. "German Aims in Southern Brazil." *South American* 6 (Nov. 1917): 21–22.

Mahan, Alfred Thayer. *The Influence of Sea Power upon History, 1660–1783*. Boston: Little, Brown, 1890.

————. *From Sail to Steam: Recollections of Naval Life*. New York: Harper and Brothers, 1907.

Manchester, Alan. *British Preëminence in Brazil: Its Rise and Decline*. Chapel Hill: University of North Carolina Press, 1933.

Marks, Frederick. *Velvet on Iron: The Diplomacy of Theodore Roosevelt*. Lincoln: University of Nebraska Press, 1979.

Marvin, Winthrop L. "America in Foreign Trade." *American Monthly Review of Reviews* 32 (Dec. 1905): 715–17.

Maurer, John. "American Naval Concentration and the German Battle Fleet, 1900–1918." *Journal of Strategic Studies* 6 (June 1983): 147–81.

Messages and Papers of the Presidents. Compiled by James D. Richardson. Vol. 12. Washington: Government Printing Office, 1896.

Meuriot, Paul. "Un nouvel essai de nouvelle colonization au Brésil." *Les Annales Coloniales* (Paris), 15 Apr. 1905.

Meriwether, Walter. "Our Navy and Germany's." *Munsey's Magazine* (Mar. 1901): 856–73.

Meyer, Michael. "The Mexican-German Conspiracy of 1915." *Americas* 23 (July 1966): 76–89.

————. "The Arms of the *Ypiranga*." *Hispanic American Historical Review* 50 (Aug. 1970): 546–51.

Moeller, Robert. "The Kaiserreich Recast?" *Journal of Social History* 17 (Summer 1984): 655–83.

Monger, George. *The End of Isolation: British Foreign Policy, 1900–1907*. London: T. Nelson, 1963.

Morison, Elting, ed. *The Letters of Theodore Roosevelt*. 8 vols. Cambridge: Harvard University Press, 1951–54.

Morison, Samuel Eliot, and Henry Steele Commager. *The Growth of the American Republic*. New York: Oxford University Press, 1937.

Morris, Edmund. " 'A Few Pregnant Days': Theodore Roosevelt and the Venezuelan Crisis of 1902." *Theodore Roosevelt Association Journal* (Winter 1989): 2–13, 37–54.

Moses, John A., and Paul M. Kennedy, eds. *Germany in the Pacific and Far East, 1870–1914*. St. Lucia, Australia: University of Queensland Press, 1977.

Müller, Hugo. *Die Deutsche im brasilianischen Urwald*. Stuttgart, 1883.

Munro, Dana. *Intervention and Dollar Diplomacy in the Caribbean, 1900–1921*. Princeton: Princeton University Press, 1964.

Münsterberg, Hugo. *The Americans*. Translated by Edwin B. Holt. New York: McClure, Philips and Co., 1904.

Nabuco, Carolina. *The Life of Joaquim Nabuco*. Translated and edited by Ronald Hilton. Stanford: Stanford University Press, 1950.

Nordholt, Jan. *Woodrow Wilson: A Life for World Peace*. Translated by Herbert Rowan. Berkeley: University of California Press, 1991.

Nørregaard, Georg. *Vore Gamle Tropekolonier*. Vol. 4, *Dansk Vestindien, 1880–1917*. Copenhagen: Fremad, 1966.

Nunn, Frederick. *Yesterday's Soldiers: European Military Professionalism in South America, 1890–1940*. Lincoln: University of Nebraska Press, 1983.

Offner, John. *An Unwanted War: The Diplomacy of the United States and Spain over Cuba, 1895-1898*. Chapel Hill: University of North Carolina Press, 1992.

Ogg, Frederic. "German Interests and Tendencies in South America." *World's Work* 5, no. 5 (Mar. 1903): 3169–70.

O'Shaughnessy, Edith. *A Diplomat's Wife in Mexico*. New York: Harper and Brothers, 1916.

———. *Intimate Pages of Mexican History*. New York: George H. Doran Co., 1920.

Parsons, Edward. "The German-American Crisis of 1902-1903." *Historian* 33 (May 1971): 436–52.

Perkins, Dexter. *A History of the Monroe Doctrine*. Boston: Little, Brown, 1941.

Pierard, Richard. "The German Colonial Society, 1882-1916." Ph.D. diss., State University of Iowa, 1964.

Pflanze, Otto. *Bismarck and the Development of Germany*. Vol. 2, *The Period of Consolidation, 1871-1880*. Princeton: Princeton University Press, 1963.

———. *Bismarck and the Development of Germany*. Vol. 3, *The Period of Fortification, 1880-1898*. Princeton: Princeton University Press, 1990.

Platt, Desmond. *Latin America and British Trade, 1806-1914*. New York: Harper and Row, 1972.

Pletcher, David. "Reciprocity and Latin America in the Early 1890s: A Foretaste of Dollar Diplomacy." *Pacific Historical Review* 47, no. 1 (Feb. 1978): 53–88.

Plummer, Brenda. *Haiti and the Great Powers, 1902-1915*. Baton Rouge: Louisiana State University Press, 1988.

Lt. Pohl. "Die Tätigkeit S.M.S. *Irene* in den Gewassern der Philippinen, 1896 bis 1899." *Marine-Rundschau* 7 (July–Dec. 1902): 760–62.

Pommerin, Reiner. *Der Kaiser und Amerika: Die USA in der Politik der Reichsleitung, 1890-1917*. Cologne: Böhlau, 1986.

———. *Quellen zu der deutsch-amerikanischen Beziehungen, 1776-1917*. Darmstadt: Droste, 1996.

Pringle, Henry. *Theodore Roosevelt*. New York: Harcourt, Brace, 1931.

Quirk, Robert E. *An Affair of Honor: Woodrow Wilson and the Occupation of Veracruz*. New York: Norton, 1962.

Rausch, George. "The Exile and Death of Victoriano Huerta." *Hispanic American Historical Review* 42 (May 1962): 133–51.

Reid, Wemyss. "Last Month." *Nineteenth Century and After* 53 (Jan. 1903): 145.

Ricard, Serge. *Théodore Roosevelt: Principes et pratique d'une politique étrangère*. Aix-en-Provence: Université de Provence, 1991.

Ricard, Serge, and James Bolner, eds. *La République impérialiste: L'expansionisme et la politique extérieure des États-Unis, 1885-1909*. Aix-en-Provence: Université de Provence, 1987.

Rich, Norman, and M. H. Fisher, eds. *The Holstein Papers*. Vol. 4, *Correspondence, 1897-1909*. Cambridge: Cambridge University Press, 1963.

Rippy, Fred. "The European Powers and the Spanish-American War." *James Sprunt Studies in History* 19 (1927): 22–52.

———. "German Investments in Latin America." *Journal of Business of the University of Chicago* 21 (Apr. 1948): 63–82.

Roche, Jean. *La colonisation allemande et le Rio Grande do Sul.* Paris: Institut des Hautes Etudes de l'Amérique Latine, 1959.

Rodríguez Campos, Manuel. *Venezuela, 1902: La crísis fiscal y el bloqueo.* Caracas: Ediciones de la Facultad de Humanidades y Educación, Universidad Central de Venezuela, 1977.

Röhl, John. *Germany without Bismarck: The Crisis of Government in the Second Reich, 1890-1900.* Berkeley: University of California Press, 1967.

————. "The Emperor's New Clothes: A Character Sketch of Kaiser Wilhelm II." In Röhl and Sombart, *Kaiser Wilhelm II,* 23-62.

————, ed. *Der Ort Kaiser Wilhelms II. in der deutschen Geschichte.* Munich: R. Oldenbourg, 1991.

————. *Wilhelm II: Die Jugend des Kaisers, 1859-1888.* Munich: C. H. Beck, 1993.

————. *The Kaiser and His Court: Wilhelm II and the Government of Germany.* Translated by Terence Cole. New York: Cambridge University Press, 1994.

Röhl, John, and Nicolaus Sombart, eds. *Kaiser Wilhelm II: New Interpretations.* Cambridge: Cambridge University Press, 1982.

Roosevelt, Theodore. *Selections from the Correspondence of Theodore Roosevelt and Henry Cabot Lodge, 1884-1918.* 2 vols. New York: Scribner's, 1925.

Rosenberg, Emily. "Anglo-American Economic Rivalry in Brazil during World War I." *Diplomatic History* 2 (Spring 1978): 131-52.

————. *Spreading the American Dream: American Economic and Cultural Expansion, 1890-1945.* New York: Hill and Wang, 1982.

Ryden, George. *The Foreign Policy of the United States in Relation to Samoa.* 1933. New York: Octagon Books, 1975.

Sandos, James. "German Involvement in Northern Mexico, 1915-1916." *Hispanic American Historical Review* 50 (Feb. 1970): 70-88.

Sartorius von Waltershausen, August. *Schriften der Centralstelle für Vorbereitung von Handelsverträgen. II Heft: Deutschland und die Handelspolitik der Vereinigten Staaten von Amerika.* Berlin: Siemenroth and Troschel, 1898.

Schieber, Clara. *The Transformation of American Sentiment toward Germany, 1870-1914.* New York: Russell and Russell, 1923.

Schierbrand, Wolf von. "Our Tariff Differences with Germany." *American Monthly Review of Reviews* 32 (Aug. 1905): 205-7.

Schiff, Warren. "German Military Penetration into Mexico during the Late Diaz Period." *Hispanic American Historical Review* 39 (Nov. 1959): 568-79.

Schilling, Warner. "Admirals and Foreign Policy, 1913-1919." Ph.D. diss., Yale University, 1913.

Scholes, Walter, and Marie Scholes. "Wilson, Grey, and Huerta." *Pacific Historical Review* 37, no. 2 (May 1968): 151-58.

Schoonover, Thomas. *The United States in Central America, 1860-1911: Episodes of Social Imperialism and Imperial Rivalry in the World System.* Durham, N.C.: Duke University Press, 1991.

Schoultz, Lars. *Beneath the United States: A History of U.S. Policy toward Latin America.* Cambridge: Harvard University Press, 1998.

Schröder, Hans-Jurgen. "Twentieth-Century German-American Relations:

Historiography and Research Perspectives." In Trommler and McVeigh, *America and the Germans*, 147–67.

———, ed. *Confrontation and Cooperation: Germany and the United States in the Era of World War I, 1900–1924*. Providence, R.I.: Berg, 1993.

Schulte Nordholt, Jan Willem. *Woodrow Wilson: A Life for World Peace*. Translated by Herbert Rowan. Berkeley: University of California Press, 1991.

Seager, Robert. *Alfred Thayer Mahan: The Man and His Letters*. Annapolis: Naval Institute Press, 1977.

Seager, Robert, and Doris Maguire, eds. *The Letters and Papers of Alfred Thayer Mahan*. 3 vols. Annapolis: Naval Institute Press, 1975.

Sellin, A. W. "Indians in the Hansa Colony." *Export* 23, no. 34 (22 Aug. 1901): 472–74.

———. "Germany's Interests in Southern Brazil." *Amerika* (Dec. 1906).

Seymour, Charles. *The Intimate Papers of Colonel House*. Boston: Houghton Mifflin, 1926.

Shippee, L. B. "Germany and the Spanish-American War." *American Historical Review* 30 (July 1925): 754–77.

Shufeldt, Robert. *The Relation of the Navy to the Commerce of the United States*. Washington, D.C.: J. L. Ginck, 1878.

Small, Melvin. "The United States and the German 'Threat' to the Hemisphere." *Americas* 28 (Jan. 1972): 252–70.

Smith, Joseph. "Britain and the Brazilian Naval Revolt of 1893–4." *Journal of Latin American Studies* 2 (Nov. 1970): 175–98.

———. *Illusions of Conflict: Anglo-American Diplomacy toward Latin America, 1865–1896*. Pittsburgh: University of Pittsburgh Press, 1979.

———. *Unequal Giants: Diplomatic Relations between the United States and Brazil, 1889–1930*. Pittsburgh: University of Pittsburgh Press, 1991.

Smith, Robert. *The United States and Revolutionary Nationalism in Mexico, 1916–1932*. Chicago: University of Chicago Press, 1972.

———. "Latin America, the United States, and the European Powers, 1830–1930." In Bethell, *Cambridge History of Latin America*, 3:27–52.

Snyder, Jack. *Myths of Empire: Domestic Politics and Imperial Ambition*. Ithaca, N.Y.: Cornell University Press, 1991.

Snyder, Louis. "The American-German Pork Dispute, 1879–1891." *Journal of Modern History* 17 (1945): 16–28.

———. *Roots of German Nationalism*. 1978. New York: Barnes and Noble, 1996.

Sondhaus, Lawrence. *Preparing for Weltpolitik: German Sea Power before the Tirpitz Era*. Annapolis: Naval Institute Press, 1997.

Spector, Ronald. "Roosevelt, the Navy, and the Venezuela Controversy: 1902–1903." *American Neptune* 32 (Oct. 1972): 259–63.

———. *Admiral of the New Empire: The Life and Career of George Dewey*. Baton Rouge: Louisiana State University Press, 1974.

———. *Professors of War: The Naval War College and the Development of the Naval Profession*. Newport, R.I.: Naval War College Press, 1977.

Speeches Incident to the Visit of Secretary Root to South America. Washington: Government Printing Office, 1906.

Sprout, Harold, and Margaret Sprout. *The Rise of American Naval Power*. Princeton: Princeton University Press, 1942.

Sprout, Margaret. "Mahan: Evangelist of Sea Power." In *Makers of Modern Strategy: Military Thought from Macchiavelli to Hitler*, edited by Edward Earle, 415–45. Princeton: Princeton University Press, 1943.

Stallings, Barbara. *Banker to the Third World: U.S. Portfolio Investment in Latin America, 1900–1986*. Berkeley: University of California Press, 1987.

Steinberg, Jonathan. *Yesterday's Deterrent: Tirpitz and the Birth of the German Battle Fleet*. London: Macmillan, 1965.

———. "A German Plan for the Invasion of Holland and Belgium, 1897." In Kennedy, *War Plans*, 155–70.

Steiner, Zara. *The Foreign Office and Foreign Policy, 1898–1914*. London: Ashfield, 1969.

Stephenson, George. *John Lind of Minnesota*. Minneapolis: University of Minnesota Press, 1935.

Sternburg, Herman Speck von. "The Phantom Peril of German Emigration and South American Settlements." *North American Review* 182 (May 1906): 641–50.

Stolberg-Wernigerode, Otto. *Germany and the United States during the Era of Bismarck*. Reading, Pa.: Henry Janssen Foundation, 1937.

Stone, N. I. "How the Germans Revised Their Tariff." *American Monthly Review of Reviews* 32 (Dec. 1905): 719–21.

———. "The International Aspect of Our Tariff Situation." *North American Review* 180 (Mar. 1905): 381–93.

———. "The New German Customs Tariff." *North American Review* 181 (Sept. 1905): 392–406.

———. "Most Favored Nation Relations between Germany and the United States." *North American Review* 182 (Mar. 1906): 433–45.

Stürmer, Michael, ed. *Das kaiserliche Deutschland*. Darmstadt: Droste, 1976.

Sudhaus, Fritz. *Deutschland und die Auswanderung nach Brasilien im 19. Jahrhundert*. Hamburg: H. Christians, 1940.

Sullivan, William. "The Rise of Despotism in Venezuela: Cipriano Castro, 1899–1908." Ph.D. diss., University of New Mexico, 1974.

Tansill, Charles. *The Purchase of the Danish West Indies*. Baltimore: Johns Hopkins Press, 1932.

Taylor, A. J. P. *The Course of German History*. London: Harry Hamilton, 1946.

Taylor, Henry. "The Study of War." *North American Review* 162 (Feb. 1896): 181–89.

———. "The Fleet." *Proceedings of the United States Naval Institute* 29, no. 4 (Dec. 1903): 52–87.

Taussig, F. W. *The Tariff History of the United States*. 8th ed. New York: Augustus M. Kelley, 1967.

Teitelbaum, Louis. *Woodrow Wilson and the Mexican Revolution, 1913–1916*. New York: Exposition, 1967.

Terrill, Tom. *The Tariff, Politics, and American Foreign Policy, 1874–1901*. Westport, Conn.: Greenwood, 1973.

Tilchin, William. *Theodore Roosevelt and the British Empire: A Study in Presidential Statecraft*. New York: St. Martin's, 1997.

Tirpitz, Alfred von. *Erinnerungen*. Leipzig: K. F. Koehler, 1919.

Tonnelat, Ernest. *L'expansion allemande hors d'Europe*. Paris: A. Colin, 1908.

Trommler, Frank. "Inventing the Enemy: German-American Cultural Relations, 1900–1917." In Schröder, *Confrontation and Cooperation*, 99–125.

Trommler, Frank, and Joseph McVeigh, eds. *America and the Germans: An Assessment of a Three-Hundred-Year History*. Vol. 2, *The Relationship in the Twentieth Century*. Philadelphia: University of Pennsylvania Press, 1985.

Tuchman, Barbara. *The Zimmermann Telegram*. New York: Ballantine, 1966.

Turk, Richard. *The Ambiguous Relationship: Theodore Roosevelt and Alfred Thayer Mahan*. Westport, Conn.: Greenwood, 1987.

Turlington, Edgar. *Mexico and Her Foreign Creditors*. New York: Columbia University Press, 1930.

U.S. Department of State. *Papers Relating to the Foreign Relations of the United States*. Washington: Government Printing Office, 1880–1914.

Usher, Roland. *Pan-Germanism*. Boston: Houghton Mifflin, 1913.

Vagts, Alfred. *Deutschland und die Vereinigten Staaten in der Weltpolitik*. 2 vols. New York: Macmillan, 1935.

———. "Hopes and Fears of an American-German War, 1870–1915." *Political Science Quarterly* 54, no. 4 (1939): 514–35, and 55, no. 1 (1940): 53–76.

Vernassa, Maurizio. *Emigrazione, diplomazia e cannoniere: L'intervento italiano in Venezuela (1902-1903)*. Leghorn, Italy: Stella, 1980.

"Vigilans sed Aequus" [pseud. of William Thomas Arnold]. *German Ambitions As They Affect Britain and the United States of America*. New York: G. P. Putnam's Sons, 1908.

Wagner, Adolf. "Germany and Pan-Germany." *Contemporary Review* 84 (Aug. 1903): 173–88.

———. *The Pan-Germanic Doctrine: Being a Study of German Political Aims and Aspirations*. London: Harper and Brothers, 1904.

Waibel, Leo. "European Colonization in Southern Brazil." *Geographical Review* 40 (Oct. 1950): 529–47.

Wainwright, Richard. "The General Board: A Sketch." *Proceedings of the United States Naval Institute* 48, no. 2 (Feb. 1922): 189–201.

Webb, Steven. "Agricultural Protection in Wilhelminian Germany: Forging an Empire with Pork and Rye." *Journal of Economic History* 42, no. 2 (June 1982): 309–26.

Wehler, Hans-Ulrich. *The German Empire, 1871-1918*. Leamington Spa, U.K.: Berg, 1985.

Wendlandt, Wilhelm. "A German View of the American Peril." *North American Review* 174 (Apr. 1902): 555–64.

White, Andrew. *Autobiography of Andrew Dickson White*. New York: Century, 1905.

Wile, Frederic. "German Colonisation in Brazil." *Fortnightly Review* 79 (Jan. 1906): 129–38.

Willems, Emilio. *Assimilação e populações marginais no Brasil*. São Paulo: Companhia Editora Nacional, 1940.

———. *A aculturação dos alemães no Brasil: Estudo antropologico dos imigrantes alemães e seus descendentes no Brasil*. São Paulo: Companhia Editora Nacional, 1946.

Williams, William A. *The Tragedy of American Diplomacy*. Cleveland: World Publishing Co., 1959.

———. *The Contours of American History*. Cleveland: World Publishing Co., 1961.

———. *Empire as a Way of Life*. New York: Oxford University Press, 1980.

Wilson, Henry Lane. *Diplomatic Episodes in Mexico, Belgium, and Chile*. 1927. Port Washington, N.Y.: Kennikat Press, 1971.

Wilson, H. W. "The New German Navy." *Harper's Monthly Magazine* 103 (Sept. 1901): 529–36.

Winzen, Peter. *Bülows Weltmachtkonzept, Untersuchungen zur Frühphase seiner Aussenpolitik 1897–1901*. Boppard-am-Rhein: Boldt, 1977.

Wolman, Paul. *Most Favored Nation: The Republican Revisionists and U.S. Tariff Policy, 1897–1912*. Chapel Hill: University of North Carolina Press, 1992.

Yerxa, Donald. *Admirals and Empire: The United States Navy and the Caribbean, 1898–1945*. Columbia: University of South Carolina Press, 1991.

Index

Dresden (German navy), 200
Dresdner Bank, 173

Edelsheim, Franz von, 46
Edward VII (king of England), 73, 97, 99, 100
England: in Western hemisphere, 6, 41, 64–65, 211, 221, 223; and U.S.-German trade, 12, 19, 20; and Germany, 23, 34, 48, 67, 70, 117, 183; and Spanish-American War, 26, 27, 29, 31, 32, 68; and Samoa, 35; and Japan, 48; and France, 49, 104, 132; at Algeciras, 49, 132; in war plans, 50, 53, 60; and Guatemala, 76; and United States, 81, 153, 190; and Russia, 104, 132; and Brazilian naval mutiny, 111
—blockade of Venezuela, 71–75, 80–81, 83–87, 170; and Patos, 78–79; and bombing of Puerto Cabello, 86, 92, 94; and arbitration, 87, 97
—interests in Mexico, 162–63, 173; and Díaz, 166; and recognition of Huerta, 170–72; and policy, 176, 184; and Lind, 178; and Benton affair, 195
See also Foreign Office; Royal Navy

Fall, Albert, 195
Fiebig–von Hase, Ragnild, 5, 46, 222
First Fleet Bill (1898), 3, 21, 24, 26, 38–39, 46–47, 65
Fischer, Fritz, 5, 6
Fiske, Bradley, 56, 192
Fletcher, Frank, 192, 198
Florianópolis, 123, 142
Florida, 48
Forbes, Ian, 146, 148
Foreign Office (England): and Patos, 79; and Venezuela, 80–96 passim, 246 (n. 69); and Brazil, 148; and Mexico, 176, 178, 186, 214, 270 (n. 34); records of, 243 (n. 27)
France: in Western hemisphere, 1, 3,

35; and U.S.-German trade, 12, 14, 16, 19, 20; and Germany, 23, 70, 183; and Spanish-American War, 26, 29; and Russia, 48; and England, 49, 104, 132; at Algeciras, 49, 132; German war plans against, 50; and Venezuela, 71; and Guatemala, 76; and *Suchet*, 76–77; and Brazil, 150; and Mexico, 162, 163, 164, 166, 171, 173, 176, 188, 192

Gamboa, Federico, 179
General Board of the U.S. Navy: and war plans, 9, 43, 55–62, 107, 159; and Dewey, 45; foundation of, 54; and Venezuela, 102–3; and Brazil, 108–9, 131, 151; and limiting Monroe Doctrine, 128, 219; and Mexico, 197; and State Department, 220. *See also* U.S. Navy
Gerard, James, 188, 190
German Brazilian Society, 114, 119
German Colonial Association, 117, 125
German Colonial Congress. *See* Colonial Congress of 1902
German navy: growth of, 3, 62; war plans of, 5–6, 46–53, 62–63, 64, 132, 159, 160, 217; bureaucracy of, 24; Reichsmarineamt (Imperial Naval Office), 24, 67; Oberkommando (High Command), 25, 126; compared to U.S. Navy, 42–46, 219; Admiralstab (Admiralty Staff), 51–52, 54; and blockade of Venezuela, 67, 68–69, 82; and visits to Brazil, 151–52; and *Panther* incident, 156. *See also* First Fleet Bill; German Navy League; Second Fleet Bill; Tirpitz, Alfred
German Navy League, 5, 117
Germany: trade rivalry with United States, 2, 10–21, 42, 52, 63, 133, 155–56; colonies of, 4; emigration from, 4, 112–14; and Europe, 48, 132, 154, 159, 183, 211; and Guate-

mala, 76; and Haiti, 77–78; and
Latin American policy, assessed, 217,
220–22
—and Venezuela: community in, 65;
claims against, 65–66, 71; decision
to blockade, 66–71, 82–83, 98–101;
cooperation with England against,
71–74, 84–87; notification of United
States, 79; cooperation with Italy
against, 83–84; sinking of ships, 86,
94, 104; acceptance of arbitration,
87–89, 97–101, 104; shelling of San
Carlos, 101–2, 104; assessment of
relations between, 105–7
—and Brazil: communities in, 108,
111–12, 122–26, 151; trade with,
108, 145–48, 159, 163; emigration
to, 109–10, 115–16, 135–36; and
naval mutiny of 1893, 111; interest
in southern secession, 111, 116;
Germanness of, 122–26; consuls in,
123, 145; banking in, 139–41; German schools in, 143–44; German
churches in, 144; citizenship laws
and, 144–45; arms trade with, 148–
52; relations with, 157–59. *See also*
Hansa colony; *Panther*: incident
involving
—and Mexico: policy toward, 145,
160–62, 182, 184–85, 192–94, 208–
11; interests in, 161–64, 173; and
Díaz, 166; and businessmen's views,
170, 175, 193, 209; and recognition
of Huerta, 171; and Lind, 178; and
views of Wilson's policy, 182, 189–
94, 211–13; and *Ypiranga*, 197–200,
207–8, 211; and unloading weapons
at Puerto México, 200–208; and
origin of *Ypiranga*'s arms, 206–7.
See also England: and Germany;
Monroe Doctrine; Pan-Germans;
Roosevelt, Theodore: and Germany;
Wilhelm II; Wilhelmstrasse; Wilson,
Woodrow
Greece, 13
Grey, Edward, 171, 176, 178, 188, 190

Griscom, Lloyd, 141
Guam, 30
Guatemala, 76

Haggard, William, 69, 71–74, 78, 81,
85, 99, 246 (n. 69)
Hague, The, 79
Haiti: and German threat, 1, 9, 37; and
U.S. interventions, 5, 107, 153, 222,
225, 226; and war plans, 47, 54–56,
59; and *Crête-à-Pierrot*, 77–78
Hale, Edward Everett, 104
Hale, William Bayard, 174, 269
(n. 18), 272 (n. 44)
Hamburg, 201, 204; senate of, 206–7
Hamburg American Line (Hapag):
and Brazil, 114, 135; and Mexico,
162, 200–208, 277 (n. 124), 278
(n. 131)
Hansa colony, 135–43, 157, 159, 217,
258 (n. 50), 260 (n. 96)
Hanseatic Colonization Society (HKG),
135–43, 157, 159
Hapag. *See* Hamburg American Line
Hartmann, Hans, 25
Hasmann (German sailor), 154
Hay, John: and German threat, 27; and
Venezuela, 73, 80, 103, 253 (n. 128);
and Guatemala, 76; and Patos, 79;
and Brazil, 153
Hay-Pauncefote treaty (1901), 81
Hebbinghaus, Georg, 64, 132
Heinrich (prince of Prussia), 27, 68, 99,
165
Hell, Jürgen, 5, 144
Herbert, Michael, 73, 74, 244 (n. 38)
Herwig, Holger, 5, 7, 46, 51–52, 57,
71, 149
Heydt, August von der, 110
Heydt'sche Rescript, 111, 113–14, 135,
136, 256 (n. 19)
Heynen, Carl, 199, 203–8
Hintze, Paul von: alarmism of, 160;
influence of, 164–65, 209; and
Madero, 166; and coup, 167; and
Europeans, 182–83, 192; and inter-

and Brazil, 111, 147–48, 152–55, 226–27; rise to hegemony, 153–54
—and Mexico: and decision to recognize Huerta, 161–62; interests in, 162–63, 173; and Díaz, 166; and European relations, 168–69; and reaction to European loan, 174, 177; and praise of Germany, 187–88, 198, 218; and occupation of Veracruz, 195–200, 205; and *Ypiranga*, 196–208; and reaction to occupation, 200; and analysis of policy, 208–15
—press, 31, 38, 43, 53, 62, 217, 218; and Venezuela, 82, 88, 91–92, 102, 103; and Brazil, 109, 119, 121, 131, 135, 141, 144, 155; and Mexico, 176, 210
See also General Board of the U.S. Navy; Monroe Doctrine; Naval War College; Pork War; Roosevelt, Theodore; U.S. Congress; U.S. Department of State; U.S. Navy; Venezuela; Wilson, Woodrow
U.S. Congress: and U.S.-German trade, 11, 18; and U.S. Navy, 32, 45, 61, 133, 224; and Brazil, 155–56; and Mexico, 173, 197
U.S. Department of State: and German threat, 6, 37–38, 135, 218–20, 222–24; and U.S.-German trade, 16, 18; professionalism of, 62; and *Suchet*, 77; and Venezuela, 87, 93, 103; and Brazil, 109, 124, 132, 142, 144, 155; and Mexico, 167, 180, 184, 218; and *Ypiranga*, 196–97, 202–3, 205, 207–8
U.S. House of Representatives. *See* U.S. Congress
U.S. Marine Corps, 54
U.S. Navy: growth of, 3, 31–33; compared to German navy, 42–46, 219; and war plans, 43, 53–61, 107, 216; and Black Plan, 57–63, 127–28; and concentration of fleet, 62, 133; and exercises in Caribbean (1902–3), 87–88, 91–93, 251 (nn. 107, 108,

112); and Brazil, 108, 127–32; and Brazil war plans, 131–32; and Mexico, 195, 198. *See also* General Board of the U.S. Navy
U.S. Senate. *See* U.S. Congress
U.S. Virgin Islands, 1, 9, 37, 46, 107
Usher, Roland, 117

Vagts, Alfred, 4, 57, 61
Vatican, 26
Venezuela: boundary dispute (1895–96), 3, 34, 81
—Anglo-German blockade of, 7, 48, 64–107, 109, 153–54, 160–61, 170, 183, 188, 215; type of, 67, 80, 84; and claims against Venezuela, 68, 71; and *Suchet*, 77; and seizure of Venezuelan navy, 85–86, 90; and arbitration, 87, 91; and claims negotiations, 101, 254 (n. 142); and war scare, 102–3
Veracruz, 184, 196–200, 205, 206, 207
Victoria (queen of England), 100
Villa, Pancho, 165
Villa Germania, 129
Villiers, Francis, 72, 73, 79–81, 83–84, 87, 246 (n. 69)
Vineta, 67, 86
Von der Tann (German navy), 151

Wehler, Hans-Ulrich, 5
Weltpolitik, 3, 23–26, 33–35, 69–70, 118
West Indies, 26, 37, 41, 57
White, Andrew, 10, 20–21, 22, 27, 29, 31, 38, 100, 125, 244 (n. 38), 253 (n. 128)
White Paper on Venezuela (1902), 94–96
Wilhelm II (kaiser of Germany): and Brazil, 1, 111, 114–15, 118, 121, 124, 129–30, 136, 143, 150, 154–57; and German expansion, 6; and "personal rule," 22–26; and Spanish-American War, 30; and Weltpolitik, 33, 35, 131; marginalia of, 35, 40,